John E. Trent

Modernizing the United Nations System

To Merwa
The best driver in
the world — with thanks

John E. Trent
with the assistance of Monika Rahman

# Modernizing the United Nations System

## Civil Society's Role in Moving from International Relations to Global Governance

Foreword by Walther Lichem

Barbara Budrich Publishers,
Opladen & Farmington Hills 2007

A CIP catalogue record for this book is available from
Die Deutsche Bibliothek (The German Library)



**ISBN 978-3-86649-003-1**
ISBN 3-86649-003-8



Die Deutsche Bibliothek – CIP-Einheitsaufnahme
Ein Titeldatensatz für die Publikation ist bei Der Deutschen Bibliothek erhältlich.

Verlag Barbara Budrich Barbara Budrich Publishers
Stauffenbergstr. 7. D-51379 Leverkusen Opladen, Germany

28347 Ridgebrook. Farmington Hills, MI 48334. USA
www.barbara-budrich.net

Jacket illustration by disegno, Wuppertal, Germany – www.disenjo.de
Printed in Europe on acid-free paper by
Paper & Tinta, Poland

# MODERNIZING THE UNITED NATIONS SYSTEM: CIVIL SOCIETY'S ROLE IN MOVING FROM INTERNATIONAL RELATIONS TO GLOBAL GOVERNANCE

John E. Trent
With the research assistance of Monika Rahman
Centre on Governance, University of Ottawa

"Perhaps our most urgent task today is to persuade nations of the need to return to Multilateralism." Gro Harlem Brundtland, Chairman's Forward, *Our Common Future: Report of the World Commission on Environment and Development.* New York, Oxford University Press, 1987.

"This current system for running the world is based on rules that were set in the middle of the 20th century, in the wake of World War II. It is based on assumptions that a handful of great powers will make most of the decisions with other national governments involved as needed and with intergovernmental efforts at times coordinated through treaties or international organizations such as the United Nations. It was designed for a time when war between countries seemed the greatest threat to international well-being, when national economies engaged in trade but otherwise operated quite separately, and when environmental concerns were scarcely a blip on the radar screen."

Ann Florini, *The Coming Democracy: New Rules for Running A New World*, Washington, Island Press, 2003.

"In fact, all these currents intermingle in a variable and contradictory manner in most minds without resulting in any theory of change, of globalization, of going beyond the nation-state, of global integration." Maurice Bertrand, *l'ONU*, Paris, Éditions la Découverte, 2000.

# Contents

**Boxes**



**Tables**

# United Nations system Glossary of acronyms

| | |
|---|---|
| **ACABQ** | Advisory Committee for Administrative and Budgetary Questions |
| **ACC** | Administrative Co-ordination Committe |
| **CEBC** | Chief Executives Board for Coordination |
| **ECA** | Economic Commission for Africa |
| **ECE** | Economic Commission for Europe |
| **ECLAC** | Economic Commission for Latin America and the Caribbean |
| **ECOSOC** | Economic and Social Council |
| **ESCAP** | Economic and Social Commission for Asia and the Pacific |
| **ESCWA** | Economic and Social Commission for Western Asia |
| **FAO** | Food and Agriculture Organization |
| **FCCC** | Framework Convention on Climate Change |
| **GA** | General Assembly |
| **IAEA** | International Atomic Energy Agency |
| **IBE** | International Bureau of Education |
| **IBRD** | International Bank for Reconstruction and Development (World Bank) |
| **ICAO** | International Civil Aviation Organization |
| **ICC** | International Criminal Court |
| **ICJ** | International Court of Justice |
| **ICSC** | International Civil Service Commission |
| **IFAD** | International Fund for Agricultural Development |
| **ILO** | International Labour Organization |
| **IMF** | International Monetary Fund |
| **IMO** | International Maritime Organization |
| **INSTRAW** | International Research and Training Institute for the Advancement of Women |
| **ISCC** | Information Systems Consultative Committee |
| **ITC** | International Trade Centre |
| **ITU** | International Telecommunications Union |
| **MIGA** | Multilateral Investment Guarantee Agency |
| **OHCHR** | Office of the United Nations High Commissioner for Human Rights |
| **SG** | Secretary General |
| **SC** | Security Council |
| **UN** | United Nations |

| | |
|---|---|
| **UNCHS (Habitat)** | United Nations Centre for Human Settlements |
| **UNCIVPOL** | United Nations Civilian Police |
| **UNCTAD** | United Nations Conference on Trade and Development |
| **UNDCP** | United Nations International Drug Control Programme |
| **UNDP** | United Nations Development Programme |
| **UNEP** | United Nations Environment Programme |
| **UNESCO** | United Nations Educational, Scientific and Cultural Organization |
| **UNFPA** | United Nations Population Fund |
| **UNGA** | United Nations General Assembly |
| **UNHCHR** | United Nations High Commissioner for Human Rights |
| **UNHCR** | (Office of the) United Nations High Commissioner for Refugees |
| **UNICEF** | United Nations Children's Fund |
| **UNICRI** | United Nations Interregional Crime and Justice Research Institute |
| **UNIDIR** | United Nations Institute for Disarmament Research |
| **UNIDO** | United Nations Industrial Development Organization |
| **UNIFEM** | United Nations Development Fund for Women |
| **UNITAR** | United Nations Institute for Training and Research |
| **UNOG** | United Nations Office at Geneva |
| **UNON** | United Nations Office at Nairobi |
| **UNOPS** | United Nations Office for Project Services |
| **UNOV** | United Nations Office at Vienna |
| **UNRISD** | United Nations Research Institute for Social Development |
| **UNRWA** | United Nations Relief and Works Agency for Palestine Refugees in the Near East |
| **UNSC** | United Nations Security Council |
| **UNU** | United Nations University |
| **UNV** | United Nations Volunteers |
| **UPU** | Universal Postal Union |
| **WFP** | World Food Programme |
| **WHO** | World Health Organiztion |
| **WIPO** | World Intellectual Property Organization |
| **WMO** | World Meteorological Organization |
| **WTO** | World Trade Organization |

# Foreword

Post-enlightenment history has been marked by the evolution of an intellectual discourse about the institutional framework within which society, political processes and government were to develop. During the 20th century the focus on state structures and processes gave way to increasingly addressing the evolving international institutional framework and its capacity for responding to the challenges of the time. What will probably be characteristic of the 21st century are the responses we find to the institutional challenges in relation to the increasingly trans-national, global quality of interactions, the relativization of the role of state and interstate structures and processes accompanied by a rising complexity of issues and of the respective necessary responses.

Non-state institutions, interests and actors have become key partners in global processes of governance. The citizen today is both victim and actor in the process of global change. Civil society, more than some state or interstate institutions have shaped our international agenda over the past decades. The issues of the human environment, of human rights, of disarmament (in particular as regards nuclear weapons, anti-personal mines, small arms) and of development cooperation have been promoted by civil society both on the policy front and in the provision of concrete contributions of implementation.

At the same time traditional diplomacy seems to have faded in its impact. The former UN Secretary-General Boutros Boutros-Ghali considered that, in fact, more than two thirds of the UN member states had difficulties following and acting on the ever more complex international agenda. And yet, even before, UN Secretary General U Thant in the early sixties recognized the need for a closer relationship between knowledge and global policy-making leading to the creation of the UN Institute for Training and Research (UNITAR) which, due to the limited resources provided, could never achieve its original purpose. Other attempts regrettably did not mature either. So far, only one major UN conference has seen a preparatory meeting by the scientific community – the International Conference on an Agenda of Science for Environment and Development into the 21st Century (ASCEND 21) in preparation of the United Nations Conference on Environment and Development, Rio de Janeiro, 1992.

Over recent years, the call for adjusting the international system, in particular the United Nations, to the new conditions of global governance has become more articulate. So far, the institutional development of the international system has been characterized by continuous "under-cover creativity" by the international secretariats in partnership with a group of "good citizen" countries (just keep in mind that today nearly two thirds of UN activities are carried out by institutions based on nothing else but a General Assembly resolution), by a total lack of resources, by attempts to institutionally anchor national interests in the international system, and by policies of containment by those interests and powers who seem to perceive the evolution of international institutions as a threat to their absolute sovereignty. Critical, knowledge-based analysis and clear constitutional criteria by which institutional options could be judged have too often been missing.

Yet an understanding of the institutional options available to the community of nations has acquired an ever more central significance if we keep in mind that the quality of institutions has an immediate influence on the quality of the decisions taken and implemented.

In this context there is an urgent need for new sources of knowledge and understanding which can support and guide this institutional development process not only on the diplomatic front but among the global community of citizens represented by civil society.

Concretely, there is a need for the contribution by the social sciences. In spite of the creativity applied in the institutional responses to new challenges, many of the new institutions and organs established over the past four decades have been flawed, often by sectoral segregation at a time when the key element of our Global Agenda is its evermore pertinent interrelatedness.

In this context, the publication of this book by Prof. John E. Trent has to be celebrated as a most valuable contribution to our knowledge and to our understanding of the options and the decisions to be taken with regard to our global governance system. Its wisdom will be available to all the partners in the global governance process, to civil society but also to the governments and their diplomats, to the political parties evermore seized by the local effects of global change, to the business community, to academia and to the media. It will be the basis and a source for the long-needed discourse on the evolving constitutional framework for humanity.

Walther Lichem
Ambassador, ret.

# Preface

The world has a major problem on its hands. The globe is spinning out of control and no one seems to be able to do anything about it. We hear about it in the media every day. The gap between rich and poor is expanding. Despite the end of the Cold War and the supposed "peace dividend," by 2006 the world's governments were still spending in the realm of one trillion dollars U.S. annually on their war machines while investing less than ten percent as much on economic development. Avian bird flu threatens humanity with a new pandemic. Global warming, climate change and pollution put the whole planet at risk. Criminal gangs—international mafias—are running the drug trade and laundering money across borders. Single-hulled tankers belonging to rogue, numbered shipping companies pollute our oceans and shores with tons of oil when they sink. In recent years, some of the worst civil wars in history have devastated populations with genocide, rape, torture, and mutilation–to say nothing of the use of child soldiers.

And the list goes on. Corporations, rebels, terrorists, pirates and gangs act with impunity against the common good. Governments kill more of their citizens than wars do. Everyday we hear of suicide bombers brutally murdering innocent civilians. American authorities are preparing for fallout from possible nuclear bombs planted by new waves of terrorists. In many countries, women are still treated as second-class humans. Some huge companies pay little in taxes, falsify their books, steal their employees' pensions and exploit the environment. We are mesmerized by the bottom line as though the market and profits were the only values. Journalists are killed while doing their duty in an anarchical world. To top it all off we have the special threat posed by the possible use of nuclear weapons, preemptive first strikes, and threats of overwhelming force to impose national will. International institutions are available but do not seem to be able to cope with the global threats and problems. A decade after the genocide in Rwanda, we have been faced with a new butchery in Darfur in the Sudan with terrible delays in effective international action. In recent decades, the gap between rich and poor and starvation in Africa has grown astronomically. One billion individuals are still trying to live on less than a dollar a day. To try to cope with some of these problems, the leaders of the world came together in September 2005 in New York to try to modernize the structures of the UN—and left with hardly any achievements.

Today's challenges are global yet authority systems are founded on national sovereignty. Sovereignty is weaker and power is shifting so there are international voids of authority. There is a lack of a supra-national authority with military enforcement capacity. Sovereignty is also complicated by the arrival of new international actors (transnational corporations, religions, international associations, the media, intellectuals etc.) who reduce the effectiveness of governments. Many of the 191 sovereign states are dictatorships and international organizations have no public participation so there is a perceived democratic deficit in the world. The multilateral system is going through a period of ambiguity and transition shot through with institutional gaps and asymmetries and the lack of a coordinating governmental body.

Well, one might say, the world has faced pretty awful problems in the past, so what's new? What's new is that some of these problems could destroy humanity. We are mutually vulnerable to all of them. Because of global interdependence, complexity and diversity in a turbulent world, a recent international commission demonstrated that most of the problems are interrelated, therefore augmenting their cumulative danger. No country is capable of dealing with these problems or protecting itself. National problems have now become global in scope, flowing across out-dated frontiers. Since the end of the Cold War, there has been a period of transition heading toward global governance but we don't know what it means or how we are going to get there.

So why not reform the United Nations to deal with these global problems? Among the most important reasons is that the UN's member are more preoccupied by their national interests than they are by the collective good. Second, any meaningful reform would mean changes in structures and power. Most states are fearful of losing the advantages they perceive they have in the present system. Third, the UN was set up, at least in part, to favour the victors, especially the five permanent members of the Security Council who have a veto over changes they don't like. Generally speaking, there is no political will to reform international institutions and, as the song says you can't have the one without the other.

So what about setting up some other power regime composed say of the major states or all the democratic states? The problem with this is the UN owes its respect and legitimacy to the fact that it is a universal organization in which all states are members, theoretically with equal rights. It represents the whole world with all its complexities. It has worked long and hard for peace, development and human rights. When it is able to act it is representative of the world and it tends to be accepted. Any other state or grouping of states, no matter how well meant their intentions, would fail this test of legitimacy and, like any interloper, its actions would tend to be rejected.

How about a world government? While someday it may be possible to form a world federation, it is generally agreed that the time has not yet arrived. Most states large and small, old and new still see national sovereignty as their best form of protection and promotion. For most élites, world government is still unacceptable. Not the least of the reasons is that there still is no consensus about the old problem: if we had one world authority, who would guard us against our guardians? For the time being then, most specialists are striving after the elusive concept of 'global governance', that is to say, various forms of diverse and overlapping authorities in the world that have legitimacy in their field of endeavor so that their decisions are accepted and carried out. But, this is a stop-gap in a period of transition.

So the question remains, is there anything we can do to promote the transformation of the United Nations so it can cope with global challenges and the globe can stop spinning out of control? This book responds with a resounding yes – or at least a yes if… We start from the proposition that the resolution of global problems requires effective multilateral institutions. Their functions must be modernized to fulfill the needs of the global system. Over the years most ideas about UN reform have concentrated on *what* type of changes have to be made to make the organization effective. As we will see there is a surfeit of propositions about what to do. Although in this study a survey of criticisms and reforms of the UN is presented, no position is taken on one type of reform over others because the principal objective is to deal with the 'how' rather than the 'what' of institutional reform. Samantha Power put it cryptically; "The reform of the United Nations has been a subject of debate, which has generally accomplished nothing useful, since the Organization exists" (*Le Monde diplomatique,* Sept. 2005: 18). Moreover, the Secretary-General Kofi Annan dedicated much of his term of office to the question of reform without much success. In other words, finding a method for transforming international organizations has become a problem that is as important as knowing what modifications have to be made. The goal in this study, then, is to concentrate on *how* to arrive at decisions about modernizing the UN and *how* they can be put into practice.

The problem with much academic writing is that it concludes just when it should be starting to get serious about the real problems its ideas create. In the case of literature on the United Nations system, there is a large consensus that it is no longer able to deal with today's global problems. So authors conclude the UN must be reformed. They use words like "need to", "must", "ought", and especially "should" – as in "the United Nations needs to be more professionilized and streamlined", "it must find a creative way to keep the United States engaged"; "the Security Council ought to be more preventive than punitive"; and "the UN should have as its goal to eliminate anarchy". One is tempted to propose that whenever we see an author or a speaker finish with the demand that some vague change "should" be made, we should stop paying attention because we know he has not put his mind to thinking about the really tough problem of exactly *how* to get these goals achieved.

Obviously, thinking about the moral imperatives of multilateralism is a very important first step. We have to have a clear idea about the values, norms and objectives of international institutions. The questions then become who will put them into practice? How do we instill in our countries the desire and will to modify the international system? How do we turn a normative discourse into a policy project? What sort and what categories of leadership are required and where do we find them? What is the optimum process and organization for bringing about reform? And, to be practical, how can the reform process be funded in a legitimate and continuous manner?

Though we are not likely to find a miracle cure for all our problems, we can be innovative in our international institutions so they can better manage our problems. No less a person than the Secretary-General of the United Nations has told us our current international institutions are not capable of working effectively and responsibly. For years he has called on business and governments—supposedly the only ones with the resources and powers—to reform these international organizations. But they have turned a blind eye. That is why this book is not addressed just to politicians or executives or even to academics but to all citizens who are concerned about the state of their world. It is especially addressed to those who have organized themselves in what have come to be called "civil society" institutions.

This book proposes that the best solution is for citizens to band together to press corporations and politicians to work on the reforms. International Non-Governmental Organizations (INGOs) have shown both in the past and the present that they are able to mobilize people and governments for institutional transformation. Civic associations are already lobbying for global reform. But to have the desired effect, more of us must participate. Now there I go, you see, using that "must" word. In practical terms this means reformers will have to pressure leaders to act. It's a big task, so it's not likely any one person or group can come up with a simple solution. To this end we will need a process that will bring concerned advocates together to develop agreement about how to change the UN system. The historical record plus the tendency of states to protect the status quo suggest that the UN will be unlikely to reform itself. Institutions themselves rarely adopt systemic changes. It usually requires outside impetus. This study comes to the conclusion that the most likely candidate to provide the reform momentum is civil society, organized in international associations (Non-Governmental Organizations, NGOs),– working eventually with those governments that are on the same wavelength.

Not everyone believes in the goal of the modernization of multilateralism. Some élites believe that little has changed since 1945 and it is sufficient for states to work together in the United Nations as it was designed six decades ago. Some have figuratively thrown their hands up in despair and have come to believe that only incremental change is acceptable because structural change is neither necessary nor possible (described by Donini 1988). Others, such as the conservative right, actually fear the furthering of global governance because it will strengthen a "multilateral technocracy" that "inevitably devolves into corruption" because it "lacks democratic accountability" and "overrides national power and sovereignty" which alone can protect the democratic world (Brooks 2005). The least one can say is that there is presently a battle royal between various perceptions of international institutional change.

As a study of the field of international institutional reform, this text is not just a personal statement. It brings together the results of research on a broad (but never complete) cross-section of thought and analysis concerning global change and the development of international (and eventually global) institutions. As Marx said, we build on the shoulders of others. As both a policy analysis and a normative project, the book should be of interest to two types of audiences in particular. Students of global studies or international relations will be able to follow the history and theory of international institutions and the roles and functions of the United Nations system. They can study the criticisms and proposals to reform the UN made over the decades and analyse the groups that are leading the reform movement now. At the end, they can evaluate a model for modernizing the world's leading multilateral organization. Activist citizens concerned more about the practicalities of improving global governance can read the book as a normative project about techniques of institutional transformation. They will see some of the difficulties Kofi Annan faced in trying to reform the UN and then become aware of the changes to our global system that require the modernization of multilateral institutions. They will learn how civil society contributed to the evolution of international organizations in the past and how it might become the prime mover in transforming the UN in the future.

Why is it urgent that citizens of the world take the time to read a tome on the reform of international institutions? A number of thoughtful analysts have observed similarities between historical trends in collapsed civilizations and current trends in our modern world. With growth in technology, production and pollution, change is running out of control. The world population has multiplied by four in the last century. Jingoistic nation-states still engage in arms races and sales. Social exploitation, urban slums, contamination of air and water, and cultural imperialism are still with us. One cannot fail to observe "the massive onslaught of 'progress,' whether it is the loss of farms to suburbs, jungles to cattle ranches, rivers to dams, mangroves to shrimp farms, mountains to cement quarries, or coral reefs to condominiums" (Wright 2005: 124).

What does this analogy with past civilizations tell us about the need to study international institutions? First, it shows us that humans have a tendency to over-exploit their natural and social environment until they drive it to collapse. There are many indications that we are nearing the carrying capacity of our globe. Second, no one—rich or poor, old or young, weak or powerful—is spared by generalized destruction. Third, we must think about institutional innovations that would allow human society to work together to forestall a drift to our downfall. History teaches us that the solution cannot be a centralized, hierarchical empire that acts in the interests of the powerful. Nor can it simply be national governments of potentially warring states, whose clans cooperate only too little and too late. We need to understand the limits of past and present models of governance so we can go beyond them to combine the local and the global.

Finally, if the main task of these institutions is to develop our capacity for cooperative management of global problems, they must aim at democratic norms. They must also inspire trust and confidence in the diverse peoples of the globe so they will cooperate. Institutions that foster cooperation will, at a minimum, have to be based on a form of equitable representation, and be seen as fair, just and responsible. These challenges for institutional innovation offer sufficient reasons for interested world citizens to participate in the modernization of multilateralism.

This has been an independent study. Nevertheless, I want to thank the Centre for the Development of Canadian Foreign Policy and its former Director, Stephen Lee, for grants for research assistance and for bringing together international specialists. Thanks go also to the thoughtful colleagues who participated in these meetings. John Langmore was particularly generous with his advice on a preliminary draft. No book can survive without the help and friendly editorial advice of such specialists as Beth McFee, John Hayes and my publisher. Thanks also to John Duggan for his keen editorial eye! I want especially to express my appreciation to Monika Rahman who turned out to be more than a research assistant. As well as research she contributed a number of first drafts and advice beyond her years.

John E. Trent,
Chelsea, Quebec.
Summer, 2006

FOR COLETTE
FOR EVERYTHING

# Introduction: Recent Attempts at Reform

*"We need to rethink the goals and instruments of the United Nations so that it can deal effectively with these increasing challenges of the state-centric system and with the complexities of a turbulent world largely out of control."*

W. Andy Knight and Joseph Masciulli, "Conclusions" in W. Andy Knight, *Adapting the United Nations to a Postmodern Era,* Houndmills, U.K., Palgrave-Macmillan, p. 246.

## Kofi Annan: the Reforming Secretary General

It may be a little unusual, but perhaps the most effective manner of introducing the topic of modernizing the institutional structures of the UN system is to observe the efforts of the Secretary-General, Kofi Annan, to move in that direction. One of the most determined and sustained attempts to reform the United Nations came to a head in New York at the World Summit of September 2005. A summary of it will serve to introduce the various themes and considerations that will teach us that how you go about reform is as crucial as what you try to do. Like a great sailing ship of the line, Kofi Annan worked assiduously to get the UN in fighting trim to wage the battle of reform. History might declare him the 'reforming Secretary-General'.

If he failed it was not for lack of trying but because he could not mobilize the members and because events and politics conspired against him.

In fact, it is worth recalling the political events capturing the headlines during this period. Before the Millennium, a growing number of social and economic issues from debt and poverty to the environment and trade rules had overflowed into the international arena and become known as "global challenges". The inequality of world institutions and their incapacity to deal with these "global challenges" had been mirrored in the frustration and rage of younger people from Seattle to Quebec City. Following the glowing days of the Millennium came the 9–11 "Attack on America" which led to the international "war on terrorism" and the ensuing invasions of Afghanistan and Iraq. With the Iraq war dividing the United Nations, and with the approach of its $60^{th}$ Anniversary, Secretary-General Kofi Annan decided the time was ripe to push member states to consider structural reforms to the international organization.

Here is a summary of the ten steps to reform pursued by Annan.

1. One of his first acts upon becoming Secretary-General in 1997 was to appoint Maurice Strong as executive coordinator for UN reform (Strong, 2000: 291).
2. Together they initiated a two-track reform process. Track One was what the Secretary General could carry out on his own authority. It was the single most radical restructuring of the Secretariat since its inception and included bringing together some thirty departments, funds and programs into five

executive groups (development, political and security, economic and social, humanitarian, and human rights).

3. These modifications were furthered in 2002 by a second report (A/57/150) aimed at: public information, the overburden of meetings and reports, the need for unified country teams, a Partnerships Office, establishing a high-level panel on relations with civil society and results-based budgeting. For the first time, the position of Deputy Secretary-General was established, in part to concentrate on reform.
4. Track Two reforms of a more fundamental structural nature, already described in Annan's annual reports, were the prerogative of member governments. The Secretary-General started working on practical, concrete goals to improve the conditions of humanity. The UN Millennium Declaration resulting from the World Leaders Summit in 2000 aimed to express their resolve to free their fellow humans from extreme poverty. The Declaration clearly shows world leaders are not in any doubt about the requirements of global governance. In practical terms this came down to the Millennium Development Goals (MDGs) eventually signed by 189 heads of state and government committing them to attain by 2015 eight goals aimed at reducing poverty that are time bound and concrete, with 18 targets and 48 indicators for measuring achievements. (www.un.org/milleniumdevelopmentgoals includes data on achievements to date.)
5. One section of The Millennium Goals on "Strengthening the United Nations" corresponded to Annan's Track Two objectives. This included reform of the Security Council, strengthening the Economic and Security Council (ECOSOC) and the International Court of Justice, better coordination among all the agencies, improved management, and reaching out to the private sector and civil society. However, no actions were taken on this 'structural transformation', a key concept that means going beyond organizational and management adaptation to modify the actual constitution of the units and rules of the institution.
6. In 2003, Annan named a High Level Panel on Threats, Challenges and Change to recommend reforms to provide a collective response to global challenges. Its report, *A More Secure World: Our Shared Responsibility* (www.un.org/secureworld) outlined six clusters of threats that are interconnected and which no state acting alone can defeat. Given the gravity of the threats, the world needs more commitment to prevention. The Panel made a considerable leap by recognizing the connection between development and security.
7. The High Level Panel report was followed in 2005 by the report of the UN Millennium Project entitled, 'Investing in Development: A Practical Plan to Achieve the Millennium Development Goals' (www.unmillenniumproject.org), also known as the Sachs Report after the anti-poverty campaigner Jeffrey Sachs. The Report showed that the eleven remaining years would be enough time to achieve the MDGs - if the global community really started taking them seriously.
8. Annan then consulted with governments and made his own recommendations for a security system that would be efficient, effective and *equitable,* synthesized

in his 2005 report to the General Assembly "In Larger Freedom". (www.un.org/inlargerfreedom). Based on the two former reports it again made a pitch for structural change. Proposed as a total reform package of reforms, it formed the basis for further negotiations in preparation for the September 2005 UN Summit of World Leaders to celebrate the UN's 60[th] anniversary, recommit to the MDGs, and implement institutional reform.

9. Enter John Bolton, President Bush's new ambassador to the United Nations, who told envoys to the UN three weeks before the Summit that the United States had 750 amendments to propose that could scrap 400 passages in the Draft Outcome Document that had been negotiated for six months. With negotiations re-opened, Russia and the Group of 77 (G-77, in fact 132 developing states) submitted hundreds more amendments. (www.reformtheun.org)
10. The negotiations led to a consensus "Draft Outcome Document of the High-level Plenary Meeting of the General Assembly of September 2005" (UN document A/59/HLPM/CRP.1/Rev.2). Unlike the relatively focused reports of Sachs, the High Level Panel and the Secretary-General, which reflected greater conceptual coherence, the drafting and revision process led to a document that read more like a wish list of the desires of every constituency within the UN.

Outside observers were hard pressed to know whether the Americans were out to sabotage the process or to negotiate from a position of strength. It seems the latter was the case as Bolton accepted to negotiate on the basis of the Draft Negotiating Document and items such as the Millennium Development Goals were still included. Following the conference, President Bush was at pains to say he endorsed the MDGs. However, the Americans had succeeded in reducing references: to multilateralism as a fundamental value; to the UN as a main actor with increased resources; to greater use of the International Court of Justice; to enhancement of the General Assembly; and to creating a strategic military reserve for the UN. The U.S. also had success in emphasizing peace and security, international law, the private sector, and the obligation of developing countries to provide good governance to attract investment. There was agreement to disagree on setting 0.7 percent of GNP as a target for development aid and on the language for achieving disarmament. Some states tried to fight back with attempts to include passages affirming multilateralism and rejecting unilateralism, but without success. Members found it impossible to come to agreement on a simple definition of terrorism or on the regulation of arms of mass destruction and nuclear proliferation. (For further elaboration see the end of Chapter 4).

## Impediments to Reform

This brief summary of the latest but most comprehensive and sustained attempt to reform the United Nations system had as its objective to introduce us to several major issues relating to the modernization of multilateral institutions. First and foremost, despite all the efforts of the Secretary-General, his reform process did not lead to any fundamental institutional modernization. The Final Outcome Document was a half empty glass. Indeed, as regards principles and objectives, it is in many ways a step backward from the Millennium Declaration.

If ever there was any doubt, it has been removed by section 146–156, which makes it clear that the World Leaders had no intention or plan for the reform of the UN's major institutions. In this section, euphemistically called "Strengthening the United Nations", we find that all the major organs of the UN will continue functioning largely as they have. Even slight innovations in the draft documents were eliminated. These included the minimal inter-agency coordination plea that UN bodies "should not duplicate their work"; or that the General Assembly might create a small representative group to interface with the Secretariat for greater efficiency; or that the ECOSOC might convene timely meetings to deal with emergencies or focus on the linkage between peace and development – all are gone, as is (once again) any specific proposal for the reform of the Security Council which had been hotly debated during the negotiations. We must surmise that no amount of effort by the Secretary-General, who, in the final analysis is the servant of the Member States, can surmount a lack of interest in reform by those same states.

The only significant exception to this general observation is the "Responsibility to Protect" paragraph, which potentially opens the door to move the world from Westphalian, sovereignty-based 'inter-national' relations toward some form of global governance where states are neither the only actors nor the final arbiters. In an important step toward the limitation of sovereignty, the Summit leaders did make the definitive statement, "We are prepared to take collective action, in a timely and decisive manner, through the Security Council, in accordance with the UN Charter, including Chapter VII, on a case by case basis and in cooperation with relevant regional organizations as appropriate, should peaceful means be inadequate and national authorities manifestly failing to protect their populations from genocide, war crimes, ethnic cleansing, and crimes against humanity." However, we must note that this was the result of world disgust over Darfur and consequent heavy arm-twisting over a three-year period by a civil society coalition and "like-minded" states such as Canada. Looking down the road, for such a principle to be put into action, the Security Council will require a set of criteria (already developed by the High Level Panel) that would guide their "collective action" i.e. use of force to intervene, when necessary, to protect populations against predatory behaviour within their own state. These criteria are an important corollary to the effective operation of the "Responsibility to Protect" (R2P). But the leaders were not even willing to include a clause saying they were ready to continue discussing such criteria.

Which leads us to a second point: the United Nations does, and always has, managed to adapt itself to the evolving international context. We have to be careful to distinguish "adaptation" from fundamental, institutional "transformation". In a speech at the University of Quebec in Montreal at the beginning of 2006, the former Deputy Secretary-General, Louise Fréchette, made a vibrant defence of the capacity of the UN to evolve despite many recent crises that had befallen it. "The UN coped much better in recent years than one might think. It is capable of evolving and does so constantly" (UN/DSG/SM/278). She gave many eloquent examples (See Chapter 2). In the specific case of the UN Leaders Summit, the meeting did lead in the months that followed to the creation of a new Peacebuilding Commission and the restructuring of the Human Rights Council. In both cases these were helpful but timid (and unproven) reorganizations of the administrative apparatus rather than a basic structural transformation.

Despite her defence of the organization, the Deputy Secretary-General also pointed out weaknesses (in veiled terms, of course) that have a strong effect on reform issues. These include: the capacity of the Permanent Five to prevent consideration of questions about which they are reticent; UN mandates that lack political support or are subject to indifference, contradictory pressures from divergent commercial or political interests; inadequate military and financial resources; a tendency to drop emergency aid once media cameras leave; and a disparate application of collective security with different rules for the rich and the poor and the strong and the weak. She concludes that, "Their exists a multitude of reasons that favour reinforcing universal, multilateral institutions like the United Nations."

A third lesson we can take from the 2005 Summit is that, when it comes to UN reform, the international context and the players at a particular time and situation appear to be of strategic significance. Let us look at several examples. To start with, the media did not give either the reforms or the Summit much public support if one judges by the lack of coverage in the years and months preceding the event. Nor was there much pressure from civil society and the public for governments to support Annan's reform process. One might have thought that normally a conference of 160 heads of state and government to reconsider the governance of the world would have drawn some public attention. But it did not. In part perhaps this reflected the oft-commented indifference or even hostility of the American government of George W. Bush for the United Nations, another contextual problem. This was part of what some authors have called a "disconnect" between the High Level Panel's reform proposals and reality. They are "ignoring the real-world incentives and disincentives to which states actually respond" (Glennon 2005: 4). More generally, if one accepts that global reforms will require a considerable consensus, then "At the heart of this is the idea that successful cooperation happens only when certain conditions are met" (Maxwell 2005: 416). In the past, one of these conditions has been the leadership or the acquiescence of the U.S. However, the Panel and Secretary-General cannot be blamed for not having foreseen other contextual problems such as the U.S. nomination of an ambassador noted for his disdain for the UN. The same is true of the scent of corruption from the Iraq oil-for-food scandal and the Volker report. These tarnished the UN's image and even Annan's reputation to the point he was not able to give full leadership to the reform effort during the summer preceding the Summit.

A fourth problem one could observe preceding the Summit was what we might call some 'inbred impediments' to reform in the UN system. For example, enlargement of the Security Council to more adequately reflect current political and economic realities was systematically undermined by regional neighbours who attempted to offset the chances of almost every aspiring candidate. The Permanent Five could just sit back and watch with joy as everyone else protected their turf. The same sort of forces hamstrings almost any major reform proposal (or even some minor ones). Although it has become customary in the new century to blame the United States for all the blockages at the UN, the Summit taught us that the UN is, in fact, the sum of its mutual vetoes. States and group of states rarely fail to protect their interests or sovereign concerns. One notorious example was a little block of members that obstructed a definition of terrorism, supposedly because they wanted to protect "freedom fighters" (for instance, Palestinians).

These impediments drive down reform negotiations to their lowest common denominator or take them right off the table – as was the case with proliferation of arms of mass destruction. In other cases the watered-down paragraphs in the declaration are just a reiteration of shop-worn principles without any action. Another tactic of member states we saw in the negotiations is to insist on seemingly small changes in wording, which can trivialize a passage or completely change its intent. If all that doesn't work and a delegate does not wish openly to oppose a measure, it is possible to hobble it by restricting its resource or putting off action to a later date. States can get away with such obstructionism because each one has interests to protect and there is no representative of collective interests present to gainsay them.

These four impediments to institutional reform – lack of governmental interest, the distinction between adaptation and transformation, the significance of the political context and actors, and the inbred narrow self-interests of states – will come back time and again in this study. Other lessons will also be drawn from the 2005 Summit when we analyse it in detail later on. For now, Annan's 1997 – 2005 reform process serves as an introduction to the need to find a more effective method for transforming the United Nations system, which is the subject of this study.

## The Plan of the Book

Despite some recent claims about the value of American hegemony, global management can be achieved only through multinational cooperation (Albright 2003a; Annan 2003). But the international institutions must be up to the task. It is urgent and imperative to think through the process of innovation in international institutions so they become better equipped to handle the challenges of global governance.

Our analysis works its way through the theoretical, historical, political and practical problems raised by this problem.

The first chapter provides the context for the study. We bring together the various strands of the theoretical literature dealing with the evolution of international relations, changes in the world order and the potential role of civil society in the reform of global governance and international institutions. A related task is to give an overview of the current international political context that impinges on international organizations. As was said four decades ago, "The UN did not invent these pressures. It mirrors them" (Boyd 1964: 186). More recently, the same thing has been reiterated, in different words: "There have always been connections between the general climate of world politics and the functioning of the United Nations…" (Puchala & Coate 1989: 100).

The book then goes on to look at the origins of international organizations to see if their creation and evolution offer us any lessons about how one should proceed today in the task of institutional innovation. In this area, as in so many others, while we cannot replicate history, we are wise to pay attention to what it can teach us. Recalling the roles, functions and achievements of the UN system completes chapter two. The next task (Chapter 3) is to attempt to demonstrate that there has been fundamental change in the world since the founding of the UN in 1945 and this warrants our efforts to transform international organizations. Once again, political organizations have to play 'catch-up' to technological and economic advances. Chapters 4 and 5 go on to an extended summary of many of the criticisms and reform proposals for the United Nations system and major global issues that present a challenge for international institutions.

But it is our thesis that the basic problem of international institutional reform has less to do with the "what" than with the "how." This study is mainly concerned with innovative techniques for transforming the UN, detailed in the last chapter. Faced by the harsh reality that international organizations have so far not been able to transform themselves to any significant degree, a process for overcoming this problem through civil society-led "second-track diplomacy" is proposed. It calls for the formation of a "campaign coalition" of international associations (INGOs) to take the lead in a triple implementation agenda of political pressure, global governance reform, and public opinion formation.

Before finishing this introduction a brief presentation of several key concepts that are central to the book's argument is in order, because they too will help to 'introduce' the book. More of the concepts will be dealt with in the first chapter.

## What is Meant By 'Reform'

There are three difficulties: the etymology of the term 'reform', its use in the context of the UN, and its place in the family of words about change. Strictly meant, reform is improvement by the removal of imperfections, abuses, or faults. In its 19th-century political roots in the Reform Acts and movements of Great Britain, the word reform had a liberal and progressive sense. It meant ending economic and political abuse via greater inclusion in the democratic franchise, greater social justice, and a more active government. In recent decades, since Thatcher, Reagan and Mulroney, the term was taken over to generally mean "change," and more particularly to cover a return to less government and to conservative economic policies that tend to benefit the wealthy. In this book, "reform" is used in its original sense to refer to improvements of international institutions. This is to make them more devoted to development and more representative, democratic and effective – a balance not easily maintained – so that they might contribute to the betterment of humanity through their improved ability to deal with global problems.

However, there is another difficulty with the term "reform" as it is understood at the United Nations. There the staff equates it with the attempts by President Reagan and succeeding Republican administrations to limit the Organization by reducing its personnel and budgets. Needless to say the word "reform" is anathema at the UN. Unfortunately, it is a term that is so widely used that it is difficult to avoid. So we can only confirm that the intention here is to reinforce the UN, not reduce it. So from time to time reform will be used as a catchall term to include the whole spectrum of change at the UN.

The third difficulty entails the use of the word within the family of words referring to change, especially political change. With regard to organizations, we must be at pains to differentiate between reform, adaptation and transformation (see Krause, Knight and Dewitt 1995 and Knight 2005). Reform connotes process modifications such as we expect in an organization in everyday life, including improvements to policies, administration, budgeting and personnel. Borrowing from organizational theory, reform is specified as 'purposeful', 'managed change process', that involves conscious, deliberate, and collaborative efforts to improve the operations of a system. However, when an institution modifies its programmes and organization only on an ad hoc basis to conform to the demands of its evolving context, we call it 'adaptation'. The adaptation of an international organization to impulses from its environment involves "vaguely intuitive or haphazardly venturesome" actions. Adaptation is incremental as in intergovernmental concerns to deal with short-term problems and their immediate consequences. For the most part, the behaviour of UN representatives is habit-driven and reactive. Knight lumps the two types of change together under the heading of the "tinkering mode of change" that is minimalist and incrementalist dealing only with effectiveness and efficiency of an organization rather than making it more relevant (see Chapter 1 for further elaboration).

'Transformation' (or what Knight now also calls 'rethinking') questions the ends, purposes and goals of organizations to modify their fundamental principles and radically alter their features and functions. Those who prefer incremental change tend to think UN structural changes are neither necessary nor possible. Others think that 'muddling through' is insufficient to meet the challenges of globalization and the time has come to consider a new strategy of change that requires standing outside the prevailing wisdom.

This study focuses on transformation, that is, fundamental structural modifications of the composition, units, norms and rules of the UN to allow it to cope better with the effects of globalization. Structures are meant in the double sense of imbedded norms and also organizational composition. Transformation means going beyond managerial and organizational adaptation and reform. Transformative learning is usually frustrated during the on-going life of an organization by "institutionalized routines, ideological wrangling and narrow interest-based decision-making (Knight 2005: 28–36). To symbolize 'transformation', the sub-title of this book speaks of *moving from international to global institutions*, the former centered on the sovereign nation-state and the latter looking more to the collective good of the whole world and the implication of a multiplicity of actors, not just governments.

## What is 'Civil Society'?

This neologism of the 1990s is enjoying such extensive usage that it should be defined a little further. Two surveys of "civil society" have shown that the concept is being used in three different ways, sometimes over-lapping. They are: analytical-descriptive, concerning strategic or public policy, and as a normative ideal (Edwards 2004, Keane 2003). The 'analytical' trend studies the composition of civil society which it sees as forms of associational life that are "a part of society distinct from states and markets" aimed at advancing common interests and facilitating collective action. It includes all associations and networks except firms but there is no assumption of a common political agenda or a normative consensus. The 'strategic or public policy' school of thought sees civil society as "an arena for public deliberation, rational dialogue, and the exercise of active citizenship in the pursuit of the common interest" especially in democracy and development. The third usage are theories that define civil society in 'normative' terms as "the realm of service rather than self interest and a breeding ground for attitudes and values like cooperation, trust, tolerance and non-violence" … a different way of being that is identified as 'civil'. Edwards: vii-viii).

The collective term 'civil society' is used here to refer to associational life in national and international non-governmental organizations (NGOs and INGOs) that deal with or are concerned about global issues, international institutions and the system of global governance. 'Un-civil' criminal types of organization are excluded, as are business corporations, except when they have projects aimed at the collective good. Although there is no teleological argument that they will necessarily produce the public good, there is an assumption that associational life tends to produce behaviour that is other-oriented and non-violent. Empirically, it is understood that non-governmental organizations can bring to international politics a wealth of relatively disinterested experience and expertise in such fields as the social and physical sciences, law and constitutionalism, economic development and humanitarian aid, and institutional philosophy and organization. It is recognized that this is still a rather unorganized, uneven and fragmented field in which some associations can exhibit unacceptable behavior – to be discussed later.

It is to be hoped that this study and its conclusions may to some small degree encourage concerned citizens of the world, and particularly those in forefront international non-governmental organizations, to move beyond the limits of today toward the necessities of tomorrow and the formation of a global governance campaign coalition.

# 1 The Current Context of Multilateralism

## 1.1 The Analytical Context

*"There is all too little effective governance capable of ameliorating, if not resolving these and numerous other problems that crowd high on the global agenda. Perhaps even more troubling, our generation lacks the orientation necessary to sound assessments of how the authority of governance can be brought to bear on the challenges posed by the prevailing disarray."*

James Rosenau, "Governance in a New Global Order"
in David Held & Anthony McGrew (eds.) (2002).
Governing Globalization, Cambridge, Polity Press, p. 70.

This study asks one basic question: how can the United Nations system be transformed into an organization more capable of dealing with global problems? It should be a clear enough question. Unfortunately, it grows and grows. First there are ancillary questions. What do we mean by transformation and reform? What types of transformation should be envisaged? What groups and individuals might be implicated in this reform process? Then there are prior questions. Why does the UN need to be transformed? Have there been changes of a sufficient degree in the world society that we must contemplate the transformation of the UN? What's wrong with the United Nations as it is? Why do we need to worry about this issue – why don't the UN members just get on with the job if it is so necessary? The chapters that follow aim to answer these questions.

### 1.1.1 The Study of International Relations

While it is not our aim here to offer a majestic new theory of the world polity, it will be helpful to situate the study of international organizations such as the United Nations system within the broader context of the theory and analysis of international relations to see what it tells us about the need to transform international organizations and our particular focus on civil society and the modernization of multilateralism. A brief overview will introduce the main issues.

### 1.1.2 Overview

Since 1945, the international system has been marked, both in fact and in theory, by a gradual evolution from a strict domination by sovereign states to a slow move toward globalization and concerns for global governance. In reality, this dichotomy was embedded in the Charter of the United Nations, which focused on the sovereignty of nation-states but also included the vehicles for it being overtaken by the notions of "we the peoples", human rights, and development. This tension between the individual state and the world collectivity has been reflected in international relations analysis by pressures on realist theorists to adjust their state-centric convictions to account for the changes to the world which can no longer be accommodated in their sovereignty-based "Westphalian" theory. States are no longer the only influential actors in the international system, nor are they any longer complete masters of domestic and foreign policy. Economics has become as important as politics. Sovereignty has become porous. Numerous studies of globalization, both by its supporters and detractors, have demonstrated the growing integration of the world. States are being challenged by threats and problems that entangle the whole world and cannot be controlled by individual governments.

'Realists', both academic and governmental, have not hesitated to strike back to reassert the authority of the state. Traditionalists, both in great powers like the United States and in newly decolonized states, want to affirm their sovereign constitutional right to govern their people and repulse external interventions, including those of international governmental organizations (IGOs) like the UN. These international organizations find themselves in a crossfire between reformists who want them to become much more active and democratic and traditionalists who want to control them for their own interests. Theorists study how the UN system might change either through planned reform, adaptation to international evolution, or rethinking its principles and functions. So far, although it has slowly adapted to its changing milieu, the UN has been stopped by "institutional routines, ideological wrangling, and narrow interest-based decision-making" from transforming its structures (Knight 2005: 58). In the meantime, growing interest is being paid to new global actors. Studies analyse their possible contributions to the UN and, more broadly, to global governance. They are able to foster domains of authority in which international decision-making will be accepted, thus leading to greater stability. Now, let us look at each of these steps from internationalism to globalism (although it is by no means a linear progress) in a little more detail.

### 1.1.3 Limits to 'Westphalian', 'State-centric' Analysis

Ever since the Treaty of Westphalia in 1648 inaugurated the era of 'international relations' (IR) between sovereign nation-states, most IR analysis has traditionally focused on what has been called the "classical paradigm" or, if one is angry with it, the "state-centric" model (among the post-1945 authors see Morgenthau, Hinsley, Aron, Bull and Deutsch). This "realist" school assumed that essential world politics took place between the governments of independent states which sought to maximize their interests and power in an anarchic international system where there was no superior authority. In this situation, international theorists concentrated their enquiry on three main questions: the nature of power in war and peace; the essential actors who carried out the relationships; and the structure or "image" of the international system (Holsti 1985: 8).

Since the 1970s numerous critics have whittled away at the state-centric model. One of the first attacks pointed out that the classical paradigm ignored other than state relations and participants. Therefore 'realists' set aside a growing number of alternate "transnational" processes that were flowing across borders and a number of significant, new non-state actors (Keohane & Nye 1972). It was clear that there were now manifold non-political, transnational relationships in fields such as religion, culture, economics, ideology and pan-nationalism that tended to contest notions of national sovereignty and the impervious state. Also, one could already distinguish at least six types of actors on the international scene: interstate governmental actors (IGOs or international organizations), both universal and regional, composed of governmental representatives; international non-governmental organizations (INGOs), that is, associations with transnational membership of individuals who are there of their own volition; the central governments of nation-states; sub-national and regional governmental organizations; intra-state, non-governmental actors, now most often called NGOs or civil society (the former being the organized part of the latter) including all sorts of grouping, movements and associations from Green Peace to philanthropists to unions and churches; finally there are leading individuals such as the Swiss founder of Red Cross or Ted Turner, the founder of the UN Foundation (Mansbach et al. 1976: 39–41). Interestingly enough, James Rosenau has more recently produced a typology of global governance based on a similar categorization of actors (2002: 81). He includes elites, business, and public opinion as additional players.

Other international relations specialists thought it was necessary to deepen and broaden the analysis to understand the empirical roots of international behaviour and also to conceptualize it as a total system. It was therefore necessary to study the physical and social foundations of the actions of nation-states (Sprout, Harold and Margaret 1962). It was the lack of an adequate study of the "sociological" bases of international relations including territory, population, technology, divergent interests and inequalities, and ideas and values that caused the classical paradigm to devalue the changes in transnational flows and in the diversity of influences on the balance of power (Merle 1987). The fundamental question then becomes: what are the needs and the resources of the world as a whole. As a consequence, the agenda has to be expanded to include issues of global demand and supply, development and inequality, the transnational economy and society and the need for justice and human rights (Sterling 1974).

The state-centric image of international politics misses the big picture and condemns itself to the status quo by limiting itself to relations between states. Even while political relations have become more fragmented and diverse the world has at the same time become a "total system" linked by economics, biology, communications and culture (Boulding 1985). In such a world we have to view the international system as a whole and not just from the perspective of actors if we are to include the total activity of all participants. A "global system" would have to deal with vast economic disparities, ecological overload, social relations and human rights as well as war and security (Brown 1992). We are living in a world of increasing mobility, interdependence, interpenetrability and vulnerability. If, then, we are to properly understand peace and conflict in a "turbulent" world we must conceptualize the global system and also the discrete, decision-making and influencing sub-systems and the relations between them. The state is no longer automatically accorded superior status in looking at governance within economic, ecological, cultural, and value sub-systems (Rosenau 1990, Brown 1992).

As time went on interest continued in "unraveling the paradigm" by subjecting assumptions of the state as a bounded entity to additional forms of enquiry concerning its capacities for transformation and stability. Questions were raised about the "diffusion of power" as the state attempted to adjust to the pressures of globalization and "the territorial boundaries of states no longer coincide with the extent or limits of political authority over economy and society" (Strange 1996: ix). "Neo-realists" attempted to integrate political economy into the classical paradigm as the state-market problematic became central under the pressures from the neo-Marxist/dependencia school (Wallerstein 1979) and the decolonized states at the UN. But the critical school did not consider their efforts very convincing because the conceptual parameters of the state remained dominant. Critics also found that the "territorializing logic" of the realists effectively sidelined consideration of knowledge processes and normative issues – and didn't even subject their model to analysis of the new challenges to territorial integrity from modern weaponry and economic transnationalism. A whole school has grown up around the normative bases of cosmopolitanism (world citizenship) and particularly the role of human rights and democracy in global affairs (Held 1995, Archibugi 2003, Appiah, 2006). The realist model also failed to incorporate learning from feminist studies about the social relations of power, of social-sexual divisions of labour, and of patriarchy, which operates across both public and private settings to impact on gender inequalities (Youngs 1999).

While the political economy approach was out in front during the 1970s and 80s the dark horse coming up on the inside was the global society school which, with the forces of globalization behind it, finally became the main challenger to the state-centric paradigm. It will be recalled that the core concern of realists was to explain "why and how nation-states go to war, conduct their diplomacy, construct institutions or customs leading to peace, order and stability, and how they organize power in pursuit of their objectives" (Holsti 1985: vii). This theoretical paradigm had a number of corollaries. States were more or less impervious, moral entities whose first task was to protect their citizens. While there might be a broader range of international relations across borders, international politics were handled by central governments of these separate political communities, none subject to a central authority. Ideals were a costly add-on in a world of states that had interests, not friends.

### 1.1.4 Global Society

Global society theorists have gradually challenged all of these principles. They propose a broader agenda concerning the units of analysis and the images of the world (Maghroori & Rambagh 1982). A "smaller world" of interdependent humans obliges us to think in terms of a unity of interests and the bonds of a connected humanity. The limited conceptualization and vision of the realists is at odds with socio-economic and technological realities. Empirically, there are disaggregated sets of issue areas where all sorts of actors and agents process issues. Governments appear to have lost a great deal of their previous freedom of choice. Undue focus on the search for power tends to deny common interests. Problems are global in scope but the way the world is currently organized means it cannot generate sufficient managerial capacities to solve or contain them. The fundamental transformations of an increasingly interdependent world call for values in addition to peace if the goal is human development. In these new conceptualizations of the world society there is a greatly expanded problematic in which norms of equality and justice, economic and ecological balance are as important as order and stability. To put it another way, you cannot have order without sustainable development. Theorists like Mendlowitz and Falk of the World Order Models Project (WOMP) were well ahead of their time and had to preach in the desert for many years: "Today we may be in the throes of an epochal change – away from particularistically based territorial settlements serving a variety of agro-industrial units upon which the nation-state system was based, on to a truly global society with a global economy and global culture, and involving global governance" (Mendlowitz 1977: 261). More recently it may be said that this message no longer falls on deaf ears after the publication of so many studies, texts, and world commission reports and the establishment of so many courses on globalism, globalization and global governance.

We now live in a world in which the capacity to do great harm is in the hands of many actors other than state governments. Unprecedented vulnerabilities such as terrorism, miniaturized weapons of mass destruction, avian flu and global warming, require global solutions. And present threats to human existence are interconnected and not all are amenable to state-centric solutions. "You cannot deter, balance or form an alliance against environmental decay" (Falk 1977: 98). There is plenty of evidence of trends toward a world economy and a global society, but one that is characterized by great disparities and conflicts. The agenda of unsolved global problems seems endless. As the media concentrate on the occasions when the UN drops the ball, people are losing confidence in the capacity of our international institutions to deal with global challenges as they are presently established.

While this study is very pragmatic and empirical in nature and concentrates on the process of international institutional reform, it will nonetheless be helpful to the reader to situate it within the major issues that have just been reviewed. I have come to two conclusions. At a very practical level, most evidence would seem to suggest that state governments are still in control of the major decisions and activities in international politics. State sovereignty seems to be so desirable that the number of states has doubled in recent decades! At the same time, global society and global problems are also a reality of our world. The quandary with which international organizations and their reform must contend is that these two, often contradictory, facts of life co-exist. Robert Keohane has recently called this multiple reality, "Governance in a Partially Globalized World" (Held and McGrew 2002: 325). In the same volume, James Rosenau calls it a "Transformative epoch" (p. 71). Mihaly Simai had earlier dubbed it, "a global system in transition" (1994: xi). So I would accept Holsti's formulation that we now must work within "the classical tradition, expanded but not superseded" (1985: 132). Further, as Holsti contends, regardless of underlying technological and cultural trends, states still accord prime importance to their own interests in the struggle for peace, security and superiority. And the fact of political anarchy has not been overcome by proclamations of mankind's unity. Marcel Merle substantiated Holsti's conclusions. In this quote we see that there are indeed additional actors but the state comes back in every sentence.

> "While the states remain as privileged actors, they figure on the international scene in very different ways, in major roles or in walk-on parts, and it is not only governments which count. Behind the actions of 'authorities' there are often business, social and ideological groups whose activities direct or influence those of their rulers. Between these private groups there are also transnational links which can, in favourable conditions, create centres of resistance or influence of which governments are obliged to take notice. There are also areas of complicity or conflict between states, which transcend national frontiers. Finally, international organizations, while not constituting real sources of power, nevertheless play a special role as an enforced link between governments which either facilitates or complicates government action" (1987: 397).

The state-centric model of the 'realists' is in tatters. Non-state actors now not only influence the ultimate decisions of states but have also demonstrated their capacity to affect structures and processes. The international agenda is no longer determined only by power and military capabilities. As we have seen in Iraq and elsewhere, war is no longer even a very effective option. There are unprecedented levels of interdependence that breakdown the traditional distinction between domestic and foreign politics. And issues such as weapons, crime, pollution, the environment, disease, water, resources and energy can affect the security not only of countries but also of humanity. This evidence of globalism incites us to construct new models of institutional competence to illuminate the paths that will transcend present limits. While the preoccupations of states must be integrated within new proposals, there is no need either to think or to act within the status quo. In particular, new values such as social justice and sustainable development need to be included not just for moral purposes (although that's not a bad idea in itself) but because we have had sufficient evidence that improved institutions cannot have legitimacy without being endowed with trust and loyalty and long term preoccupations. That is why this book can be considered within Seymon Brown's concept of the "world polity as a normative project". However, this is not just the old idealized dream that theorists projected and then hoped would be realized either by trends going in their direction or by mankind's common sense and goodwill (for example Sterling 1974: 574–6). Normative projects suggest concrete measures for moving ahead. They accept the givens of the current world but are not limited by them. Humans can take part in the process of effecting change by visualizing alternative patterns and redefining political legitimacy. We are not just observers but active participants in contributing to the discourse on a more just world polity (Brown 1992: 172–3).

Let us now focus in on the literature concerning our central analytical issue: change in the international system. We will approach this in three steps, first looking at change in the global order, then more specifically in globalization and global governance and finally in the multilateral system.

### *1.1.5 Change in the International/Global Order and World Politics*

By *world order* is meant, "the structure of world politics and in particular the number of power centers" (Dingwerth & Pattberg 2006: 197). These authors also qualify *world politics* as a neutral concept that refers to political structures and processes which cross borders. Let us start by studying the various elements in the analysis of change and reform in the global order such as growing interdependence, changes in the capacities of actors, and the nature of globalization and global governance. In his "*The Future of Global Governance*", Mihaly Simai paints with a broad brush but he shows us how international institutions fit into the current period of transition in global orders. He finds that the "State-centred character of the international political system is in increasing conflict with the transnational nature of the world economy" (p. xx). Simai summarizes many of the fundamental changes in the world order. The growing transnational economic flows have produced technological and income gaps, global ecological crises and the need to harmonize economic and ecological demands. Simultaneously there has been a rise in political problems such as ethnic and religious fundamentalism, devastating civil wars, the ballooning number of states, a growth in interdependence and interaction, an erasing of the boundaries between domestic and international domains, and a general weakening of the Westphalian state system faced by the forces of globalization.

Simai puts our quandary in a nutshell when he proclaims that "Change cannot be prevented, but its consequences must be managed" (p. vi). That is why he concludes that the strong international convergence of problems requires multilateral cooperation and the help of the UN for their solution. A growth in interdependence should produce incentives for its management. Simai argues in favour of a multilateral approach and multilateral institutions to deal with present and future global problems. However, the international community has yet to create a grand design for a new order and change has produced more academic debate than concrete measures.

The dominant patterns of international cooperation would appear to be increasingly "inefficient and irrelevant" (Simai, Mihaly 1994: vi–viii). Changes in the state system and new global actors are outstripping international organizations and their capacity to deal with unilateralism and the overflow from domestic conflicts and international economic instability.

> "By contrast, multilateralism is founded on international dialogue, mutual tolerance and respect, consensus building, accommodation of interests and values, and mutual understanding." (Simai 1994: xi)

It is well known that there are few things under the sun that are completely new. Of course, this is as true of policy research and model building as of any other field. A case in point is the 1996 study of Charles Hauss on *Beyond Confrontation: Transforming the New World Order.* He had to take the first fifth of his book to demonstrate that there had been sufficient changes in war, economics, the environment and minorities to require new thinking in international relations that goes beyond confrontation as the only solution (our Chapter 3). Although Keohane and Nye (1989) had already discussed the concept, Hauss took the second fifth of his book to establish 'interdependence', which requires some sort of cooperative, win-win solution, as his central organizing principle. Today, thanks to these authors, more and more scholars accept international interdependence as a key principle of global politics. Hauss then asked how new thinking consistent with the implications of interdependence could replace values and assumptions based on imposing one's will in international relations. He believed a political paradigm shift akin to scientific revolutions (Kuhn 1969) was the key and he thought he could already see some geopolitical examples of countries cooperating in new and interesting ways. Unfortunately, they were not validated by the neo-conservative revolution, the conflict of civilizations and the war on terror – a warning to us about how difficult it is to predict the near future in international relations.

However, in looking at models of change and political paradigm shifts Hauss was ahead of the game. A paradigm can be said to be the "mental lens" through which people make sense of the world around them. Hauss saw a paradigm shift as a "dramatic adaptation to dramatically changed circumstances." (p. 155) Moreover, a new mindset offers a more accurate view. According to him:

> "There are times when a community can get away with incremental reforms which tinker with the status quo. There are other times when there is so wide a gap between what can be done with business as usual and what has to be accomplished that incremental approaches just won't work"

Having analyzed several paradigm shifts that both succeeded and failed, Hauss hypothesized that it takes a protracted period of struggle during unusually charged moments in history before a new consensus is formed. They start with a small number of visionaries who innovate new concepts that are adopted by another small number of public opinion leaders who are not afraid of risk. They in turn communicate it to larger numbers including widely respected social leaders who see to the education of others until the new concept gains credence and decision-makers can no longer avoid dealing with the issue. He concludes that if there is to be a global paradigm shift based on this model, it would come most quickly among educated individuals and small groups with resources of time and money that have the opportunity to experiment with new ideas and practices. In particular, since their expanded role at the 1992 Rio Summit on the environment and development (UNCED), this leadership role has fallen to NGOs (Hauss 1996: 162–7).

Finally, the author claims that states are no longer the only actors and the study of international regimes shows that in fact they gain their impetus from NGOs and international organizations. This is because they can operate outside a single nation's interests for the collective good and because they have expertise and they can develop plans and strategies for the longer term.

> "The record of the NGOs is in many ways even more impressive, because there are so many more of them and they have more latitude in what they chose to do. They have, for instance, been major players in protecting the rights of indigenous peoples, setting up international forums, lobbying national governments, sharing and spreading information, and even convincing private companies such as McDonald's to stop or reduce their polluting practices." (p. 232).

### 1.1.6 Globalization and Global Governance

Just as there are great debates about world orders and the phenomenon of integration, so there are over the meaning and impact of globalization and global governance. Both the practice and the analysis of these two phenomena are important to us because they very much form the context in which multilateralism is evolving and to which the reform of international organizations must respond. To a large extent one can say that the movement towards the analysis of global governance was a result of both the integrative and disaggregative impacts of globalization.

A survey of the literature shows that *globalization* can be defined as an "historical process, which transforms the spatial organization of social relations and transactions, generating transcontinental or inter-regional networks of interaction and the exercise of power" (Held & McGrew 2002: 2). Originally intended to focus on international economic integration, the definition has been enlarged to capture change in interactions in key domains such as the economic, the environmental and the political.

The traditional understanding of *multilateralism* was as a hierarchical, intergovernmental activity to coordinate national policies mainly developed around inter-governmental organizations, the main one being the United Nations. It was largely assumed multilateralism was only amendable to incremental change (Keohane 1990). It is also a deeper organizing principle that includes the principles and norms of international society. But its effect on the international system was to perpetuate the dominance of states and piecemeal reforms (Coate, Knight & Maximenko 2005: 15). A newer conceptualization of multilateralism sees it adapting to, even being radically transformed by, material circumstances in the international environment. Thus its scope is broadened to include other international actors such as NGOs and to be of long duration so that the post-World War II period was just one building block in its evolution. Through regime building, multilateralism fosters consensual practices via common norms and decision-making practices. Its continued evolution will likely lead to "third generation" "successor organizations". In part, they will result from the current critical analysis of problem-solving techniques. It is the destiny of multilateralism to continually surpass itself (Ruggie 1993, Weiss & Gordenker 1996, Krasner 1983, Cox 1992, Bertrand 1988, UNA-USA 1987, Coate et al. 2005).

*Global governance* includes "those procedures and practices that exist at the world or regional level for the management of political, economic and social affairs" (Coate, Knight, Maximenko 2005: 17). This definition is in line with that of the *Commission on Global Governance* (1995: 2). Various international institutions can be responsible for organizing particular spheres of multilateral action. It can take place at different locales and as it evolves it can be understood to include non-state actors and to cover global issues by establishing authoritative rules and procedures to govern interaction among multiple forces. Global political issues refer to "broad issues involving the contestation of power and transcending the narrow interests of states" (Coate et al. 2005:17). Aside from guiding our analysis to political processes beyond the state, global governance is an analytical concept that goes beyond specific actors to study the existence of norms, rules, and standards that structure and constrain social activity in the world. It draws attention to the emergence of spheres of authority beyond the national/international dichotomy and analyses linkages between societal actors and governmental institutions (Dingwerth and Pattberg 2006: 197–99).

Fuchs and Kratochwil are particularly critical of earlier studies of globalization that tended to be a repeat of 'modernization' theory that assumed the world inevitably progresses in linear stages that can be analyzed as an apolitical, functional and fairly harmonious process. They find these studies were pitched at a macro-trend level, which ignored the highly differentiated and contingent distributional outcomes that actually happen across the world when one analyses the actions of the transformative agencies. They provide a devastating portrait of a vulnerable world where information infrastructures "steer" other infrastructures; virulent ethnic conflicts are leading to "failed" states; marauding "nomads" have access to information and financial networks even when they are supposedly hiding out; and where political entrepreneurs are able to mobilize their followers through the modern media.

> "Precisely because of much denser information and transportation networks, potential warlords competing with the state by establishing a protection racket can plug into "networks" of mercenaries, weapons purveyors, drug distributors, and smugglers, thereby gaining access to resources – earning money by selling drugs or even engaging in slavery – or raising funds in the various diasporas abroad." (Fuchs and Kratochwill 2002: 231)

This type of "bottom-up" analysis leads Fuchs and Kratochwil to conclude that conventional understanding of ethnic and civil conflict (and hence of security) is "woefully inadequate" and the reality of globalization is much more complicated than overly optimistic evaluations suggest (p. 232). While there are positive achievements of globalization, the overall record is rather bleak with evidence that: fewer and fewer people are owning more and more of the world's resources (Scholte 2000); there is a decline in various dimensions of security; and the democratic bases of governance are severely limited. They believe that interpretations of globalization are highly dependent on one's point of view. We therefore require detailed, disaggregated studies to discover the differences in its geographic and social impacts "for the identification of steering needs and instruments" (p. 239). We return to such studies of globaliztion in Chapter 3.

Let us turn to one of the early authorities in the field of global governance for some up-dated definitions and conceptual distinctions. James Rosenau agrees with Coate et al. in proposing that "global governance is a summarizing phrase for all the sites in the world where efforts to exercise authority are undertaken. It neither posits a highest authority nor anticipates that one is likely to evolve in the long run. On the contrary, it argues that an irreversible process is underway wherein authority is increasingly disaggregated, resulting in a system of global governance comprised of more and more centres of authority in every corner of the world and at every level of community" (2002: 71). Rosneau goes on to assume that the study of global governance is a normative enterprise that tries to answer the question of how to develop the order and authority needed for "an improvement of the human condition" – a goal to which this book subscribes.

As Rosenau elaborates, governance consists of rule systems and steering mechanisms that are authoritative because their directives are heeded, even if through informal processes and repeated practices. Compliance is the key to ascertaining its presence. There are, he maintains, two types of world politics, one an inter-state system and another multicentric system of diverse types of other collectivities that has lately emerged as a rival source of authority, which often cooperates with the state system. He thinks of such entities as international non-governmental associations, coalitions of them, corporations, professional societies, advocacy movements and others. Often they constitute international regimes (Krasner 1983: 2). States are still the main players but there is a continual diminution of their authority as more wealth, ideas, power and people move across their borders in private transactions. There is no longer a simple territoriality of power. And in such a world, Rosenau believes hegemonic power can neither flourish nor endure. Much power is migrating to non-state actors who can organize sprawling networks. It is likely that whoever masters the mobilization of networks stands to gain great advantage. This essentially is the way that civil society organizes itself. It is one of the main reasons this book sees civil society as a key player in the modernization of multilateralism.

The extraordinary variety of new forms of multilateral action and global governance is both complex and politically motivated. We have two trends. There is an enormous movement toward multi-centered global governance with diverse actors, sectors and locales. In addition, the American Ambassador to the United Nations, John Bolton, has let it be known the UN is in a competitive field and the Americans and others can chose to carry out their multilateral relations in other venues. For military action the Americans seem to prefer to turn to NATO. For economic affairs they turn to the G8 of the Bretton Woods institutions, and so on. The proliferation of alternatives to the UN is quite remarkable. Just think of the various Groups (G8, G20, L20, G77 etc.), Coalitions of the Willing, various Summits, regional and sub-regional organizations, special Panels and Commissions, hybrid institutional arrangements like the Global Environmental Facility (created by the World Bank, UNDP and UNEP), inter-agency coordinating mechanisms (e.g. UNAIDS), public-private partnerships (Global Alliance for Vaccines and Immunization) or private initiatives like the Carter Center or the Center for Humanitarian Dialogue which carried out the peace negotiations between Indonesia and Aceh. One motive for this explosion of alternatives is the inefficacy of UN decision-making; another is the political will to avoid the UN. Both are equally good motivations for its reform.

Moreover all these alternative, semi-institutional settings for multilateral negotiation and action have severe drawbacks. Keohane (2002) and Forman and Segaar (2006) have posited a number of components of the efficacy and legitimacy of international institutions. These include the procedural rules, accountability, transparency, and representation. On the output side there are questions of generalized policy, efficiency, sustainability and predictable funding. It is demonstrable that these new coalitions and partnerships can draw in new actors, energy and funding for specific short-term goals. However, there are already instances when these new, ad hoc, targeted measures have the effect of drawing away from the funding, the generalized representation and the global policy making of UN agencies. There is also the matter of the sustainability of these new partnerships because of issues of the unpredictability of funding and thus of human and financial resources. There is also the question of the legitimacy of these operations, which, by definition, have asymmetrical power relations, narrow representation, and lower levels of access for

NGOs. More generally in governmental activities, there is the whole question of the appropriateness of private actors that are not generally subject to public accountability. In the longer term, there is also the likelihood that public-private partnerships and coalitions, which deal with particularistic issues and do not exhibit permanent authority or continuity, may also have deleterious effects on the capacities of inter-governmental organizations and their ability to develop global governance.

To try and put in place a degree of structure for understanding this "messy world", Rosenau posits a six-fold typology of structures and processes that sustain current flows of authority. He imagines top-down and bottom-up governance, market governance, network, side-by-side and mobius-web governance. The collectivities that crowd his global stage include: governments, trans-national corporations, inter-governmental organizations, non-governmental organizations and INGOs, elites, mass publics, and markets. Rosenau admits his typology in no way resolves the problems of accountability, transparency and effectiveness required in global governance but it gives him some grounds for optimism. He finds there is safety in numbers and a crowded, pluralistic global stage is a healthy form of politics. The numbers also suggest that the numbers of those concentrating their talents on the human condition is growing. And the advent of networks means potentially greater participation in the on-going dialogue. These are all quite positive reasons for espousing a key role for civil society in global governance and its reform.

Fuchs and Kratochwil (2002: 11–20) have very well summarized the pros and cons of global governance that can be found in the now extensive literature. However, almost everyone agrees, as we saw with Rosenau, that global governance does not mean global government both because of considerations of undesirability and infeasibility. There are, though, disagreements about the actual and potential extent of global governance and whether or not it is necessarily virtuous. Global governance optimists base their hopes on civil society that has sources of power in its specialized local knowledge, its technical expertise, and its public participation in networks and activities and telecommunications. INGO Internet websites allow the public relatively easy access to relevant information. And civil society has benefited from the legitimacy crises of the IGOs and the state. In addition, there is a generalized, creeping undermining of sovereignty. The critics point to evidence that, in fact, global governance regime development and effectiveness fall far short of ambitions and expectations. There is a persistent "enforcement gap" that shows that global civil society does not have the "steering competence" that some claim for it. There are doubts about the capacity of new actors to contribute substantially to global governance and there is a lack of access to them by large sectors of the global population. It is also claimed that many NGOs do not intentionally pursue politics and there are huge variances in their political capabilities. As for international organizations, they are still substantially under the control of their member states, which are still the only actors legitimately able to raise resources through taxes and to implement collectively binding decisions. It is unlikely civil society will have real influence until its participation is sufficiently supported by international law. In other words, while it is possible to be optimistic about the potential of global civil society, one must be very aware of its limits when making projections about its future activities.

### 1.1.7 Changing the Multilateral System

> *"The key question on UN reform has always been not "why" or "what" but "how".* (Maxwell 2005: 415).

What lessons can we learn from the recent history of attempts to reform international organizations, which are at the heart of the multilateral system? Let us start to zoom in on the core of our study, the actual process of organizational transformation and how this process can be initiated and mobilized.

While our concern is with international institutions in general, this book deals mainly with organizations that have universal membership—mainly the United Nations system. This is a short hand that will be used to speak of the UN, all of its agencies, funds and programmes, including the specialized agencies and courts and also the international financial institutions (IFI, sometimes called the Bretton Woods institutions made up of the World Bank and the International Monetary Fund, IMF, and with which we now include the World Trade Organization, WTO). Although the IFI are not strictly speaking under the control of the UN because they are based on their own treaties, they will be included under the rubric of the System.

Institutions can be defined as the norms, rules, conventions and codes of behaviour that provide a framework for human interaction (North 1990). Although they usually involve organizations, institutions may be informal as well as formal. On the international scene, we are particularly interested by "regimes," which are "sets of implicit or explicit principles, norms, and rules and decision-making procedures around which actors' expectations converge in a given area of international relations" (Krasner 1983: 2). In other words, they are formed of codes of behaviour that international actors follow out of their own perceived interests without the structures and enforcement power of institutional authority. Security regimes and the effects of globalization are of particular concern because, in a sense, it is regime formation that provides dynamism to international relations.

Because international institutions have become so large and complex, when analyzing change, it is necessary to make distinctions concerning levels of significance. In this text, as we saw in the Introduction, *change* is used to refer to ongoing, low-level continuing political evolution as in regular elections to the Security Council or nominations of secretary-generals. *Transformation*, on the other hand, is when the nature of politics is modified, including constitutional (Charter) objectives and values or structural modification of an institution's norms or components. In between, we may speak of managed and purposeful *reform* of an institution's internal administrative or financial functions to improve efficiency and adjust to a changing agenda or the growth or retraction of resources. Sometimes there may be a process of *adaptation* on an ad hoc, incrementalist, and reactive basis to changes in an organization's environment. The terms *reform* and *change* also have to be used on a catch-all basis to include all sorts of forms and proposals for modifications to present institutions. Needless to say, as in any categorization, there may be gray areas between each of the types of change.

Modernization is used in its generic sense of "bringing up-to-date". As regards international organizations, it means bringing their functions into line with the challenges imposed by the global society. The term has been adopted here because it moves us away from all the controversy surrounding the term "reform" in the context of the United Nations.

The process of on-going change which does not question underlying principles has also been categorized and specified under the headings of 1) incremental growth, 2) turbulent non-growth and 3) downsizing, by Ernst Haas who includes them all under the rubric of 'adaptation' (Haas 1990: 27–29). With incremental growth, an organization adapts reflexively by adding new tasks to suit newcomers and new demands. It is probable the current UN would fall under the heading of turbulent non-growth, which is characterized by a "lack of consensual knowledge, loss of control by the dominant coalition, a phenomenon of shifting coalitions, an incompatibility of goals, the inability to monitor the performance of the organization's sub-systems and basic confusion in the organization's task domains". Rigidity and retrenchment set in and, Haas forecasts, one can expect calls for downsizing and/or reorganization. In each of these situations the organization proves to be incapable or unwilling to face up to requirements for fundamental transformation to face new realities.

However, Haas is also interested in the conditions of more fundamental institutional change that he dubs 'organizational learning'. It includes new world-views that redefine world problems and set aside outdated ideologies at the same time as it abandons established organizational ideas and routines. To arrive at such transformational change, Haas proposes four conditions: 1) there needs to be a dominant coalition of member states with similar goals; 2) the coalition needs to be supported by a credible epistemic community that provides a knowledge base; 3) a sufficient consensual set of ideas is necessary to reformulate problems and propose solutions; and 4) a reflective mode of thinking must exist in the organization that accepts the need for its reconceptualization (Haas 1990: ch. 7).

These innovative proposals are very stimulating. Too often, the UN is seen as a whole, instead of as a system of competitive coalitions of states. The need for a consensual set of ideas as a prior condition for fundamental change has been underestimated. On the other hand, under Kofi Annan the UN has been willing to consider structural change and this is an immense advance that seems to be ensconced in the Organization. As will be proposed later, under certain conditions civil society could act as 'epistemic' community to provide a knowledge base for reform. However, it is to be noted that the conditions refer to the need for new ideas and 'rethinking' and do not include the necessary forces for mobilizing for change and organizing the reform process. Haas leaves it in the hands of the very states whose national interests are blocking the modernization of the organization.

Haas also represents a particular approach to UN reform. One wants to leap head first into the fray. Once one has perceived problems with the current organization and its capacity to deal with world challenges, it is assumed, then, that everyone will rush head long into holistic, uncompromising, long-range reforms. This is not the position taken by Andrew Knight in his latest book, which proposes a combination of "both tinkering and rethinking" (Knight 2005: 35).

As one author has recently pointed out, while institutions are intended to facilitate human relationships, they may become an impediment because their inherently slow evolution can lead to gaps between decision-making structures and the scope of the issues with which they are supposed to deal. While global issues cut across borders, the most powerful institutions are still within states. The distinctions and limited interactions between sectorially based institutions often result in "deeply fractured public management systems" (Kaul & Le Goulven 2003: 378).

Although many people think change is beneficial, bringing about political change is difficult because it runs headlong into established interests and human habits. It is usually the wealthiest and most powerful groups, communities and individuals who support the established order because they benefit the most from it. States protect their national interests before they worry about the common good. The sovereignty paradigm protects existing political regimes. Many businesses seem content with the present world anarchical system. While we have gotten used to stability in the nation-state, it seems very difficult to convince new generations of business that an orderly market would diminishes risk and uncertainty. Additionally, those with wealth and power are comfortable in the system they understand and that recompenses them. Intellectual gatekeepers sometimes make nice sounds about the need for change and reform, but writers such as Ann Florini have noted the gap between rhetoric and reality:

> So far, although people are becoming more aware of the global nature of humanity's most urgent problems and opportunities, the responses, with some notable exceptions, add up to imaginative muddling through. The thousands of international conferences, treaties, and declarations of pious intent have, with some notable exceptions, done more to salve the conscience than to save the world (Florini 2003: 6).

We have already seen that Knight (2001–05) and his co-authors propose a straddling position on the modernization of multilateralism. They think we must improve reform techniques within the UN at the same time as we rethink its basic principles and operations. They make interesting suggestions with regard to both. First, they use case studies of multilateral action to provide experience from which the UN can learn to be more effective and relevant. These lessons suggest that even "enlightened realists" like Henry Kissinger, who still believe the world can be run by a "concert-based coalition" of great powers and regional organizations on an ad hoc basis are out of date. The world has now moved into a "post-modern" era defined by global integration and characterized not by states but by a polycentric system of both hard (military-economic) and soft (persuasive influence) determinants of power. It is in a transitional period with tensions between state governments, a world capitalism that is largely out of control, and global clashes of identity. Knight and Masciulli therefore propose a "neo-idealism or idealpolitik" that is "cosmopolitan and democratic, humane global leadership in the pursuit of world interests." (Knight 2005: 246). For them, idealpolitik combines moral principles with a notion of world interests, advocates reform of the UN for human, not national, survival in dignity, and advanced global leadership and governance centred in the UN but not limited to it. They assume that multilateralism must of necessity undergo periodic change and therefore the UN must be equipped with procedures for learning so it can continually adapt to the needs of the world.

Central to the world's needs is a new ethical consensus founded in human dignity and rights. Human dignity must be bolstered by democracy, solidarity (the global common good and world interests) and subsidiarity (the larger community leaves to the smaller ones or individuals what they can to do best). A new universal imperative will seek to protect all human beings against cruelty, oppression and fear. All humans ought to be treated humanely. The UN should therefore intervene against gross violations even at the expense of state sovereignty.

In the context of their neo-idealism they advocate for the United Nations holistic, institutional, social learning rather than reformist, ad hoc tinkering. Social learning engages in questioning and revising means and ends on the basis of consensual knowledge. This means a rational re-examination of the UN's goals (including the Charter) and a realignment of its structures to meet world challenges. The UN needs to be more aware both of the historical trends in multilateralism and also the forces for change coming from its environment. To plan for a process of change through learning, UN leadership must be self-critical and well enough informed to be able to coordinate change at all levels. An autonomous intelligence capacity must be created to collect, analyse and disseminate information. Because information and its analysis are now so large and complex, the UN must act as a coordinator, fostering networks of cooperation between its own learning mechanisms and those of civil society and also of universities and think tanks acting as an epistemic community (Knight 2005: 245–55). For instance, the more we move toward major institutional change, the more it is necessary for the authorities or the leaders of change to undertake wide public consultation and/or participation at the agenda-setting and ratification phases, even if the negotiation phase is carried out in more restrained groups (Stein 1990).

But, Knight and his colleagues also want to rethink the UN's principles and operations. The 'third generation' multilateral institutions that they imagine operating in polycentric global governance will have a new set of goals and values. At their centre will be a reconceptualization of security, which will no longer be limited to national security but will focus on world interests and human security. As suggested in the UNDP 1994 report on Human Development, human security will be one of the "five new pillars" of a people-centred world order which will also include new models of sustainable human development, new partnerships between state and markets, new patterns of national and global governance and new forms of international cooperation. Human security is not only protection from violence but also must be based on human focused sustainable development. This entails integrating economic and social issues with war and peace priorities and legitimizing supra-national governance so that the psychological end-state is that individuals feel more secure. "Human Security" is considered one of the major conceptual shifts (Jolly, Emmerij & Weiss 2005: 33) in the UN's history and after 12 years of gestation has been accepted as the basis of the UN resolution on "responsibility to protect" which eventually will come to challenge the Westphalian notion of sovereignty.

But, there is more. Development requires peace but it also should be centered on human needs, which go beyond survival to include growth, learning, identity and control of one's environment. Historically, the satisfaction of human needs conflicts with institutional values, "between the structures and norms created and supported by powerful elites and the human needs that must be met at the individual level if societies are to be functionally efficient and harmonious" (Burton 1979: 83–4). This highly significant concept is further elaborated by Coate, Knight and Maximenko who specify that the "historical dialectic of societal needs and allocation and control structures versus processes of human needs fulfilment lies at the heart of human evolution." (Knight 2005: 22) Good governance must include human needs. It will also require new forms of cooperation and partnerships that go beyond the state to include NGOs, epistemic communities, global civil society and transnational social movements – although the authors worry that there are areas of the globe that are not covered by international associations (Knight 2005: 18–23). The problem with the idealized projections of these authors is that they stop short of proposing how they can be attained in a real world.

Finally, two articles specifically targeting techniques for reforming the UN and published at the time of the September 2005 New York UN Leaders' Summit, deserve special attention. Edward Luck, director of the Centre on International Organization of Columbia University, believes Kofi Annan ignored all the lessons of former campaigns to reform the UN. Luck establishes a number of important historical principles to which reformers should pay attention.

1. A limitation to change is the precedent-bound nature of the UN and the intrinsically political nature of its decisions. When the true implications of potential reforms for national interests become clear to member states, "their conservative instincts and fear of change come to the surface" (Luck 2005: 408).
2. The problems of international organizations are first of all political rather that institutional, and these problems must be addressed within the member states. "Political convergence precedes institutional change" (p. 410).
3. If the aim of reform is to bring states together in support of a common platform, then starting with the remodeling of the Security Council is a "surefire formula to exacerbate tensions" (p. 411).
4. As Annan himself said, "Reform is not an event; it is a process" (Annan 1997: par. 165). Sometimes it is helpful to delink the most controversial items and not insist on the acceptance of a complete package at one time (p. 412).

However, aside from this wise advice, Luck is also opposed to radical restructuring and prefers "modest and sensible renovations" (p. 407). The UN should be sharpening the tools of management, implementation and agenda setting to make the UN work better. Modest expectations are in order. His main thesis is that the UN is in the state it is in precisely because a world with profoundly divergent interests and perspectives needs its institutions and norms to evolve peacefully. Moreover, "those hoping to strengthen the institution should be wary of raising public expectations about the rate and depth of likely change" (p. 412).

His vision of "glacier-like" change reposes on the view that reform must be brought about by member states and that history tells us that while broad packages are sometimes proposed they are never adopted (p. 411). Reform is hard to achieve when commitment of members is "shallow and self-serving", they are divided among themselves and they are fearful of unpredictable renovations. In brief, based on a traditional, state-centric view, Luck is saying that reform has not worked in the past so it will not work in the future and the best the UN can do is adapt to circumstances. Such a view has two problems. It does not take into consideration that the structure of international politics has changed making new demands and offering new potential for system transformation. Second, it falls in an old trap of empirical political science, which is limited by what it observes, that is, by historical precedent. But, as political philosophy teaches us, politics also appeals to values and hence to normative projects that go beyond what is in order to seek what can be. To quote the former Prime Minister of Canada, Paul Martin, "There is such a thing as a global conscience" (8-12-05). So let us accept Luck's wise advise and set aside his undue pessimism.

Simon Maxwell, director of the Overseas Development Institute of London, offers an eight-step program to help reform multilateral institutions. Theory from a number of disciplines (Gillinson 2004, Ostrom 1990) on how to develop cooperation is married to more specific proposals about multilateral institutions (Maxwell 2005).

1. Trust is central. Build trust and shared vision. Trust is harder to achieve in large groups. Keep core groups small.
2. Develop trust-building measures from the start. Provide opportunities both for informal interaction and also for formal negotiation. Complex agreements can be broken down into component parts and sequential steps to build momentum.
3. Use the same core group for many issues to keep transaction costs down. Like-minded people working together establish ways of doing things.
4. The likelihood of cooperation increases through strong reinforcement: non-cooperators are simply frozen out. Use "network closure" to make it embarrassing or awkward for those who refuse to cooperate. Civil society can play an important role in provoking severe political consequences through targeted demonstrations and "naming and shaming".
5. Cooperation is a matter of self-interest and ensues when actors have something to gain and when defection entails significant costs. So choose the right issues where all the actors have something to gain and something to lose. Collective action is often most successful when costs of defection are high, like expulsion or suspension. On the other hand what do the big players really want and need to work together for?
6. Now start to think about positive incentives. "Cooperation requires a combination of an enabling social environment and a rational exercise of ruthless self-interest: a mutually reinforcing mix of culture and calculus" (p. 417). Sometimes you need packages, sometimes trade-offs.
7. Certain benefits accrue when cooperation is broad and lasting. It is easier to sustain community when it performs more than one function. Cooperation tends to build over time and is greater when longer lasting.
8. Establish institutions that will manage these interactions. It helps when there are the right rules, the right spaces and the right procedures.

So we should recall here the conclusions we drew from Annan's ten-year attempt in the real world to reform the structures of the United Nations. It was found that the roadblocks to reform included: a lack of leadership and the narrow self-interests of governments; the use of short-term adaptation to put off long-term transformation; the capacity of the Permanent Five to prevent consideration of unpalatable issues; real-world incentives and disincentives of the current political context including the attitudes of major actors and the media; the "inbred-impediment" of blocking vetoes by various coalitions of states opposed to specific issues that adds up to a form of obstructionism that drives reform efforts down to the lowest common denominator.

## *1.1.8 The Role of Civil Society and NGOs*

Recently there have been a plethora of studies on the growing role of NGOs and civil society in global politics (Edwards, Kaldor, Keane, Keck & Sikkink, Khagram, Tarrow). They look at the influence of advocacy "beyond borders" in "restructuring" world politics. Kaldor even sees civil society as an answer to war. Whether or not this is tenable, certainly the increased international activism of international non-governmental organizations (INGOs) has been demonstrated.

At this point, an additional, parenthetical clarification about terminology will be useful. Often in the UN, they refer to "civil society *and* NGOs". One has to assume that this is to allow for the fact that one has to include in civil society not only formally organized associations but also such categories as academia, churches, unions, the media, social movements and even some embryonic groupings (especially in developing countries). Because the UN hates to knowingly exclude anyone, they therefore have the habit of referring to the two entities – NGOs and civil society. When speaking of civil society, this study refers mainly to organized associations operating internationally (which, in addition to advocacy groups, may represent such groupings as unions, churches or the media). Traditionally, these have been called INGOs but today many writers seem to be using the shorthand of just NGOs. As stated earlier, civil society is used in this study as a catch-all term to include especially advocacy groups and NGOs, but also the broader grouping of transnational social movements and also unions, churches, academics, media etc. but excluding criminal activities and for-profit business operations.

Citing numerous analytical-descriptive studies between 2000 and 2002, Keane showed there were an estimated 5,000 world congresses held annually and some 50,000 not-for-profit non-governmental organizations operating internationally (3,000 in 1994 in Simai: 347). Thus, nearly 90 percent of them have been formed since the 1980s and 90s. World wide, they employ several millions of people and can count on the volunteer labour of as many more. Many have larger staffs and budgets than the UN agencies with which they deal (Keane: 5). "The normative concerns that inevitably attend their strategic approaches are treated as a given; their main preoccupation is with the means of achieving or stabilizing a global civil society" (Keane: 3).

The debate over civil society has been waxing fast and furious. Some see it as an adjunct to international democratic and cosmopolitan life (Held 1995, Archibugi et al. 1998). Others are more critical noting the lack of resources and access in large parts of the globe; the imbalance of resources between civil society and corporations and states; and a lack of democratic credentials, transparency and accountability of many civil society actors. Further, they maintain that NGO activism tends to strengthen the influence of developed countries to the point that "current governance efforts at the global level have a club quality" (Fuchs and Kratochwil 2002: 235).

Edwards gives an intuitive definition starting from a church quote that "Fellowship is life", which is an idea that has echoed down the centuries for "anyone who has ever joined a group, formed an association or volunteered to defend or advance the causes they believe in. It is collective action in search of the good society" (Edwards 2004: 1). Most recently civil society has been in the forefront of promoting good governance, civil and political rights, and mobilizing opposition to the agglomeration of power and authoritarian rule and the defence of the democratic public sphere. However, there is also recognition that in civil society there are dangers of cooptation, of 'privatization by stealth', of exaggeration of political importance, of 'loonies and paranoids', and of a narrowness of purpose and constituency that can lead to illegitimacy, corruption, lack of accountability and external dependence (Edwards 2004: 1–17). Given both this potential and its limits, Edwards maintains that associational life is a handmaiden to much broader change in social, economic and political structures. The essence of civil society is collective action. "The determination to do something because it is the right thing to do, not because we are told to do it by governments or enticed to do it by the market, is what makes associational life for good ..." (p. 111).

Another potential role for civil society is to fulfill the function of an 'epistemic community'. When an organization is in a reform mode and moves toward questioning its initial beliefs and goals it needs to do so on the basis of consensual knowledge. Peter Haas has proposed that this can be supplied in part by what he calls an epistemic community, "a network of professionals with recognized expertise and competence in a particular domain and an authoritative claim to policy-relevant knowledge within the domain or issue area" (P. Haas 1992: 3). As Haas refers to people coming from various disciplines, one may assume he is generally thinking of academics and other experts. But NGO leaders either have or could develop the aptitudes to fulfill his criteria, which include a shared set of normative beliefs oriented toward social action, shared causal beliefs, and criteria for weighing and validating knowledge based on the end result of enhancing human welfare. NGOs also fulfill the criteria suggested by Robert Keohane of taking a critical stance toward the traditional view of current thinking about reform or adaptation by being able to stand outside multilateral institutions (Keohane 1988).

A study by the recognized specialist in social movements, Sidney Tarrow, brings us full circle to some of the original theorizing about the current role of the state. After a broad reading of the literature on "transnational activism", Tarrow reaches a number of conclusions. He makes us aware that international social movements are just one component in the spectrum of international contention that also includes NGOs, labor movements, transnational coalitions and elements of international organizations. However, Tarrow maintains that while new actors are appearing, the state remains the fundamental framework for contentious politics. Transnational activism does not "float above the earth" but is shaped by states' domestic structures and international institutions. The most effective transnational activists are what he calls "rooted cosmopolitans", that is people who remain rooted in domestic networks and opportunities. They are constrained and supported by domestic networks.

> "Even as they make transnational claims, these activists draw on the resources, networks, and opportunities of the societies in which they live. Their most interesting characteristic is how they connect the local and the global. In today's world we can no longer draw a sharp line between domestic and international politics" (Tarrow 2005: 2).

Secondly, while globalization may provide the incentives and themes for transnational activism, it is what he calls "internationalism" that offers the framework, focal points and structure of opportunities. Students of social movements know that it is not enough just to trace their roots to grievances and social cleavages. There must be intervening processes that lead people to engage in the politics of contention. "Acting collectively requires activists to marshal resources, become aware of and seize opportunities, frame their demands in ways that enable them to join with others, and identify common targets" (Tarrow 2005: 8).

Tarrow believes that it is internationalism that channels resistance to globalization. His concept of internationalism includes increased: horizontal relations across states, governmental officials and nonstate actors; vertical relations among subnational, national and international levels; and enhanced formal and informal structures that invite transnational activism by making the threats of globalization more visible and offering resources, opportunities and alternative targets. Thus, internationalism is a loose framework of institutions, regimes, practices, and processes that include state actors and penetrate domestic politics. Internationalism impinges on the state but does not destroy its power base. States still have armies and the taxing power. To understand this *complex* internationalism requires identifying the major processes and mechanisms by which nonstate actors bring new issues to the international agenda. "My central argument is that there is no single core process leading to a global civil society or anything resembling one, but – as in politics in general – a set of identifiable processes and mechanisms that intersect with domestic politics to produce new and differentiated paths to change" (2006: 9).

Of the three orders of processes that link domestic activists to the international system, the one that concerns us the most is "international coalition formation". Coalitions are defined as "Collaborative, means-oriented arrangements that permit distinct organizational entities to pool resources in order to effect change" (2006: 164). Tarrow makes the very useful distinction between 'instrumental' coalitions (low level, short term involvement around a conjuncture of interests), 'event' coalitions (e.g. Seattle), 'federated' coalitions (formally organized umbrella groups), and campaign coalitions (combine a narrow focal point and a high level of structured, long-term involvement). 'Networks' are much looser arrangements within which groups and individuals communicate and join together for specific purposes. 'Social movements' tend to be more confrontational and are defined as sustained interactions between challengers and authorities on matters of policy and culture. We will return to Tarrow's detailed analysis of processes for campaign coalitions in the final chapter. In general, the extent of cooperation and the duration of the different types of coalition vary. Groups join when they see their efforts are urgent and efficacious and they form around threats and opportunities. There is a striking capacity to produce new institutional forms. Often the campaign coalitions become distinct organizations in their own right.

> "That is why campaign coalitions, which are less exciting than short-term event coalitions and have narrower ambitions and more concrete issue-foci than federations, may be the wave of the transnational future. Their focus on a specific policy issue, their minimal institutionalization, their capacity to shift venues in response to changing opportunities and threats, and their ability to make short-term tactical alliances according to the current focus of interest make them among the most fruitful strategies for transnational collaboration" (Tarrow 2006: 179)

In a nutshell, a campaign coalition is the structural form I propose for pursuing the reform of multilateral institutions by civil society, specifically, by qualified and dedicated INGOs.

Again taking the practical, empirical approach, I see civil society as a relatively new organized actor and force on the international scene that has already had a significant influence and that could have a much greater one if it were to give itself the institutionalized means. It is one of the few political forces that can have influence both domestically and internationally. INGOs are becoming more and more global in their composition and conceptions. They are also becoming much more sophisticated. Thus they are and will be a force to be reckoned with at a time when other players may not have or want the mandate to reform international organizations. This being said, if some of the leading players in civil society decide they want to play a larger role in global governance they will have to take the criticisms seriously. In particular, they will have to work collectively and be more globally representative and more transparent and responsible. One cannot call for these characteristics in world governance if one does not exhibit them oneself.

However, to be complete and develop a normative project, the role of civil society in the modernization of multilateralism must be conceived in the current context of globalization and of a guiding set of values. Philip Cerny has taken us a long way in this direction. He insists that civil society must be analyzed in the context of the political economy of globalization. In other words, civil society's actions must be investigated alongside markets and states to understand the politics of globalization. He presents pluralism as an empirical and normative platform for exploring political action in a globalized world. The normative theory of pluralism asserts that groups, operating in the context of competitive liberal democracy, inherently develop a system of checks and balances, which is a normatively desirable condition that promotes a quasi-democratic political market place that is a "good" (or "least worse") system of governance. Pluralism can thus be used as a normative base for developing a democratic project for civil society within globalization. Cerny proposes an expanded 'neopluralist' analysis of globalization that shows how various configurations of interests and globalizing trends operate on each other. The result is a complex and conflictual world that "creates possibilities for a fairly broad range of actors at multiple levels and pressure points to influence and manipulate outcomes and to reshape global political processes in significant ways, in both empirical and normative terms" (Cerny 2006: 82).

The inference is that if we want to transfer pluralism and its normative and active potential to global politics, we must assure that there is in fact a viable base of socio-political forces and secondly that they can find a way to interact to generate a structural/institutional world context similar to liberal democracy that allows them to have effective influence. But, the key element would be the existence of groups and leaders from civil society who are able and willing to act in a creative, entrepreneurial fashion to structure such a global political market place. "Pluralism, like all political projects, has to be imagined and constructed by means of a normative political project that is always contested" (Cerny 2006: 91). It will continually be opposed because of inherent inequalities, clashing values and new claimants. We are also warned that ideal-type pluralism in which no groups are overly dominant is never realized in practice in the real world. Rather we are searching for self-stabilizing rules of the game for relatively competitive groups somewhere on a continuum between political monopolies and perfectly equal groups. There may be relatively dominant groups or coalitions but they must be able to be contested by coalitions of outsiders, or outsiders aligned with insiders. Thinking through this process is the aim of this study.

Cerny's central thesis is that the world of globalization, despite all its opponents and critics, actually opens up *opportunities* for pluralist groups and entrepreneurial leaders to have greater influence on global governance and to manipulate the development of structures and institutions. It has become a set of permissive conditions. "The changing constellation of actors in a globalizing world *plus* the increasing complexity of the structured field of action creates opportunities for reactively and/or proactively restructuring that playing field itself as particular problems arise and are confronted in practice" (Cerny 2006: 109). There are new coalition-building opportunities. Key actors can rethink the substance of their interests. In this period of transition, actors have a strategic institution-building role – as at other moments of transition in modern history.

According to Cerny, there is as yet no conclusive evidence whether globalization will support genuine competitive pluralization or will merely entrench new forms of oligopoly or monopoly. However, he points out that new economic and political entrants are emerging, and the latent power of Indian, Chinese and Latin American groups (to name but several) is incalculable. Existing hierarchies are being challenged by new coalitions of transnationally linked interest and value groups seeking to promote or restrain change. Left-right politics appears to have been displaced by other kinds of linkages like multiculturalism, diasporas, world cities, business markets, epistemic communities of scientists and experts, and transnational advocacy networks and coalitions. There are various mixed arenas of public-private, transnational regimes and global governance. These new intermediaries are running well ahead of our consciousness of the changes. At the institutional level, little can be achieved without the nation-state but the state itself can do less. Control of the state no longer means the control of policy outcomes. "Contracting out" (writ large) of governmental responsibilities has created new spaces for special interests to inhabit and capture. The multiplication of sites of governance and of conflict, competition and coalition-building means that groups and institutions must be continually rethinking their strategies. "The development of multi-nodal politics is both an existing reality and a pluralist project in the making" (Cerny 2006: 108).

The globalizing world with trends of internationalization, transnationalization, trans-local networks and uneven pluralization within webs of global governance offers unprecedented opportunities to shape change. Globalization and pluralization are mutually constituted. The paradigmatic concept of pluralism as a dynamic, "great moving process" plus the skills of civil society political entrepreneurs could place it at the centre of the action of the 21st century. They are the best hope for the pursuit of the common good, economic growth and social development – what has come to be called "enlightened self-interest". They have shown their capacity to go beyond the vested self-interest of politicians and capitalists to start to create a new normative order (Ehrenberg 1999). With their solidaristic, cross-border social agendas, they act as "cause groups" to "think globally and act locally" (Keck and Sikkink 1998). Not that everything is in their favour. Governing and economic elites will also be looking to restructure their institutions, with their rewards and constraints, to their own advantage. New and old inequalities, conflicts and destabilizing events will intervene. Often, NGOs will be conflicted on whether to become virtual parts of the growing bureaucracy of global governance or to maintain their outsider status. The institutional and policy outcomes are far from certain. As yet, civil society has not sufficiently penetrated economic and political structures. But, as Cerny concludes, "globalization is increasingly what actors make of it" (Cerny 2006: 110).

Although Cerny's theory is aimed at a much larger constellation of actors, I consider it to be an analytical foundation for thinking about the *potential* role of civil society associations and leaders and specifically about their role in the transformation of the United Nations into a third generation institution for global governance. The hypothesis of this study is that civil society, and more particularly international associations, is strategically placed to have the *opportunity* to influence the modernization of international institutions. Because of their numbers, their flexibility, their knowledge and information, and their experience, they have the possibility to influence global change. Globalization has opened up the access points and the fluidity of the world situation. Because of their value base as normatively oriented groups they are likely to orient reform in the direction of the common good. Their plurality can be molded to form a global foundation for democracy. But this will only happen if they become conscious of their potential and reconstitute their structural base to give themselves the capacity for institutional influence.

Ramesh Thakur believes NGOs are already a significant policy-influencing actor. The reasons for their rise to prominence include new 'political space' at the end of the Cold War, new issues such as human rights and the environment, their comparative advantages such as experience, expertise and credibility, the multi-layered complexity of governance, modern communications technologies for mobilization, and the quality of their personnel. "They are partners in policy formulation, information dissemination, standard-setting advocacy, monitoring and implementation" (Thakur 2002: 277). Those who learn to exploit the new opportunities for partnerships between all the new actors will be among the most effective new-age diplomats, concludes Thakur.

In closing, it is worthwhile recalling that we live in difficult times in a difficult world. It's not that our era is necessarily any more dangerous or lethal. Rather, it is because it is so difficult to understand, so unclear – so indeterminate. As citizens, we live this indeterminacy everyday. At one moment we are asked to be local citizens worrying about municipal water supplies, at the next to be national citizens trying to cope with problems of employment or immigration, and then, without the time to draw a breath, we are expected to be global citizens concerned about the tragedy in Rwanda or Darfur or about global warming that most of us can't understand. And the media don't help, turning at lightning speed from our town's traffic accidents, to the country's latest murder, to the death toll in Iraq but usually leaving out any in-depth analysis of global affairs. Nor is there anything steady on which to hang our hats. That is why we call it an era of 'complex turbulence'. Within a few years the United States went from being a colossus bestriding the whole world to a struggling nation that couldn't find enough soldiers for its army or taxes for its debts – and had learned the hard way that weapons can start wars but not make the peace. At the same time, the United Nations had gone from being a much-admired diplomatic centre to being "scandal ridden" and "irrelevant". The only reality is instability and indeterminacy.

This global situation is reflected in global governance (or its lack) and in our concepts for understanding the world (or not). No longer can we simply leave international relations to our governments. Although undeniably important, the "state-centric" world has given way to a stage crowded with new actors such as transnational corporations, fundamentalist religions, international associations, world criminal syndicates, the Olympics, ethnic nationalities, warlords and so on. Interstate relations of governments are slowly sharing the stage with multiple players at multiple levels in a complex process that tries to grapple with global challenges. But, as of yet, nothing has come to replace the Westphalian theory of international relations and so we go on playing the out-dated charade of sovereign states running the world. Even the United Nations now has economic, regional and social competitors.

As the international scene has felt the pressure of change, so too has international relations theory. We have seen how the classical realist paradigm of 'Westphalian' sovereign states has been challenged by the political economy school and by globalism. It is worth noting that underlying these battles of empirical theory has been a less recognized renewal of the normative struggle between realists and idealists. Wilsonian idealists were ridden out of town in the period leading up to the Second World War for their failure to deal with the challenges of nationalism, communism and fascism. But, they took a lot of intellectual baggage with them including not only international law but also the role of group and individual actors, or as it is sometimes called "voluntarist ideas" or "human agency". These have made a comeback in recent years, aided and abetted by human rights, which as a concept has done so much to undermine the rigid idea of sovereign independence.

Voluntaristic transnational actors, in the form of advocacy networks including social movements and INGOs, have quite different purposes and processes from governments and it is their study that helps us to understand how change occurs in the world polity, according to Keck and Sikkink (1998: 199–217). In the emergence of new global norms there are intense domestic and international struggles over meanings and policy that are best explained by human agency and international indeterminacy. For instance, globalization is not an inevitable steamroller but the sum total of thousands of individual decisions that could be oriented in a different manner. Individuals in transnational advocacy networks are motivated by principles for transforming the global scene. The motors of profound change are not just states but individuals and groups in internally differentiated societies who determine the preferences of states, which in turn determine final outcomes. These individuals and groups in national and transnational advocacy networks constitute new actors who transform understandings and interests through persuasion, socialization and pressure but also through a process of mutually transformative negotiation. Political learning takes place in these INGOs and civil society. Moreover, this process of negotiation within an emergent cosmopolitan community is not "outside" the state but involves state actors. Together society and state determine international policy. "Our initial research has suggested that networks have considerable importance in bringing transformative and mobilizing ideas into the international system…" (Keck and Sikkink 1998: 217).

As a last consideration, one of the problems of political theory is the claim that politicians pay no attention to all that academic twaddle. A remarkable article by British Prime Minister Tony Blair after nine years in power gives the lie to this pretension by taking up many of the arguments just put forth. Blair starts off by saying there is universal agreement that we are living in an interdependent world. Therefore we all have an interest in stability and a fear of chaos. This makes a mockery of traditional views on national interest. Only global development and international agreement can manage the problems of globalization. A coherent view of national interest must be wedded to a sense of international community. "But common action will not be agreed unless it is founded on common values – of liberty, democracy, tolerance and justice." Despite the scale of the agenda, there is a "hopeless mismatch between the global challenges we face and the global institutions to confront them." They need to be renewed. The greatest obstacle to multilateralism is the fear by states that they will have to give up some of their independence. But, Blair continues, there is a common basis for working together: countries can sub-contract out the problems they cannot manage on their own and everyone has an interest in stability.

> "I have not become more cynical about idealism. I have simply become more persuaded that the distinction between a foreign policy driven by values and one driven by interests is obviously wrong. Globalization begets interdependence. Interdependence begets the necessity of a common value system to make it work. In other words, the idealism becomes the *realpolitik*" (*The Globe and Mail* 27-05-06: p. A15).

### 1.1.9 Summary: Propositions for the Modernization of International Institutions

Now let us pull these various theoretical strands together to draw a portrait of the analytical context that will interpret the content of this study on how to modernize institutions like the UN.

- The post-World War II inter-national system, dominated by inter-state political relations, is slowly ceding place to a global system characterized by multiple actors, economic regimes, and considerable integration, interdependence and mutual vulnerability. International organizations such as the United Nations are driven by both inter-state and global realities.
- There is a consensus that in this current transformative epoch, international relations must of necessity be dualistic (not either/or but both/and) in nature. Here are some illustrations of politics in our inter-regnum between the end of the Cold War and whatever comes next. While sovereignty is continually being undermined, state governments remain the most powerful international decision-makers. We now must work within "the classical tradition, expanded but not superseded". As Hedley Bull predicted in 1977, "the new system will have overlapping authority and multiple loyalty." There are now two types of world politics: intrastate and multicentric. Change of the UN must include both "tinkering and rethinking". Global security must include "human as well as national survival". A new mindset is required to go beyond confrontation as the only solution to include cooperative, win-win solutions. World politics is now about both hard and soft power.
- There are now multiple actors that must be taken into account because they have an influence on global relations including: state governments, inter-governmental organizations (IGOs – both universal and regional), transnational corporations, international non-governmental organizations (INGOs, associations), broader 'civil society' including intra-state NGOs, religions, academics, media etc., sub-national and regional governmental bodies, and influential individuals (not to mention criminal organizations and warlords).
- Due to increased mobility, interdependence, interpenetrability and vulnerability, international relations have become global relations including all aspects of

society and worldwide problems. It is a total system that looks more and more like traditional nation-states, writ large. Any form of (state-centric) analysis that ignores the global system and its economic disparities, ecological overload, social mobility and human rights is likely not only to misread global relations but to condemn decision-making to the status quo.

- Problems are global in scope. At the same time, state boundaries no longer demark the limits to political authority. Unprecedented common vulnerabilities require global, not just national solutions. Critical analysts also envisage an international citizenship that more and more is calling for normative changes that include democratic principles and respect for human rights. Thus, we must think of a "smaller world" with a unity of interests and a connected humanity. But for this we need a better managerial capacity to deal with common problems.
- The UN has been hampered from reforming itself to keep up with global challenges because of its sovereignty-based Charter, a lack of state leadership, the habits of institutional routines, ideological and regional wrangling, a negative political context, and narrow, interest-based decision-making. Change runs headlong into established interests, the precedent-bound and political nature of the UN and the conservative instinct that fears loss from change. To change the UN one must understand its groups and coalitions.
- We are living in an era of transition that can be dubbed 'complex turbulence'. This is a charged, transformative period in history announcing a protracted struggle that will require visionaries, leadership and education. The messy world stage, crowded with actors, is also a sign of healthy politics that has a potential for greater participation.
- Change cannot be stopped, but it must be managed. Unfortunately, international organizations, due to their members, have become increasingly inefficient in dealing with global problems. Nevertheless, multilateral approaches are necessary because they are based on mutual respect, complex learning and global legitimacy. The goal is multi-centric global governance, not world government, which would at present be both undesirable and infeasible.
- In such a sprawling world the advantage goes to those who can organize widespread networks. Leadership has fallen to international non-governmental organizations (INGOs) that have the knowledge, time, and money to experiment and the latitude to operate outside the interests of single countries and to develop long-term strategies. The power base of these global associations and more generally of civil society is their specialized information, technical expertise, telecommunications, networks and relative ease of public participation and access.
- Nevertheless, while civil society might be the potential motor of change, steps must be taken to minimize its weaknesses, including: a still relatively weak capacity to penetrate corporations and states; a certain 'club' quality than has less than optimal participation from the Third World; a lack of resources and

of transparency and responsibility; and no coordinated capability for thought and action. There are ever-present dangers of cooptation, of airs of exaggerated importance, a certain paranoid outlook and a narrowness of purpose and constituency.

- If there is to be a transformative reform of the UN, there must be (based on Ernst Haas' formula) a dominant coalition (presumably of state and non-state actors) supported by a credible and knowledgeable ('epistemic') community that develops consensual ideas for an organization that has already demonstrated that it is in a reflective mode of thinking. The most effective organizations for building and coordinating transformative momentum are "campaign coalitions". Such a coalition is required to provide leadership, establish trust and cooperation, and to plan and manage the transformation process.
- As part of the transformation of the United Nations, there will be a requirement for rational re-examination of its norms and goals to meet global challenges and enhance effectiveness. Networks of cooperation between civil society, universities, think tanks and the UN's own 'thinking' units could undertake this 'constitutional' debate.
- This re-examination of requirements for "third generation" multilateral institutions will include, at a minimum, a reconceptualization of security to include world interests and human security based on human needs, and the integration of economic and social objectives with sustainable development. To gain momentum in the movement toward transforming institutions, common action must follow from common values – liberty, democracy, tolerance and justice (in the words of Tony Blair).
- There is consensus that the study of global governance is a normative enterprise that seeks how to develop the order and authority needed to improve the human condition. This 'idealpolitik' aims to give rise to a new ethical consensus based on human dignity and human rights and to make human security as compelling a goal as national security. This normative project must suggest concrete measures for moving ahead by visualizing alternative patterns and redefining political legitimacy. Without exaggerating the normative nature of civil society, there does seem to be sufficient evidence that its main preoccupation is to use its collective fellowship and policy-relevant knowledge in the search for the good global society.
- Despite its negative aspects, globalization has created the opportunities for wider participation in the transformation of international institutions into global governance. The changing constellation of actors in this period of transition, the new economic and political entrants such as China, India and Latin America, recent transnationally linked interest and value groups all seeking to promote or hamper change, plus the multiplication of sites of governance and conflict – have all opened up possibilities for rethinking power strategies and for new coalition building. Still, the problems of international organizations are first and foremost political in nature. Political problems and the building of convergence must

> still be addressed within the states as well as internationally. An era with these characteristics opens up opportunities for pluralistic, transnational groups and entrepreneurial leaders to manipulate the development of global structures and institutions. "Globalization is increasingly what actors make of it" (Cerny 2006: 141).

Not everyone will agree with this transformative guide. Some do not want a more effective form of global governance because it may interfere with sovereignty and the market place. However, the benefits of stability, order and justice trump the short-term gains of anarchy for the few. Some will think it is time to sideline ineffectual and self-interested state governments. Nevertheless, they are a present-day reality and they do have resources and make decisions. Better to woo them and to convince them it is their obligation to serve their citizens by moving toward world community. Some will find it too idealist. But the weight of research indicates that, as never before in recent decades, the international scene is open to the venturesome. And because our goal is transformative reform of the global system, it is safe to say that this will not be accomplished by the comfortable. It takes normatively driven entrepreneurs with an alternative vision of the future to bring about institutional change.

## 1.2 The International Politics Context

When analyzing Kofi Annan's attempts to reform the United Nations in the Introduction, it was noted that 'the context' in which reform is undertaken is crucial for designing a strategy for success. Judging both by the problems facing Annan and the theoretical proposals of Ernst Haas, the 'context' of international institutions can be considered to be composed of the current international regime, competing coalitions and power structures, consensual ideas about reform, and the actions of key players. For greater clarity let us call these the underlying conditions in the international system, power structures and coalitions, current policy orientations, and major recent events. One should add ancillary events, but unfortunately they are unknowable. The best one can do is to advise reformers to keep a weather eye on current international events and to include them in their defensive strategy. Because the descriptive task we have before us is so immense (usually filling a text book), only the context directly affecting the UN will be included.

While the centrality of the UN was once a given, it can no longer be taken for granted – ever since President Bush proclaimed it "irrelevant" in 2002 when faced with the possible defeat of the second Security Council resolution on the Iraq arms inspectors. Barely six months after Bush made his threat of "irrelevance," the U.S. and Britain felt obliged to come back to the UN to seek support for the rebuilding of Iraq. Even so, the Iraq episode also led to accusations against both the moral and the utilitarian value of the UN. Proposals were even made for its replacement. This reinforces the importance of context. It also shows why it should not be surprising to see the United States taking a central place in this analysis of the current context of the UN. The 2006 mid-east war between Israel, Palestine and Lebanon can be taken as another instructive example. It was the United States that said how long the war would go on. It was the Americans that laid out the ceasefire conditions and led the negotiations. It was the Americans who sponsored the UN resolutions. Each proposal by the UN Secretary-General or his officials was repulsed. No credible peace action was taken until the American president decided to say something. Everyone waited for the Americans. In any description of the UN context circa 2006, the Untied States must indeed be central.

### 1.2.1 Underlying Conditions

In the era of globalization since the end of the Cold War in 1990, business, technologies, production, markets, investment, transport and communication have become transnational. Knight and Masciulli believe the era is characterized by polycentric determinants of hard and soft power and is defined by globalization of communications, transportation, technology, economics and culture and renewed clashes of identity. There is a primacy of economic concerns in this transitional period. Boundaries between domestic and international politics continue to erode as situations rife with famine, civil war and violations of human rights cry out for international intervention. "The explanations of the dynamic underlying the parametric transformations include internal and external processes vis-à-vis world politics. Above all, central forces include dynamic technologies, shrinking social and geographical distances, and the proliferation of actors. The latter includes a series of transnational, large-scale and powerful social movements, addressing the non-conventional issues of women's rights, peace, environmental pollution and ecology, AIDs, the flow of refugees, drugs and currency crises in the context of interdependence and the centralizing dynamics that compel cooperation on a global scale" (Knight 2005: 246).

Globalization, according to Philip Cerny, opens up new possibilities for pluralism and civil society in the global community. Although the state is not disappearing, it is disaggregating under pressures from new and old inequalities, the global market place and new points of international access. "Multi-level governance" presents a structurally open and problematic global playing field. States are also losing a part of their policy coherence to transgovernmental networks of central bankers, regulators, lawyers and judges (Slaughter 2004). The macroeconomic policies of states are constrained by global flows of trade and finance, so they turn from the welfare state to the "competitive state" thus weakening internal unity. Specialists maintain that government sovereignty is increasingly being drawn into transnational webs of governance, regulatory diffusion, and global markets. Multiculturalism, transnational Diasporas, and fundamentalist religions increasingly confront national identity. National institutions of all types are losing their hold on public opinion. Partly this reflects the way in which consumerism and internationalized financial markets are undermining collective solidarities. Multi-national corporations are finding it increasingly difficult to be monopolistic in the context of new multi-continental competition, especially from India and China. In addition, new groups and extended networks are arising to play a role in international relations beside states and their governments. Trans-national advocacy groups (INGOs), business organizations, social movements and specialized pressure groups participate in a range of advisory, coordinative and pressure functions. They also form alliances and coalitions, coordinate local and international activism, and bring pressure to bear through the media and new Internet networks (Cerny 2006: 112–115).

Sovereignty has not been eliminated but it has been limited. Global, multi-polar governance is gradually replacing the traditional, state-centric international system, during this period of transition characterized by complex turbulence. It is an era that clearly calls for the restructuring of international institutions. Ironically, as states feel more pressured and vulnerable, they have taken to bolstering the remnants of their sovereignty rather than working to improve their collective capacities. Not only is the state no longer the unique player, but also international organizations must compose themselves with a whole new panoply of players.

Thus, international relations have become more economic and cultural and new actors challenge the preeminence of governments. At the same time the world socio-economic system has also been modified. Under the impulse of neo-liberal economics, the world wealth gap has widened considerably. The World Food Program is feeding 100 million people, and the UN High Commissioner for Refugees (UNHCR) brings aid to the world's 22 million refugees and displaced persons and every year UNICEF has to look after children in 140 countries (Rock 2006: 3). Thakur points out the facts that the combined gross domestic product (GDP) of the world's 48 least-developed countries is less than the assets of the world's *three* richest people. The annual income of nearly half (47 percent) of the world's poorest people is less than that of the richest *225 individuals* (Thakur 2002: 284). The world's first study of global wealth distribution presents the revealing fact that 10% of the richest adults own 85% of global wealth (*Globe and Mail* 05-12-06: A16). Moreover, violence and governmental depredations continue: during the 20th century, while 30 million people were killed in international wars and 7 million in civil wars, people's own governments killed an additional 170 million. Half of the world's governments spend more on supposed protection from enemies than they do to promote health (ibid, 273, 275). The world system is unfair because under the oppression of their own leaders and the pressures of the World Bank and the IMF, many citizens have been deprived of education, employment and health and social services. It is also undemocratic. The people are barely represented in their foreign policies and many developing countries are mostly excluded from the decision-making of the international financial and economic institutions. The wealth gap contributes to the fact that a North-South split has replaced the East-West one in the UN and other institutions such as the WTO.

Another major change in the international system is the prevalence of global threats that render all countries and humans vulnerable to problems that go beyond state boundaries. Problems that used to be managed by the nation-state now must be managed at the international level. We can think of climate change, environmental pollution, international crime and drug syndicates, failed states, global hunger and poverty and infectious diseases as just a few of the problems that can no longer even be called 'inter-national' in the sense that they potentially put every one at risk. They are global. Thus, governments and international organization must now think in terms of three types of threats: national, human and global: national security focuses on threats to a state and its citizens; human security deals with threats to individuals' rights, safety or lives worldwide; global security is aimed at threats to the vital interests of the planet (Intriligator 2006: 7).

Lest one think our analysis concentrates only on horror stories, let us also recall that the 20th century has seen extraordinary advances in health, life-expectancy, and satisfaction of basic human needs. The number of people living in peace and security was never higher. Even in the last decade we have research that indicates the number of people killed in conflict and the number of refugees has declined while the number of people taken out of poverty in China and India and other East Asian countries is truly astounding. There are also a number of countries that have been brought to the favorable side of peace and security, including South Africa, Namibia, Mozambique, Cambodia, Libya, Ireland and Spain. Here, though, we concentrate on the problems that modernized international institutions will have to deal with in the 21st century.

The new conditions, actors and wealth gaps, as well as extraordinary levels of international competition, have multiplied the opposing coalitions inside and outside the UN. There are new or rejuvenated powers such as India, Japan, Brazil, Germany, Nigeria and South Africa seeking seats on the Security Council. However, as Ed Luck has pointed out, regional neighbours are not necessarily friends and allies. Virulent animosities bubbled to the surface during the 2005 struggle for Council seats. Some of these powers have also formed the G-20 to confront the G-8. American demands for managerial reforms and the empowerment of the Secretary General were brought to a screeching halt by the developing countries in the G-77, which feared the reforms were aimed at sidelining the General Assembly where they have a majority.

At the time of his retirement in 2006 as Canadian Ambassador to the United Nations, Allan Rock, presented a very forthright description of the divisions of the UN into various "allegiances, groups, coalitions and political blocks" (Rock 2006: 4). The dynamic now is North-South. Global South is represented by the G-77 with 132 countries in various stages of development, which are "for the most part unhappy, suspicious, resentful, angry, negative, and bring that perspective to almost every negotiation" (p. 4). China wants to broaden its influence over this group. It is however, not monolithic, not even within its component regions of Africa, Latin America and Asia. For instance "socialist populist" countries like Venezuela and Cuba can cause quite a bit of mischief – as when they opposed a consensus definition on terrorism. Asia is neither a coherent block nor predictable. The European Union, on the other hand, is normally a cohesive and coherent group where states rarely break from the pack. "The United States is in a category by itself… It can make things happen and it can ordinarily prevent things from happening… it also engenders resentment… reaction to an American edict… is often skeptical, critical, dubious and inclined to go in the other direction" (p. 5). Rock concludes that religious, economic and political allegiances are complex and always shifting, there are increasing tensions and the United States often finds itself at odds with everybody else. His sage advice to reformers or anyone else is that while this situation within the UN offers great opportunities for influence, "Before you try to advance an idea or project, or seek support for something you want approved, you have to understand where the groups are, where they're coming from, what they want to achieve, and what they want to prevent" (p. 4).

Although by definition it is almost impossible to categorize our current 'complex turbulence era' (multiple causality, rapidly changing), let us summarize by saying that it is characterized by a certain number of 'key words'. The present era is multipolar (several power centres), polycentric (numerous actors and decision-making locales), globalized (interdependent), transnational (heavy degrees of activity across national borders) and undemocratic (secretive, unrepresentative, exclusive). In this era there is a rise of identity politics (race, religion, ethnicity), sovereignty and state power are present but constrained, and security concerns are global and human as well as national. Economic policies have often excluded social and political considerations so the wealth gap has become a central issue. These are the conditions with which the UN and its successors must contend.

## 1.2.2 Power Structures and Coalitions

The world's power structure of sovereign states has been characterized since the 1990 Gulf War by the absolute dominance of the United States, the only hyperpower. With a defense budget in the $500 billion range (with special allocations for Iraq), the United States is spending more on its military than are the 12 next-highest spenders combined. To see the power of the United States in context, one must realize that even with recent increases, the rate of American defense spending is still less than during the half century of the Cold War, when in terms ofGDP per capita it averaged 6.8 percent from 1948 to 1988 (Ferguson 2001: 127). Despite its vast expenditures, the U.S. is not stretching its potential military capacity. Another comparison shows that in 1913, at the height of the power of its Empire, Britain's share of world output was 8.3 percent while the equivalent figure for the U.S. in 1998 was 22 percent (Ferguson 2001: 126). Furthermore, an extraordinary amount, both in absolute and relative terms, of the American defence spending goes into research and development and transport and logistics. The U.S. is far ahead of any other country in armaments and being able to project its power worldwide. For example, the vaunted British navy no longer owns a troopship.

Nevertheless, the U.S. is not alone as a power centre and its strength is diminishing. China and Russia have considerable military capacity. There are half a dozen other nuclear powers. There are numerous regional military powers. But power cannot be sufficiently calculated in military terms alone (Nye 2002). Japan, the European Union, China and India are economic rivals to the Americans in every sense of the term. Like every other hegemonic power before it the U.S. is squandering its wealth on foreign adventures and internal waste. Stiglitz has estimated that in real terms the Iraq war and occupation will end up costing the U.S. taxpayer between one and two trillion dollars. American savings rates are negative, its consumer debt explosive, its government debt out of control, and its international debt so high that it must attract 70 percent of the world's capital flows to finance its current account debt (Dodge 2006). In fact, the American economy is for the first time dependent on the rest of the world. For instance, China holds $1trillion in foreign exchange reserves, while its defense budget multiplied by a factor of six since 1990 and its gross domestic product multiplied eight times in the past 25 years (*Globe and Mail* 05-12-06: A16). Thus we live in a contradictory era where everyone still waits on the United States to lead the world but its overall power base is rapidly diminishing.

While the nature of the international regime remains what we are calling 'complex turbulence', it is quite amazing how quickly its components change. According to Oxford professor Timothy Garton Ash, the "unipolar moment" of American supremacy after the Cold War has ended and we are now in a period of "new multipolar disorder" (*Globe and Mail* 20-07-06: A13). Ash points to three trends: the rise or revival of other states such as China, India, Brazil Russia and Japan, which have competitive power resources; the growing power of small numbers of people in non-state actors including not only NGOs but al-Qaeda, Hamas, Hezbollah, the Tamil Tigers, corporations, regions and religions; and, third, developments in information technology and globalized media that open up the battle for public opinion approval. The net effect of these trends is to reduce the relative power of Western States and insure that global challenges can only be met through multilateral diplomacy such as that of the Americans and Europeans with regard to Iran or the six party talks on North Korea. Where the "multipolar disorder" will lead us is far from clear.

### 1.2.3 Policy Orientations

It is not so much the structure of international politics that has changed since September 11, 2001, but rather the policies and attitudes, especially in the United States. President Bush has announced his policy priority as "unilaterally determined pre-emptive self-defense." The White House's *National Security Policy* (United States 2002 and restated in a second Statement on National Strategy, 2006) has turned American defense policy on its head, replacing defensive containment with aggressive pre-emption (Judt 2003: 12–17). However, some American strategists have called it a doctrine of preventive war and not of preemption (Kissinger 2006). A precursor to this Strategy was the neo-conservative Project for a New American Century of 1997, which aimed to reverse the thesis of American decline and use American global leadership to spread liberalism and democracy by ensuring "the U.S. army is unrivalled in the world. Washington can dictate its law wherever and whenever it wants" (Gonzalez 2003).

The Pentagon's Nuclear Posture Review (2002), called for a combination of offensive and defensive, nuclear and non-nuclear capabilities and called for possible use of nuclear weapons in various contingencies including against non-nuclear weapon states and in response to conventional weapons. This casts into doubt the Nuclear Non-Proliferation Treaty. The Review also led to the end of the Anti-Ballistic Missiles treaties with Russia and promotes research on a smaller, tactical generation of aggressive nuclear weapons with new delivery platforms, which will quite possibly cause additional proliferation (Weinberg 2003, Intriligator 2006). Military policies around the world were leading to annual expenditures of one trillion dollars on armies, but less than $100 billion, that is less than 10 percent, on development assistance.

Under Bush, selective American unilateralism has given away to generalized unilateralism and general disdain for international organizations. Active promotion of "liberalism and democracy" in bilateral relationships is the result of the Bush administration's philosophy that political regimes are more important for maintaining world peace than international institutions and arrangements. The greatest threat, it is perceived, comes from states that do not share democratic (American) values. Changing these regimes and spreading democracy is seen as the best way to reinforce American security and peace (Frachon & Vernet 2003: 13).

We should not be surprised that these factors have been erected into a theory of an American tradition of international conservatism that Bush is said to follow. Henry Nau who served in the Ford and Reagan administrations, suggests there are four major elements of this policy orientation that have been followed by various leaders since the time of Jefferson. 1) Freedom, not stability, is the essence of democracy and should be the motivating ideal of American foreign policy. 2) One must react to attacks and to war fiercely and unilaterally in an instinctive and protective manner. 3) Conservative internationalists are not strong believers in international institutions, so Bush is more comfortable with "coalitions of the willing" and "NATO à la carte" rather than multilateral decision-making committees. He is sceptical of the United Nations, where non-democracies have veto power. 4) They are selective internationalists, not institutional ones. For instance, they shun or delay structured negotiations in order to alter the balance of forces on the ground to improve their bargaining position (Nau 2005).

Needless to say, the conservatism we are talking about is the maximization of the American sovereign right to pursue its leaders' perceptions of international power in the national interest. "Bush's views rest on two fundamental pillars. The first was that in a dangerous world, the best – if not the only – way to assure America's security was to shed the constraints imposed by friends, allies and international institutions. The second was that America should aggressively go abroad searching for monsters to destroy" (Daalder and Lindsay 2003: 47). As if to signal his power-oriented, unilateral intentions, in March 2005 President Bush nominated two of his most conservative supporters to deal with international institutions – John Bolton as U.S. ambassador to the United Nations, and Paul Wolfowitz as President of the World Bank.

Many analysts, this one included, like to think there is more than one America and a change of governing party could lead to a return to a policy of multilateralism. The former National Security Advisor, Zbigniew Brzezinski, suggests that new structural conditions may make such a change less than automatic. He posits the present reality of American world hegemony and that such a situation, as in the past, requires an imperial "elite endowed with its own special sense of mission, destiny and privilege". The responsibilities of the Cold War and the American hegemony have generated the American equivalents of a "hegemonic elite". It includes the staffs of the U.S. Commanders-in-Chief of Unified and Specified Commands deployed in security zones around the world; the "enormous" U.S. professional bureaucracy serving abroad; and a "colossal" apparatus of diplomatic relationships, military deployments, intelligence-gathering systems; and bureaucratic interests coalesced to manage America's global engagements. "Animated by a forceful concentration of knowledge, interests, power and responsibility, the imperial bureaucrats view themselves as singularly equipped to determine America's conduct in a complicated and dangerous world" (Brzezinski 2005: 201). This political-military web surrounding the executive branch increases the pressure on American democracy. Although supposedly tempered by Congressional oversight, Brzezinski points out that in the most powerful state in the world there is the complete absence of any central, strategic planning organ and no formal consultative relationship between White House policy-making and Congress. Far-reaching strategic decisions are made by a small circle of insiders whose personal impulses, group interests, political calculations, and questionable evidence are obscure to the public (see also Rothkoff 2005).

In 2003, France, Germany and Russia reciprocated American intransigence and seemed determined to maintain the autonomy of the United Nations (and their own authority). They aimed to reject "the interventionist global role claimed by George W. Bush's America" (Ignatius 2003). Competing interests but similar values keep the U.S. and the EU in complex relationships. As noted, another competing coalition is G77 with its 132 developing countries members. For many of them, especially the Muslim countries, the U.S., "is seen not as a symbol of opportunity but of a threatening modernity: trampler of tradition, mouther of hypocrisies, poor listener, bully, robber baron, disguising its intent in a cloak of noble convictions" (Roger Cohen, *International Herald Tribune* 04-05-05: 2).

However, for the most part these competing coalitions seem incapable of taking international policy leadership. In his classic critique of the UN, Maurice Bertrand explains.

> The diverse hypotheses we have seen have, for the moment, no influence on government policies. Political reality is that the United States of America remains convinced that it must exercise its *leadership* in international politics and that the military, technical and economic means it has at its disposal allows it to do so. The European countries, preoccupied by the problem of European construction, accord only a limited attention to world institutional problems. Japan has not put forth any new idea; developing countries have other worries. There doesn't seem to be any chance to see the initiation of negotiations on a new, more effective system of world security. The Secretary-General of the UN can certainly explain he needs more authority and means of action but no one is ready to give him a positive answer. The political situation is such that no consensus is possible.... Who would dare propose today any reform that would not please the United States? And the susceptibilities of numerous countries on the subject of their sovereignty leaves little hope that a system of supranational intervention will see the light of day in the near future (Bertrand 2000: 115).

Another component of policy is the influence of public opinion. In the post–September 11, U.S.-dominated world, a *New York Times* writer asked if the American public was up to the task. "What scares me most, however, is the home front.... These serial embarrassments went almost unreported by U.S. domestic news media. So most Americans have no idea why the rest of the world doesn't trust the Bush administration's motives" (Krugman 2003). But the distrust of the United States, or at least its government, does seem to be a growing phenomenon. "I have never seen the United States and an American president so unanimously hated around the world," wrote *New York Times* columnist, Thomas Friedman (04/05/04). The treatment of prisoners at Guantánamo Bay as sub-humans, and the revelations of degrading torture and even killing of prisoners in Iraq, has combined to do more harm to the human rights reputations of Western democracies than any other actions in history. The West has been losing the world public relations battle in recent years and most Americans are oblivious to it.

Nevertheless, some research suggests that international public opinion is not a component that policy makers can afford to ignore. There is a larger, worldwide "attentive public" than one might think, which is more aware of international affairs and holds values that have some limiting effect on world politics. This rudimentary international public opinion is the result of growing education, potential mass participation in politics, and communications networks (Etzioni 2004: 109–11).

Policy contradictions appear to be a major component of this era of complex turbulence – and nowhere more so than in the United States. It is very hard to know what the future will hold for us. In 2006 the U.S. was still considered the economic motor of the world and yet it has become a dependent economy in decline. It is no longer the undisputed technological leader but its culture fills the TV and movie screens of the world. The government is aggressive in its actions but defensive in its posture. At one moment it is the only leader on the international scene, in the next the world goes on without it (Criminal Court, Landmines, Law of the Sea, Kyoto Accord etc.). It is said to be the super power but has so few soldiers it must contract out to mercenaries. It acts on both a unilateral and multilateral basis whenever it suits it. America wants to lead the world to liberty and democracy but has shown a decline in moral integrity. The greatest incongruity of all is that George W. Bush may have done everyone a great favor by demonstrating conclusively that hegemonic unilateralism does not work in the 21st century and multilateralism is the logical choice for managing a complex world. Just to confuse matters further, the Democrats, having won both houses of Congress, found they had to live in concubinage with the unilateralist President Bush, when their own last candidate for the presidency, John Kerry, had been strongly in favor of multilateralism. The world must accomodate to these changes.

### *1.2.4 Recent Events and Actions*

Since Seattle in 1999, protestors have been demonstrating against the destructive impacts of an anarchic marketplace and free trade agreements that unleash giant corporations in a globalization that pays scant attention to local economies and cultures. International organizations, especially the international financial institutions (the World Bank, and the IMF and the WTO) were seen by many to be part of the problem.

The September 11, 2001, attack on America, which led President George W. Bush to declare war on terrorism, pushed these factors into the background. It went largely unnoticed that the UN did everything demanded of it in Afghanistan, from Security Council resolutions legitimizing the Coalition's intervention to humanitarian aid and nation building. As partial recognition, the U.S. started paying its back dues to the UN. However, In short order, Bush transferred the wrath of the United States from the terrorists to the government of Iraq. The "battle of the Security Council" that pitted France, Germany and Russia against the U.S., Britain and Spain led to the war in Iraq being carried out without UN legitimacy. Many believe the U.S. has squandered the global good will and support against terrorism it had gained on 9-11. By the time of the war between Israel, Palestine and Lebanon in 2006 it appeared as though the U.S. and Israel were incurring the wrath of the entire Muslim world and the UN was sidelined once again.

In yet another domain, the UN was not receiving many plaudits. The 2002 Johannesburg World Summit on Sustainable Development was a great disappointment in the eyes of environmentalists and their allies. More generally, "The giant global conferences organized by the UN are becoming more unmanageable as they are overtaken by special interests or become the battleground for clashes between competing ideologies of a cultural or religious kind" (Axworthy 2003: 253). Even the intrepid World Trade Organization (WTO) met demands for structural reform. After the failure of its September 2003 Cancun conference as part of the new "Doha round," Canada's Trade Minister, usually in the diplomatic background, went public with a demand for a revision of the WTO's rules. However, because of the West's refusal to cede ground on agricultural protectionism the Doha Round was almost dead by 2006 and some were predicting the same for the Organization (*Globe and Mail* 31-07-06).

Nevertheless, it is the UN that was called upon to provide a peacekeeping mission of 15,000 for Liberia, as well as to assist the transitional government and facilitate humanitarian aid and an even bigger force for the Congo as it headed for an election. These are just two examples of the 18 peacekeeping missions the UN had in place on four continents by 2006 with over 90,000 personnel, a deployment only second in size to that of the United States (Rock 2006: 3).

The "war on terrorism," became so focused on the hunt for bin Laden that no one asked why terrorism exists and is growing. A lesson from 1919 might give us the inkling of an answer. "If Bolshevik ideas were permeating Western society, it was because people were fed up. Remove the causes of Bolshevism, both Wilson and Lloyd George argued, and you would take away its oxygen. Farmers without land, workers without jobs, ordinary men and women without hope, all were fodder for visionaries promising the earth" (MacMillan 2002: 68). Today, Muslim fundamentalists promise heaven, but the fodder is still ordinary people facing poverty and authoritarian regimes.

A recent example of deep international divisions was the "rough row" that broke out between the United States and a host of other countries over the protection of cultural diversity, with the U.S. trying to halt an international treaty on the subject, based on the Motion Picture Association of America's view that "cultural diversity should not be used as an excuse to raise new trade barriers (Godoy 2005).

Finally, the potential irrelevance of the UN is not just a passing thought but also a political intention. Several times in recent years, the United States has offered its leadership in place of the United Nations, for instance in the "war" on terrorism, the post-tsunami relief and the rebuilding of Iraq. The issue is profound and far-reaching. In the 21st century, who will drive international politics, the one or the many, the United States alone, perhaps with a few selected friends, or the U.S. within international organizations, representing all the states of the world?

What does all this portend for the future of international institutions? Based on consultations with NGOs around the world and looking 15 years into the future it is forecast that by 2020, "Increased pressures on international institutions will incapacitate many, unless they can be radically adapted to accommodate new actors and new priorities" (National Intelligence Council 2004). They must also take into consideration the growing strength of the rising powers. Regionally based institutions will be particularly challenged to meet the complex transnational threats posed by economic upheavals, terrorism, organized crime, and WMD proliferation.

Both supporters and opponents of multilateralism agree that Rwanda, Bosnia, Somalia and the Sudan demonstrated the ineffectiveness, lack of preparation, and weaknesses of global and regional institutions to deal with what are likely to be the more common types of conflict in the future. The problem of state failure – which is a source or incubator for a number of transnational threats – argues for better coordination between institutions, including the international financial ones and regional security bodies.

Building a global consensus on how and when to intervene is likely to be the biggest hurdle to greater effectiveness, but to many experts this is essential if multilateral institutions are to live up to their potential and promise. Many states, especially the emerging powers, continue to worry about setting precedents for outside intervention that can be used against them. Nevertheless, most problems, such as failing states, can be effectively dealt with only through early recognition and preventive measures.

Other issues that are likely to emerge on the international agenda will add to the pressures on the collective international order as well as on individual countries. These "new" issues could become the staples of international diplomacy, much as human rights did in the 1970s and 1980s.

Ethical issues linked to biotechnological discoveries, such as cloning, genetically modified organisms, and access to biomedicines, could give rise to hot debates among countries and regions. As technology develops, the capabilities of states to track terrorists, concerns about privacy, and extraterritoriality may increasingly surface worldwide. Similarly, debates over environmental issues (connected with climate change) risk scrambling the international order, pitting the U.S. against its traditional European allies, as well as developed countries against the developing world, unless more global cooperation is achieved. Rising powers may see in the ethical environmental debates an attempt by the rich countries to slow their progress by imposing "Western" standards or values. The issue of institutional reform might increasingly surface. Many in the developing world believe power in international bodies reflects the post–World War II world rather than the current one.

What can we surmise about the impact of post-9-11 international politics on international institutions?

First, as many analysts have pointed out, war is proving to be a tool of very limited value for managing international issues in the 21st century.

Second, no state or group of states has the legitimacy to intervene in another country and control a people without the combined will of the international community.

Third, the complexity of international politics requires a diversified, experienced and complex capacity for governance.

Fourth, the United Nations and the multilateralist cause have been seriously wounded not just by the Iraq war, but also by a growing number of issues. These include antagonism to globalization, the UN's often "fantastical nominations and policies," the oil for food crisis, the enmity of the superpower, and a growing perception that its activities are dominated by the rich and powerful. Worse, in some quarters the UN has become a subject of ridicule.

Fifth, leaders and the media are ignoring the fact that the UN did everything asked of it with regard to terrorism and Afghanistan. They also forget that despite rhetoric about the Charter, the United Nations has never played a major role in security crises. But, it has played an important role as a negotiation forum, a legitimator, a mobilizer of world opinion, and as a humanitarian resource.

Sixth, global governance requires both more effective international institutions and the leadership of the United States. There could be no better time to sound the call for a process of reform of international institutions to make them more responsive to the needs of global management. Let us look at the historical record to shed some light on how international institutions have been formed and reformed.

# 2 The History and Development of International Institutions

*"The challenge is to build a viable international order without the impetus of having survived catastrophe"*

Henry Kissinger, "American strategy and pre-emptive war", *International Herald Tribune,* 14-4-06

## 2.1 The Origins of International Organizations

Our objective in this study is to see how we might more effectively promote the process of innovation, reform and transformation in international institutions (where "innovation" means making more creative use of the institutions we have and "reform" and "transformation" encompasses deeper types of change of these institutions).

One source of inspiration would be past experience about international organizations. How and why were they founded? What have been their roles, functions and contributions to date? These are our goals in this chapter. While one cannot directly analogize from the past, we *can* learn from history. For this we need to find the best possible interpretations of the founding of international institutions.

Many studies of the United Nations simply assume that it, like the League of Nations, was founded in reaction to the crisis of a world war, and it responded to that war and the experience preceding it. Thus,

> The immediate stimulus, however, for its establishment is to be found in the events of World War II. Paradoxically, as with the League before it, war provided the impulse for creating a new organization for peace.... The nation-state has sheltered so much that civilized man rightly prizes, it is not surprising that it takes a world cataclysm to break the mould.... (Nicholas 1962: 1).
>
> The UN came into existence as a result of the most terrible war in history. During World War II, American President Franklin Roosevelt, British Prime Minister Winston Churchill, and the leaders of several other major combatant nations agreed that it was necessary to create a world organization that would help insure the peace in future years (Fasulo 2004: 1).

As we shall see, there is some truth in this assumption, but it is far from the whole truth. This "big bang" theory of the origins of international organizations is being supplanted by an "evolutionary" theory that places the roots of international institutions at the beginning of the 19th century rather than the 20th.

In the International Political Science Association, Yves Schemeil (2003) and colleagues have been looking at that lessons the past holds for today's international institutions. Bob Reinalda (2003) presented a survey of what we may call the "evolutionary school" as a prologue to his new history of international organizations. Although the writings he pulls together include such classics as Innis Claude's *Swords into Plowshares* (1964), most of them are quite recent. Another major writer on the origins of international organizations is Clive Archer, whose *International Organizations* (2001) has become a classic. Newer works on peaceful change in international relations (Kupchan et al. 2001) and neo-diplomacy, referring to the founding of new international institutions and regimes by a combination of private and public actors acting outside the UN system (Cooper et al. 2002), provide further evidence and suggestions on how innovations come about in international institutions.

The overviews of the literature by Reinalda, Archer and Schemeil allow us to tease out the following: a) the steps in the creation of international institutions, b) the socio-economic changes concomitant to their founding and c) the tensions within the Westphalian international system that render international organizations so necessary. Let us look at these in succession. Box 1 synthesizes some of the events and activities demonstrating the growth and innovation in international institutions during the 1800s.

**BOX 1: The Growing Web of International Institutions 1815–1914**

**Vienna Congress and Founding of the Concert of Europe 1815**
The first multilateral conference, this peace treaty ending the Napoleonic Wars included a major power alliance to which other states could adhere. As a "security regime," it held regular meetings on common interests and preventative diplomacy, as well as for consultations, common rules and monitoring.

**Central Commission for the Navigation of the Rhine 1815–32, 1832–68**
This system of agreements limited sovereignty over the common waterway and opened it to international commercial traffic. It gradually extended to other river systems and canals, starting the "global commons."

**International Private Conferences and Movements**
Inspired private citizens took their right of participation seriously on issues such as the abolition of slavery, promotion of peace, and improved labor conditions. For instance, Mary Goegg founded an international women's organization in 1868 that initiated an international movement. They were based on either individuals or issue-oriented, national, non-governmental organizations with few transnational networks. Today we would call them "epistemic communities," with private leadership taken by scientists, humanists, academics, lawyers, artists, etc. (Haas, Young, Moravscik).

**Public International Unions Conferences 1860s to 1910**
These international governmental organizations were mainly in functional areas such as the post office and telegraphy. They were called "unions" in the same sense as the "European Union" means the bringing together of states to cooperate within a number of concrete policy domains. It was the experience of these public international unions, such as the current Universal Postal Union and the International Telecommunications Union that created international functionaries, experimented with conferences, innovated in organizations, set standards, and empowered individual participants as well as governments.

**Paris Peace Conference of 1856**
This conference marked the beginning of the codification of international maritime law with the *Declaration of Maritime Law.*

**International Red Cross 1864**
Founded as a private initiative by Henri Dunant and other Swiss citizens, the Red Cross became responsible for the government-sponsored Geneva Convention for the Amelioration of the Condition of the Wounded in Armies in the Field, the first of many Geneva Conventions.

**International Law Associations 1873**
International lawyers founded two private associations, the Institute of International Law and the International Law Association. As well as helping governments by preparing arbitrage schedules for conferences, these associations, along with the peace movement, helped to develop international public opinion.

**International Union of American Republics 1890**
This union, which preceded the Organization of American States, attempted to cover all the topics of the European public international unions.

**Hague Peace Conferences 1899, 1907**
To supplement his waning power, the Tsar convened governments and individuals every seven years to promote understanding and avoid conflict. These conferences gave rise to the Hague Permanent Court of Arbitrage.

**International Association of Labour and International Labour Office in Basel 1900–1901**
These organizations were established by international lawyers and economists to improve labor legislation, under pressure from Swiss unions and with the aid of the Swiss government. Conferences followed.

**J. E. Trent, 2003, with reference to Reinalda 2003, Archer 2001, and Schemeil 2003.**

While this is only a partial list of events and activities concerning international organizations, it is sufficient to show us that they truly had their origins in the 19th century. A strange mixture of public and private endeavor created them. This activity involved governments, and budding non-governmental organizations, and concerned citizens, international lawyers, scientists and economists. But organizations and meetings there were. Between 1840 and 1914 there were nearly 3,000 international gatherings. More than 450 private or non-governmental international organizations were created between 1815 and 1915. The number of governmental international organizations increased from 7 in the 1874 period to 37 in 1909 (Lyons 1963: 12; *Yearbook of International Organizations 1974*, Vol. 15, tables 1 and 2).

They seemed to grow topsy-turvy, without any particular plan or leadership. However, it appears from the evolutionary perspective that one thing led to another in an expanding circle. By 1815, and to an ever-increasing extent afterwards, European governments were torn between their desire for sovereign independence and at the same time the requirements of technological, economic and social cooperation. The same quandary exists today with governments trying to preserve their sovereignty and respond to the demands of the global market and of collective security. Thus, the 19th century governments sometimes supported international meetings, both to bolster security and for mutual interests. The Europeans learned from the conferences how to overcome problems of protocol and procedure. But eventually, demands of efficiency and effectiveness required the help of the expertise that had grown up around these conferences in order to staff the organizations needed to structure the agreements reached at the meetings, and to prepare the subsequent rounds.

In the meantime, the civil populations used the newly won rights of citizens, their liberal philosophy and their growing number of contacts to create non-governmental organizations, at first national and then international, to furnish the growing needs for technological, economic and social services. When the governmental will was lacking, civil society leaders created international movements to promote their causes. They invited themselves to the international governmental conferences and worked the margins until eventually their expertise or their political clout got them invited as regular participants. A prime illustration of the potential role of individuals and groups in developing international organizations was writer Leonard Woolf, founder of the Fabian Society, the reformist discussion group within the British Labour Party. His Fabian Committee plan called for an international high court, a council of states, and an international secretariat and sanctions as tools to prevent war. All of these found their way into the League Covenant (Archer 2001: 132). Woolf was also one of the first to write extensively on international organizations, which he considered to be the beginning of world government (Woolf 1916).

Behind the scene were the changing technological, economic and social conditions that characterized Europe in the 19th century and that stimulated the demand for international organizations (Box 2). Today we would call this the demand for creation of global public goods. Technological developments such as the telegraph, postal system and railways made cross-border communications and commerce more practicable. At the same time, the new communications systems and enhanced trade gave rise to a need for their international organization and regulation. In turn, the new industrialists pressured their governments to provide continent-wide systems of stable security for their investments.

### BOX 2: Contextual Inducements to Forming International Institutions

**An economy that extended beyond national boundaries** required international regulation. "The simultaneous industrialisation, the development of transport and communication, the migrations of men, capital and goods, the search for markets and raw materials, all contributed to an economy which far transcended national units" (Lyons 1963: 11).

**Industrialization** also sought continental security for markets and investments (Murphy 1994: 2–4), which broadened common issues and the consequent search for rules of procedure, mechanisms of consultation, feedback and monitoring, and the development of personnel with the temperamental attributes of give and take that make multilateral negotiations possible (Claude 1966: 23).

**Public international unions, as institutional prototypes** for international governmental organizations, experimented with secretariats, policy directorates and procedures with regard to language, documentation and precedence in large multilateral meetings. Without breaking with sovereignty, the PIUs' new conventions (agreements) built on the traditional techniques of inter-state treaties (Claude 1966: 33).

Within a world of sovereign countries, **the new conference system gave credibility to experts** and professionals, both governmental employees and private advisors, who became the new architects of international institutions and international standards (Murphy 1994: 62, 64).

Development of **modern forms of communication** required taming of competition, protection of public health and infrastructures, and common legislation and regulation, so public international unions grew up in communications and transport, weights and measures, trade, intellectual property, agriculture, labour, science, policing, sanitation, etc. (Reinsch 1911: 156–8). "States could hardly afford to stay outside" (Reinalda 2003: 8), and they gradually learned to deal with the tension between cooperation and sovereignty and contradictions between equality and hierarchy.

**Success breeds success** Between 1815 and 1914, some 30 intergovernmental organizations were formed as well as 450 international non-governmental organizations. From 1840 to 1914, 3,000 international conferences were held (Lyons 1963: 11). Also, international movements formed public opinion on slavery, peace, women, workers etc.

Not all developments were government sponsored. **Issue-oriented non-governmental organizations (NGOs) appeared** at the end of the 1700s. They became international by the 1850s, when they began to organize for influence and traveled to international conferences to pursue their interests. NGOs recognized their abilities to influence governments, and governments learned the benefits of their expertise and societal support (Reinalda 2003: 3; Charnovitz 1997: 212). Private individuals (professionals, academics, humanists) played a major role too.

**Domestic policy shifts** and changes in political personnel also greatly influenced chances for international innovation. For instance, international lawyers and economists formed the International Association of Labour Legislations in 1900 and the International Labour Office a year later. Their good relations with states encouraged the Swiss to call an international conference in 1905, but a breakthrough came only at the second conference, in 1906, once Great Britain had elected a Liberal government with a social welfare agenda (Reinalda 2003: 9; Lyons 1963: 153).

**J. E. Trent 2003, with reference to Reinalda 2003, Lyons 1963, Claude 1966, Murphy 1994, Reinsch 1911, Charnovitz 1997.**

The influence of technological-economic innovations on socio-political transformations has long been hypothesized. Hendrik Spruyt has reconfirmed it in an in-depth study of the transition from feudalism to the nation-state. In a first stage, technological innovations in manufacturing, plus developments in transport and communications and creation of a new class of producers and merchants permitted the emergence of "translocal trade". In a second stage, the changed socio-economic environment led to new political alliances vying to understand and control the changes and to reorient public policy. This led to a third stage of conversion to transform the new political coalitions into longer-term structural modifications to capture the benefits of the changes in new political institutions (Spruyt 1994). These stages are not purely chronological and tend to overlap as we saw in the continuous international institution building going on in the 19th and 20th centuries, egged on by cumulative technological and industrial advances. And, as we know, even the institution-building was not linear in nature but succumbed to numerous setbacks. The hypothesis here is that a similar period of global politico-institutional transition is underway in our era to cope with the techno-economic changes of the last half of the 20th century.

Though environmental conditioning and evolutionary development are important elements of innovation in international institutions, they alone cannot explain the creation and the nature of the League of Nations and the United Nations. Clive Archer believes that the League was not fashioned by the ideas of 17th-century writers, but by the immediate experience of wartime cooperation. "Whilst schemes abounded for innovations, the statesmen present at the Paris Conference drew heavily on their own experience of co-operation in the war and of previous institutional developments" (Archer 2001: 17).

At the beginning of this chapter, we alluded to the hypothesis that growth and innovation in international institutions took their impetus both from the logic of evolution (our "evolutionary" theory) and from the necessities and lessons inspired by world crises (our "big bang" theory).

> The statesmen moulding the new League of Nations found that the plans before them relied heavily on the experience of the previous hundred years: the congress and concert systems, the public international unions and their private counterparts, and the Hague meetings. They also had something else on their minds: the wartime experience. One side of the coin was the determination to prevent the collapse of international relations into general war; the other side was the experience of Allied cooperation during the war… (Archer 2001: 15).

### BOX 3: Influences of the First World War on the Creation of the League

#### Ideas

- President Wilson was committed to a "general association of nations"; Colonel House drew up the plans.
- The British accepted the idea of a more organized diplomacy, but did not think international relations could be radically changed.
- Jan Smuts wanted deliberation and delay for a cooling-off period of dispute.
- The French opted for a robust international tribunal, a council and an international force with a permanent staff.
- "The Covenant of the League of Nations reflected the somewhat jumbled hopes and fears of the Allied and Associate powers' leadership" (Archer 2001: 15; Armstrong et al. 1996: ch. 1).

#### Precedents

- The Hague meetings stressed the need to harness the sinews of war. Article 8 of the Covenant recommended the reduction of armaments and the limitation of their private manufacture.
- "Concert-like" additions included the members of the League Council advising on territorial aggression; any threats of war being of concern to

the whole League (Art. 11); and Article 19 calling for the prevention of conflict through the prior consideration of threats to peace.

- Like its Hague predecessor, the new Permanent Court of International Justice (Art. 14) stressed arbitration, mediation and conciliation.
- Based on American power and the experience of the American hemisphere, Article 21 referred to "regional understandings such as the Monroe Doctrine."
- The colonial powers were able to block intentions to have the League cover the world. All that remained was the minor compromise to include "just treatment" in articles 22 and 23, establishing the "mandate system," which assigned the ex-colonies of the defeated powers to the victorious ones.
- The International Labour Office gave birth to the first and continuing international agency, the International Labour Organization (the ILO). The work of the Red Cross was mentioned in Article 25.

**Experience of the War**

- Although the inclusion of economic and social issues (Art. 22–25) reflected the work of the public and private unions of the 1800s, the "real stimulus" for their inclusion was work of the Inter-Allied Committee to make recommendations to governments on technical and administrative matters, and for the organization and maximization of use of rare economic resources.
- The Inter-Allied Supreme Council, established during the war, became the basis for the Council of Ten at the Peace Conference, and then the Council of the League of Nations.
- While the Hague conferences have often been cited as the model for the Assembly of the League, the impetus for the inclusion of the small and medium powers likely came from the role of the British Commonwealth during the Great War, and from the United States' desire to have the Latin American countries strongly represented.
- While some have maintained that the bureaux of the international public unions furnished the example for the Secretariat of the League, the answer lies more in the wartime experience of the Secretariat of the Supreme War Council, "which was just brought up from Versailles and attached to the Secretariat-General of the Peace Conference" (Hankey 1946: 26–7).

**J. E. Trent 2003, with reference to Archer 2001, Armstrong et al. 1996, Hankey 1946.**

While we have been referring to international organization specialists for the most part to study the mechanics of institutions, one cannot do much better than to listen to historian Margaret MacMillan to get a feel for the underlying politics of international structures. In her much-praised study of the 1919 Paris Peace

Conference that founded the League of Nations, she draws a deft portrait of the players and their ambitions that has held true from the League until now.

> On January 12, the day after his arrival in Paris, Lloyd George of Great Britain met Clemenceau of France, Wilson of the United States and the Italian Prime Minister Orlando, at the French Foreign Ministry on the Quai d'Orsay for the first of well over a hundred meetings. Each man brought his foreign secretary and a bevy of advisors. The following day, in deference to British wishes, two Japanese representatives joined the group. This became the Council of Ten, although most people continued to refer to it as the Supreme Council (the name of the wartime leadership). The smaller allies and neutrals were not invited, an indication of what was to come. At the end of March, as the Peace Conference reached its crucial struggles, the Supreme Council was to shed the foreign ministers and the Japanese to become the Council of Four: Lloyd George, Clemenceau, Wilson and Orlando" (MacMillan 2001: 53).

MacMillan points out that these men were the virtual world government for the next six months, and they made decisions that still have repercussions. "We are the league of the people" said Clemenceau. Wilson replied, "We are the State." Even in their early meetings, the members of the Supreme Council started to act as a cabinet. Part of their task was to handle the lesser powers that were full of complaints and demands, and for whom even a chance to appear before the Supreme Council bolstered their reputation back home.

The leaders also had to deal with the intense scrutiny of the world media, which complained incessantly about the secrecy of the meetings when President Wilson had proposed, among his Fourteen Points, "open covenants openly arrived at." The press demanded the right to attend meetings but Clemenceau thought this would be "a veritable suicide." Finally, Lloyd George proposed they tell the media straight out that the negotiations would be long and delicate and they had no desire to stir up unnecessary controversy by publicizing their disagreements. In the first weeks, the Supreme Council also spent much time talking about procedure.

> In December, the French Foreign Ministry had sent out invitations to every country from Liberia to Siam, that could claim, ever improbably, to be on the Allied side. By January there were twenty-nine countries represented in Paris, all expecting to take part. How would their role be defined? Would they all sit together with the British Empire having the same vote as Panama? None of the great powers wanted that, but where Clemenceau was willing to start the delegates from lesser powers on relatively harmless questions such as international waterways, Wilson preferred as little structure as possible. "We ought to have," he said, "no formal Conferences but only conversations." Clemenceau found this exasperating: if the allies waited until they agreed on all the main issues, it would be months before the Peace Conference proper could begin, and public opinion would be very disappointed. Anyway, he added, they would have to give all the other powers, who were assembling in Paris, something to do. Lloyd George proposed a compromise, as he was to do on many occasion, there would be a

> plenary session at the end of the week; in the meantime, the Supreme Council would get on with other matters. The members of the Supreme Council, even Wilson, had no intention of relinquishing control of the conference agenda, which promised to be huge… (MacMillan 2001: 56).

These few paragraphs by MacMillan act like a director's introductory notes to the theatre of international organizations that would unfold before our eyes during the next century. They show how the essential structures of the League of Nations and the United Nations took shape. We see the origins of the restrained executive group of great powers that would become the Security Council where the real decisions would be taken—even if other states would be "given something to do." The intention of the Great Powers to dominate the international agenda, and their utter disdain for lesser powers, are revealed. The more crucial the issue, the more restrained the decision-making group. The plot, in which the major states, despite all their great power, are surrounded, hounded and limited by the smaller countries, the media and public opinion, is made clear. Both the need for secrecy and its limits become evident. The importance of procedure and of precedents is laid out. We are introduced to an issue that is coming back to haunt us: the question of the rights and obligations of membership in international organizations, and the role and powers of states of various sizes. We are also introduced to some facets of foreign policy: the unilateralist desire of the United States to be as little constrained as possible by international institutions, and the need of small powers to look good to their constituents. And behind the scene, we see the need for diplomacy if anything is to be achieved.

The League of Nations itself was certainly a seedbed for more "centralized and systematic" world relationships. Archer claims that in some ways the founding of the UN resembled the creation of the League in that "the wartime cooperation was crucial in determining the institutions and aims of the United Nations" (Archer 2001: 21–4). Thus, the Great Power cooperation became a model for the Security Council dominated by the Permanent Five (P5). But, once again, the founders looked to recent experience for their models. The secretariats of the International Labour Organization and the Relief and Rehabilitation Agency provided examples for a UN secretary-general and secretariat that had political and executive prerogatives as well as administrative ones. Final commissioned reports on the League (such as the Bruce Report) also furnished ideas for the economic and social reforms.

But the League also furnished negative examples that the framers of the UN Charter were determined to overcome. Responsibility for peace and security would be clearly lodged in the numerically restrained Security Council, where only the P5, and not every sovereign state, would have a veto. The UN was also to be a more forward-looking organization, based more on practical politics than on theoretical legalities. Not only was peace in the hands of those who had the means, but a number of adaptive tools were set up to carry out the job under varying conditions

(Chapter VI: Pacific Settlement of Disputes; Chapter VII: Action with Respect to Threats to the Peace; Chapter VIII: Regional Arrangements).

As did the League before it, the UN had to respond to the political realities of the time. Thus, the Charter, signed at the San Francisco Conference six weeks before the end of the war in 1945, had to reflect the demands of all the Allied powers, which had so greatly contributed to the war effort. For instance, small and medium powers were added to the Security Council. Private organizations, particularly in the U.S., also produced many proposals. These were fed into the process. The Charter was also the result of ongoing, tough negotiations during the war. Thus the UN reflects the political conditions and power structures of the time: it is the negotiated result of private and public inputs, examples from previous international institutions, and Allied cooperation in response to the wartime crisis.

It is often said that not even a comma has been changed in the Charter of the United Nations since the organization was founded in 1945, almost six decades ago. While, technically there have been two reforms to the Charter, it is also true that much of the UN has been changed over the decades to adjust to changes in the international environment.

One can think of the UN-fostered decolonization, which led to the defining feature of the organization: its universal membership. In operations, the UN took on the task of being the world's peacekeeper and leader in development, democratization and nation rebuilding. The little-used possibility of consultation with a relatively small number of international non-governmental organizations (INGOs) has blossomed into a vast network of interaction with, and often dependence on, thousands of INGOs; links with highly placed, individual "friends of the UN"; and a "compact" with business corporations. At the same time the secretary-general is now a world leader and not just an international public servant, although he is that too, of course. In the policy domain, after years of negotiation, the UN led the way in the creation of the Law of the Sea. The UN's declaration and covenants on human rights have created a rights-based regime that is slowly competing with sovereignty, as can be seen in the recent document on the "responsibility to protect" that is likely to guide humanitarian intervention in the future (see Jolly et al. 2005). What is striking about these major changes in the foundations and activities of international organizations is that almost all of them were mediated by a combination of outstanding individuals within the intergovernmental organizations, determined INGOs, and activist small and medium powers.

This evidence of recent change in the UN, as presented by Reinalda, Archer and Schemeil and the myriad authors whom they cite, as well as their own thinking on the subject, shows how the experience of the 19th century suggests conclusions that can explain the process of innovation in international institutions in our own era.

1. There have been a great number of influences on the development of interna-tional organizations, including "epistemic" communities of private citizens, bankers

and traders, state interests, and the innovation of the personnel of the organizations themselves. But, in general, an evolutionary or "genetic" perspective seems best suited for us to gather the explanatory variables that are both national and international, both public and private (and indeed these two mixed), and that include a progressive internal learning process through the very act of conferencing (Reinalda 2001). This is especially true the more the organizations inhabit the functional rather than the security/political end of the institutional spectrum.

2. This evolutionary process of institution building is defined as "new forms of consultation, decision making, implementation, and correction, which slowly got a more permanent character. There are experiments leading to variation. New inventions are both planned and coincidental... Hence, there is imitation, mutual influence, selection and learning, both by engaged politicians, experts, civil servants and private representatives and by organizations themselves" (Reinalda 2003: 6–7).
3. Evidence suggests that in international organizations, innovation often comes out of lively and continuous debate originating in scientific, technical and humanistic communities. Philosophical ideals play a leading role in inspiring pragmatic policies. Discussing intellectual, universalistic propositions forces people to take sides in the debates; debating in turn leads to organizations; informal exchanges transform themselves into official preparatory meetings; publicly made commitments tie the hands of those who make them (Reinalda 2001; Schemeil 2003: 12, 17). Indeed, the conferencing process creates a temporary equality among unequals, and encourages the sort of open discussion that often gives rise to innovation (Murphy 1994: 62).
4. Governments have to become involved when participants become too numerous to cooperate freely and are too unequal to contribute evenly, and when rules and fair representation must be imposed (Schemeil 2003: 16). Governments also learn that the tentative, experimental nature of exploratory international meetings helped to minimize the domestic costs to politicians of desirable international innovations (Murphy 1994: 61).
5. Conferencing was also conducive for developing the techniques and the psychological aptitudes required for successful multilateral negotiation (Claude 1966: 23). Engaged thinkers and practitioners found they could implement their ideas on a world scale (Schemeil 2003:1). Private institutions and individuals experimented with institutions, debated ideas and reforms, and sometimes were called on to prepare government positions.
6. In other cases, NGOs learned that governments could be moved toward cooperation by private or unofficial pressures, skilfully applied (Lyon 1963: 154). Changes in domestic politics contribute to windows of opportunity at the international level (Reinalda 2003: 9).
7. Although each of them may have a corner of the reality, no single current theory (such as neo-realist, security, rationalist, liberal or constructivist paradigms) satisfactorily explains how international institutions, especially functional

agencies, grow and innovate in a supposedly hegemonic world, use private entrepreneurs to produce public goods, and pursue universalistic goals. Neither security goals nor economic interests can adequately explain much of institutional innovation (Schemeil 2003: 4, 17).

## 2.2 The Development of International Organizations: the Recent Past

Taken as a whole, the historical analysis of attempts to reform the United Nations brings up a number of repetitive themes or undercurrents, not so much about the actual reforms themselves, but regarding the process by which international reform is handled on the international agenda.

First, international institutions hover between the demands of nation-state interests and the new requirements of global problems and opportunities. These contradictory forces, often based on perceptions of the impact that proposed modifications might have on one's power-interests, are at work every time the issue of institutional innovation is addressed.

Second, it is therefore necessary that even as reformers strive to have the harsh underlying realities of globalization more positively included in the structures and policies of international institutions, they must also keep a weather eye on the realities of international politics, and must, in effect, devote a part of their efforts to changing the perceptions of self-interest of politicians and their governments.

Third, fundamental change and innovation are very slow and difficult to achieve at the international level, just as they are at the national level. Leading democracies as diverse as Switzerland, Canada, Australia and the United States have had relatively little success when they have attempted constitutional reform during the past half-century. So the UN is not unique in having a great deal of difficulty in transforming itself. Time and again, when wise reforms have been proposed to resolve self-evident problems, nothing has happened. The changes just "wilted" on the agenda, probably to be brought back 20 years later. It is not enough simply to have good ideas. One has to have the political clout to place and keep innovative ideas on the agenda of governments, the media and global public opinion.

Fourth, there are the few cases such as the International Criminal Court when structural modifications have actually been brought about. Usually it is because there has been a sense of immediacy and a convergence of interests. Reformers must be able to perceive opportunities and be prepared to strike when the iron is hot. Conversely, one has also to recognize when the time is not ripe. Some have argued that without the active leadership, or at least support, of the United States, Kofi Annan was hitting at a steel wall with his 2005 reform efforts.

Fifth, no group of reformers, no matter how representative or how wise and alert to political realities and needs, has a crystal ball that allows them to accurately perceive "the foreseeable conditions of the world" or "the desires for institutional change of the international community." The main reason is that most proposals for change are highly context-specific. They depend on the political realities of the situation, especially the political will for radical change imbedded in the mindsets and knowledge of office-holders. September 11, 2001, and the advent of the Bush administration should remind us we do not even know what profound forces may move the world next year. In such conditions, where the only tea leaves we can read are the long-term trends and forces within the world and the underlying currents of the reform process we have just described perhaps we should endow multilateralism with a learning mechanism that will allow it to continually adapt and modernize.

Now let us look at each of these repetitive themes of institutional renewal in a little more detail.

Gene Lyons entitled his 1995 review article of proposals for UN reform "Competing Visions." And competing visions there are. They run the gamut from Burton Pines of the Heritage Foundation in Washington, who would just as soon see "A World Without a UN" (Pines 1984) to Peter Wilenski, former Australian permanent representative to the UN, who observed "that radical reform of the United Nations is unlikely" (Wilenski 1991: 125). Innis Claude thought, "Particular international organizations may come and go, but international organization is here to stay" (Claude 1956: 123). Offering its "successor vision" of the UN, the United Nations Association of the USA tried to provide a strategic approach to UN reform through the concepts "global watch, consensus building, and consensus conversion" (United Nations Association of the USA 1987: 29). Also, of course, there are national and regional visions of international institutions, and scholarly ones, and the ones of the North and the South—the current great divide. In any case, particular visions of international organizations are likely to become outdated because, as Ernest Haas theorized, their change and reform rarely goes in a straight line. Rather, it cycles through periods of "incremental growth, turbulent non-growth and managed interdependence" (Haas 1990).

However, one thing we all can agree on is that the determining factor is the foreign policy of member states. Their actions depend on their perceptions of their national interests that may be more or less in conformity with collective needs at any given time. Robert Cox tells us that "visions of international institutions" are based on power structures, and a new vision requires "a power structure of stable dominance" (Cox 1983: 252).

Similarly, a comparison of foreign policies toward the UN in 1995, made clear that what differentiated the policy position of states toward international organizations was their place in the international power structure and their desire to use the UN (or not) to further their power goals. There are struggles over representation by population or territoriality, and representation for elites or masses (Trent 1995:

464–72). Lyons repeatedly asked if member states are willing to provide support for collective action by the UN (Lyons 1995: 42, 45, 65). The Nordic UN Project cautioned that the persistent weakness of UN programs is due not only to absence of policy guidance and effective management, but also to inconsistent and conflicting policies of member states. Donor countries contributed to development programs because of their own national interests (Nordic UN Report 1991: 81–2). The UNA-USA study pointed out that even the Charter proved to be flexible enough when members could agree on taking collective action (United Nations Association of the USA 1987: 6–10). When analyzing how to choose a secretary general, Urquhart and Childers first asked, "What do governments, which make the key decisions in this matter, really want from the Secretary-General?" (1990: 17).

The situation seems clear. If they want to have any degree of success, people who propose models for international institutional reform should also think about how their proposals are likely to be received by governments, and how they can influence governments to move toward the desired changes. This does not mean that new models must be limited to the status quo or to current state interests, but that they must take them into account and consider how to deal with them. Otherwise, we are making proposals that are doomed to stay on the printed page.

Historical analysis also confirms the great difficulty that exists in getting reforms accepted at the UN. "These reform studies and recommendations," writes Maurice Strong, "had become something of an industry, and the fact that actual reforms had thus far been minimal was not for lack of ideas but for lack of political will and a sufficient degree of consensus among member governments" (2000: 289).

Two reports were commissioned, one in the 1960s under Sir Robert Jackson and one by a group of experts in the 1970s, to rationalize UN development programs. One result was the creation of a Director General for Development and International Economic Cooperation, but "he was given few resources and made little or no dent in the system" (Study of the Capacity 1969; Report of the Group of Experts 1975; Lyons 1995: 52).

Twenty years later an entirely new group of experts repeated proposals originally made by Jackson—and they were still not adopted. *The Group of 18 Report* on the functioning of the UN in 1986 was so tied to its context of responding to specific American demands that it could only recommend more long-range studies; it left major issues largely unresolved (General Assembly 1986: 8).

An immediate follow-up study could not come to agreement and wilted in committee. The carefully crafted, multi-year reports of the much-respected Nordic UN Project and the UNA-USA international team got no response from governments. The two year, in-depth "Blue Book" study of UN finances from Canada's Department of External Affairs barely saw the light of day before it was buried and forgotten. Despite much analysis and focused proposals on improved methods for selecting secretary-generals (see Urquhart and Childers 1992), there was no evidence in the appointments of Boutros-Ghali or Annan or Ban Ki-Moon that the process had been changed. Finally, the Security Council and the General Assembly never subjected to serious review the much heralded and clear-sighted report of Boutros-Ghali on international intervention, *An Agenda for Peace*. It seems evident that if even the finest reports, at the highest levels and with the most judicious recommendations, get little response from governments, then alternative methods of promoting the modernization of multilateralism must be found.

Despite the foregoing, the members of the UN (or at least a good majority of them) have united for action on a number of occasions. One can think of the 1960s when it was necessary to broker a deal to break the East-West logjam over the entrance of new members in fulfilment of the principle of universality. In the 1950s, in the absence of the Soviet Union, the General Assembly was used to bypass the Security Council and pass the "Uniting for Peace" resolution that made the Korean War a UN operation. The Charter has been amended several times to change the number of members on ECOSOC and the number of non-permanent members on the Security Council. More recently, the International Criminal Court has been created despite the opposition of several major members, including the United States. At another level, it is likely the sovereign nation principle will be somewhat curtailed in favour of the humanitarian intervention principle as the "Responsibility to Protect" concept gradually becomes a global norm.

In looking back over UN experience, the USA-UNA reform study concluded that success came when there was a convergence of interests among countries centrally involved in any issue, and when this convergence could be converted into a common view of the problem, followed by cooperative action (UNA-USA 1987: 33). Taking the long view, Rosenau has suggested that in this period of historic transformation, when we are shifting from a world of states to a global system, we are passing through a period of "turbulence" when people are more focused on levels of human loyalty and attachment than on collective organization. In any case, Ernst Haas advises that we keep our eye on a) the interplay of substantive forces of social transformations such as science, technology and economics; b) decision-making processes within the UN; and c) the foreign policies of member states. "States acting on their perceived interests … are the architects that will design the international organizations of the future" (Haas 1990: 6). At any given time, this is the question: is there is a pragmatic convergence of interests, or is there is a political center through which broad support can be mobilized (Lyons 1995: 57)?

This leaves us with the all-important context within which each set of reform proposals is made. For instance, the Group of 18 and the Davidson reports of 1986 on the functioning of the UN did indeed lead to a cut of top-level staff, simplification of cumbersome procedures, and a long period of zero budget growth in the Secretariat, as well as a form of budget "veto" for the U.S. based on "consensus" decision-making. But all this was achieved in the context of several years of intense lobbying by a superpower, and finally by American non-payment of its assessments (which amounted to 25 percent of the UN's regular budget) and its decision to quit UNESCO. Even so, the

U.S. was in harmony with all the other major contributors who had been pressing for reductions to the UN budget and rationalization of its programs (Lyons 1995: 46).

Maurice Strong's on-the-ground experience confirms the importance of context. In January 1997, on his first day as Secretary-General, Kofi Annan called Strong to New York and named him executive coordinator of UN reform, with the rank of undersecretary-general. Annan also appointed him chairman of the newly constituted Steering Committee for Reform made up of the most senior UN officials. The new secretary-general was determined not to repeat the errors of his predecessor and to move expeditiously with radical internal reforms, led by a respected and experienced external advisor and senior UN personnel. "The U.S. had been pushing cost savings, staff reductions and greater efficiency (the whole fashionable 'downsizing' rigmarole), and developing countries were suspicious that the net effect would be to weaken the UN…." (Strong 2000: 289). The U.S. had accumulated $1 billion in arrears. Attempts to pay it got mixed up in the extreme demands of right-wing Republicans, led by Senator Jesse Helms. Madeleine Albright, the American Secretary of State, was cool to Strong's appointment because there were "competent" (meaning "American") people in place to lead the reforms. However, Annan had to prove two things: that he wasn't in the Americans' pocket, and that he was more than just a "nice guy" and could take tough decisions. He also had to move fast because of the erosion of support for UN peacekeeping and peacemaking, and the shift of developmental initiatives to the World Bank.

Because of their short mandates, the reports done on UN reform in the 1980s could barely skim the major operations that needed repairs in an organization that was "too top-heavy," "too complex" and "too fragmented" (General Assembly – G18 1986:12)—repairs that it would take another decade to tackle. Nevertheless, internal reforms have been the only major changes to the operations of our major international institution. We have seen the amassing of forces it took to achieve just minimal internal modification. The reform focused on one topic area; it was limited to a few internal, administrative changes; and it required the heavy hand of American diplomacy and the consensus of other major contributors. Because the UN was feeling more and more vulnerable, there was a compliant secretary-general who, with external help, whipped the senior staff into support for the changes. For institutional changes to take place, the stars really do have to be aligned.

All the reports of the 1980s focused on the UN's economic and social programs because they were the source of the greatest budget growth and the greatest resentment between North and South. But by the 1990s, when the developing countries had been induced to pursue export-oriented economic policies and rely more on private sources of capital, the development issues had been largely transferred to the International Financial Institutions. With new global threats, the UN had turned to the environment and security issues that became the subject of the Secretary General's "Agenda for Peace," as well as of various summit conferences.

A landmark study of UN reform, the United Nations Association of the USA project, set as two of the major roles of the United Nations: that it reflect the current and foreseeable conditions of the world; and that it respond to the desires for institutional change widely expressed in the international community today (United Nations Association of the USA 1987: 11). Wise and realistic, one would say. But with what we now know about the rate of change in the international system, who knows the "foreseeable conditions" and "the desires for institutional change" of tomorrow? When will we get around to discussing the reform propositions of today? The answer seems to be a continuing process of world reform that evolves with the world context.

In recent years, the partnership between INGOs and "like-minded states" has become more and more a practical and theoretical reality. They try to "end run" the status quo-oriented, established hierarchy of powers and structures of the Permanent 5 in the UN. The aim is to create institutional change through a "new diplomacy," as Andrew Cooper, John English and Ramesh Thakur have hypothesized in *Enhancing Global Governance: Towards a New Diplomacy* (Cooper et al. 2002). It was triggered by accumulated frustration with the hierarchical state system, closed agenda setting by the great powers, and the stagnant institutional structure. The challenge has been met through the Ottawa Treaty to ban anti-personnel mines, the campaign for the International Criminal Court and more recently by the "Responsibility to Protect" resolution. It demonstrated the capacity for alternative innovation in the United Nations system.

The hallmarks of the "new diplomacy" start with an often awkward, uneven and ever-changing partnership between an expanding diplomacy of civil society and leading NGOs, aided and abetted by a growing number of like-minded middle powers and bureaucrats, and often with the collaboration of the UN Secretary-General. The activist states augment their power through diplomatic skills and focused concentration of their resources in specific policy areas. They have moved from "being helpful fixers to being gadflies … nudging and tweaking the P5 and especially the USA" (Cooper 2002: 4–11). The focus remains very much on dealing with blockages in the UN system through new problem-solving techniques. Often public diplomacy has replaced quiet diplomacy. The NGOs play multiple roles, going from catalysts having a triggering effect to joint managers and agents, and putting pressure on governments as an alternative form of leadership. Transnational social movements act as mobilizers and opinion makers. They provide speed and energy. Strategic and tactical alliances are adapted to changing situations and goals. Often their expertise trumps that of their bureaucratic opponents.

All this proves that when it comes to innovation, reform and change in international institutions, whether in the 18th century or during recent decades, it is not necessary to wait for a crisis. Much preventative and evolutionary change can be brought about by activist partnerships that concentrate their ideas and energies. Nor is it necessary to wait on the great powers. In fact, they are the least likely to support changing of the status quo (Halliday; Reed). While it may be true that it takes a crisis to create transformational situations, it is the combined efforts of strong individuals, committed middle powers, activist INGOs and social movements—and often the international organizations themselves—that can stimulate innovation in international organizations.

## 2.3 The Three Primary Roles of International Organizations

The above account shows how a changing political environment, an increased number of overlapping domains of activity, varying interaction between individuals and groups across states, and other factors have played a part in the evolution of international institutions. The various roles and functions of these institutions are manifest in two main realms of activity: the security/political and the functional. What has evolved is how the maintenance of peace and security, as well as the provision of functional services, have been carried out in recent years.

It is useful to remember what is meant by "roles" and "functions" in the context of international organizations. Archer expresses this clearly. In determining the role of international organizations, Archer asks whether they are "one of the many participants...mere instruments of other players... [or] forums for meetings, commongrounds for gatherings." In examining the functions of international organizations, he asks how they affect the functioning of international affairs (Archer 2001: 65).

If the world is our stage, what roles do international organizations play? Many have endeavored to answer this question with overlapping themes and content (Claude 1966; Keohane & Nye 1989; Knight 2000; Roberts & Kingsbury 1995; Taylor 1999). Archer's typology identifies three main roles of international organizations to date (see Table 1).

TABLE 1: The Three Roles of International Organizations

| Role | Description | Examples |
|---|---|---|
| Instrument | ...for members states in gaining their foreign policy objectives, or as a tool | Wealthy/powerful countries controlling policy in their interest. The use of the UN by multilateralists as a tool for diplomacy |
| Arena | ...where members meet for dialogue and events to take place, and values to be established | • Less-powerful states have forums to coalesce<br>• Global values can be established |
| Actor | ...that independently participates in the international system, and can direct member activity through resolutions, etc. | • The UN's peacekeeping or socio-economic activities<br>• The ability of INGOs to pressure governments and international institutions |

Source: Archer 2001: 68–92

### 2.3.1 Instrument

The roles of international organizations often reflect an ideal–reality dichotomy. While the outline in Table 1 is quite simple, reflecting the ideal picture of the UN often portrayed in the media and in political statements, the complexity of each role must not be understated. As an *instrument* of member states, the UN is often ideally portrayed as directed by the collective will of its member states. For states that prefer a multilateralist approach, the UN is seen to have significantly developed as a tool for diplomacy, whereby multilateral decision-making has become an "ordinary occurrence" (Alger 1995: 15). John Ruggie has convincingly argued that multilateralism—the desire to pursue common problems cooperatively—has become "a generic institutional form of modern international life." An adherence to multilateralism also implies a preference for conflict resolution through negotiation and cooperative interaction (Ruggie 1993: 7).

Although less-powerful countries do achieve foreign policy goals at times by using the UN as a tool for conducting diplomacy, the organization remains primarily an instrument of the most powerful states in the international order. The veto power of the five permanent members of the Security Council is a clear example of this. Steve Holloway has concluded from his study of great powers in the UN: "Greater power enable[s] greater capacity to act and to influence outcomes to greater power's liking" (Holloway 2000: 64).

Similar critical sentiments were put forth at an expert round-table discussion early in 2003 in Ottawa by Yale professor James Sutterlin. Sutterlin made the provocative statement that a rejected resolution on the war in Iraq maintained only an *image* "that the UN is not just an instrument of U.S. policy, but rather, what it's supposed to be—an instrument for the protection of the global whole…." (DFAIT 2003). Many at the UN believe the collective good has ceded place almost entirely to the national interest of great powers, and that their claims to sovereign will is one of the greatest obstacles to the UN's fulfilling other roles and functions.

### 2.3.2 Arena/Forum

As an arena or forum, the UN has allowed a diversity of opinions and views to be voiced, and innovative activities to take place. Even in the worst of times, harsh antagonists may be brought together to seek out consultative, exploratory solutions. Within the notion of world forum is a whole bundle of forum roles.

There is the peace and security role, if the membership is of a mind to act together to confront security issues, such as Iraq's invasion of Kuwait in 1991. For the first time in history, the international community has an "emergency standby capacity" because the states sitting in the Security Council are obliged to have permanent representatives at the UN to provide round-the-clock reactions to crises. Individual states constantly use international organizations as a locale for lobbying other countries and world institutions in their country's national interest. As they say, if it didn't exist it would be invented, as an (inexpensive) place where everyone is located for "continuing diplomacy."

The UN plays a mentor role for new, young and small states, where they can be welcomed into the international fraternity and taught the tricks of international negotiation. Part of the relative smoothness of decolonization was attributable to this role. Many groups of states "caucus together" in international institutions to improve their relationships and work for their mutual interests on the world stage. Building of world awareness can be achieved through the global media that is often located at the UN to enhance the public profile of crucial causes, such as human rights, terrorism and the ozone hole. Similarly, there is also the "plaintiff" role, which allows aggrieved parties in international disputes to focus world attention on their side of the story.

The UN system also acts as a world forum in a secondary sense. It has been able to remain a somewhat neutral arena, facilitated partly by the inclusion of non-state groups that have interests in international affairs. This has been managed through consultation procedures (such as the consultative status that may be granted to non-governmental organizations through ECOSOC), or at world conferences. People's movements, environmental groups, academics, and the private sector are just some examples of those who regularly participate in UN proceedings.

Additionally, international non-governmental organizations (INGOs) have been able to provide crucial services and work with governments and international leaders. An example is the work of the International Committee of the Red Cross in times of war and disaster. Furthermore, using international forums as continuing sounding boards, they have been able to exert pressure to achieve results on behalf of citizen's movements, such as placing human rights and the environment on the international agenda, halting the establishment of the Multilateral Agreement on Investment (MAI), and aiding political prisoners. INGOs provide specialist knowledge and expertise in many areas, and often assist governments and other international organizations in technical tasks, such as the implementation of development policies and projects. Because of the participation of a wide variety of actors, including INGOs, the UN has remained the primary forum for the establishment of global values.

Less-powerful states are also able to take advantage of the UN as a place to coalesce, and to voice their common discontent in a unified manner. One example of such coalescing was the expression of the need for a New International Economic Order (NIEO) by the bloc of developing countries known as the Group of 77 (G77). Although the UN system did serve an invaluable role as an arena where the existing economic order could be challenged during the 1960s and '70s, there is now a clear imbalance of real power in so-called neutral forums. Less powerful countries are often unable to influence economic policy due to the concentration of wealth and resources in a few powerful member states. Because most global economic policy is formulated in the World Bank, the IMF and the World Trade Organization, where decision-making power depends upon the number of dollars that are being contributed to the institutions, powerful countries effectively control development priorities and monetary policy. This is one of the reasons why the 'global South' is so determined to use its majority control over the General Assembly to stop changes that would extend the power of others, such as the Office of the Secretary General, which is seen as too dependent on the P5 and the U.S. in particular.

### 2.3.3 Independent Actor

The UN is often excused by sympathetic observers who explain away its weaknesses and failures by pointing to its nature as an organization dependant on the will of the members. The membership does play a significant role in directing UN activities. However, this underplays the reality that international organizations can and do act in a relatively independent manner and influence the international order.

This was illustrated by the activities of INGOs that have been able to influence the international agenda through international institutions. The Secretary-General has become a major world figure whose influence it is difficult to ignore. The specialized agencies are often where the action is in each major international field of endeavor as they create regime norms and conventions that become the accepted rules of behavior. The Security Council creates international law by its resolutions, but also by its practices. International institutions act as go-betweens and negotiators to oil the wheels of all forms of global exchanges so that things can get done and disputes get resolved. If humanitarian supplies are delivered, if failed states are rebuilt, if refugees return home or find asylum, if women and children are helped, if local conflicts are defused—it is often because the UN, its agencies or its emissaries have intervened.

Other examples of the independent work of international organizations on the world stage are most clearly noted in the functional aspects of their work. This is most obvious in the institutions upholding international legal justice, and the various peacekeeping and socio-economic development activities in which the UN system is involved. These activities are discussed further in the next section.

## 2.4 The Functions of International Organizations

As mentioned in the beginning of this section, the primary roles and functions of international organizations are apparent in both security/political and functional realms of activity. In order to analyze how international organizations, in whatever role, affect the functioning of international affairs in these two realms, Paul Taylor summarizes their main dealings as addressing "order" between states and "justice" within states (Taylor 1999: 280–3). (And he might well have added justice between states and order within states.) These "dealings" are the functions of international organizations: the raw services provided to meet human needs across states, stripped of any theory and, unfortunately, any glory. Because the functional advantages of international organizations are often assumed to exist without any necessary justification, most fail to appreciate their value.

The functional approach to international organization reaches back to the activities undertaken by 19th-century public unions under the common understanding "that it made sense to co-operate across frontiers on specific matters of a technical or administrative nature" (Archer 2001: 14). The approach was developed and established in the modern era through the work of David Mitrany, who began from the idea that if we first identify human and societal needs, then this should prompt individuals and groups to create institutions that can satisfy those needs. Institutions and authority are linked to specific functions and activities, rather than to states. Since Mitrany, many others have sought to study international organizations in a functional framework (Mitrany 1975; Eastby 1985; Haas 1964; Jacob et al. 1972).

The nature of the UN system is clearly a result of thinking in increasingly functionalist terms. Activities promoting peace and security between states, as well as justice within states, have become crucial to the UN's overall objectives. This is because it has become clear that order within states is not only intrinsically important, but also crucial to maintaining order between states. Below, a snapshot of the various activities of the UN system demonstrates the functional scope of international organizations.

*Peace-enforcement and peacekeeping (Security Council, various peacekeeping missions).* Activities in this area are premised on chapters VI and VII of the UN Charter, which laid out guidelines for dealing with disputes. Tasks in the realm of peacekeeping include "fact-finding and reporting, mediation, negotiation, truce-monitoring, observation of cease-fire zones, disarming of military forces, election monitoring, and even national administration and reconstruction" (Durch & Blechman 1995: 4).

*Humanitarian assistance and intervention within states (UNDRO, UNHCR, Security Council).* Humanitarian assistance may merely be state-approved provision of services in the face of natural disasters, post-conflict disorder, famine and other emergencies. However, the increasing concern of the international community with standards of justice within states has led to a more "flexible view of sovereignty," allowing external actors such as the UN to become actively involved in cases where citizens' rights are not being protected by the state (Taylor 1999: 281).

*Economic and Human Development (ECOSOC, UNDP, World Bank, IMF, UNCTAD, FAO, WTO, UNICEF, UNIFEM, UNFPA).* Alongside and with governments and NGOs, various UN agencies and programs and the World Bank have implemented development projects and programs under general guidance from UNDP and ECOSOC. Specialized agencies, such as FAO, WHO and UNICEF, are heavily involved in developing countries, in their specific focus areas.

*Human Rights and Social Justice (UNHCHR, ECOSOC, UNICEF, UNIFEM, ILO, UNESCO, ICC).* In this area, the UN is mostly concerned with setting international standards through conventions and monitoring within states. However, recent years have seen increasingly active defence of human rights, including the trial of individuals committing serious breaches of international human rights law.

*Inter-state social and technical functions (WHO, FAO, IAEA, ICAO, WMO, ITU, UPU, UNESCO).* This is the area of global service provision to resolve overlapping problems and address areas of common interest, such as health, climate monitoring, administration of the international mail and aviation system, etc. These tend to be the functions of international organizations that are universally enjoyed but rarely seen.

*Stewardship over the Global Commons (UNEP, CSD).* The global commons, a fairly new concept, includes the atmosphere, outer space, the oceans, and other environmental and life-support systems (Commission on Global Governance 1995: 251). Progress toward conserving and protecting the commons for present and future generations has been largely due to the work of the Commission on Sustainable Development, and to various conventions and frameworks dealing with such topics as climate change, fisheries, forests and biodiversity.

*International Legal Justice (ICJ, ICC, ILC).* The UN has spent considerable energy consolidating and expanding international law. Over five hundred multilateral treaties and agreements have been concluded, including customary laws and judicial decisions. Some examples include the Law of the Sea, the Framework Convention on Climate Change, and the Convention against Illicit Traffic in Narcotic Drugs and Psychotropic Substances. The International Law Commission usually prepares drafts of international laws, which then go to conferences to be incorporated into a convention.

### 2.4.1 Accomplishments

No doubt there have been many sources of frustration over the lifetime of the UN system, leading to sceptical references to its decreasing relevance and legitimacy. However, as the Commission on Global Governance has pointed out, "The ramifications of the cold war cracked and weakened the very foundations of the Charter.... Given that the United Nations system was so hobbled from the outset, it is remarkable that it accomplished so much in so many areas of international co-operation" (1995: 231).

The former Deputy Secretary-General, Louise Fréchette, in 2006 provided a vibrant defence of the institution's capacity to adapt itself to changing conditions within its original mandate. In the field of peacekeeping, Mme. Fréchette pointed out, there were only 13 operations in the first forty-five years of the UN, whereas there have been twice the number during the past fifteen years. Now these operations may use force not only to defend themselves but also to defend the civilian population. Their mandate has been completely transformed to include assuring police services and training, disarming militias, facilitating political transition, managing the courts, organizing elections, protecting and coordinating humanitarian workers, and much more. In East Timor and Kosovo, the UN was even called upon to act as the administrator. Similarly, sanctions have been modified to make them much more targeted and viable to avoid hurting the captive populations. For instance, offending leaders are prohibited from travelling; their foreign bank accounts are frozen; and trade in illegal natural resources curtailed. Experimentation with three ad hoc criminal tribunals led to the eventual creation of the International Criminal Court, which while not a part of the UN, came into being because of the UN. Human rights have a much more central place in the UN than ever before, starting with the creation of the Office of the High Commissioner for Human Rights at the beginning of the 1990s. A new Human Rights Council has been created to replace the discredited Commission. With its resolution 1373 following the 9–11 Attack on America, the UN set up an anti-Terrorism Committee and placed strict obligations on all countries to draw up lists of potential terrorists and freeze their assets.

The UN, Fréchette suggests, is relatively successful because of its flexibility, its legitimacy as a universal organization, and its founding principles of peaceful settlement of disputes, economic and social development of peoples, and respect for human rights. In practical terms, it was the UN that assured humanitarian services in Afghanistan, created an interim government, set the bases for a new constitution and managed elections. Similarly, despite disputes in the UN about its support for the Iraq war in 2003, within a year the UN was requested to establish a provisional government and oversee elections. In 2006 the UN had 70,000 soldiers deployed under its flag, more than any country except the United States. Its humanitarian agencies aid millions of people a year; it leads in the fight against communicable diseases; its Millennium Goals mobilize the world against poverty; and it has a new fund to support democracies (UN/DSG/SM/278).

A listing of the UN's many accomplishments and contributions in three broad-ranging areas will set the record straight about its continuing importance in a new era. This is not to claim the UN is perfect and needs no reforms. Rather, it is to demonstrate the pertinence of international institutions and hence the validity of attempts to maximize their usefulness through reform. Of course, this list is illustrative rather than exhaustive.

### 2.4.2 Post-Conflict/Emergency

- The UN Civilian Police Division maintains local law and order in coordination with peacekeeping missions. They also train and monitor local police forces. In countries such as Cyprus, Haiti, Bosnia and Herzegovina, Kosovo, and the Eastern Slavonia region of Croatia, the UN has established local police forces trained to operate with respect for the human rights of local residents (www.un.org/Depts/dpko/dpko/civpol/civpol1.html). A new Peacebuilding Commission has been formed.

- Humanitarian mine clearance, along with training of local de-miners, has become an essential role for UN peacekeepers. These operations not only include mine surveying and mapping, but also mine-awareness education. Mine clearance programs, which have been carried out in several countries (including Afghanistan, Angola, Bosnia and Herzegovina, Cambodia, the Lao People's Democratic Republic, Mozambique, Rwanda and Yemen) allow civilians to return home—to everyday life—after conflict (www.mineaction.org/misc/dynamic_overview.cfm?did=87).
- In post-conflict situations, such as in Nicaragua, El Salvador, Mozambique and Guatemala, UN peacekeepers have supervised the "de-weaponization" of societies by demobilizing soldiers. The UN has sometimes been successful in transforming armed opposition movements into organized political parties (disarmament.un.org/dda-activities.htm).
- The contributions of the United Nations Refugee Agency can best be recounted with statistics of the number of refugees—men, women and children—who were assisted in emergency situations.
  1. In the following countries, UNHCR assisted these many people go home after they had left their native country in an emergency or conflict: Afghanistan: 2.6 million; Guatemala, El Salvador and Nicaragua: 1.9 million (internally displaced); Mali and Liberia: over half a million; Mozambique: nearly 400,000; Vietnam: 109,000.
  2. Additionally, UNHCR has provided the following numbers of refugees with humanitarian assistance (including the establishment of schools and medial clinics): Africa's Great Lakes: 1.7 million Rwandan refugees; Bosnia and Herzegovina: 2.7 million refugees (over four years—the longest running humanitarian "air-bridge" in history); Armenia, Azerbaijan and Georgia: 450,000 refugees and asylum seekers and 970,000 internally displaced persons.

  (Statistics from www.unhcr.ch/cgi-bin/texis/vtx/statistics.)

## 2.4.3 Human Condition/Rights

- The Universal Declaration of Human Rights has been translated into over 300 national and local languages, and is close to being universally accepted as a standard for the rights of all the world's citizens (http://www.unhchr.ch/udhr/index.htm).
- The UN was instrumental in overseeing the process of independence for most of the former colonies, and may have helped avoid many more conflicts than did occur (Alger 1995, 8).
- Since 1992 when the UN established the Electoral Assistance Division, UN-supervised or monitored elections have helped open the way to "establishing and advancing the principle of democracy and political rights" for many members states. These countries include Albania, Cambodia, Eastern (Croatia), Eritrea,

East Timor, Kosovo, Mozambique, South Africa and Uganda (www.un.org/Depts/dpa/ead/ea_content/ea_context.htm).

- The International Decade of the World's Indigenous Peoples (1995–2004) increased recognition of issues important to indigenous peoples within the United Nations system. Most importantly, the Permanent Forum on Indigenous Issues was established as a sub-group of the UN's Economic and Social Council to deal with issues ranging from human rights, to environmental, educational and development issues affecting indigenous peoples. A declaration of the rights of indigenous peoples is being drafted. This is but one example of how the UN uses its symbolic powers (UN Year of …, UN Decade of …, UN Commission on …, Secretary General's Special Representative on … etc. to draw attention to particular issues (www.unhchr.ch/indigenous/main.html).
- Increased awareness of the diversity of human rights abuses worldwide has led to the development of various international legal instruments protecting the rights of various groups (although not all have been signed by all members). These instruments include the Geneva Convention Relative to the Treatment of Prisoners of War (1950), the International Convention on the Elimination of All Forms of Racial Discrimination (1969), the Convention on the Elimination of All Forms of Discrimination Against Women (1979), and the Convention on the Rights of the Child (1989). The adoption of the Convention against Torture and Other Degrading Treatment or Punishment, another landmark, declared torture as an international crime (www.unhchr.ch/html/intlinst.htm).
- Children have received special attention from the United Nations in an attempt to successfully provide a legal basis for the protection of their rights. All 191 member-states have ratified the Convention on the Rights of the Child (except the U.S. and Somalia), and almost all states that did not previously have local legislation to implement this convention have taken measures to do so.
- The needs and health of millions of children are also addressed through international partnerships between UN specialized agencies (such as UNICEF, UNDP and WHO), non-governmental organizations, and governments. For example, it is estimated that because of such programs, more children now are immunized, go to school, and have access to sanitation and safe water than ever before.
- The UN has been pivotal in defining HIV/AIDS as a development issue. Under the direction of UNAIDS, UNDP and the WHO, countries that have dealt with the multisectoral nature of the issue (such as Thailand and Uganda) have significantly reduced the number of expected new cases. Stephen Lewis, the UN's special representative on this issue, has been tireless in his efforts to make the world aware of the calamitous nature of this issue and of extent remedies.
- The first international judgment on genocide was handed down in May 1999 by the International Criminal Tribunal for Rwanda (International Criminal Tribunal for Rwanda 1999).

- Accomplishments that are universally enjoyed but rarely seen are mostly in the area of global service provision to resolve overlapping problems and address areas of common interest. For example, ensuring the safety of travelers or the distribution of mail worldwide is the job of the International Civil Aviation Organization, the World Meteorological Organization, and the Universal Postal Union. Furthermore, smallpox, polio, malaria, tuberculosis, leprosy and yaws are all on the brink of elimination due to worldwide campaigns and the work of the WHO (Kenworthy 1995: 91).
- Human development has traditionally been one of the cornerstones of UN activity. Although starved for funds during the 1990s, what has been called the FfD Monterrey Conference got the UN back in to the international economic game in a significant manner, and gained promises of billions of dollars in aid money (Official Development Aid). The UN had bent over backward to be self-effacing, to garner cooperation among its agencies as well as with the international financial institutions, and to lobby for coordination among the disparate ministries in donor countries.

### *2.4.4 Research/Training*

- The UN has been significantly instrumental in establishing cooperative research and training among experts and scholars across the world. The foremost example of this is the leading research in agricultural development facilitated by the Food and Agriculture Organization (FAO). The FAO brings together expertise in programs that emphasize local knowledge from all parts of the world, and gathers, interprets and disseminates information (ibid: 92).
- Walden Bello has praised UN agencies for "provid[ing] a hospitable home for Third World economists and economic thinkers to conceptualize the problems of development and to come out with concrete development strategies" (Bello 1998: 209).
- UN conferences, the UN University, and the UN Institute for Training and Research have provided a forum for research in the area of international organization, including evaluations of development projects, the role of new actors in the UN system, and the training of new delegates in multilateral diplomacy (Alger 1995: 32–3).

The broadscope of UN accomplishments can be found in the 2005 publication *60 ways the UN makes a Difference* (www.un.org/works). A more in depth presentation of UN achievements can be found in *The Power of UN Ideas: Lessons from the First 60 Years* (Jolly et al. 2005). We learn that the UN played a leading role in promoting global goals, human rights, sustainability, gender equality, human development, human security, global governance and civil society.

Nevertheless, we should note that all along, major thinkers about the UN have been astonishingly prescient in their understanding of the United Nations and its future problems and orientations. In a book published in 1965 to commemorate the first 20 years of the Organization (Norman Padelford and Leland Goodrich, eds. *The United Nations in the Balance: Accomplishments and Prospects*), two of the godfathers of UN analysis accurately forecast the future. Harland Cleveland (former U.S. Assistant Secretary of State for International Organizations) concluded:

> These *four great issues (the spread of nuclear weapons, the ethics of intervention, the dilemma of human rights, and the reconciliation of resources with representation in the UN system)* are major issues visibly ahead of us in UN affairs. On their outcome depends the success or failure of the primary aim of United States foreign policy—to help create a world safe for diversity (Padelford 1965: 470).

These comments are so startlingly prescient of the problems confronting the UN in the first decade of the 21st century that it seems the only thing that has not held steady is the orientation of the American government! For his part, Innis Claude, an early major writer on the UN, also handled his perception of continuing issues with deftness and foresight. He forecast that the movement toward universality (he was pleading for the entry of China) would be the foundation of the future UN function of *collective legitimization*, not because of its power but because statesmen act as if it matters. The concentration of the international body's attention upon the economic and social aspirations of developing countries would grow in intensity, although it was not certain the political incentive to meet the demand would undergo corresponding growth. The UN would always find frequent opportunities to promote the peaceful settlement of disputes through methods of investigation, mediation, conciliation, and preventive and quiet diplomacy. His wish for the international organization was that it be in the position *of encouraging and facilitating rather than discouraging and inhibiting, and that the value of the UN would lie not in becoming stronger but more useful. Its great potential lies in promoting the stabilization of international relations and accommodation of divergent interests.* Claude was so sure-footed in his analysis because of his understanding of the UN's strengths and weaknesses at that time:

> … the reaffirmation of the Organization's fundamental premise: the proposition that the United Nations should seek to limit the disturbance of international relations caused by conflict between states and that it must acknowledge the limitations imposed upon its functioning by conflicts arising between the Great Powers (Padelford 1965: 474).

However, times change and it is difficult for international intergovernmental institutions to keep in step with technological and economic developments. In fact, it is difficult for all of us to conceive of just how much the world has changed since the founding of the United Nations six decades ago. That is the task of the next chapter.

## BOX 4: The Elimination of Smallpox

They say that a picture is worth a thousand words. The campaign for the elimination of smallpox is a picture of international institutions in action. Plagues of smallpox have been the scourge of humanity since at least 1000 BC. As we learn from Richard Preston's *The Demon in the Freezer,* the World Health Assembly of the World Health Organization (WHO) launched the Smallpox Eradication Program in 1966. Imitating President Kennedy's program to place a man on the moon, they gave themselves a 10-year deadline. As it turned out, the last naturally occurring case of smallpox was contracted in 1978—the international campaign lasted 12 years.

The Smallpox Eradication Program mobilized hundreds of thousands of doctors and health workers. At its core was a little team of experts and administrators at the WHO headquarters in Geneva. Their cubicles were usually empty because at any one time, half the staff was in the field. For instance, during the height of the campaign in India, 150,000 people were working for the program—most on very small salaries. With a fleet of 500 jeeps they called on every house in India once a month for a year and a half (120 million homes, for a total of two billion house calls). "Firewalls" of vaccinated people were erected around any outbreaks of smallpox to choke them off.

Not only were medical workers mobilized, so was the world. Inspired doctors marshalled their resources. National efforts were led by cooperation between the United States and the Soviet Union. When serious outbreaks occurred, other countries such as Sweden poured in resources. Service clubs such as Rotary and Lions paid huge sums to help the eradication, and NGOs such as Oxfam contributed large quantities of money and people. Of course, these are only a few examples.

Preston concludes by saying, "In the years just before the Eradication began, two million people a year were dying of smallpox. The doctors who ended the virus as a natural disease have effectively saved 50 to 60 million human lives. This is the summit of Everest in the history of medicine and yet they have never received the Nobel Prize" (Preston 2002: 277–8).

These words are written on Remembrance Day, when countries around the world honor their soldiers fallen in wars past. Why is there no special day when we commemorate the good things that humans have done for each other? Why is it that while almost all countries have war memorials, so few have monuments to peace? The answers to these questions would explain why some still think that international institutions are "irrelevant." The lesson of all this is that the world can achieve miracles when people work together, and when effective institutions are there to help countries, individuals and NGOs to cooperate.

# 3 A Changed World?

Our last chapter taught us that not only governments but civil society as well can make serious contributions to international institutional innovation. Equally important, we saw that the origins and evolution of international organizations were greatly conditioned by their economic, social, and political environment. For instance, in a large measure, the expansion of the industrial revolution across whole continents in the 19th century motivated business to pressure government to provide predictable international conditions to allow them to work in new markets – and the international laws and organizations to make them effective. Today we must see if the world has been transformed to a degree that necessitates a mirror transformation in international organizations so they can carry out new functions in a global era. The idea here is that reform is needed to correspond to change. "Institutions must reflect society" (Seara-Vazquez 2003: 19). But first we must see if change in the environment is sufficient to necessitate institutional transformation.

We may hypothesize that the more changes transform the international system, the more they confront current international institutions with problems they are not designed to handle. For instance, take Margaret MacMillan's description of the founding of the League of Nations in her book *Paris 1919.* She maintains that the League did represent "a recognition of the changes that had already taken place in international relations… The way states behaved toward one another had undergone a transformation in the century before the Peace Conference met" (2003: 84).

- "War increasingly was seen as an aberration, and an expensive one at that.
- The people themselves, not just monarchs, constituted nations.
- It was no longer fashionable to seize the territory of another nationality.
- The spread of democracy and nationalism, the web of railways and telegraph lines, and mass-circulation newspapers created public opinion that government did not like but dared not ignore.
- Prosperity and progress encouraged the belief that the world was becoming more civilized. A growing middle class produced a natural constituency for peace" (MacMillan 2003: 84–5).

So our task is to demonstrate that the world has changed to such a degree since the founding of modern international organizations in the 1940s that institutions must be transformed to allow them to deal with current and future global challenges. First, we need a 'base-line' to remind us of conditions in 1945 so we will be able to estimate the degree and nature of change since that time.

In 1945, the world was just coming out of the Second World War. The victorious powers decided they needed an intergovernmental organization to promote peace and security between states and encourage human development. To overcome the blockages of the League of Nations, the victorious powers granted themselves permanent seats and a veto on the all-powerful Security Council and made sure the UN could not interfere in their vital affairs. The UN would accomplish its goals by encouraging diplomacy, acting as a permanent meeting place and forum, and fostering negotiation to impede inter-state wars. It was recognized the states needed an organization to help them cooperate to collectively halt wars and promote development in a world that still maintained non-intervention in sovereign affairs.

The UN corresponded to the essential features of the world of 1945. The world was composed of sovereign states and colonial powers. It was soon to be dominated by the stalemate of the bipolar nuclear weaponry of the United States and the Soviet Union and would remain divided for four decades into the Western and Communist camps of the Cold War. International relations were largely political (and not economic, cultural or social) between impervious states thought to be mainly homogenous in nature. Interest groups and elites acted on and through the foreign policy of their countries. International relations to maximize state power were carried on mostly by governments and their diplomatic and military representatives. The power balance leant heavily toward North America which had come out of the War empowered and largely unscathed. Note the use of adjectives such as "largely" to convey the understanding that this map of the post-war world had exceptions to all its elements that portended future changes (for an enlightened overview, see Deutsch 1968).

Already by the 1970s, a groundbreaking study on transnationalism noted a massive development in trans-border exchanges. Keohane and Nye identified four types of interactions:

- communication: the movement of information
- transportation: the movement of physical objects
- finance: the movement of money
- travel: the movement of persons

Each was found to have become much more frequent, regular and widespread. This growth in *transactions*; would lead to the creation of a *common agenda* for the world and the transformation of the *international system*. The most important evolution of our times has been the gradual transference of functions to the international level that used to be handled inside the nation-states. In a sense, it is the gap between the transferal of our socio-economic problems to the international level and the capacity of our international institutions to cope with them that is the subject of this book. To start our study of change, let us illustrate this trend of problems moving beyond national borders by summarizing a small selection of the more dramatic changes under the titles we normally use for ministries or departments within state governments. A second section describes how a number of specialists have analyzed the most significant of all changes – globalization – and its relationship to governance. Then it will be possible to draw some conclusions.

## 3.1 From National to International Transactions

*Department of Social Services*: In most countries where the public has a voice, there is some form of social safety net to help those suffering from poverty. Often referred to as "unequal globalization," world poverty and the growing gap in wealth within and between countries has become an international scourge that would not be tolerated in our countries. In 1998, there were 1.2 billion humans living in dire poverty, usually meaning less than $2 a day. The number had not improved an iota during the 1990s. During that decade, foreign aid had dropped not increased, while school enrolments—particularly girls'—and infant mortality rates had barely improved (The Economist 07/03). Illustrative of the concentration of wealth, we learn from a 2004 headline in the *Sunday London Times* that the "Rich increase their wealth by 30% in one year." The article explained that since the Times started following the 1,000 richest Britons 16 years previously, this was the largest year-over-year growth, and represented a gain of £200 billion (18/04/04).

Aside from the inhumanity of these wealth gaps and levels of destitution, they also put a huge burden on the international system. Poverty may not be the direct cause of terrorism, but it underlies the sense of humiliation that is the seedbed for terrorist recruiters. Unstable and unsustainable governments lead to civil wars (as many as 30 of them at any given time), and eventually to failed states where the UN must send peacekeepers, humanitarian aid and nation-builders.

The President of the World Bank, James Wolfensohn, has issued a dire warning:

> One fifth of humanity takes home four fifths of global income... more than one billion people lack drinkable water; women are dying in child-birth at the rate of one a minute.... So what can be done about it? Trade barriers that prevent the poor from exporting their way to a better life should be torn down, and development assistance should be doubled.... Doubling aid... would only cost one fifth of 1 percent of the income of the richest countries.... During the next 20 years the world's population is projected to grow from 6 billion to 8 billion, with nearly all that increase concentrated in poor countries. People in rich nations who think that this has no impact on their security are kidding themselves.... There is no wall. We are linked by trade, by migration, by environmental degradation, by drugs, by financial crisis and by terror (*International Herald Tribune* 13/03/02).

Three years later, when little had been done, Jeffrey Sachs' 2005 book, *The End of Poverty* laid out for world leaders in clear and unambiguous terms a relatively straightforward plan for overcoming global poverty. He shows how extreme poverty is not an individual sin but a collective trap. To get out of it requires not handouts but investments in agricultural techniques, basic health clinics, no fees for school children who also require a meal, and electrification, primary roads and communications services (p. 233). He calls this investment in human, business, and natural capital and in infrastructure and public institutions. Such development requires a sustained plan that can only come from a partnership between more effective and committed developing state governments and foreign aid from donor countries.

Sachs demonstrates, based on World Bank calculations, that such a world compact to overcome extreme poverty is eminently doable. It is estimated that basic needs can be met for $1.08 a day per person. Around the world, approximately 1.1 billion people have a shortfall for a total $124 billion in 2001 (U.S. dollars). At the same time, the income of the 22 donor countries of the Development Assistance Committee (DAC) was around $20.2 trillion. "Thus a transfer of 0.6 percent of donor income would in theory raise all the 1.1 billion of the world's extreme poor to the basic-needs level" (p. 290). Moreover, this percentage is relatively small because there are now many fewer in extreme poverty (it was 1.5 billion in 1980) and the donor countries are proportionately much wealthier. So Sachs goes on to show what each donor country could and should be doing to alleviate world poverty. The catch-22 is that this sort of plan requires will-power. Based on his experience in setting up the Global Fund to Fight Aids, TB, and Malaria in 2001, he believes that if you can put people into a room and infuse their discussions with factual information and "analytical deliberation" you can bridge seemingly irreconcilable positions (p. 204). But it takes time, background studies, data and determination. It is obvious that these conditions did not exist within the world leadership when they met for the UN World Summit in 2005 because they all but eviscerated Sachs' most simplified Millennium Project proposals. Better international institutions would help the debate but we can see how hard it will be to get fundamental UN reform and why it will take enormous determination, debate and political pressure.

*Department of Justice and Attorney General:* When one speaks of world anarchy, one is usually thinking about sovereign countries looking after their own interests. But a newer meaning is the crime wave that has been unleashed on the world in the past several decades. The dramatic dangers of international crime are starkly depicted by a simple list: drug lords and their trade, piracy, international mafias and crime cartels (the person who mugs you in Barcelona may come from Rumania and be controlled from Moscow), ship hijacking (up 40 percent in Southeast Asia in 2003 alone), smuggling of humans, diamond trafficking to support civil wars, the trade in stolen cars, and kidnapping of foreigners for ransom. Interpol – another international institution – needs legislative and material support for international policing to restore some semblance of legal order.

*Departments of the Environment and Natural Resources:* Known internationally under the title of "sustainable development," the task is to marry concerns over economic development with problems of resource depletion and environmental degradation. The aim is to preserve the world for future generations.

Why do city dwellers need SUVs? It seems a whole generation forgot the lessons of energy conservation. Why is it that the only way to fish is with enormous factory ships that drag up everything on the sea bottom that might produce life?

How is it the forests of Russia and Canada and the jungles of Brazil and Africa have been taken over by international forestry corporations that thrust in roads, build tentative towns of thousands, maximize profits through slash and burn, and, in the case of Africa at least, pay such low wages that the workers slaughter the apes and monkeys for food? And why are single-hull oil tankers, flying flags of convenience, still polluting the oceans? With each practice multiplied many times over, the result is smog in our cities, pollution in our waterways, oceans empty of fish, denuded forests, fossil fuel pollution of the atmosphere, global warming and acid rain, and the list goes on. These issues touch us all. The biggest problem is that no one country can resolve them alone. Pollution and economics do not respect frontiers (see, for example, Roodman 1999; *Options 2002*; The Johannesburg Declaration, Heinrich Böll Foundation 2002).

In our Preface the thesis of Ronald Wright's *A Short History of Progress* was introduced. He shows that that historical civilizations throughout the world had gone to their doom because they were not able to adapt their ecological policies and institutions to the harsh environmental conditions that were confronting their societies. But he did not stop there. He up-dated his study to give us a thumbnail sketch of how our current abuse of nature and unconcerned élites are potentially condemning today's global civilization. Natural disasters, from mudslides to flooding, are on the increase. "Species are going extinct 1,000 times faster than at any time in history, with up to 30 percent of all mammal, bird and amphibian species in danger of disappearing", according to the UN's four-year Millennium Ecosystem Report involving 1,300 experts from 95 countries and released on March 30, 2005. Species are the root of biodiversity that underpins ecosystems. Their loss becomes irreversible and can have a greater impact than climatic change. A forest, for example, is an ecosystem that produces 'services' such as oxygen, cleaning water, preventing erosion and flooding, capturing excess carbon dioxide, and providing habitat for many species.

In addition, weapons of mass destruction, worldwide pollution, the conflict of civilizations, and international anarchy could threaten our very existence. But, once again, elites are digging in their heels and refusing to heed the signs of impending hazards. Wright points out that the postwar consensus on the use of collective, international institutions and democratically managed forms of Keynesian economics has been undermined. Tax cutting and deregulation have hobbled governments' capacity to deal with collective problems. In the United States, messianic evangelism and market extremism have united to hobble policies on the environment and climate change. The levers of power have been transferred from elected governments to unelected corporations. The revolt against redistribution adds to the gap between rich and poor. There is hostility to change from vested interests, and inertia throughout most of society.

At the very least, these lessons from the past should make us think. These accumulated technological dependencies and over-extensions, along with the accumulated accelerations in growth, population and pollution, should make us wonder what humanity is doing to its world and what we can do—together—to change course before we face the fate of previous civilizations.

*Department of Health:* For the most part, we think our health problems will be looked after by our regional and national governments. After all, what could be more local than a hospital? But when an infectious disease such as SARS (Sudden Acute Respiratory Syndrome) comes from another continent and closes down our local hospital—and even kills patients, nurses and doctors—then we start to see how the dots are connected.

Since 1973, 20 well-known diseases, including tuberculosis, malaria, cholera and syphilis, have returned with a vengeance, and 30 new infectious diseases without cures have appeared. Together these are responsible for a 500-percent increase in induced deaths in 20 years. The world *is* able to take action against infectious diseases, as demonstrated by the control of smallpox, yellow fever, polio and measles, thanks to dedicated programs of the World Health Organization. Still, we keep being threatened by pandemics such as HIV/AIDS, mad cow disease, influenza, and hemorrhagic fevers such as Ebola, Lassa fever, Hantavirus, and Avian Birdflu. These diseases "present a direct and significant long-term threat to international governance and prosperity" because global cooperative surveillance and public health policies are needed to deal with the disease amplifiers, such as ecological and antibiotic misuse, warfare, climate change, fast travel, famine, natural disasters and increased trade (Price-Smith 1999: 427; Oldstone 1998).

*Department of Research and Industrial Development:* New technologies are the driving force behind globalization. They are also one of the main contributing factors to the wealth gap in and between countries. The continuing problem is that "technical innovation inevitably proceeds at a faster pace than legislators and policy makers can address the implications of the changes" (Wiltshire 2001: 6). Globalization itself was made possible by technological change: rapid and cheaper travel, instantaneous, worldwide communications (including financial transfers), and huge cargo ships and airplanes for expanded trade.

Biotechnology, for instance, has raised international controversy over bio-diversity. Genetically modified organisms allow half a dozen hyper-corporations to have a monopolistic stranglehold on plant patents that even extends to implanting "terminal genes" in seeds to prevent their being replanted. These corporations also feel little need to develop products for poor countries with weak markets; on the contrary, their plants may give additional advantages to the farmers of the wealthy countries. In other cases, genetically modified crops have devastated huge commercial trading markets because some countries refuse imports tainted with these products.

All this raises immense international issues about ethics, control, access, benefits (the corporations often use patents developed by publicly funded universities), fairness and ownership. Should anyone be allowed to own seeds that used to be developed and made available to all by agricultural departments? As *The New York*

*Times* concluded, "The real crime of genetic modification is not its risks but that of squandering its promise by widening the gap between rich and poor" (13/9/03; Mulligan & Stoett 2000).

New information technologies are another vast domain with paradoxical twin influences that augment both international cooperation and dependence. Revolutionary advances in communications and computing technologies have the capacity to alter relationships and redraw boundaries. They also erode the traditional separation between domestic and foreign policy, as well as reduce the power of governments while empowering non-state actors and making possible transnational civil society (Matthews 2000). But once again, not all citizens or countries can equally benefit from these new technologies. According to Jeffrey Sachs, states with only 15 percent of the world's population innovate nearly all the world's technology. Innovation spawns innovation, and requires a critical mass in ideas and market. A second category, with a further 50 percent of the population, is able to adopt these technologies for production and consumption. This leaves about 2 billion of the globe's people "technologically disconnected, neither innovating at home nor adopting foreign technologies" (Sachs 2000: 81).

Having passed from the industrial to the technological revolution, the world is divided into a new form of haves and have-nots. This has implications for international governance. On one hand, because of rapidly advancing technologies, much of the globe is more integrated and interdependent and therefore requires better international organizations and regimes. On the other hand, vast groups of humanity live in abject poverty and technological disconnect, which can be surmounted only by international cooperation and aid.

*Department of Defense:* In the modern era (let's say, since the Treaty of Westphalia, in the 1600s), first the European and then the world scene has been dominated by international power politics, the game of alliances, and, from time to time, balance-of-power politics. The United Nations promised to change this. Then came the Cold War, where a nuclear standoff between two superpowers assured a certain form of stability. Since the fall of the Berlin Wall in 1989, we have been sliding back toward a condition of complex international anarchy. Benjamin Barber has portrayed it this way:

> In Hobbes' famous blunt portrait, this condition is one "of continual fear, and danger of violent death; and the life of man, solitary, poor, nasty, brutish, and short" but the point of politics is to get out as soon as a covenant can be contrived.... Hobbes captures our own experience today of an international realm wracked with terrorist violence and Third World desperation, as well as with the First World fear and uncertainty they breed. Weak local government, poverty, and religious fanaticism constitutes a recipe for uncertainty; international predators, whether they are financial speculators, drug syndicate criminals, or enraged terrorists, leave billions of people in the world in a state of perpetual fear, unable to govern their destinies, as frightened of their own government and sometimes their own neighbours as they are of distant superpowers that intimidate them with their splendour and their hegemony. Terrorism has now displaced fear from the Third to the First World, giving

> those in Europe and America who have conquered anarchy within their own borders a taste of the its grim rewards in the borderless world of interdependence that lies beyond …. To overcome insecurity, men may be tempted to forego liberty—unless they can discover a formula in which they can abdicate nature's anarchy without surrendering their freedom. That formula is the social contract (Barber 2003: 70–2).

The nature of international security has radically changed since the formation of the United Nations and its Security Council in 1945. Then the fear was of renewal of war between sovereign states. The goal was collective security. Without underestimating this possible international threat, the fear today is of terrorists who can sneak behind borders, possibly with weapons of mass destruction, and of rogue regimes and of horrendous civil wars that threaten both national and international stability. Decision makers are caught in between these two worlds, as can be seen in the Bush administration: they call for multilateral unity to wage war on terrorism, while thinking they can act alone to protect the U.S. by using the sovereign right of self-defense to wage war on foreign regimes it suspects of harboring threats to its security.

In such a changed world, it is best to ask the generals in our "Ministry of Defence" for a threat analysis update. Just what has changed in the military field?

- The Cold War threat of nuclear annihilation that gave rise to mutual deterrence has ceded place to a single global power plus a bevy of smaller states with atomic weapons, and a consequent loss of discipline and control over weapons of mass destruction. "Nuclear proliferation is on the rise…. If the world does not change course, we risk self-destruction," warned the Director General of the International Atomic Energy Agency, Mohamed ElBaradei, at the beginning of 2004 (*The New York Times* Op-Ed 12-2-04).
- Supposedly banned by international treaty, chemical weapons, including vicious gases, returned in the Iran–Iraq war.
- A newer category of weapon of mass destruction—easy to make and transport—are biological weapons such as anthrax, of which the U.S. got a tiny whiff at a terrible cost. Before the fall of the Berlin Wall, the Soviets had 20,000 tons of weapons-grade smallpox bacteria loaded on multiple warhead missiles and ready to go (Preston 2002: 112).
- Costly helicopters have become as necessary and ubiquitous as jeeps were for surveillance, search and rescue, transport and aerial attack.
- Giant, powerful, so-called "conventional" weapons have recently come on the scene. These include laser-guided bombs and missiles that can go to the bottom of underground hideouts, and "daisy-cutters" that parachute clusters of copper bomblets that can wipe out entire infantry or armored regiments and also act as landmines (which are supposedly outlawed).
- Not only have these weapons been made larger and more deadly and sophisticated, they have also been miniaturized for battlefield use—and for easy transport and hiding.

- Just as cannons were invented to destroy mighty fortresses, terrorists have invented ways of using undetectable weapons to attack their powerful enemies behind their defenses—with devastating results, first in Europe and now in the Americas, Africa and Asia.
- Not only are terrorists more audacious, they are also better financed, organized, trained and led. They even control territory. Their threat is more sustained and the fear they arouse more contagious.
- There appear to be new links of mutual aid between terrorist cells and international criminal organizations.
- Both groups have turned massively to kidnapping.
- The continuing availability of small arms, plus the breakdown in Cold War controls, has fueled ethnicity- and religion-based civil wars, genocide and crimes against humanity on an enormous scale. This availability also eventually led to humanitarian disasters, massive numbers of refugees and displaced persons, and the breakdown of states that can be used by criminal gangs.
- Fear of rogue states, terrorism and the dissemination of weapons of mass destruction has caused the United States to turn its back on its policies of dissuasion, deterrence and containment in favor of a new strategic policy of pre-emptive attacks on perceived enemies. They do this to take anticipatory action against emerging threats and building a defense system that is beyond challenge (Barber 2003: 78–101, Intriligator 2006).

What are the results? First, there are the costs of high-tech warfare (almost 500 billion dollars annually in the U.S. alone) and their potential destructiveness in an anarchic world. Collateral civilian deaths are unacceptable. Second, vulnerability is universal. The starkest result is the massive economic, cultural and democratic cost of this universal vulnerability. Like a huge boulder being thrown in the sea of international affairs, state breakdown and terrorism and their causes have washed waves of fear-based reactions over our societies. Airlines and tourist industries were decimated.

Politicians are perverted by a paranoia that is often combined with their ulterior motives. For example, the famous "peaceable kingdom" of Canada passed an anti-terrorism act that gives virtually unreviewable power to the Solicitor General to brand activities and organizations as "terrorist," and powers of preventative arrest and investigative hearings that override fundamental freedoms in an unprecedented manner. Canada went beyond U.S. and British legislation by defining as "terrorist" almost any activity that intentionally disrupts essential services. "The overall effect is to lengthen the reach of the criminal law in a manner that is complex, unclear and unrestrained" (Morden 2003: 6–7). Similarly, George W. Bush undertook "egregious presidential overreaching" to use executive authority to fight terrorism without Congress or the judiciary (*New York Times* 19-12-03).

The most powerful state on earth lives in fear of terrorism. The cost of its mysterious "alerts" is enormous.

> Terror Alert is Raised to "High," Increasing Scrutiny of Travelers
>
> Washington, December 21, 2003 – The Bush administration raised the nation's antiterrorism alert status a notch Sunday (to orange, the second highest level), indicating a newly heightened concern about the possibility of an attack in coming days….
>
> Coming at the peak of the holiday season, the change in alert level will subject millions of travelers to tighter security measures at airports and elsewhere and will set off more intense surveillance by federal, state and local enforcement agencies at borders around vulnerable targets….
>
> It came after intense consultations over the weekend among intelligence agencies, which had picked up recent talk among extremists about some unspecified but spectacular attack….
>
> New York City officials said they were putting more police officers on patrol at landmarks and important sites, establishing check points at bridges and tunnels, and calling in teams of National Guard members who are trained to detect chemical, biological and radiological substances….
>
> On Sunday in New York, suspicious packages prompted the evacuation of throngs from the Metropolitan Museum of Art and the suspension of service on a busy Manhattan subway line…. A police spokesman said the boxes contained "a nondevice."
>
> Gov. George E. Pataki, responding to the federal alert, ordered New York State's agencies to activate contingency plans, including the use of National Guard troops and state police officers to protect airports, bridges, tunnels, train and bus terminals, utilities and other "critical infrastructure" (Cushman 2003).

When we are going to start asking if there is a more effective way of limiting terrorism?

When will we realize that rising military and security expenditures offer little real protection, and that turning a blind side to the causes of terrorism is simply hiding our head in the sand?

And then there are the costs of the breakdowns of states afflicted by ethnic hatred, fundamentalism and civil wars that threaten to overflow their borders (there have been at least six armies in the "Democratic" Republic of Congo). The immense demands on world policing, pacification, UN peacekeeping, humanitarian aid, and nation building are prohibitive. They distract the world from development, as Kofi Annan stated in his 2003 year-end report. To put it another way, "It is a challenge … to ensure that global riot control does not get in the way of global problem-solving" (Groom & Taylor 1975: 406–7).

It is clear that most of the problems that were outlined above—economic gaps, cultural conflicts, global terrorism, arms diffusion, international criminal gangs, civil wars, the conflict of civilizations, refugees, world policing, peace making, nation rebuilding, etc.—can be dealt with only on a collective, multilateral basis. When we have universal vulnerability, it is becoming painfully obvious that no state, no matter how powerful, can police the world unilaterally.

*Department of Immigration and Refugees:* At the beginning of the 1960s, there was a worldwide campaign to empty out refugee camps. Four decades later, the refugee situation is worse than ever, and is accompanied by masses of internal displaced persons and international migrations of people in search of security and a better livelihood. In 2003, the United Nations High Commission for Refugees was concerned about 20.6 million persons, of whom 10 million were refugees in the strict sense of the term and the rest were internally displaced persons, asylum seekers, returned refugees, and stateless persons. In the past 25 years, the number of refugees (persons outside their country who cannot return due to well-founded human rights persecution or because they fled war or civil conflict) varied between a low of 8 million in 1980 and a high of 17 million in 1990.

One recent longitudinal, comparative study noted a global trend toward the growing mobility of people. In the mid-1990s, the global stock of immigrants was about 125 million. These movements of people can be unsettling, leading to cultural and ethnic tensions and eroded territorial political control. Migrations are also partially responsible for the number of humanitarian crises, which has roughly doubled in every decade from an average of 53 disasters annually in the 1960s to 223 in the 1980s (Nafziger et al. 2000: 47–8). The authors of this study analyse the major causes of mass migrations, refugee flows, and humanitarian crises.

> In summary, the propensity of societies to humanitarian crises is affected primarily by two sets of factors: dissolution of political order and increasing vulnerability of the people in exposed groups and societies. The decline of the state permits non-state actors to resort to sub-national violence, weakens the capacity to meet the basic human needs of the citizens, and gives a greater role to fear and revenge. Vulnerability increases both as a result of poverty and social inequality, which marginalize increasing numbers of people, and the deterioration of economic and environmental living conditions. Usually, the decline of the state and the increasing socio-economic vulnerability interact with each other, bringing about a humanitarian crisis (Nafziger et al. 2000: 49).

Is it not striking that the World Bank, despite its long-time policies, also concluded as long ago as 1997 that the state is a crucial factor in modern development?

> This Report shows that the determining factor behind these contrasting developments is the effectiveness of the state. An effective state is vital for the provision of the goods and services—and the rules and institutions—that allow markets to flourish and people to lead healthier, happier lives. Without it, sustainable development, both economic and social, is impossible (World Bank 1997: 1).

Then there are the costs to the international community. Aside from the myriad NGOs, it supports four large UN humanitarian agencies: the UN High Commission for Refugees (UNHCR), the UN Relief and Works Agency for Palestine Refugees (UNWRA), the World Food Programme (WFP), and the United Nations Children's

Fund (UNICEF). Each has a budget of between one and two billion dollars a year, of which only about 3 percent comes from the UN's regular budget (Bertrand 2000: 76). All the rest is in voluntary contributions, and is therefore subject to political pressures. Despite its more than six thousand employees on the public payroll, UNHCR still is able only to collect money from UN members and transfer it to its "partner" NGO charities contracted to do the fieldwork (Hancock 1989: 10). UNWRA has acted for five decades almost as a national social service administration for the Palestinian people.

Still we are left with growing numbers of unprotected child soldiers, sex slaves and urban urchins, and, of course, refugees and impoverished migrants.

Perhaps the largest social and economic cost is that paid by the countries hosting the refugee camps, and particularly by the countries receiving the refugees and immigrants. In spite of the long-term benefit of the contributions of these future new citizens, there are immense short-term policy and administrative costs in choosing who is to be accepted and in protecting their borders. Countries have become so inured to these expenses they are hardly noticed anymore. But in almost every country in Western Europe and in North America and Australia, there have been considerable policy debates over the merits of large-scale immigration flows that have distracted these countries from other objectives. There have also been considerable national backlashes, leading to some racial strife. However, none of these reactions get to the roots of high rates of migration: extreme poverty, enormous international wealth gaps, uncontrolled ethnic conflict, and human rights abuses. And none of these challenges can be resolved by one country alone, or by many countries without coordination.

*Ministry of Trade and Commerce:* "Trade in goods and services is growing faster than the global economy as a whole, accounting for more than 4$ trillion per year in a global economy of some $30 trillion" (Florini 2003: 163). More than one dollar in ten in our pockets takes part in international trade. However, when the overall trade figures are broken down, we find that "trade accounted for 37.4 percent of the economies of the rich countries in1999, but only about 8 percent of the economies of the low-income countries" (Florini 2003: 160). Eighty percent of the world's people live in countries that produce only 20 percent of the world's total income. Fewer than 20 developing countries (such as Taiwan, South Korea and Brazil) have large trade and capital flows. Most trade is between Europe, North America and Japan and now China and India. Of the 40,000 multinational companies, almost all the larger ones are located in the technologically advanced countries.

The intention of free trade was to gain economic efficiency by allowing countries to trade in the goods and services they produce best. But corporations have also used it to improve their economies of scale. This has led to the concentration of production and ownership. The World Trade Organization's rules on non-discrimination do not have the flexibility of the former General Agreement on Trade and Tariffs that acknowledged the different degrees of development of countries. Nor do the WTO's rules allow for non-economic factors such as the environment, safety, labor standards, human rights, wages, education and child labor.

*Department of Finance:* Following World War Two, there were considerable attempts to stabilize international exchange rates and maintain confidence in money supply via the IMF and the gold standard, and then by pegging of currencies. Under the theory of international liberalization, money markets were to be deregulated. More and more currencies floated freely, protected only by interest rates. Combined with advanced information and communication technologies, deregulation now means that vast sums of money flow across national borders.

It is estimated that $1.5 trillion in international exchange transactions now occur per day. The exchange transactions are concentrated in huge banks, multinational corporations, pension funds, mutual funds and insurance companies run by professional money managers. These transactions, aimed at producing short-term maximization of returns, lead to the volatility and instability that were major causes of the 100 world financial crises between 1980 and 2000. "The fluid transfer of funds across national borders is the single most dramatic element in global economic integration" (Florini 2003: 157).

*The Economist* estimates that only 5 percent of these transactions are for the financing of trade, and less than 15 percent are for investment. The *Wall Street Journal* estimated that less than 10 percent of this sum of $1.5 trillion per day has anything to do with trade and services (18/9/92). "It would seem that the remaining 80+ percent of the ebb and flow is attributable to speculative and/or 'money-laundering' motives that are in large measure beyond the bounds of serving a beneficent social purpose…." (Miller 1995: 66). Some estimates suggest that one million or more "anonymous corporations" are run by criminal gangs to launder as much as $500 billion a year (United Nation 2001: *Report on the World Social Situation*: 22). The problem is that the IMF which was meant to curb these problems now lacks both the means and the mandate.

*Foreign Aid:* Official Development Aid (ODA) is running in the range of 60 billion to 100 billion dollars per year (depending on who is doing the calculating). Compare this with Foreign direct investment (FDI), which is in the range of $250 billion to $300 billion per year. About 80 percent of ODA flows to 10 developing countries, leaving 164 others with the leftovers. Similarly, 10 countries receive 75 percent of FDI—and most of this goes to *developed* countries. Of the rest, most goes to 10 large developing countries; the 47 poorest countries obtain less than 1 percent. But even together, all the foreign funds account for less than 15 percent of the capital invested in developing countries (Miller 1998: 5).

As ODA decreased during the 1980s and 1990s, and interest rates exploded, the foreign debt of developing countries increased. Despite all the efforts of Jubilee 2000 to get wealthy countries to forgive the debts of the poorest, the low- and middle-income countries of the world saw their total external debt increase from $1,421,578 million in 1990 to $2,332,621 million in 2001 (World Development Indicators 2003: 248). Debtor countries may pay 25 to 30 percent of their foreign exchange earnings to servicing foreign debt. Payments often exceed new funds coming in. Although the donor countries have made new commitments in recent years, the reality is that the rich are living off the poor.

In sum, we may conclude that vast sections of all sorts of human activity now take place as part of inter-national relations. This is far different from the world of 1945. While international organizations have adapted as best they can, the fact remains there have been no structural institutional changes to reflect the transformation of global society.

## 3.2 The Generalized Transformation of the International System: Globalization

If international change means anything, it means globalization. Globalization is "The removal of barriers to free trade and the closer integration of national economies …" Stiglitz 2003: ix). In its most limpid and narrow form, globalization can be defined as "the increasing volume and speed of flows of capital and goods, information and ideas, people and forces that connect actors between countries (Keohane 2002b: 194). The immense growth and global movement of goods, services and financial transactions is our last and major subject under the heading of transformation of challenges to international institutions. Globalization has been made possible by technological developments, but it is also the result of the political economy policies of transnational corporations and the wealthy countries. "The resulting rules largely reflect the interests of the governments of a few rich countries, in particular the United States" (Florini 2003: 146). The ideology is neo-liberal, with its emphasis on free trade, less government and more market, deregulation and privatization. The aim is to end all barriers to the free flow of goods, services and capital and the reduction of government's role. This has become known as the "Washington consensus" for the "structural adjustment" conditions of the IMF and the World Bank. This orientation has been summarized as:

> The prevailing view among globalization's supporters is that markets and democracy are a kind of universal prescription for the multiple ills of underdevelopment. Market capitalism is the most efficient economic system the world has ever known. Democracy is the fairest political system the world has ever known and the one most respectful of individual liberty. Working hand in hand, markets and democracy will gradually transform the world into a community of prosperous, war-shunning nations, and individuals into liberal, civic-minded citizens and consumers. In the process, ethnic hatred, religious zealotry, and other "backward" aspects of underdevelopment will be swept away (Chua 2004: 8–9).

Indeed, globalization has enjoyed some successes. In effect, as the *World Development Indicators 1998* report stated, "the developing world today is healthier, wealthier, better fed and better educated." However, as we shall see, the major challenge to the international community is that this slight development is so skewed, so disproportionate, so unbalanced that while some get rich, others—the vast majority—remain distressingly poor. More and more conflicts are breaking out and disasters occurring, making the world politically destabilized and ethically demoralized.

So many books have been written on globalization that it is impossible to summarize them. Our aim is more restrained. We want to look at some data that will illustrate the rapid and extensive economic changes in the international economy and then look at the effects of these changes on the global system.

In general it can be said that globalization has policies that have increased world wealth and its distribution but also its inequalities – but it has no policies to enhance global economic and social justice.

- More people are living in poverty now than there were in the 1990s. Almost half the world's population gets by on an income of less than $2 a day (World Bank 2000).
- A century ago, the average person in the richest country was only nine times richer than the average person in the poorest country. Now the disparity is 60 to one (adjusted for purchasing power parity) (Birdsall 1998).
- As a common example of poverty, we may meditate on the fact that 70 percent of rural Filipinos own no land (Chua 2004: 5).
- In the 35-year period from 1965 to 1999, of 95 developing countries surveyed, 28 suffered a decline in GDP per capita, and 46 others did not even double their GDP (which would double in 35 years if it grew at just 2 percent annually) (UN 2000: 122). In relative terms, the rich are getting richer and the poor are getting poorer.

This raw data gives us numerous indicators that the world has indeed changed massively in the past quarter century. It will help us to give context to these facts if we now turn to some interpretations of the meaning of globalization, which has served as sort of envelope for all the factors we have just noted. Also, if we are to truly understand proposals for the development of international institutions we must place them in the general context of globalization and its challenges to the international system. At the core of the world's current problems is the redistribution of wealth and power, the growing gap between rich and poor and between advanced and developing nations, and the problems of interdependence ranging from the environment to crime. We can be helped in our understanding of globalization by four quite diverse American authors. We chose them because many people consider the United States to be the main progenitors of globalization. Even if the four avow to be friends of globalization, they all are very critical of the problems it causes.

At its heart, the major world issues are relatively clear and simple. The solutions are less so. Amy Chua sees it as the increasingly explosive relationship between the three most powerful forces in the world: markets, democracy, and ethnic hatred (2004: 6). Benjamin Barber has characterized the major world issue as a struggle between tribalism and reactionary fundamentalists versus the forces of integrative modernization and aggressive economic globalization (crystallized in his phrase "Jihad versus McWorld"). It leads to a clash of two sorts of fundamentalism in which democracy is likely to be the principle victim (Barber 1995–2001: xii–xv; 2000). Joseph Stiglitz points out that international financial institutions have been part of the mismanagement of globalization, which has neither reduced poverty nor ensured stability (2003: 6). Ann Florini explains the multiple, stunning changes in the world that require changes in global governance, because "the current global economy is deeply unjust, and in some ways it is becoming more so" (2003: 146).

While it is not very startling that each of these authors should perceive poverty as the central problem, it is surprising that, although approaching the problem from different angles, each points to the same causality: rampant capitalism without proper democratic safeguards. Everything from East-West, North-South, Christian-Muslim conflicts, ethnic wars, socio-cultural dissolution, political corruption, environmental decline, massive unemployment, global terrorism and ineffective institutions has the common root of savage economic exploitation without the political balance to protect the collective good. Let us look in a little more detail at their criticisms and proposals as examples of the situations to which UN reforms must respond.

Amy Chua, a law professor, describes the repeated situation around the world where a small ethnic minority controls huge portions of national economies. She studies the cases of the Chinese in Southeast Asia, the whites in Latin America, the Lebanese in West Africa, the Ibo in Nigeria, the whites in Zimbabwe and South Africa, the Croats in the former Yugoslavia, the Jews in post-Communist Russia, the Tutsis in Rwanda, and the Americans in the world.

As an example of the extreme wealth in the hands of what Chua calls "market-dominant minorities," she presents the case of the Chinese minority in the Philippines. With just one percent of the population, the Chinese control 60 percent of the private economy, the country's four major airlines, and almost all of the banks, hotels, shopping malls and major conglomerates. Seventy percent of rural Filipinos own no land (Chua 2004: 3–4). This type of example leads to her thesis.

> Unrestrained markets—superimposed on postcolonial societies with massive initial ethnic imbalances in financial and human capital—have helped create intolerable and volatile conditions in these societies, the very conditions that unrestrained democracy detonates (Chua 2004: 263).

Addressing the causes behind these extreme cases of ethnic wealth and poverty, Chua looks first at globalization, representing "five decades of American foreign policy" to consciously promote capitalism through international financial institutions, multinational corporations, development agencies, and giant foundations that generated "modernization" projects and exported capitalist institutions. Privatization programs, foreign investment, trade liberalization, and market-friendly laws favoured the already wealthy "outsider" minorities, fuelling ethnic envy and hatred of the impoverished majorities (2004: 19–21). Free markets do not spread wealth evenly.

When linked with Western-sponsored "democratization" programs centered on implementing immediate elections with universal suffrage, no time is left for the development of an all-important democratic culture to underwrite the political processes. Nor does it include such principles as equality under the law and protection of minorities and property.

Chua stresses that at no point did any Western country ever implement laissez-faire capitalism and overnight suffrage at the same time (2004: 14). Without the safeguards, rapid democratization has differential effects in ethnically divided societies, where rather than promoting a civil competition for votes, it fosters the emergence of demagogues who scapegoat the resented minority, as with Mugabe in Zimbabwe. Those who have studied only the generalized impacts of globalization have missed this worldwide subset of economically dominant minorities and the ethnic resentment and conflict they inspire and the difficulties of too rapidly imposed democracy.

Benjamin Barber, a political philosopher, is an authority on democracy. He claims that neo-liberal (and then neo-conservative) antagonism to all international political regulation, to all institutions of legal and political oversight, to all attempts at democratizing globalization and institutionalizing economic justice, has been a sign to transitional democracies and developing countries that the West is not interested in their welfare or their claims for justice (2001: xvii). We have globalized markets in goods, currencies and information without globalizing the civic and democratic institutions that have historically constituted the free market's indispensable context. But now in the global context our vices have been globalized (crime, weapons, drugs, prostitution, pornography, trade in women and children, child soldiers, poverty, disease and starvation) but few of the virtues of constitutional society. In addition, jobs defy borders, hemorrhaging from one country to another in a race to the bottom. Safety, health and environmental standards lack international benchmarks. All this creates fertile ground for recruiting terrorists. Globalization's current structures breed anarchy, nihilism and violence.

Joseph Stiglitz, a Nobel Prize economist has been on the Council of Economic Advisors to the President in the United States and also chief economist of the World Bank. Writing in the context of the international financial institutions (the World Bank, the International Monetary Fund and the World Trade Organization), Stiglitz states from the outset,

> I have written this book because while I was at the World Bank, I saw firsthand the devastating effect that globalization can have on developing countries, and especially the poor within these countries. I believe that globalization—the removal of barriers to free trade and the closer integration of national economies—can be a force for good and that it has the *potential* to enrich everyone in the world, particularly the poor. But I also believe that if this is to be the case, the way globalization has been managed, including

> the international trade agreements that have played such a large role in removing those barriers and the policies that have been imposed on developing countries in the process of globalization, need to be radically rethought (Stiglitz 2003: ix–x).

Stiglitz has a number of criticisms of the international financial institutions. Decisions are often made, not on the basis of economics, but because of ideology and politics that fit with the interest or beliefs of the people in power, and without considering the effects on poverty. This mindset ignores advances in economics in the past 30 years: first, that there are market imperfections because of asymmetries of information and lack of transparency; second, that markets can be improved by desirable government intervention, especially with regard to inequality, unemployment and pollution; and third, that there are changing patterns of global competition. Many of the policies are based on the outworn presumptions that markets, by themselves, lead to efficient outcomes and fail to allow for desirable government interventions in the market, measures that can guide economic growth and make *everyone* better off. Government can play an essential role in mitigating market failures and in ensuring social justice in such fields as education, infrastructure, the legal system, financial regulation, a safety net for the poor and the promotion of technology—all activities that countries in the West take for granted but which the IMF limits every time it deals with a crisis in the Third World.

Stiglitz believes globalization has been mismanaged. It is therefore not perceived to be legitimate. It is also based on a wrong-headed mind-set.

> The greatest challenge is not just in the institutions themselves but in mind-sets: caring about the environment, making sure the poor have a say in the decisions that affect them, promoting democracy and fair trade are necessary if the potential benefits of globalization are to be achieved. The problem is that the institutions have come to reflect the mind-sets of those to whom they are accountable (Stiglitz 2003: 216).

Because globalization creates interdependence, it also creates the need for effective global institutions to help set the rules. There are circumstances when there is need for collective action such as when markets do not result in efficient outcomes or when impacts are global and call for efforts for stability. Finally, international financial and trade governance need an increase in openness and transparency, so there can be direct accountability to the public. Too many decisions are taken behind closed doors, where special interests are heard and mistakes are hidden. This undermines concepts of democracy.

Ann Florini, with the Brookings Institution in Washington, discovers a world where barriers to the flow of goods, services and money have fallen dramatically, but which is plagued by ethnic conflict, environmental deterioration, terrorism, and a global economy that is both unstable and inequitable. She asks if we cannot improve global governance, and especially the rapid, global decision-making that is required. After summarizing the changes both in communications technology and also in group identity that have made civil society possible, she then addresses the appropriate roles for governments, private enterprise, and civil society in global governance. Her thesis is that none of the interveners can resolve global problems alone, that broad participation is required in rulemaking and implementation, and that transparency in decision-making is the best means of promoting accountability. An augmented role for civil society will help provide the accountability and voice for the public that will move us toward a form of global democracy.

With regard to globalization, Florini believes, "The problem is not with the fact of integration itself; the problem is with the manner in which that integration is being carried out" (Florini 2003: 145). She supports Stiglitz in providing convincing data and examples to demonstrate that international economic rules and decisions are made by and for the wealthy and powerful. Decision-making often excludes developing countries and is unduly secretive. The WTO's mandate is to increase trade, not to balance out competing concerns such as the environment, safety, worker protection, and human rights.

However, Florini maintains that foreign exchange transactions are the single-most dramatic element in global economic integration. Managed by transnational corporations to make the largest short-term profits, vast sums of money can leave a country overnight and push it into recession (100 countries experienced financial crisis in the 1980s and 1990s). To get IMF and World Bank loans, weak countries had to adopt "structural adjustment" programs. These austerity policies crippled local economies, with devastating effects for workers and their families. Simplistic policies paid too little attention to the specific needs of individual countries. "There is no reliable international financial architecture to support the increasingly globalized economy" (Florini 2003: 158). In part this is because too much attention has been paid to economic efficiency and too little to public goods.

One of the reasons it is so difficult to get people on the same wavelength about the provision of collective goods is this:

> With the private sector ever more powerful and the wealthy ever more isolated from the rest of society, governments find themselves unable to compel those with money to help pay for such basic public needs as defence and police functions, economic infrastructure, environmental protection, or a social safety net (Florini 2003: 3).

All the wealthy need to do, or just threaten to do, is to move their money offshore and they impede the functioning of the national and international societies. We are returning to the times of an aristocracy riding about on their armored chargers and living safe in their castles high above the hidden masses. Today, the super rich need have little contact with ordinary people. They sail though the streets in air-conditioned limousines, and fly high above the huddled masses in their private jets on the way to a sojourn on a luxury yacht before returning to their security-surrounded mansion or gated community. No wonder the elites have little know ledge of, or care for, global society.

In summary, these four perspectives on the "raging bull" of globalization describe the context in which the modernization of multilateralism must take place. These specialists believe that globalization must be understood and not simply praised, pilloried or parodied. We must understand not only the processes of globalization (meaning, at its root, free trade and closer economic integration), but also the political and ideological forces behind it and the institutions through which it operates.

Those who are concerned about the costs of globalization believe it rages along at such a rate that social and political balancing mechanisms cannot catch up. Nor does it recognize the immense differences between countries and between individuals' capacities to cope with change. It leaves aside human rights and the protection of labour, social security and national culture. In negotiations, trade deals are hammered out to the exclusion of concerns about the environment, health, salaries and safety. Pro-market reforms undermine national democratic decision-making and participation. "The historical symmetry that paired democracy and capitalism within societies and made the democratic nation-state the free market's most effective regulator, humanizer, and overseer has gone missing" (Barber 2003: 158).

By far the greatest worries about globalization are the uneven consequences of economic integration and its increase in inequities between developed and developing countries, and between the rich and poor within countries. During 2003 alone, the world gained 111 new *billionaires*, to bring the total to 587. Their total wealth comes to $1.9 *trillion* (*International Herald Tribune* 1/03/04). Economies of scale have led to the concentration of wealth in a small number of vast transnational corporations. "In the international sector, the age of robber barons has returned… fostering predatory practices and global anarchy" (Barber 2003: 159).

Privatization has led to the general depreciation of national and international rules. Government is made over into a useful tool of global firms in international negotiations and financial institutions. Rules and procedures favour private over public interests. There is no transparency or equality of representation in the IFI, so the rules that exist are made behind the scenes in favour of the wealthy states and the corporations—the lenders. When the donor countries have the preponderant votes (unlike in the UN system, where all states have equal votes), the laws of the market are made to suit the powerful. Developing countries have been generally excluded from the decision-making that affects them. Thus, globalization is the nub of the conflict between North and South in international institutions. The South tried to use its votes in the United Nations to outflank the Northern control of the financial institutions. But they ended up being frustrated as development issues were more and more transferred to the World Bank, while endless UN debates turned in circles, and resolutions had no binding force (Lyons 1995: 79).

Of course, globalization is only an image, a symbol, or, as we say in the social sciences, a reification. We must still seek to understand the forces behind globalization, which include not only economic and technological impulses but also the people who make the decisions. Its ideological foundations benefit certain interests and therefore it is supported by certain economic and political forces and international institutions. These start with the countries that hold almost 40 percent of the votes in the IMF and the World Bank: the United States, Japan, Germany, France and Great Britain. But fundamentally, its market-oriented, capitalism-promoting orientation is rooted in the Anglo-American philosophy of neo-liberalism. These ideas are held, promoted and put into practice by the executives of banks and transnational corporations, finance ministries and central bankers, major business interest groups, the leadership of American foundations, right-wing political leaders in Western governments, and long-term officials in the World Bank, the International Monetary Fund and the World Trade Organization.

It may be argued that this analysis presents a rather negative picture of globalization. There are a number of answers. The first is, as mentioned before, one can agree with the proponents of globalization that it can bring greater economic benefits to everyone. Freer trade and fewer protected industries will bring greater specialization, comparative advantage, competition, efficiency and, hence, wealth. Despite numerous economic crises, World Bank studies claim that more people, especially in East and South Asia, have experienced better jobs, incomes and opportunities and a slow convergence of wages with those of the West. Trade has been growing faster than the world economy. Through transnational corporations, globalization also spreads capital, employment, technology, managerial know-how and export markets. Free trade had to be promoted because states had learned how to use non-economic issues (such as health, the environment and corporate loans) to mask protectionism. Deregulated capital flows should allow for greater flexibility and efficiency, as investment moves where it can make the highest returns. Aside from its reputed economic benefits, by furthering integration globalization also potentially erodes the bases of virulent nationalism. All this can be agreed in principle even if one might not go so far as to claim that the purpose of global governance should be "to facilitate free trade, freedom of capital movements, and unrestricted access by multinational firms to markets around the globe" (Gilpin 2001: 401).

We saw that our four authors can also agree with these arguments. Each claims to be a "friend" of globalization. Their aim was to understand not to condemn. Other answers to possible claims of negativism stem from the problems of empirical social science. First, it reports the world as it is, which can become a conservative bias in favour of the policies that exist and the powers that be. Second, each human can only know so much, so the portrait of society is never complete. Third, the result will tend to be selective and will depend on what the researcher is seeking. In our case, we are seeking to understand the problems that globalization produces and that a new generation of international organizations will have to surmount.

As the unrepresentative, international political processes have been corrupted, they have provoked numerous difficulties for developing countries including environmental destruction, massive unemployment, urban violence and social dissolution all compounded by a lack of time for cultural adaptation (Stiglitz 2003: 8).

Economic integration may create pressures within countries to lower health, employment, safety and environmental standards if they are to compete with cheaper imports (Florini 2003: 145). These in turn lead to frustration, resentment and the threat of backlash when governments have been weakened to the point where they can no longer protect their citizens. It can even be hypothesized that the new world capitalism is undermining its own foundations as it undermines the democratic stability and the state's capacity to function (Martin & Schumann 1997: 9). "Globalization's current architecture breeds anarchy, nihilism, and violence" Barber 2001: xvi).

The causes and consequences of the current international situation have been summarized in the United Nations *Report on the World Social Situation 2001*:

> Disparities in income and wealth are growing in many countries, and the distance between richer and poorer countries is also widening.... A complex set of variables and circumstances explain the differential social impact of varied economic fortunes among and within countries.... Themes that have risen to the surface... include emerging patterns in production and distribution, such as globalization and technological innovations in information and communication; fiscal constraint and resistance to taxation; structural adjustment programmes and liberalization policies, including privatization and deregulation; the introduction of users fees for the provision of social services; and hardened attitudes toward social welfare and unemployment compensation (p. 1).

As we have seen, one of the major problems is that the international economic game is not staged on a level playing field. But just wishing for fairer rules of the game will not bring about change. After decades of debate about the worthiness of state-centric models, we are still forced to conclude with Hoffman that, "The highest allegiance of each actor remains either to himself or to a fragment of mankind—a bloc he belongs to out of necessity or conviction" (1978: 144). If the international financial institutions are biased and if they, rather than the more representative UN, have the big end of the stick with regard to development economics, it is because the major economic powers will it to be so. They prefer working through the IFI precisely because they are unrepresentative and therefore can be controlled by the wealthy states.

To accept this unpalatable reality is not to say we have to continue living with it. It does mean that we must take it into account when imagining an improved system. If we believe with the authors cited (who simply exemplify a wider school of thought) that only a much broader, more open system of decision-making will produce well-designed and legitimate international policies then we must contrive a plan that will achieve that end. As Ann Florini reasons, "Making those policy choices well requires a wide-reaching debate about the broad goals to which economic integration should contribute and about what rules and processes will get us to those goals" (Florini 2003: 145).

In this chapter, we have not been able to inventory all global change, but our sampling should convince us of the great socio-economic changes that require a political counterpart if they are not to spiral out of control. With such extraordinary changes in the world system, some have argued in favor of world government. However, such a modification would require a growth in the sense of community among citizens of the world to warrant larger degrees of cooperation. Political community is based on mutuality and trust. In a study in 1995, I found that current globalization had an integrating effect only on a relatively thin stratum of elites (mainly from the North) who have the know-how and wealth to invest, trade and travel and to participate in high-tech communications such as the Internet (Trent 1996). It would seem this situation has not evolved in the past decade despite great increases in transactions and interdependence between states. With just 15 percent of the world producing new research and technologies, we have seen that fields such as computers, information and communications, genetics and biotechnology have the power to hasten integration *and* widen the gap between haves and have-nots. This creates a need for more effective international organizations as well as more cooperation and aid.

We have seen that the enormous costs in money, effort and suffering caused by global terrorism, arms diffusion, civil wars, the conflict of civilizations, refugees, world policing, peace making, and nation rebuilding, etc. can be dealt with and perhaps remedied only on a collective, multilateral basis. We have seen that the equally extraordinary costs in terms of human misery, crime, political conflict and organizational effort engendered by enormous flows of migrants, refugees and displaced persons can only be minimized by joint international efforts. And we have seen that the trade and financial flows of global integration have not only created a sort of international economic anarchy—the ineffective and unrepresentative decision-making has brought in its wake mistakes, crime, pollution and inequity.

Since 1945, massive socio-economic changes have not been reflected by change in our political institutions. The threats and challenges we now face affect many countries at a time, if not all of humanity. Issues that used to be handled within states or between several of them have now become global in nature and can only be dealt with collectively. We have moved from internationalism to globalism. There are new types and scales of difficulties facing humans. They have in fact become a new type of threat to security. There is unprecedented vulnerability for all. Many of the world problems are interconnected and require "interdisciplinary" policy-making. Because new threats challenge many countries at one time, the world has become truly interdependent, it is one system, and requires renewed institutions to cooperate better. A prior necessity is to think about how to foster global values and a sense of community.

Within the context of globalization we see that that our problems are in part man-made. Our unrepresentative international financial institutions have in many ways augmented world problems and the increasing gap between rich and poor.

These lessons pose new challenges for global governance. Just as our national governments and their various departments and agencies look after the common affairs of their citizens, so we need global institutions capable of dealing with the vast mobilization of humanity we have just discussed. The world's major task is to modernize multilateralism to deal effectively with this range of newly evolved global problems. Only multilateral institutions have the legitimacy and the scope of vision and experience to cope with the complexity of global challenges. The United Nations has the legitimacy but it has many other failings. To these we now turn.

# 4 The UN: Criticisms and Proposals for Reform

*"I find it difficult to conceive that men who conduct the foreign relations of states will ever again consider that they can dispense with a comprehensive institutional mechanism, or that they will, in the foreseeable future, contrive a global mechanism fundamentally different in character from the United Nations." (Innis L. Claude, Jr. "Implications and Questions for the future" in Norman Padleford and Leland Goodrich, The United Nations in the Balance: Accomplishments and Prospects, 1965.*

*"We can no longer take for granted that our multilateral institutions are strong enough to cope with all the challenges facing them. I suggest in my conclusion that some of the institutions may be in need of radical reform."*
(Kofi Annan, Report to the United Nations General Assembly, 2003: 2).

In the previous chapters, we have concluded that there have been two areas of massive change in our world. First, to a very large degree what once were national problems that could be managed by states have now gone beyond state boundaries and require ever-increasing amounts of collective management, in part by multilateral organizations. Second, globalization has generated enormous degrees of integration and hence of interdependence – which is another way of saying mutual dependence. The result is that continuously heavier demands are placed on international organizations for which they often have not been provided the mandates or the resources. Thus there has been a growing body of criticisms of international institutions and demands for their reform. This chapter provides an overview of the criticisms that have been made of the United Nations system and the international financial institutions. It also offers a sampling of the various proposals that have and are being made to modernize multilateralism. It deserves to be said once more that when we refer to international organizations we are not referring to some sort of independent agencies that are entirely responsible for their own fate. The UN system is a treaty organization dependent for its existence and its evolution on the will of its member states. While the UN is not an inanimate object and is the target of some of the proposals for change, a great deal of the responsibility for its failings (and successes) falls on the shoulders of its members.

It is not intended to present here a cohesive and detailed critique of international organizations and proposals for their reform. Many others have done or are undertaking this task, including the Secretary-General's High-Level Panel on Threats and Challenges and Change. We offer our analysis of the panel's report, *A More Secure World* (2004; www.un.org/secureworld at the end) of chapter 5. Two other recent initiatives that will provide the reader with examples of broad treatments of proposals for transforming international institutions are the 2001 report of the International

Commission on Intervention and State Sovereignty entitled *Responsibility to Protect* (www.ciise-iciss.gc.ca). The evolving concepts of sovereignty and humanitarian intervention are crucial for understanding the future role of collective institutions. Second, the Report of Ubuntu, the World Campaign for In-Depth Reform of the System of International Institutions (www.reformcampaign.net), includes its *Proposal to Reform the System of International Institutions: Future Scenarios*. This is one of the most holistic and complete treatments of reform of the UN system and its sister agencies.

The objective in this chapter is double. First, it is to offer a compendium of examples and an overview of the critical analysis of the UN system (writ large) and the myriad proposals for its improvement. Second the aim is to demonstrate that where there is smoke there is fire. If international institutions have been the subject of so much criticism and creative suggestions for change from varied and highly competent sources it is because there are indeed problems that require resolution. We will pay particular attention to a selection of reputable commissions, study groups and experienced individual experts who have undertaken intense analysis of the UN. Despite these many serious, well-considered, proposals for change over the years, international organizations have not been able to transform themselves. This does not mean, and it needs to be stressed, that the UN has not been able to adapt itself over the years to changing conditions– as we have already seen. Nevertheless, there would appear to be fundamental problems because some of the criticisms and proposals have been repeated time and again, over many years. The point is that reasonable criticisms and wise suggestions may be necessary for institutional reform, but they are not sufficient to make it happen.

I am, of course, well aware that the style of presentation of the materials in this and the following chapter do not make for the easiest reading. But there are reasons and compensating factors, so let me explain. The major problem is that, when it comes to the reform of the UN, most people have their pet ideas. These ideas are very strongly held. And if you do not agree with them you are cast into outer purgatory. In other words they stop reading. Because the aim of this study is to think about methods for transforming the UN system rather than presenting a specific model or set of reforms, the problem is resolved by presenting a spectrum of proposals for basic structural modifications. The benefit to the reader is that you obtain access to a broad set of proposals made by experts over a considerable period of time – and not just what this author thinks. Each section starts off with a brief, introductory overview of an institutional sector and continues with a series of critiques and transformative proposals. Thus, it is a research source for a fairly detailed view of any particular sector of the UN system in which one is interested at the moment. So, the reader can pick and choose without have to read the whole chapter at once.

The United Nations and the Bretton Woods financial and economic institutions, in which the World Trade Organization (WTO) has now been included, have continuously been criticized ever since their founding in the 1940s. The opening of the 1947 UN General Assembly was greeted with derision: by the *Daily Mirror* ("We're not interested in the comic cuts organization"), by the *Wall Street Journal* ("degenerated from a useless debating society to a mutual vilification society"), and by the *Catholic Herald* ("Every honest and realist person knows in his heart that the United Nations is dead") (Boyd 1964: 9).

The UN has outlived its early detractors. But 40 years later, critics were already beginning to use the terrible "I" word, that is to speak of "irrelevance". "Until very recently a frequently offered evaluation of the United Nations was that the organization was neither effective nor ineffective in dealing with pressing world problems. It had simply become irrelevant" (Puchala & Coate 1989: 1). And, they reported, "The United States had long since ceased to take major initiatives within the UN or to staunchly support the institution" (ibid). That was a decade and a half before George W. Bush declared the UN "irrelevant." Although their 1988 annual report on the UN finally pronounced that this world organization "is relevant in the world political setting of our time," their 1987 report had characterized the UN as "teetering, tottering, battered and smarting" (Puchala & Coate 1988). What a difference a year can make!

Today, criticisms of international organizations come from various angles. Pointing to the distrust caused by "hypocritical" policies dominated by the P5, the South attacks the UN for not fulfilling the very principles and norms that underlie the UN Charter. Other critics stress the lack of democracy in the UN where "we the people" were meant to reign. The various organizations are castigated from the left and the right for their incompetent administration, unrepresentativeness, poor decision-making, lack of coordination and ineffective programs. Street protesters have turned their backs on international institutions because of their exclusiveness, hidden agendas, corporate connections and inability to deal with new global realities. Critics from the right say the organizations are manipulated by an unaccountable international bureaucracy. They seek the UN's replacement by a new coalition of democracies.

Just as international institutions have been criticized for decades, so have a myriad of proposals been made for their modification. Some of these proposals start at the constitutional level, with a redrafting of the Charter, including its principles and membership. Others content themselves with politically easier reforms of the organization and procedures within established institutions. A large constituency opts for democratic reforms and renewal of the global power structures. While some concentrate on redefining policies and programs, the following overview focuses on fundamental, structural transformation proposals of the last decade.

As just noted, proposals for change come from many quarters. For instance, in the last few years a number of religious leaders have called for international reform. At the time of the Millennium debates in New York, the founder of the Interreligious and International Federation for World Peace, Dr. Sun Myung Moon, sponsored "Assembly 2000" to bring together world leaders and political representatives to discuss renewing the UN. Among other things, Dr. Moon called for the formation of an assembly of religious representatives appointed by states within the United Nations especially to advocate the ideals of peace (Assembly 2000: 65–73). We have already seen that on January 1, 2004, just as he had on every January 1 since 1979 on his "World Days of Peace," Pope John Paul II emitted a message in which he called for a new world order based on the goals of the United Nations, international law, and respect for the dignity of man and equality among nations. The Dalai-Lama has proposed the creation of a planetary "Committee of Wise People," who at times of grave crisis would propose alternative pacific solutions (*Le Droit* 14/10/03).

From quite another angle, neo-liberals think the best role for international institutions such as the United Nations would be to step aside and let the business corporations do their job. One of their spokespersons, Doug Bandow, senior Fellow at the Cato Institute, observed:

> Whereas the UN, assorted specialized agencies and allied organization once played a significant role in shaping the global economic system and aiding underdeveloped states, today rampant globalization has largely passed by the UN. Huge private capital flows dwarf official aid levels. Market reforms have swept away *dirigiste* economic planning. Mobile transnational corporations have reduced the importance of international borders. Ever-accelerating entrepreneurial and technological changes have marginalized government regulation. The UN and other international organizations should promote rather than combat such trends.... The UN's most important duty is to first do no harm by impeding such liberating forces. Second, it should encourage freer and more open markets wherever possible (Assembly 2000: 105–6).

Bandow goes on to conclude that the UN can offer no panacea for development; so it should simply promote market-oriented reforms and help remove such artificial barriers as foreign aid and protectionism. Other American groups, such as the Heritage Foundation, join him in his desire to sideline governmental institutions (see Pines 1984).`

Whatever the merits of these various proposals, in this chapter we concentrate on individuals and groups that are fostering innovation in order to improve the established principles of multilateralism and develop new or transformed institutions to deal with emerging global challenges.

Most criticisms of today's international institutions—as well as most proposals for their reform—can be grouped under two headings: the structure of the UN system and the major issues in the global system that require institutional development. The global problems will be analyzed in the next chapter. The institutional issues can be handled under the four following headings.

1. International Institutions, the UN, the courts and international law
2. UN Charter, sovereignty and global constitutionalism
3. The International Financial Institutions (IFI)
4. Specialized agencies attached to the UN

## 4.1 International Institutions, the UN, the Courts and International Law

### *4.1.1 The United Nations in General and the International Institutional System*

> *"The comparative advantages of the United Nations are its universal membership, political legitimacy, administrative impartiality, technical expertise, convening and mobilizing power, and the dedication of its staff. Its comparative disadvantages are excessive politicization, ponderous pace of decision-making, impossible mandate, high cost structure, insufficient resources, bureaucratic rigidity, and institutional timidity"*
>
> (Thakur 2002: 284).

**Current Profile**

The United Nations is made up of six principal organs, all of which, except the courts (which are in the Hague, Netherlands), are based in New York:

- General Assembly
- Security Council
- Economic and Social Council (ECOSOC)
- Trusteeship Council
- International Court of Justice (ICJ), the International Criminal Court (ICC), and International Law
- The Secretariat

The activities of the UN are carried out by its programs, funds and related bodies (such as UNICEF for children, UNDP for development, and the High Commissioner for Refugees). Then there are some 14 "specialized agencies" (such as UNESCO for science, education and culture; the World Bank; and ICAO, the International Civil Aviation Association). "You may think that you have never benefited personally from the UN," says Madeleine Albright, former U.S. Secretary of State, "but if you have ever traveled on an international airline or shipping line, or placed a phone call overseas, or received mail from outside the country, or been thankful for an accurate weather report—then you have been served directly or indirectly by one part or the other of the UN system" (Fasulo 2004:13). Most of these programs and specialized agencies have their own governing bodies and independent representation bases within states, so they run their own affairs with little interference and often not much communication.

Moreover, the United Nations was born with a number of build-in, permanent contradictions. It had become necessary to found the UN in order to control the self-interested and warlike nature of states, but at the same time peace and security was entrusted to these very same states. The UN accepts all states, democracies and dictatorships alike, but expects all of them to protect the fundamental rights and liberties of their citizens. Like all organizations, the UN required a directing council, however this was entrusted to a committee of vastly different powers and political systems. Although it required strong bureaucratic leadership and coordination, the Secretary-General was designated a simple "administrator" heading a "Secretariat". The UN was founded on the principle that collectively governments must work to stop trans-border wars between states, but the real dangers to humanity now come from governments and 'rebels' and terrorists that violate citizens' rights within the states, and often the UN can do little about it. Partly this is because the UN consecrated the contradictory principles of national sovereignty and collective security. Also it was based on "we the peoples", but all power was given to state governments. And even within the principle of sovereign state equality, some states were 'victors' and the five permanent members of the Security Council, with their veto power, were definitely more equal than the others (Power 2005: 18). The point, of course is not that the founders of the United Nations were thickheaded but that they, like any group trying structure multilateral relations in this most human world, must compose not only with high-minded ideals, but also with the complex political realities that underlie them.

### The UN and the International System in General: Criticisms

Maurice Bertrand makes three fundamental criticisms of our systems of international institutions: conceptual, organizational and practical. From a conceptual point of view, the national foreign policy thinking upon which the United Nations system was founded had not advanced one iota.

> We must consider that nations and their leaders, even when they are democratically elected, have not modified their foreign policy philosophy from that of princes and kings.... They speak of "national interest" of "national sovereignty," and of "reasons of state": moral codes cannot apply to the conduct of foreign policy. The balance of power is the only way to guarantee peace.... "Realism" has been the reigning philosophy.... The idea that the world is composed of peoples who could only be potential enemies appeared natural and founded on experience. The explanation is to be found in "human nature," considered to be aggressive and power seeking (Bertrand 2000: 10–11).

Organizationally, the United Nations system suffers from the same problems as the League of Nations before it, because both were founded on the same structural premises: the institutionalization of an alliance of the victors; dividing up zones of influence; "collective security" supposing that an attack on one is an attack on all; a model based on decentralized technical agencies (assembly, smaller council, secretariat); diplomatic delegates with no political mandate; verbalism (grand statements of principle without application); studious efforts at arms reduction under the title of "disarmament"; legal procedures of arbitration; and functionalist techniques for promoting harmony through economic, social and cultural relations (ibid: 15).

Unfortunately, in practice these policies and structures did not work very effectively for the League, nor have they worked in the past 50 years. This is because an agreement between major powers does not last eternally, collective security does not work once there is disagreement among the big powers, the International Court of Justice cannot handle political cases, and the limited and weighted economic and social practices were not sufficient to create a climate of peace (ibid: 17).

> Thus, it wasn't a system aimed at maintaining the *status quo* that it was necessary to invent, but on the contrary institutional mechanisms capable of helping to manage change… an instrument handy for permanent negotiations on a world level between countries and peoples with opposing interests and ideologies (ibid: 23).

"The General Assembly has an agenda crowded with items that either overlap or are of interest to only a few states. Repetitive and sterile debates crowd out items that really matter. Decisions can often be reached only on a lowest-common-denominator basis, and once reached, command little or no attention. In the Security Council and the international financial institutions the problem is the opposite: decisions may be reached but lack legitimacy in the eyes of the developing world, which feels insufficiently represented. The composition of the Security Council is at odds with the geopolitical realities of the 21st century" (Annan 2003a, Report of the Secretary General on Implementation of the UN Millennium Declaration: 16).

—"Public debate on globalization is at an impasse. Opinion is frozen in the ideological certainties of entrenched positions and fragmented in a variety of special interests. The will for consensus is weak" (*A Fair Globalization,* 2004: x).

—"The problems we have identified are not due to globalization as such but to deficiencies in its governance…. The multilateral system is under-performing. It lacks policy coherence as a whole and is not sufficiently democratic, transparent and accountable…. Rules and policies are the outcome of a system of global governance largely shaped by powerful countries and powerful players. There is a serious democraticdeficit…. Most developing countries still have very little influence…" (ibid: xi).

—"Global governance is not a lofty, disembodied sphere. It is merely the apex of a web of governance that stretches from the local levels upward" (ibid: xi).

—"In this ever more globalizing context, world citizens are increasingly affected by decisions taken at the global level, which needs to be more transparent, accountable and democratic. Moreover, world problems and challenges—poverty, inequality, violence, injustice, environmental deterioration, and cultural homogenization—can only be dealt with by global policies; and the current multilateral system—designed for a fairly different world than ours—is not very well equipped to face such an interconnected world" (Ubuntu, 2004: 3).

Ubuntu summarized the "Shortcomings of the original design of the present system of international institutions" where victors gained a privileged position:

- The restricted membership of the Security Council limits its legitimacy.
- Unbalanced decision-making undermines the Bretton Woods institutions.
- The Bretton Woods institutions act independently, without coordination.
- The UN's development mandate has been hamstrung and lacks funding.
- The World Trade Organization was established outside the UN.
- UN summit meeting and Millennium plans of action have not been implemented (Ubuntu 2004: 5).

> "In the second half of the last decade, the rise of social movements and mass mobilizations on the occasion of intergovernmental summits and gatherings brought to the fore the discontent of the world population vis-à-vis the politics operating at the global level, the de-legitimization of global institutions and distrust with political leadership. At the same time, they evidenced the rise of a sense of common interest and global citizenship amongst the world's peoples" (Ubuntu 2004: 5).

—"Present efforts to reform the UN either are of the housekeeping category… or consist of regional powers importuning to become permanent members of the Security Council. Neither really gets to the nub of the problem: the flawed nature of a multilateral body designed around power alignments and policy ideas stemming from the Second World War. One of the most egregious of these leftovers is the secretive and exclusive exercise of power by the five permanent members of the Security Council. They have too much power, the members of the General Assembly too little…. The other serious consideration is how to apply certain basic tests of membership…. Should a member state be allowed to take a seat endowing certain responsibilities, especially in the Security Council, if it is in flagrant violation of a UN resolution, has refused to pay its membership dues, is governed by a military dictatorship, and is under inquiry for suppressing the rights of its own citizens" (Axworthy 2003: 254–55)?

—"I have to confess to a sense of real disappointment that the political will on the part of the governments that 'own' the UN is at a low ebb. While it is gratifying that the Secretary-General's reform program has somewhat muted, if not satisfied, the critics of the UN, notably in the U.S. Congress, it has also given rise to an attitude of tiredness and complacency…" (Strong 2000: 307).

"It's not easy to devolve issues away from the UN. The UN agenda included 166 specific items in 1999, which have accumulated over the years. Each one remains the special interest of one or more member governments, often allied to the units in the secretariat that service the item" (ibid: 313).

—"When governments or people speak of reform of the United Nations, they address a process of change that has to begin in national behaviour" (*World Commission on Global Governance*, 1995: 225 – *afterwards, Commission on GG*).

"The people of the world never developed a sense that the UN was theirs. It did not belong to them. It belonged, if to anyone, to governments – and then only to a few of those." (ibid: 226)

"The United Nations was there to be used, and not infrequently abused; to be an instrument of national interest where it could be; and to be bypassed where it could not be made to serve that interest" (ibid: 226).

"The newer countries… simply could not prevail over the minority that exercised power in the Security Council or the world economy…. And the UN bureaucracy, once fired with imagination and zeal, became frustrated and disillusioned" (ibid: 227).

—"The end of the Cold War has essentially added to the dilemma posed by the Secretary General, not resolved it. The UN still has to deal with disparities in development, the legacies of imperialism, threats of environmental deterioration, and human rights violations, while taking on the added burdens of an expanded role in maintaining peace and security" (Lyons 1995: 44).

"Multilateral organizations have been under ideological attack from Washington since the Reagan administration in 1981, driven by deep resentment over U.S. loss of control in the 1970s" (ibid: 46).

—"Various factors have contributed to the present difficulties of many multilateral organizations. We are still adjusting to the new and uneasy distribution of forces in the world resulting from the Second World War, from the revolution of decolonization, from demographic and technological changes, from the mixed patterns of development, and, of course, from the advent of nuclear weapons" (SG report on the work of the organization, New York, United Nations 1986: 4).

## The UN and the International System: Proposals

> *Our governments are no better than we are. The United Nations is no better than its governments. Gen. Roméo Dallaire, "Lessons from Rwanda", International Herald Tribune, 12-4-05*

A good place to start is with the proposals of the former UN Secretary-General in order to waylay any thought that reform has to be imposed on the Secretariat staff. It is more likely that the Secretary-General and the members of the Secretariat have a pretty good idea of the reforms required by international institutions, but they do not have the power to bring them about. Action belongs to the member states and to political forces within member states.

—Kofi Annan noted in his 2003 report *The Implementation of the UN Millennium Declaration*, "We can no longer take it for granted that our multilateral institutions are strong enough to cope with all the challenges facing them. I suggest in my conclusions that some of the institutions may be in need of radical reform" (p. 2). He went on to state, "The General Assembly needs to be strengthened; the role of the Economic and Social Council—indeed the role of the United Nations as a whole in economic and social affairs, and its relationship to the Bretton Woods institutions—needs to be rethought and reinvigorated; the Trusteeship Council needs to be reviewed in light of the new kinds of responsibilities given to the United Nations by its members in recent years; and the Security Council needs to be reformed in a way that will enable it to confront the changing nature of conflict and the new challenges to peace and security..." (p. 17). Given that the more he proposes specifics, the more he becomes a target for all and sundry, the Secretary-General could hardly be clearer about his motivations and about the directions in which the reform of international institutions should move.

—*Fair Globalization*, a report of the International Labour Organization Commission on the Social Dimensions of Globalization, made three packages of proposals for reform. Reversing the usual trend of blaming international institutions, they anchored their analysis in a broad set of principles for change at the national level. The report calls for good political governance within countries (democracy, rights, law, equity and devolution); an effective state including not only economic growth but education, social services and gender equity; a vibrant civil society based on freedom of association and expression; and representative organizations of workers. Of all these, the highest priority is for decent work to improve productivity and competitiveness.

The second set of proposals called for improved international economic regulation. Among these recommendations we find the following: greater policy autonomy for the developing countries that would take into account their level of development and specific circumstances; fair rules for the cross-border movement of people, including the problems of trafficking in humans and exploitation of migrant workers; fair rules for trade and capital flows, including new rules on foreign direct investment (FDI) and competition, core labour standards (as codified by the ILO), reducing agricultural and textile protectionism in rich countries; minimal levels of social protection and decent work, and greater mobilization of international resources for development aid to attain the Millennium Development Goals.

A third set of proposals targets the strengthening of global institutions, of which the UN multilateral system forms the core.

- To deal with new challenges and improve the quality of global governance, there should be improvements in democratic representation and decision-making, accountability to people, and policy coherence.
- Member states must increase their financial contributions to the UN system especially in the mandatory (as opposed to the voluntary) categories.
- Policy coherence would be improved by a focus on the well-being of people and the formation of a Parliamentary Group to provide Parliamentary oversight of decisions by state representatives and accountability of UN agencies.

- There should be increased representation for developing countries in inter-national financial institutions.
- Greater voice should be given to non-state actors, including business, organized labour, and civil society (especially representatives of the poor).
- The responsible media has a duty to develop a well-informed public opinion to underpin change.
- International agencies need to create interagency Policy Coherence Initiatives, a new operational tool to deal with the major issues impeding a fair and inclusive globalization. These would be buttressed by multi-stakeholder Policy Development Dialogues.
- The UN and its agencies should organize a Globalization Policy Forum to review the social effects of globalization on a regular and systematic basis (*A Fair Globalization* 2004: xi–xv).

—Ubuntu proposes three future scenarios, each leading to deeper reforms of international institutions. They aim at improving the efficiency, legitimacy and democratic credentials of the institutions. The "elementary reform scenario" seeks areas of greatest political agreement where immediate improvements can be made in the functioning of existing organizations. The "substantive reform scenario" includes first steps to achieving the major goals of democratization via greater participation, redistribution and human rights; a more balanced and legitimate capacity to enforce peace and security; more emphasis on sustainable development; and more independent financing to attain global justice. The "in-depth reform scenario," which aims to enable global institutions to effectively confront the issues of peace, development and justice in a more democratic manner, will be presented under Section 8 on Global Democracy (Ubuntu 2004: 4).

—"Since it is not the Charter that has failed but the policies and practices of its members, much of the necessary reform of the system can be affected without amending the Charter—provided that governments have the will to inaugurate real change" (Commission GG 1995: 233).

## 4.1.2 The Secretariat, Internal Administration

**Current Profile**

"The Secretariat shall comprise a Secretary-General and such staff as the Organization may require. The Secretary-General shall be appointed by the General Assembly upon the recommendation of the Security Council. He shall be the chief administrative officer of the Organization" (Article 97 of the UN Charter). The least one can say is that the Charter is not overly wordy about the Secretariat and its head.

The Secretariat has approximately 8,900 staff members, from 160 countries. It is meant to hire people of the "highest standards" from "as wide a geographical basis as possible" (Article 101.3). There is considerable debate about the degree of national intervention but many believe that governments exert pressures to ensure employment of their countrymen, so there is often a conflict between the principles of merit and representation. It is said that Kofi Annan is committed to promoting for merit, and that he has attracted many professional and dedicated personnel and weeded out many of the "careerist" position-holders. Still, his own High-Level Panel made a recommendation that amounted to suggesting he be given funding to undertake a one-time buy-out of deadwood personnel.

Although the main headquarters is in New York, the UN also has major offices in Geneva, Vienna and Nairobi, as well as coordinating offices for UN programs in cities around the world. About 50 special/personal representatives and envoys also represent the Secretary-General across the globe. In the end, though, the Secretary-General is responsible for everything—policy, administration, communications, advising the Security Council and all crisis negotiations—so in 1997 a Deputy Secretary-General was named to help the Secretary-General manage the Secretariat, coordinate economic and social development programs, represent the UN at conferences and official functions, and promote reform.

The Secretariat and the UN programs and bodies are presently grouped around six departments: political, disarmament, peacekeeping, humanitarian, economic and social, and legal.

**Secretariat – Criticism**

Linda Fasulo, UN correspondent for NBC news, points out in her recent description of the UN that although giant strides have been made to rationalize the UN's administration, many of its remaining problems are of the members' making. A major barrier to change is the General Assembly, which insists on passing too many resolutions and giving vague and unprioritized instructions that the Secretariat cannot carry out. "Often its mandates are so obtuse that its actual ability to function is limited" (Michael Sheehan, quoted in Fasulo 2004: 10). Added to this is the complaint that no one takes a stand. This lack of clarity in options and lack of clarity in decision-making grinds down the Secretariat. Also, the UN is bound up in rules, most of them imposed by the member states.

Not all the problems are of the members' making. A somewhat exaggerated exposé by Corine Lesnes in *Le monde* demonstrated that several recent political affairs have managed to undermine the UN bureaucracy's credibility and Kofi Annan's management. The allegation that the un-analyzed "black box" of the downed plane of the Rwandan President was found in a closet in UN headquarters 10 years after the event not only made the Secretariat look foolish, it opened the possibility of collusion in a plot. When it was reported that Saddam Hussein and friends made a corrupt misuse of $10 billion during the UN administered "Oil for Food" exchange program from 1996 to 2003, it took direct American pressure to get the UN to open even an originally toothless investigation into the scandal. It turns out that after numerous warnings, UN security officers turned a blind eye to the possibility that UN personnel could be the target of an attack in Iraq. A report of the August 19, 2003, bombing of the UN headquarters there cites "widespread incompetence, negligence, and poor judgement by UN security chiefs" (*Ottawa Citizen* 22-10-03). The head of security was fired. Partly in relation to this affair, the Deputy Secretary General, Louise Fréchette, tendered her resignation (which was refused). In each of these cases, UN authorities have absolved themselves ("What administration can know everything that's in its closets?") or to blame the nefarious intentions of others ("There are clearly efforts to embarrass me and to weaken the organization."). Some people are beginning to wonder if, as in every organization, there is not a will to power in the UN (*Le Monde* 3/04/04)? These accusations did a lot of damage to the organization's reputation, even though it later appeared that members of the Security Council were at least equally responsible for the "Oil for Food" fiasco.

On the issue of coordination, while there has been some improvement in communication between the UN and its agencies, according to former U.S. Ambassador to the UN Richard Holbrooke, "The field coordination is appalling, and the agencies in the field have no real single head. They have a coordinator system that doesn't work" (Fasulo 2004: 106–8).

Studies by the US General Accounting Office and the State Department showed that in 2000 in the professional staff categories, if one considered their financial contributions to the world body, the U.S. and Japan were under-represented and the British, French and Canadians over-represented.

The Secretariat was too top-heavy, too complex, too fragmented (G18 1986). Too much was spent on meetings, conferences, services and new facilities (G18).

**The Secretariat: Reforms Proposed and Accomplished**

Although we do not intend to pursue internal reforms to any great extent, it is important to note that the United Nations has not been standing still. Responding to heavy pressures from its wealthiest members since the 1990s, Boutros-Ghali and Annan have carried out extensive internal administrative reforms of the Secretariat and the processes of cooperation with the major agencies. These have included budgetary savings, reductions in and restructuring of personnel, simplification of administrative units, and improved management capacities to make the organization more effective, efficient and accountable. The UN was criticized for not having an effective system of checks and balances. In 1994 the Office of Internal Oversight Services was established. The UN website tells us that the total number of staff in the whole system, around 52,000, is less than a single government department in some countries. It is many less than some multinational corporations. "The Secretariat's staff fell from about 12,000 in 1984–85 to 8,900 (in 2004)" (Fasulo 2004:107). Former American Secretary of State Madeleine Albright, who helped lead the charge against the UN's "bureaucracy" has now given the UN a clean bill of health. "We have made important progress. UN headquarters and the entire UN system are better led than they have ever been," she claims (Fasulo 2004: 108). Even more important, the General Accounting Office of the U.S. Congress evaluated the UN's restructuring, leadership and operations. To the surprise of many, its report was generally positive.

—Rather than giving powerful states a veto over the budget (as the U.S. had requested), the General Assembly accepted the mechanism of "consensus voting" on the budget (G18 1986) in the Committee for Programme and Coordination, which gave the U.S. (and the other 33 committee members) a virtual veto.

—In 1969, the Jackson Report required governments to project coordinated development programs for a period of five to ten years, and to provide UNDP residents with authority to coordinate. Under Annan, in 1998, the administrator of the UN Development Plan was also appointed chair of the UN Development Group, which comprised the heads of all the UN funds and agencies working on development issues.

—A group of ambassadors asked Urquhart and Childers to follow up their report by developing detailed suggestions for the reorganization of the Secretariat. These became a major part of the discussion of the ambassadors with Boutros-Ghali who had announced his intention to reorganize. Several weeks after taking office in 1991, he consolidated the headquarters activities into eight departments eliminating many high-ranking positions. Four of the departments dealt with peace and security and humanitarian assistance, one covered economic development, and three were for administration (legal, information, administration) (GL65).

—In 1997–98 Kofi Annan then brought together some thirty departments, funds and programs into five executive groups for Development, Political and Security Affairs, Economic and Social Affairs, Humanitarian Affairs, and Human Rights.

—"The UN should give highest priority to improving its capacity to collect, evaluate and disseminate information that bears on the major global issues on its agenda.... The Office of Statistics is highly respected... but it has proven awfully difficult to find a common framework to make use of capital and human resources.... It is the most important tool the UN has..." (Strong 2000: 297).

## 4.1.3 Finance and Budgets

**Current Profile**

The United Nations is financed by its "regular budget," by an ad hoc peacekeeping budget, by voluntary contributions to the various programs and funds, and by the employees, who, instead of being taxed by their country, pay a portion of their salary to the UN.

"Contributions from Member States to the regular budget ($3.8 billion for the biennium 2006–07), which pays for staff, activities and basic infrastructure, are determined by reference to a scale of assessments approved by the General Assembly on the basis of advice from a Committee on Contributions" (UN Handbook 2006: 345). The scale is based largely on a country's share of the world income. The maximum contribution of 25 percent since 1974 (the United States) was reduced to 22 percent in 2000 as part of a deal to get the U.S. to pay its past dues. This reduction allowed Washington to save approximately $35 million on an assessment of US$283 million in 2002. The American government started in 1999 to pay its arrears of nearly $1 billion over a period of three years. Japan pays almost as much (19.5%) as the Americans. All other countries pay much less. Even so, in 2002, the 15 largest contributors accounted for 85 percent of the United Nations regular budget. In 1997, the floor for the minimum assessed rate was set at 0.001 percent of the total UN regular budget, which amounts to about $11,000 a year. It should be stressed that the regular budget has remained around US$1,150 billion, since 1986. But for 2006 the UN was restricted to a half year budget until new demands for management reforms were implemented. In addition to their "legally" obligated contributions, many states also make substantial voluntary contributions that demonstrate their appreciation of the UN's activities.

The Secretary-General proposes a draft budget to the 16-member Advisory Committee on Administrative and Budget Questions (whose members serve in their personal capacity). The draft is reviewed by the Committee for Programme and Coordination. Its 34 members represent their governments (the U.S. is always represented). The committee makes its decisions by consensus; thus each member has a virtual veto. The committee recommends the budget to the General Assembly.

Given the very different economic capacity of member states, it was decided since 1973 that the UN could not use the same assessments for peacekeeping as it does for the regular budget. For many years, members were classified in four categories (now 10). Group D, comprising the least economically developed countries, pay 10 percent of their assessed rate of the regular budget. The wealthier developing countries, Group C, pay 20 percent of their reg ular assessment rates. Members of Group B (middle powers ranging from Australia to France and Japan) contribute 100 percent of their regular budget assessed rate. The Permanent Members divide up the rest of the peacekeeping budget (a surcharge of about 25 percent). By 2002, the annual peacekeeping budget was once again near the US $3 billion mark and had climbed to US$5 billion by 2006 for the 18 operations in place. This is the annual price the world pays for priveleging peacekeeping over prevention. The American share was reduced from 31 to 27 percent in 2000 (UN Handbook 2006: 68).

The infrastructure administrative budgets of the various UN bodies, programs and funds are to be covered by the organization's regular budget. However, the lion's share of their budgets is subscribed to voluntarily, as arranged by negotiation and depending on the needs and the state's interests. Even these voluntary contributions are divided into "core contributions" and donations to trust funds for special causes. So international institutional budgets are not constant. Also, from time to time the UN makes special appeals for emergency humanitarian funds. A small number of wealthy people and corporations have made donations to the UN. An example is Ted Turner, who donated $1 billion to create a new UN foundation. "It is estimated that the total cost for the regular budget, peacekeeping, the UN agencies, funds and programs, excluding the World Bank and the IMF, comes to about US$11 billion per year" (Fasulo 2004: 115). The budget of just the federal government in Canada is near the $200 billion range. The UN website points out that the UN budget for worldwide human rights is less than that of the Zurich Opera House, and the World Health Organization spends about as much as a medium-sized teaching hospital in an industrial country. Even so, the UN has difficulty in getting its members to pay on time—only about 40 percent pay their dues by the first quarter of the year, and at any given time some 20 states may be more than two years in arrears.

**Finance and Budget: Criticism**

—"The question now remains whether member states will support changes to strengthen the organization to take on new security responsibilities as well as reform the economic and social programmes" (Lyons 1995: 45).

"The failure of member states and particularly the United States to pay their obligatory contributions and their peacekeeping contributions on time has left the UN in a perpetual financial crisis" (ibid: 44).

—"Financing of the UN is the single most serious manifestation of the decline in the political will to support it" (Strong 2000: 327).

"Governments have consistently, and the U.S. most vehemently, opposed any new financing system that would accord the UN the equivalent of taxing power and relieve it of dependence on the direct contributions of governments.... Another evidence of the unwillingness of member governments to permit the UN the flexibility of managing its finances is the denial of the right to borrow funds" (ibid: 328).

"There is a general unwillingness of governments to pay fixed assessments to fund operational programmes. Governments prefer to direct their contributions... to programmes that they themselves select as deserving of their support" (Davidson 1986: 10).

**Finance and Budget – Proposals**

—At least since a *New York Times* article in 1985 by Sadruddin Aga Khan and Maurice Strong and the 1986 report by George Davidson, it has been proposed to reduce the maximum percentage any member could pay from 25 percent to 10 or 15 percent, and to have the slack picked up by the middle-sized states.

—The Nordic UN Project (1991) sought greater financial stability and predictability for the UN through a three-tier system: assessed contribution for administrative infrastructure; negotiated multi-year pledges, regularly replenished; and voluntary contributions from wealthy states.

—In 1993, Boutros-Ghali asked "a select group of qualified persons," headed by Shijuro Ogata (Bank of Japan) and Paul Volker (former chair, U.S. Federal Reserve), to act as an independent advisory group to make recommendations on funding. To ease cash flow they suggested each member's annual assessment should be paid in four equal instalments. The "Working Capital Fund" should have its cushion increased from $100 million to $200 million. The assessed budget should cover the administrative costs of all the programs. Voluntary contributions should be negotiated on a multi-year basis. There should be one peace-keeping fund, based on a continually replenished fund of $400 million (Lyons 1995: 47–50, 71–73).

The expansion of UN tasks and activities had often led to "marginal activities" and "incremental tasks without full consideration of whether they are susceptible to meaningful international action" (Davidson: 27).

—"Some of the proposals for alternative financing include: Charging interest on unpaid assessments; ... temporary debt; increasing the working capital fund; authorizing the SG to borrow commercially; establishing a $1 billion Peace Endowment Fund; imposing levies on international air and sea travel, arms sales, postage and telephone calls... transnational movements of currencies, international trade, the production of polluting materials and on all mineral raw commodities; an annual UN lottery" (Knight 2005: 90).

## 4.1.4 *The General Assembly*

**Current Profile**

There are presently 191 members, roughly four times the 51 states at the origin of the UN. Each state has one vote, signifying its "equal" sovereign status. It is the only UN organ consisting of all members. Its "one member, one vote" principle makes it a symbol of the UN's universality and quasi-democratic traditions. It is the center of the world, where the voice of every member state can be heard. That is why states go to the general debate each September.

Aside from acting as a sounding board, the Assembly is also a launch pad for new ideas, such as when the Maltese ambassador's speech in 1967 started a 15-year debate that led to the Law of the Sea. A two-thirds majority is required for questions of peace and security, elections, new members and budgetary votes. Its resolutions are non-binding, and it makes recommendations to members and the Security Council. Its mandate covers all areas, including peace and security (except when a case is under consideration by the Security Council), socio-economic affairs and human rights. From the outset, the General Assembly was only a deliberative forum, with power to debate and pass resolutions but no real authority. The bilateral and multilateral meetings that take place behind the formal speeches are of equal, if not greater, importance to the peaceful unfolding of world affairs.

The representative General Committee comprises the president and vice-presidents of the General Assembly and chairs of its five Main Committees: First Committee – Disarmament and International Security; Second Committee – Economic and Financial; Third Committee – Social, Humanitarian and Cultural; Fourth Committee – Special Political and Decolonization Committee; Fifth

Committee – Administrative and Budgetary; and Sixth Committee – Legal. The chairs are nominated each year based on their qualifications. All members have the right to be represented on each committee, which take decisions on their recommendations to the Assembly by majority vote of those present. The General Assembly has been largely eclipsed since the 1980s. As the Security Council has become more active and the wealthy states turned more to the financial institutions to drive economic development, the Assembly has become more marginalized. (On the current structures of the UN system, see UN Handbook [annual], Fasulo, Childers with Urquhart, Ubuntu seminar, and Commission on Global Governance).

**General Assembly: Criticisms**

—According to Prof. Joseph Schwartzberg, it is unlikely that additional funding and other reforms will be forthcoming for the UN until the basic flaws in its decision-making systems in the General Assembly and the Security Council are corrected. The one nation – one vote system of decision-making is unrealistic, as it bares no relationship to the distribution of power in the world. Malta and China have the same vote. No fewer than 42 members have less than a million inhabitants each, 13 have fewer than 100,000 and two barely exceed 10,000. The 64 least populous members – enough to block a two-thirds majority vote – comprise less than one percent of the world's population. In theory, the 127 least populous members, accounting for barely eight percent of humanity, are enough to provide the two-thirds majority needed to pass a substantive resolution. Once again, in theory, the 127 states which are assessed at 0.001 to 0.039 percent of the UN budget, only contribute less than 0.9 percent of the total UN budget. One result is that the GA can only make recommendations and not binding decisions so the international system is deprived of legislative authority (Schwartzberg 2004: 3–9).

—A notable failure of the Assembly has been on North–South issues. Developing countries were overly ambitious and too rigid, with their unrealistically wide agenda. Industrial countries showed an obdurate resistance to change, and stepped aside from the Assembly as a forum for negotiation (Commission on GG 1995: 245).

—Industrial countries have persuaded the Assembly that budgetary decisions must be taken by consensus. That would be a sound procedure, but it is unbalanced because of the de facto threat of a rich-country veto.

—Two thirds of the members are developing countries, representing three quarters of the world's population. Some call this the tyranny of the majority. It could more appropriately be called democracy. The question is this: are the wealthy countries prepared to let democracy function at the international level? The difficulty in reaching decisions at the United Nations is compounded by the now normal practice of arriving at decisions by consensus. This gives even the smallest countries a de facto veto. Important agreements are often held hostage to narrow special interests (Strong 2000: 321).

The General Assembly, where developing countries hold the majority, has been reduced to meaningless, repetitive debate as the advanced countries concentrate economic decisions in the Intenational Financial Institutions (Lyons 1995: 44).

**General Assembly – Proposals**

—In the "Binding Triad" proposal for weighted voting in the General Assembly (Szasz 2001), the idea is to give each vote a triple weighting according to sovereign autonomy, population and financial contributions. According to Szasz, the proposal is easy to operate, inexpensive to initiate and offers advantages to all the stakeholders in the UN. The General Assembly would become a force to be reckoned with, democratic principles would be introduced and the UN would become more effective.

—Joseph Schwartzberg proposes a system of weighted voting for the General Assembly. A country's vote would be the average of its percentage share of the total population of all UN members (99 percent of the world population); its financial contribution as a percentage of the UN budget; and its share of the UN membership. This formula embodies three fundamental principles: democratic/demographic, economic and legal (sovereign equality of nations). Calculations for 2004 would give the USA a weighted vote of 9.1%, China 7.7%, India 6%, Germany 3.8%, France 2.6%, and the UK 2.4%. Some 33 states would gain under this proposal but these states contain roughly 79 percent of the world's people and account for 92 percent of the contributions to the UN budget. The four principal gainers presently have only 2.1% of the votes in the GA, despite accounting for 45.5% of the world's people and 43.1 percent of the UN's budget. But the others would still have 38 percent of the vote and these votes would count because Schwartzberg is proposing that the newly legitimated decision-making system would allow the General Assembly to be empowered to make much needed binding decisions in (at first) carefully defined and limited spheres of concern (Schwartzberg 2004: 11–20).

—Scenario 1: Establish a GA General Committee and specific working groups. Increase the supervision of the Assembly over agencies and programs. Establish a joint SC and GA commission to organize consultations and reports. Create a forum to resolve jurisdictional disputes. Scenario 2: Create capacity to make appeals to International Court of Justice on constitutionality of Security Council actions. Adopt an increased role in humanitarian interventions. Take effective control over all UN agencies and multilateral institutions (Ubuntu 2004: 10–12).

—"One little-used power the Assembly has is to direct the Security Council through resolutions. Such resolutions are not binding, but do carry weight...Our emphasis should be on gaining strong endorsement for this principle of reorienting the definition of sovereignty and for the recommendation for reform of the UN to meet the needs of a more robust (humanitarian) interventionist mandate.... It could be prepared to act when the Security Council freezes on an issue. It should be able to deal assertively with terrorist threats" (Axworthy 2003: 252–55).

The General Assembly should establish a new, high-level, independent Financial Advisory Committee with the aim of substantially increasing the UN's access to financial resources (Reimagining 2000: 3).

The UN General Assembly should immediately establish a standing UN Reform Commission.

The General Assembly should be revitalized as a universal forum of the world's countries, and its agenda reduced and rationalized. It should meet in a theme session in the first half of each year on selected issues of major importance. An experiment could be tried with an enlarged forum. Its methods could be modified to encourage discussion among leaders rather than just talking at each other. It is within the Assembly's mandate to suggest peace and humanitarian operations that do not require a military component (Commission on GG 1995: 245–50).

"Consensus decisions should still be sought for major issues, but the practice of insisting on it should be abandoned. The Assembly would also be more effective if its agenda were streamlined" (Strong 2000: 321).

## *4.1.5 The Security Council*

**Current Profile**

The Security Council presently comprises 15 members, including five permanent members (the P5: China, France, Russia, the United Kingdom and the United States). Each holds a veto. Following a 1963 amendment of the Charter, the number of non-permanent members was increased from six to10 rotating, non-permanent members elected for two-year terms by the General Assembly. Charged with ensuring peace and security, it is the only organ of the UN with the power to take decisions that bind all member-states and to authorize enforcement action. A majority is nine. Its main responsibilities are for peace and security, economic and military sanctions, arms inspections, and electoral and human rights supervision. It elects judges to the International Court of Justice (with the General Assembly), and it nominates the Secretary-General. The veto was given to the five major powers after the Second World War on the principle that no military action could be taken against them or without their consent, but also to keep the major powers within the world organization and to avoid the unit-veto blockages by each individual member of the Assembly. All these practices were perceived to have hobbled the League of Nations. The veto was used heavily during the Cold War (e.g. more than 80 times in the decade 1946–55) but was only used 13 times between 1996 and 2004, nine times by the United States.

The Security Council was generally paralyzed during the Cold War, but it has since become much more active, at least when there is cohesion among the P5. Such was the case in the resolutions on Afghanistan and terrorism and also on the first resolution on arms inspectors in Iraq. But in 2003 the U.S. and the U.K. were opposed by their allies over the invasion of Iraq. It was not until they came back a year later to ask for the Security Council's help that an appearance of togetherness was reinstated in a unanimous resolution to end the formal occupation of Iraq and transfer full sovereignty to an interim government. In addition, it is argued that, in general, the Council is working better than it did in the 1990s. There are more open meetings, preliminary drafts of resolutions are circulated to all members, area briefings provide more information, and a new website demonstrates greater transparency.

During its last period on the Security Council (1999–2000), Canada got elected on a strategy to make the Council more open and participatory, to restore its integrity as an active player in global security, and to promote the human security agenda aimed at the need to protect individuals and not just states. During its incumbency as president of the Council, Canada took the unprecedented step of inviting the presidents of major INGOs and representatives of non-member states to address the Council on the issue of human protection. The Secretary-General prepared a report on the issue. Resolution 1296, on civilian protection, established clear responsibility and guidelines for the Security Council to act against crimes against humanity and command it to respond to violations against humanitarian personnel, displaced persons or refugees. Canada tabled a report on sanctions, and in the case of diamond trafficking in Angola the Canadian ambassador introduced the new practice of "naming and shaming" criminal practices. The rebellion came to an end (Axworthy 2003: 237–52).

At the time of its founding, the Security Council represented a certain reality. Only those powers capable of projecting force (eventually nuclear powers) were given permanent status; representativity and legitimacy were sought through the rotation of small and medium powers; cohesion and decision-making effectiveness were thought to be maximized by small numbers. "The right of the veto in the Security Council was given to those powers who would share principal responsibility for the maintenance of peace" (Russett, O'Neill, & Sutterlin 1996: 67). Now there is consensus that both the composition and the powers of the Security Council must be changed to make it more legitimate and more representative of the global system. But there is no agreement about how it should be changed. Resolution 47/62 of the General Assembly in 1992 instituted a working party on the "question of equitable representation on, and increase in, membership of the Security Council." For the last half dozen years, the working party has not met due to lack of consensus. But, debate is open on the issues of numbers, categories, regions and powers (including the veto) of members.

Permanent members do not want democratic changes that would lessen their power and influence. It is assumed the United States likes things the way they are where they are so powerful that they even have demanded the removal of several ambassadors to the Security Council whose statements they did not like, including Mexico and Chile. In each region, candidates for permanent membership have been opposed by neighbors: Nigeria by South Africa and Egypt, Japan by South Korea,

India by Pakistan, and Germany because it would mean another European state in addition to France and the United Kingdom. There is fear that if there were a move to regional representation, smaller states could be ignored. While waiting for reform, it is argued that the veto could be "surrounded" by treaties, and that, if they act together, the rotating members have a "sixth veto" because any seven of them can block any item on the Council's agenda (see Fasulo 2004; Axworthy 2003; Knight 2002; Russett, O'Neill & Sutterlin 1996).

**Security Council – Criticisms**

—The current system is neither fair nor representative. For instance, some 77 members have never sat on the Security Council. Yet, Mauritius with 1.2 million people has sat as long as Indonesia with its 211 million. With the addition of new members to the UN, the SC has gradually become less and less representative of the organization and of the world. At the founding, the combined population of the Council's 11 members comprised 63 percent of the total population of all UN members. It is now not quite 30 percent of both the UN and the world as a whole. Also the original 11 represented 20 percent of the 51 members but with expansion the percentage of SC members to total membership had fallen to just 7 percent in 2003. It is no wonder many states feel left outside the UN's power structures. In addition, the SC's anachronistic special status for the five permanent members, along with their veto power, makes many other members feel marginalized. The very legitimacy of the UN is being questioned. (Schwartzberg 2004: 29–36).

—A major charge of illegitimacy of the Council stems from the perception that it is dominated by a few states and it is not truly representative of the rest (Knight 2002: 24).

—It has not been possible to reform the Security Council because of prestige rivalries among potential new candidates for Permanent Member status, and because no consensus has been achieved on criteria for justifying the existence of permanent members. But the real problem has never been stated: whether great powers are willing to transfer to the UN real power so that a method for the prevention of conflicts could be developed. Without such a debate, any change in membership would not change the capabilities of the Council (Bertrand 2000: 110).

—The fact that the membership of the Security Council is small—15 in all—enables it to meet frequently and expeditiously, and to deal with crises. It is clearly the most effective of the UN's deliberative organs, as well as the most powerful. Its composition, however, is a problem: it continues to reflect the political power structure that emerged from the Second World War. The five Permanent Members—the United States, Great Britain, France, Russia and China, effectively control it (Strong 2000: 322).

—Is the Council sufficiently representative in the new century to provide legitimacy for its decisions (Lyons 1995: 43)?

Since the end of the Cold War, the unanimity of the Security Council had often been perceived by the poor as the will of the powerful to use the UN for their own national interests (Lyons, 1995: 43).

—The notion of enemy states or victorious powers should have no place in the Charter now.

Since the number of members of the Security Council was expanded in 1963 because the UN membership had doubled from the original 51, should it not now be increased again, when membership has once more almost doubled to 192?

If the Security Council is to be more active and fulfil the role intended for it in the Charter, it must be seen to be legitimate (that is, representative) in the eyes of the world.

We believe that the Security is too closed a shop due to frequent resort to private consultations among the five permanent members, which reduces transparency and widens the gap between two classes of members. The same is true for the practice of holding informal meetings that are closed and have no records.

Because of the veto, UN reform can be achieved only with the acquiescence of the great powers (Commission on Global Governance 1995: 236–39).

**Security Council – Proposals**

—Prof. Joseph Schwartzberg has worked diligently to propose systems of weighted voting for both the General Assembly (see above) and the Security Council. He proposes that the permanent seats along with their attendant veto be abolished and be replaced with objective eligibility criteria for a weighted vote (WV) formula based on population, contributions to the UN budget and unit share of UN membership, as in his proposal for the General Assembly. He further proposes that countries with a WV of more than 4% would be entitled to a seat on the Council. At present this would include China, Japan, India and the United States. Other countries would be encouraged to caucus within regional groupings to nominate members to the Council. One or two seats (for a total of 18) would be reserved for states not in any regional bloc. The proposed system would enable representation on the SC of more than 90% of the world's population at any one time and would foster consultation and cooperation within the regional blocs.

—At a meeting in Baden, Austria, in July 2004, the Secretary-General's High-Level Panel on Threats, Challenges and Change came up with a strong consensus around a "winning formula" for an expanded, 24-member Security Council of three tiers: the existing permanent five (Britain, China, France, Russia and the U.S.); a second tier of seven or eight potentially semi-permanent members elected on a regional basis for a renewable term of four or five years (Brazil, Germany, India, Japan and South Africa might be in this group); and a third tier of rotating members elected, as at present, for a non-renewable two year term. Only the permanent five would have a veto. It was felt that this way, "everyone wins" and nobody loses—even if some do not win all they want. More emphasis should be accorded to giving membership to those who make a real contribution to peace and security, especially when a full review is carried out in 12 to 15 years (*The Economist* 22/07/04). Unfortunately, in its final report, the panel split over this recommendation because some members insisted on the need for new permanent members with a veto.

—Scenario 1: Develop regional representation; render decision-making transparent; discourage use of veto except on security matters (Ch. VII). Scenario 2: Restrict veto, and make a minimum of two obligatory; establish public procedural rules; subject decisions to International court (Ubuntu 2004: 10–12).

—"My thought is, and always was, that the veto should be abolished and that it would be much better for the UN if everyone had to stand for election. The council could then be expanded to include more Southern members. There could be a variation on the period of election, with staggered terms, allowing certain countries longer terms. Direct accountability to the membership, however, should be the basic principle. Of course, this is not about to happen. For now we are stuck with two-tier-membership" (Axworthy 2003: 242).

—It seems to the author that the mandate of the Security Council is not being challenged.The aim of expansion should be to achieve the following goals: improve the rate of participation from poorly represented categories; improve the geographical representation; improve its democratic character by limiting the use of the veto to Chapter VII actions and ensuring the Council represents a clear majority of the world's population; maintain its efficiency by limiting its growth; improve transparency by consulting with non-members on actions concerning them, and greater involvement of rotating members (Knight 2002: 33–4).

"For an institution to be considered legitimate it must be recognized as a lawful authority; one that conforms to a particular standard and operates in such a manner that its actions and decisions are seen as legally or morally justified and proper" (Caron 1993: 552). It is said that the power of social institutions resides largely in their legitimacy.

—"The Security Council must be enlarged and reconfigured to reflect today's geopolitical realities…." (Strong 2000: 322).

—"The composition and structure of the Security Council should be changed with the phasing out of the veto power over a 15- or 20-year period. Initially, permanent members should retain the veto, but limitations would be placed on the frequency with which it is used. Great powers would retain permanent membership, but such membership would be reviewed, perhaps every 10 years. To ensure greater representation, the membership should be expanded from 15 to 23 or 25, with permanent members expanded to seven or nine, and two rotating members (each serving a three-year term) drawn from each of eight suggested regions" (Reimagining 2000: 2).

—While informal meetings and consultations can advance the work of the Council they should be the exception rather than the rule.

"The number of veto-wielding members should not be increased…. The Security Council should be enlarged to make it more representative of UN membership… 23

would be reasonable.... There should be a new class of five 'standing members' (until a full review of membership is undertaken), made up of major powers to represent all the regions and proposed by the General Assembly.... The number of rotating members should be increased from 10 to 13 and the majority from nine to 14.... There should be a phasing out of the veto with the first step with the permanent member agreeing, as a first step, only to use their veto in exceptional cases of national security" (Commission on GG 1995: 240–41).

—Canada should support an increase in the number of Security Council members to 21 from 15, and agree to an increase in permanent seats only if three states from the South are among them and if a fixed proportion of seats for the South on the Council is established. It should work toward a reduction in the significance of the veto by denying it to new permanent members, by making it valid only if exercised by at least three members acting together, and by limiting the kinds of issues on which it can be exercised (Canadian Priorities 1995: 2–5).

The UNA-USA panel suggested the Security Council not get involved beyond its capacities. It should do what it does best: behind-the-scenes negotiations, consensus-building, face-saving, proposing alternatives—rather than what it does less well: conferring legitimacy, passing resolutions with teeth, and enforcing its judgments (1987: 79).

To improve the competence of the Security Council, Canada's former director of the division of International Organizations, Chuck Svoboda, proposed that non-permanent members be elected one year ahead of their term so that they could be brought into to consultation loop and be prepared for their stint on the Council—and it does not require any structural change.

## *4.1.6 Economic and Security Council (ECOSOC)*

**Current Profile**

ECOSOC has 54 members elected by the General Assembly for three-year terms. It studies and reports to the General Assembly on international social and economic questions, oversees the UN's agencies, programs and funds, and consults with the specialized agencies. It has functional commissions on human rights and social development, as well as crime prevention and criminal justice. The Economic and Security Council has been expected to alleviate poverty, foster sustainable development, facilitate equitable participation by developing countries in the international economy, and deal with such globalization issues as humanitarian intervention, environment, gender, crime and drug trafficking. In general, however, the authority invested in ECOSOC by the UN Charter has been transferred to the international financial institutions, the World Bank, the International Monetary Fund and the World Trade Organization. However, the effectiveness of ECOSOC has been improved somewhat in recent years through the inauguration of twice-a-year meetings with the international financial and trade organizations, and through improvements in procedures and preparation.

—In general, the UN empowers ECOSOC to initiate studies and reports, make recommendations to member states and specialized agencies, to prepare conventions and to hold conferences on international economic, social, cultural, health, human rights and related matters. So ECOSOC is designed to be the principal international forum dealing with, among other subjects, the social dimensions of globalization. It is also the existing intergovernmental body with the greatest potential to link the isolated "silos" into which international economic, financial, trade, social and environmental organizations have tended to settle. ECOSOC's meetings are public, which means it is more transparent and accountable than most other international economic and financial agencies (United Nations Association of the USA and World Federation of UN Associations Conference May 2004).

**ECOSOC – Criticisms**

With 54 members, it is too large to be swiftly decisive; its principal session is held once a year during July and so does not attempt to address crises as they occur; the principal sessions last for four weeks, so attendance of high-level participants for longer than a day or two is impossible; the world's major economies are only rarely engaged with its activities at senior levels, and it has few powers and fewer resources to give influence to its deliberations (ibid).

—Admitting the fact that ECOSOC was created mainly as a deliberative and not as an operational body, it is nonetheless remarked for its talent for fostering endless debate that leads to no apparent action. It lacks a clear public profile, and its lengthy, unfocused debates do not attract as many ministers as necessary to assure its role as a capable decision-making body. These heads of state, foreign secretaries and finance and trade ministers prefer the summit meetings, the financial institutions and the WTO (Fasulo 2004: 154).

—The provision of global public goods can be enhanced only if they are cost effective. But they suffer from "free riding" because internationally (unlike in countries) there is no government that can enforce or encourage cooperation. Individual actors (corporations, countries, powerful individuals) opt not to pay the front-end costs of cooperating, and end up worse off in a state of anarchy. The international community needs a forum in which the provision of global public goods could be reviewed and decisions made to stimulate collective cooperation (Kaul et al. 2003: 35).

—"There is still much frustration among the UN's membership over the Council's apparent inability to exercise any significant influence over the specialized agencies of the UN" (Strong, 2000: 323).

—"The founders intended the United Nations to be the world community's principal instrument in promoting global economic and social progress.... But the UN, and in particular ECOSOC, has fallen far short of its envisaged role of co-ordination and overall direction in the economic and social fields.... ECOSOC and the Second and Third Committees of the General Assembly are currently the principal headquarters bodies.... Many countries have expressed concern about the effectiveness of these bodies. Overlapping mandates leading to repetitive debates, lengthy agendas and voluminous documentation are among the major complaints.... Fifty years are long enough to know what works and what doesn't work within any system. ECOSOC has not worked" (Commission on GG 1995: 263–78).

—The Cancun Summit in 1981 signaled the beginning of an era in which the major industrial countries became more unyielding in their opposition to notions of broader participation in the management of the world economy (ibid: 264).

—The Nordic Project was concerned by the failure of broad policy guidance within the organization, a failure that stemmed in large measure from the weakness of ECOSOC, which was an empty vessel because the specialized agencies operated autonomously under separate governing arrangements. It found that countries were sending low-level delegates with little authority or expertise to ECOSOC.

Even as ECOSOC grew to 54 members, developing countries preferred to bring economic questions to the General Assembly where all were represented, and they had an overwhelming majority so that the same issues were argued over and over again (Nordic UN Project).

—The UNA-USA report found the ECOSOC "neither fish nor fowl, too large for high-level consultations and flexible decision-making—not large enough to perform credibly as a plenary body" (1987: 82).

**Economic and Security Council (ECOSOC) – Proposals**

—Ubuntu Scenario 1: Establish a regio nally representative executive committee. Improve mechanisms for coordination of agencies, international financial institutions, and World Trade Organization. Enhance infrastructure, work methods and financing. Scenario 2: Effective control and coordination of agencies, Bretton Woods institutions, and all multilateral institutions.

—Most important is the creation of a new broadly based Economic and Social Security Council as a principal organ of the UN, replacing ECOSOC and accountable to the General Assembly. There would be no veto power but it would operate in its domain like the Security Council (Reimagining 2000: 4).

—"The world is becoming increasingly interdependent, a number of multisectoral issues are coming to the fore, new players are emerging in the world economy, and the economic future of some leading countries is uncertain. For these and other reasons, we propose an Economic Security Council (ESC) be established at the apex of the UN system.... What is needed, we believe, is to wind up ECOSOC, to merge the Second and Third Committees (which deal respectively with economic and financial issues and with social, humanitarian and cultural questions), and to program the dialogue and negotiation schedules of all three within the newly merged Committee. This will require Charter amendments to chapters IX and X" (Commission on GG 1995: 276).

"There needs to be a balance in the world system, and this will not be achieved by preserving economic decision-making in the hands of a small directorate.... The time has come for a much more even-handed process of reform along the lines of our integrated proposals... The UN Conference on Trade and Development (UNCTAD) and the UN Industrial Development Organization (UNIDO) should be closed down.... Our ideas on global economic governance include an Economic Security Council designed to be more responsive to the interests of developing countries (using a constituency system to represent all regions) and changes to the distribution of votes in the Bretton Woods institutions to give developing countries a bigger voice (ibid: 283).

—Amending the UN Charter to create a new Economic and Social Council any time in the near future is very unlikely, so some short-term process reforms of ECOSOC should be considered:

- Introduce a segment of its annual session on global macroeconomic management, and invite finance ministers to attend.
- Regularly review the adequacy of the provision of finance for development.
- Invite institutions such as the IMF, World Bank, ILO, UNEP, WTO, BIS and G20 to report to it on action to implement ECOSOC's resolutions, and comment on their reports.
- Use its capacity to hold short, focused sessions during the year to discuss high priority issues or emergencies. When appropriate, invite relevant ministers.

(United Nations Association of the USA and World Federation of UN Associations Conference May 2004).

The Nordic UN Project (1991) proposed that if ECOSOC could not be substantially reconstituted, a new International Development Council should be created to provide overall policy guidance. The goal "is to bring high-level ministerial participation in its deliberations."

The UNA-USA panel recommended that ECOSOC be expanded to include all members, while the Second and Third Committees of the General Assembly (that deal with economic and social issues and already include all members) be terminated. It would be managed through a small reports and agenda committee that would screen all reports and proposals and establish priorities and timetables for the debates. A ministerial board of some 25 governments would be created, as well as an advisory commission of five persons to help the Secretary-General to coordinate UN programs. Finally, a single, "development assistance board" would, in effect, merge the governing councils of all the development agencies within the UN, such as the United Nations Development Program (UNDP), the United Nations Population Fund (UNFPA), the United Nations Children's Fund (UNICEF), and the World Food Program (WFP).

—Numerous reports and commissions have suggested the transformation of ECOSOC into an "Economic, Social and Environmental Security Council" with authority to make global decisions in these domains similar to the powers invested in the Security Council for international peace and security. It would also provide oversight and guidance to the specialized agencies including the international financial institutions. See, for instance, the Commission on Global Governance (1995), Independent Working Group on the Future of the United Nations (1995), South Commission (1990), and the World Commission on Environment and Development (1987).

—A more recent proposal that would use present structures more effectively has been made by a group of researchers analyzing global public goods: Inge Kaul, Pedro Conceiçao, Katell Le Goulven, and Ronald Mendoza (2003: 35–6). To make use of structures that are already in place and avoid having to change the Charter, the General Assembly might consider making its General Committee into its "executive committee" for social, economic and environmental issues – "a true apex body." The 28 members of the General Committee already include one president and the chairs of the six main committees of the General Assembly, plus 21 vice-presidents, including the five permanent members of the Security Council. The chairs and other vice-presidents are nominated annually by each world-region group of UN member states: Africa, Asia, Eastern Europe, Latin America and the Caribbean, and Western Europe and other states. The president of ECOSOC could also be included to form a "G29." While small enough to be manageable, it grows out of accumulated UN traditions and is representative of all world regions and major states. To become effective, it should convene annually at the level of heads of state, presumably at the beginning of each year's General Assembly meetings. It could be authorized to designate socio-economic priorities for the UN and its agencies. Policy priorities would be referred back to the Assembly for debate and majority approval. As called for, the 29 leaders could act as a summit for global vision and policy guidance.

—A similar but more modest proposal has been made by Kofi Annan to unite the governing bodies of the agencies that report to the ECOSOC (UNDP, UNICEF, UN Fund for Population Activities, and World Food Programme) in one body that would become a sort of executive committee for coordination and coherence. Alternatively the Executive Committee of EOCSOC could fulfil this function. "Such changes, of course, will come about only when necessity compels them" (Strong 2000: 324).

—A former Canadian delegate to ECOSOC and later president of the International Peace Academy, David Malone, proposed that the Council could improve its stature by making itself more relevant to the UN by working more closely with the Security Council on a vital issue such as peace-building, which addresses the causes of violence rather than its effects. Many of these activities, such as fostering civic institutions and the rule of law, promoting human rights, and rebuilding economic and administrative infrastructure, are already carried out by UN agencies, so it would legitimate and valuable for ECOSOC to take the lead role.

## 4.1.7 The Office of Secretary-General

**Current Profile**

The UN Charter says very little about the Secretary-General, although there was every indication the founders thought of the post as "administrative" rather than "political" (Goodrich & Hambro 1946: 269). He was to serve, not lead. "The Secretary-General shall be the chief administrative officer of the Organization" is all the Charter documents say. Could it be otherwise in an organization of sovereign members? The functions were somewhat extended by Article 99, which called on the Secretary-General to bring to the attention of the Security Council any matter that might threaten peace and security. However, over the years the Secretary-General has become an influential political figure, both because the Security Council (when the U.S. is not taking the lead) almost always looks to the Secretary-General to implement resolutions on peace and security, and also because new offices and programs that have been developed have reported to him.

**The office of Secretary-General – Criticisms**

—"The job has become overwhelming" (Lyons 1995: 61–2).

—"Management skills and experience receive little or no weight in the highly politicized process. Annan has proven a welcome and timely exception" (Strong 2000: 295).

"Over the years, the authority of the Secretary-General has been eroded by the tendency of member governments to micro-manage the organization" (Strong 2000: 326).

There are considerable limits to the office of Secretary-General. Its incumbent is always walking on thin ice. With regard to institutional reform, Maurice Strong has pointed out, "On these matters, which include revisions to the UN Charter and an overhaul of the UN's agenda, the secretary-general could make only recommendations, and even this was seen by some governments as an unwelcome intrusion into their prerogatives" (2000: 297).

The Secretary-General is appointed, not elected, with the nomination being passed in the SC (where the veto applies) before being submitted to the General Assembly. The Charter is silent on the term of office and renewability. Urquhart and Childers found that the process of selecting a Secretary-General, in fact left to the permanent members, was "haphazard and disorganized," "the product of chance rather than foresight, consultation or planning" (Urquhart and Childers 1990: 23). Urquhart and Childers called for a more serious and rational process. Governments would have to decide what they really want from a Secretary-General, but the only response they got was "excellence within the parameters of political reality" (ibid: 18). Neither the selection of Boutros-Ghali nor of Annan has suggested the process had been enhanced. In both cases the choice was motivated by Africa's regional demands that it was "their turn."

**The Office of Secretary-General – Proposals**

—A radical improvement in the selection process for the Secretary-General would include the following elements: the veto would not apply, but, unlike now, candidates could come from the Permanent Members of the Security Council; individuals would not campaign for office; a single term of seven years; the Security Council would organize a world-wide search for the best candidates and carefully consider qualifications for the position (Commission on GG 1995: 293).

—The USA-UNA report stipulated that the office of the Secretary-General needed to be greatly strengthened if he is to use Article 99 to fulfill the UN's function of "global watch" to identify incipient conflicts and warn of dangers. He must never become too identified with "one side." The Secretary-General is the person who must carry out preventative diplomacy and negotiations. The panel saw him more of an "initiative taker" than a "caretaker." To encourage the Secretary-General in this direction, they proposed one seven-year term so he would not be concerned by reappointment (1987: 101–2).

—Urquhart and Childers called for a serious selection process with specified qualifications, an extended search, rules for nomination, and a timetable for discussion within the Security Council. They also proposed a single seven-year term (1990).

### 4.1.8 International Court of Justice (ICJ)

**Current Profile**

The ICJ includes all members of the UN. The Security Council and the General Assembly elect its judges jointly. It arbitrates between states that wish to bring cases before the court, as well as on affairs provided by the Charter or standing treaties and conventions. No individuals can appeal to the court. If its judgments are not complied with, parties may apply to the Security Council.

The global system is made up of a cacophony of international political and economic relations and a growing communications and social community, all reposing on a rather unstable bed of international law. Technically, international law that has weight and legitimacy is composed of duly signed and ratified international treaties. To this may be added decisions of the Security Council that are intended to be binding on all members. But there is also a broader sense of the concept. There are a plethora of "hard-law" instruments, including treaties, conventions and protocols that are intended to be binding on governments, and a great many "soft-law" instruments, which include declarations, statements and plans of action agreed to by signatory countries or international conferences. Together, they provide the norms, but not the coordinating framework, for an "international legal regime." It is a patchwork of individual instruments each served by its own small secretariat, located and functioning separately, directed only by those who are party to the particular agreement. There is an almost total lack of—or at least a very unbalanced—capacity for enforcement. "If the U.S. doesn't agree with any international agreement, it will not be enforced" (Strong 2000: 331).

**International Court of Justice – Criticisms**

The court has no power of legal review of Security Council actions. It is open only to states. Regional organizations, international non-governmental organizations, local governments and individuals cannot avail themselves of the ICJ (Ubuntu 2004: 6).

**International Court of Justice – Proposals**

Ubuntu, Scenario 1: Enable greater recourse to the ICJ for constitutionally doubtful actions of the Security Council. Scenario 2: Create a constitutional chamber capable of rendering judgements on the actions of all UN bodies (ibid: 10–12).

### 4.1.9 Programs, Funds and Bodies of the UN

**Current Profile**

In Article 55, the Charter requires the UN to promote higher standards of living, seek international cooperation on social and economic issues, and enhance human rights and freedoms. The UN has some 60 bodies fulfilling these functions. They can be divided into six categories: 1) programs and funds created by the General Assembly to address specific issues; 2) Other UN entities, such as the Commissioner on Human Rights and the UN University; 3) functional commissions, such as Sustainable Development and the Status of Women, which concentrate on policy while agencies are oriented more to implementation; 4) Regional Economic Commissions setting policy on economic development, reporting to ECOSOC; 5) related organizations, such as the World Trade Organization (specifically created outside the UN); and 6) some 14 specialized agencies—autonomous organizations with formal working relationships with the UN (see below).

The Programs and Funds and related bodies carry out studies, provide advice and technical assistance, and offer forms of practical support in almost all economic and social fields. They have independent executive bodies, budgets and assemblies of their member states, and therefore can establish their own line of action, although they are theoretically accountable to the General Assembly through ECOSOC. Administration costs are expected to be covered by the UN assessment budget, but most of their activities are financed by voluntary contributions. They include the International Research and Training Institute for the Advancement of Women (INSTRAW), UN Centre for Human Settlements (Habitat), UN Conference on Trade and Development (UNCTAD), UN International Drug Control Programme (UNDCP), UN Development Programme (UNDP), UN Environment Programme (UNEP), UN Population Fund (UNFPA); Office of the United Nations High Commissioner for Refugees (UNHCR), United Nations Children's Fund (UNICEF),

UN Development Fund for Women (UNIFEM), UN Institute for Training and Research (UNITAR), United Nations University (UNU); World Food Programme (WFP), and the UN Relief and Works Agency for Palestine Refugees in the Near East (UNRWA).

In more practical terms, it might be said these entities deal with human rights, economic and social development, the natural environment, disaster relief, control of dangerous materials, world trade, and international crime (Fasulo 2004: 160).

In the field of human rights the 1993 session of the General Assembly, adopted a Declaration on Violence Against Women and, most significantly, created the post of UN High Commissioner for Human Rights.

**Programs, Funds and Bodies of the UN – Criticism**

The Commissioner for Human Rights has inherited what might be described as the very antithesis of a system—one that is characterized by lack of coordination, of a national division of labour, or of any clear institutional blueprint (Canadian Priorities 1995: 49).

—The Nordic UN Project was completed in 1991, five years after the G18 and Davidson reports. It found not much had changed, and it echoed its predecessors' findings concerning duplication, inefficiency and cumbersome management. Operational activities had grown piecemeal without coherent organization. It attributed the persistent weakness of UN programs to the absence of policy guidance, deficiencies in management, and the inconsistent and conflicting policies of members.

—The Nordic UN Project (1991) reported that members contributed to programs, not from collective goals but because of their own national interests or in response to humanitarian needs and public demand—leaving program managers in uncertainty.

—Following the renewed collapse of Haiti in 2004, the UN had to once again appeal for a special $35 million humanitarian aid fund to buttress peacekeeping. A similar request for Liberia in 2003, supported by the U.S., met with great success. But it took six months just to convene the donors' conference after the end of conflict and another month before any money began to flow. During this time, young men started to riot again. In recent years, similar calls had to be made for emergency aid for Afghanistan, Angola, East Timor, Kosovo, Sierra Leone, Sudan and Somalia. According to Mark Brown, head of UNDP, these delays of needed assistance in the weeks and months at the beginning of reconstruction can determine whether a transition to stability will succeed or fail (International Herald Tribune (IHT) 20/03/04).

**Programs, Funds, and Bodies of the UN – Proposals**

—Ubuntu Scenario 1: Improve coordination. Scenario 2: Provide adequate infrastructure and financing (2004: 10–12).

—The essential of the Nordic UN Project report was to try to consolidate all activities of UN agencies, programs and funds (such as UNICEF, UNDP and UNFPA) under one governing board which would attract responsible ministers to act as a counterweight to the financial institutions and specialized agencies (1991: 19–20).

—Following the renewed collapse of Haiti and the end of hostilities in Liberia, Mark Malloch Brown, administrator of the UN Development Program, has called for a "Stand-alone, multilaterally managed post-conflict fund to be available to assist countries during the critical initial period of reconstruction." It would draw on the combined resources and expertise of all the agencies that usually respond to crises. It would have both money and experienced people already available to provide food, shelter, medicines, social services and economic and governmental infrastructure (IHT 20/03/04). In 2006 the UN created a Peacebuilding Commission as an advisory and coordinating body.

—A case could be made that the regional economic commissions of the UN could be merged with the functions undertaken by the other principal organizations rooted in the region itself. There is a need for stronger and more effective regional organizations and this would be aided by rationalization and consolidation. This need not weaken the UN because they could be accorded associate status and become the UN's principal partners in each of the regions (Strong 2000: 325–6).

## 4.2 UN Charter, Sovereignty and Global Constitutionalism

**Current Profile**

Because they are founded on international treaties between sovereign states, international organizations do not have constitutions as such. Despite the hopes betrayed in the "we the peoples" opening of the UN Charter, the UN and other international organizations may have influence, but they have no constituent communities or populations and no independent powers. They are creatures of their nation states members, created by international treaties. The world community will have to decide at some point whether it wishes to rectify this situation.

What we have now in place of a "constitution" is a series of documents: the treaties themselves, the United Nations Charter and the founding documents of the other organizations, the Universal Declaration of Human Rights and the principles and values in it and in various international conventions. The Universal Declaration is not a treaty and its provisions are therefore not law, but this was remedied in 1976 by two binding treaties—the International Covenant on Civil and Political Rights and the International Covenant of Economic, Social and Cultural Rights—which, along with the Universal Declaration are referred to as the "International Bill of Rights." Most countries have signed some 80 treaties covering aspects of civil rights, such as genocide, the status of refugees, racial discrimination, torture and migrant workers.

The major principles and values enshrined in the United Nations are these: non-intervention in national sovereignty, balanced by the concept of "we the peoples who reaffirm faith in fundamental human rights, in the dignity of the human person, in the equal rights of men and women and of nations large and small"; one country, one vote in the General Assembly; protection of the powerful via a veto in the Security Council; justice and respect for law; promotion of social progress and better standards; protection of future generations against the scourge of war via collective security when called for by the Security Council; and promotion of these values by uniting our strength and combining our efforts.

"As the Preamble to the Charter declares, the world's peoples, acting through their governmental representatives, seek to create a just, peaceful and prosperous world through common action. It could hardly be simpler…." (Fasulo 2004: 3).

Or to put it another way, "What it comes down to is a need to change the nature of who makes decisions and in whose interests. It is the classic questions of all political systems—who governs" (Axworthy 2003: 258)?

The United Nations was born with an internal contradiction that has never been resolved. Its members are states, but its goals are human values (Canadian Priorities 1995: 49).

One way to think about a global constitution is to apply to it some of the practices and tests borrowed from the model of democratic states. These would include executive, legislative, judicial, public administration, regional and federal divisions of power; checks and balances for limitation of power; surveillance of the executive branch; majority–minority rights; membership/citizenship representation and participation; weighted voting; citizen rights, obligations and accountability; resources and revenues; and coordination and communication.

The term "sovereignty" has been used several times. Since the Treaty of Westphalia in 1648, the concept of sovereignty has been the bedrock of international relations, even when it was honoured in the breach. Only in the past decade have the theory and practice slowly started to evolve.

According to the Commission on Global Governance, sovereignty is the principle that a state has supreme authority over all matters that fall within its territorial domain. Three other norms stem from this central principle. First, all sovereign states, large and small, have equal rights (enshrined in Article 2.1 of the UN Charter). Second, territorial integrity and political independence of all sovereign states are inviolable. Third, there is a corresponding obligation to respect every other state's sovereignty—intervention in the domestic, internal affairs of sovereign states is not permissible (Art. 2.7 on non-intervention). States also have the right of self-defense (Art. 51). While these principles have their detractors, the Commission points out that general adhesion to this set of norms has been responsible for much of the international stability since the Second World War. There have been very few cases of outright inter-state aggression (1995: 68).

Academics have noted the necessary evolution in the concept. "During the last decade of the 20th century, sovereignty increasingly came to be seen as conferring on states the obligation of being accountable to the international community" (Taylor 1999: 564). This trend was evident especially with regard to humanitarian crises. The provisions of the United Nations Charter are now widely interpreted as permitting the possibility of legitimate humanitarian intervention—which can be defined as "military intervention in a state, without the approval of the authorities, and with the purpose of preventing widespread suffering or deaths among the inhabitants" (Roberts 1999: 35). An emerging consensus suggests that external intervention can be legitimate, providing it is conducted according to generally accepted international norms and is based on humanitarian concerns or the desire to prevent massive cross-border refugee flows (Dowty & Loescher 1999; Wheeler 2000). In addition, the creation of international tribunals for war crimes and crimes against humanity reflects, among other motives, the determination to deter governments from violating the internationally recognized rights of the individuals within their reach (Ratner & Abrams 2001). However, so far the "international community" has been willing to enforce its standards on "failing" states only in particular circumstances (overview synthesized by Koenig-Archibugi 2002: 49).

Kofi Annan has discussed the practical and conceptual dilemma of two notions of sovereignty: one that vests supreme authority in the state and the other in the people (1999). The second has become more preponderant as democracy ("government of the people, by the people, for the people") has spread around the world. At the request of the UN Secretary-General, Canada sponsored the International Commission on Intervention and State Sovereignty. The major contribution of its 2001 report on the right of humanitarian intervention was to propose that there need not be any contradiction between the two concepts of sovereignty. "State sovereignty should be able comfortably to embrace the goal of greater self-empowerment and freedom for people, both individually and collectively" (2001: 13).

The Commission went on to propose that when a State signs the Charter as a member of the United Nations, it voluntarily accepts the responsibilities of membership. There is no transfer or dilution of sovereignty. "But there is a necessary re-characterization involved: *from sovereignty as control* to *sovereignty as responsibility* in both internal functions and external duties" (1999: 13). The report concludes that there is a threefold significance to the notion of "sovereignty as responsibility":

- State authorities are responsible for the safety and welfare of their citizens.
- State authorities are responsible to their citizens internally, and to the international community through the UN.
- The state's agents are responsible and accountable for their actions.

The report has been received by the United Nations and the basic idea that the international community has a responsibility to protect citizens when a state can or will not was finally adopted at World Leaders Summit in 2005 – but with no teeth. The leaders refused to accept the High Level Panel's proposals of a set of criteria that would direct the interventions by the Security Council. Without an established set of criteria for action it is highly unlikely the Council will move forward. The reader should note the connection between the concepts of human rights, human security, responsibility to protect, and humanitarian intervention and their cumulative impact on the concept of sovereignty. It tells us something about the linkage between innovative ideas and the pathway to change through adoption of the ideas by movements and some leading governments and then their slow operationalization until they have entered the political vernacular and are ready for adoption by the UN.

Former Canadian foreign minister Lloyd Axworthy has commented,

> In each of these cases, traditional sovereignty gets in the way; too often there is implacable hostility or outright bullying from the strongest members and defiance from many of the smaller outlaw regimes and their criminal allies. All these UN organizations are in need of a spark, something to break the ritual dance. The "responsibility to protect" principle could light a fire of real reform by establishing a new modern standard by which the behaviour of states is measured (Axworthy 2003: 257).

The notion that "ideas matter" has been picked up by the UN Intellectual History Project under Richard Jolly, Louis Emmerij and Thomas Weiss in their series of books analyzing the development of key international concepts during the past fifty years under the UN's tutelage. They conclude that, "The UN has had a more positive and pioneering record in the economic and social arena than is generally recognized. Its contributions to development thinking and ideas are among its most important achievements. Yet often these are little known". They also say the UN must not rest on its laurels. Many ideas and problems currently demand intensive analysis and debate. Their priority list includes: the clash of civilizations, human security, aid, culture and development, environmental sustainability, global economic inequalities, international competition, and the management of the global economy. The UN must reward creative thinking (Jolly, Emmerij & Weiss 2005: 3 & 61–4). Above all, the linkage between critical thinking, fresh ideas, and constitutional debate needs to be stressed when we analyse the transformation of the UN.

### 4.2.1 UN Charter: Constitutional Elements of International Institutions: Criticisms

—In a special issue of *Le Monde Diplomatique* (Sept. 2005), just prior to the UN World Leaders Summit, Monique Chemillier-Gendreau drew up a considerable list of global issues and UN weaknesses that make the case for the creation of a new "Organization of the World Community". The central global issue is violence but its causes are multiple. "Hunger, indecent development gaps, inequality in the face of natural disasters, and the major powers' encouragement of arms sales and other trafficking; ideologies that breed racism and discrimination; and globalization that is leaving many by the wayside, provoking new forms of violence and widespread terrorism." Underlying all this is the fact that the UNDP's pleas for a more equitable sharing of such vital resources as water, energy, knowledge and medication have largely gone unheard. And the complexity of a global society is completely ignored. A second set of issues is the challenge of a changing world: "wars, civil violence, poverty, infectious diseases, environmental degradation, terrorism, organized crime, and weapons of mass destruction" as elaborated by the High Level Panel on change and security.

Chemillier-Gendreau goes on to point out the deficiencies of the UN, which start with its being dominated by the victors of World War 2, its arbitrary interventions, and its bloated, inefficient bureaucracy. In practice the UN is a prey to major powers' arms sales, peacekeeping fiascos, and American unilateralism. Despite the efforts of Kofi Annan and the few efforts at reform he proposed, the UN is incapable of changing itself. The idea of reform at the UN "is empty words" because "it leaves sovereign states totally free in their commitments" and avoids "the heart of the problem: the permanent members and their veto remain unchallenged". Proposed changes to the Security Council would only consolidate the powers of the few. There has been no hint of any advance in the democratic process. "What really needs to be questioned is power itself as a criterion of appointing leading members. The history of democracy has been a constant struggle against the usurpation of power by the richest and strongest" (pp. 22–3, translation by Krystyna Horko, IPU).

—"It is clear the scorpion can never beat the ants. It is also clear that in a globalized world the old game of power politics can only lead to chaos. Today the dream of global hegemony is as far out of reach for anybody as it was in the past (Seara-Vazquez 2003: 7).

— "The enormous inequities, inefficiencies, and dangers of the current system of global governance have made reform both necessary and inevitable" (Reimagining 2000: 1).

—When the United Nations Association of the USA produced its general review and proposals on the future of the UN, it kept its eye on specific domains of considerable transformation that are of interest to those who think about international institutions: a) the structure of world power, b) the number of independent countries, c) the nature of conflict (internal and external wars), d) the globalization of economic activity, e) the emergence of global environmental risks, and f) the disruptive nature of social and political conditions illustrated by the number of stateless and displaced persons (1988: 6–10).

—We must start by recognizing that the problems of the United Nations are essentially political, despite the habit of attributing to poor management and administration the political failures of the Security Council. Since 1963 and 1971, when they managed to change the numbers on the Security Council and ECOSOC, the idea of changing the Charter has remained untouchable because of certain antiquated ideas: a) the creation of a universal institution was such an immense progress that it would be hardly reasonable to imagine another type of solution; b) it has become common to think that because the League and the UN had both been created after world wars, it would take another crisis to create a new organization; c) any modification to the Charter would be like opening a Pandora's box of demands; d)"reform" would have to be limited to the functioning of the Secretariat, evolving program priorities, and non-structural changes to organizational machinery (Bertrand 2000: 109).

—Theorists have not come up with any practical reform proposals, and they rarely consider constitutional issues that go beyond sovereignty and power politics. "Realists" defend power politics and national interest and limit their proposals to improving diplomacy and the balance of power. Marxists were more interested in analyzing relations of domination and exploitation. "Idealists" worry about the creation of world community, and they have not transferred European functionalism to a global level. "Moderate reformists" mix conservative realism and skepticism concerning world governance. They therefore count on national power, alliances and cooperation among the wealthy and powerful to maintain peace and security. The UN has only a marginal role in these domains, so why worry about its reform (Bertrand 2000: 12–4)?

—"As the need for more of what I call 'co-operative governance' increases, paradoxically there is an increasing mistrust of government in all its forms.... There has been strong support for right-wing calls to 'get government off the backs of people'.... A parallel push is for reduced support for international organizations, nourished too by strongly voiced fears that they're likely to subvert national sovereignty and, indeed, represent a movement toward world government" (Strong 2000: 309). "There is also a limited understanding, and much misunderstanding, about the nature of international organizations. They are not governments but the servants of governments, and lack the basic attributes of governments.... The United Nations cannot tax or borrow and has no source of revenue independent of its member governments. The UN has no military forces or capacity of its own to carry out missions mandated by the Council or to enforce its decisions. It has no direct relationship with the people.... Because member governments frequently fail to supply the funding and military support to carry out the decisions, the UN becomes a scapegoat for delinquent governments. The specialized agencies ... are the counterparts of the related departments of national governments, but they are not integrated into the central body of the United Nations" (ibid: 311–12).

—Yet, it is a mistake to reduce the perspective of global constitutionalism to governmental alternatives to the state system. Governance implies a cluster of various values, norms, procedures, regimes, institutions and practices that enable coherent forms of order to be common or general features of international life. This coherence entails considerable centralized capabilities with respect to the following governmental functions for the world as a whole: legislative organs to establish binding standards of behavior; administrative capacity to interpret these standards; financial powers, including revenue sources and taxing powers; rules and procedures determining membership and participation in international institutions and the status of international actors, as well as modes to render all actors accountable; verification of compliance with behavioral constraints and enforcement mechanisms; disaster, relief and refugee services; regimes for protecting and managing the global commons; regulation of collective violence and supranational police; frameworks for world economic life, including trade, monetary and financial spheres, and protection against agreed-upon categories of economic disruption; and, finally, a "global constitution," or, possibly, some "invisible document" that establishes an organic law for the community of states, nations, and peoples that frames and constitutes the political world (Falk 1993: 14–15).

— If the U.S. does not agree to a particular item of international law, it will not be enforced. Enforcement is therefore both inconsistent and unfair, reflecting the political interests, the will and the priorities of the power structure of the world system rather than the rule of law (Strong 2000: 331).

### *4.2.2 UN Charter: Constitutional Elements of International Institutions: Proposals*

—In *Le Monde Diplomatique's* special number on UN reform, Monique Chemillier-Gendreau proposes that "If the UN cannot be reformed, and the major powers refuse to give up their prerogatives and hog most of the world's resources, then a new organization of the world community must be invented soon. Those states that bear the brunt of globalization would be well advised to consider quitting the UN immediately and founding a new organization adapted to their requirements." The new organization she proposes would aim to construct a universal political community, as proposed by the democratic cosmopolitans, which would complement states in order to cater to the complexity of society and to define and defend mankind's common resources. Its headquarters would be located outside the West. There would be four political bodies: a general assembly made up of states and a second made up of representatives of national parliaments; to these would be attached two councils, one made up of 25 elected by the parliamentary assembly to promote preventative actions and peace-keeping, the second composed of 25 states elected by the state assembly to manage intervention in the event of conflict. The Secretary-General would be responsible to both assemblies. The permanent-member category and the veto would be eliminated, as would be the Economic and Security Council and the Trusteeship Council. Bicameral commissions would deal with economic, political, social, cultural and military matters in "the common interest". The International Court of Justice and the Criminal Court would be merged. A Court of Human Rights would be created. The decisions of the assemblies and the courts would have the weight of law.

The proposals are for discussion but "the imperatives behind them are: the need for democracy, for law and justice." (2005: 22–3, translation by Krystyna Horko).

—"Let us be realistic and imagine a new world, where law and order prevail over the will of the powerful, and something like a world constitution, which takes into account the ambitions but also the possibilities of our time. Let us draft a new Charter for the United Nations" (Seara-Vazquez 2003: 7).

—Robert Keohane's article "Governance in a Partially Globalized World" summarizes his proposals for institutional development based on approaches from political philosophy and knowledge from political science. The following are some main elements of his complex argument.

We are living in a partially globalized world. To live thus, we need not just effective governance but the *right kind* of governance. The analysis begins with two premises.

The first is that increased interdependence produces discord. The gains of cooperation loom larger relative to the alternative of unregulated conflict. Both realists and liberals agree that under conditions of interdependence, institutions are essential if people are to have opportunities to pursue the good life.

The second premise is that institutions can foster exploitation, or even oppression. The result is the governance dilemma: although institutions are essential, they are also dangerous. We who are unwilling to accept Hobbes's solution incur an obligation to explain how effective institutions that serve human interests can be designed and maintained. We must ask the question that Plato propounded more than two millennia ago: Who guards the guardians? Are there ways by which we can resolve the governance dilemma, using institutions to promote cooperation and create order, without succumbing to exploitation and tyranny? Our goals, or "consequences," are security, liberty, welfare and justice.

The world is so culturally and politically diverse that most functions of governance should be performed at local and national levels. Five key functions should be carried out at least partially by regional or global institutions:

- limit the use of large-scale violence
- limit the negative externalities (such as beggar-your-neighbor policies) of decentralized action
- provide focal points for coordination (such as agreeing on a single standard)
- deal with system disruptions (financial crises, climate change, powerful technologies, etc.)
- provide a guarantee against the worst forms of abuse, particularly involving violence and deprivation (tyrants, inequality, etc.).

Procedures must be based on criteria of accountability, participation and persuasion. Our standards will have to be quite minimal to be realistic and sustainable in a polity of perhaps 10 billion people. The point of presenting ideal criteria is to portray a direction, not a blueprint.

Various schools of political science help us think through the problems of the governance dilemma. From rational-choice institutionalism, we learn both the value of institutions and the need for incentives for institutional innovation. These incentives imply privileges for the elite, which have troubling implications for popular control. From game theory, the study of political culture, and work on the role ideas play in politics, we learn the importance of beliefs in reaching equilibrium solutions, and how institutionalized beliefs structure situations of political choice. Traditional political theory reminds us of the importance of normative beliefs. It is not sufficient to create institutions that are effective; they must be accompanied by ideas that respect and foster human freedom. From historical institutionalism, we understand how values and norms operate in society. We abdicate our responsibility if we simply assume material self-interest. Democratic theory demonstrates the crucial roles of accountability, participation, and especially persuasion in creating legitimate political institutions. These lessons are in tension with one another… Governance, however, is about reconciling tensions (Held & McGrew 2002: 325–47).

—"To succeed, any reform agenda must enshrine three distinct yet closely connected principles: human security, political democracy and socio-economic justice" (Reimagining 2000: 1).

—"Third-generation" or "constitutionalist" analysis of international organizations is now timidly taking its place. Still, it is made up more of critical remarks and proposals than of actual theories. It is as though these specialists did not want to appear too audacious in confronting the traditional taboos against creative thinking on multilateralism. The first step is to point out the false, out-of-date concepts on which international organizations are currently founded:

- "Collective security" built on the unreal expectation of permanent alliances of great powers willing to intervene in causes that don't touch their vital interests.
- The concept of "functionalism," which breaks the link between economics and security and reduces common action to vague discussion of possible "norms."
- The irrelevant nature of tardy "peacekeeping" efforts in intra-state conflicts.
- The ineffectiveness of "preventive diplomacy" based on simple "good offices."
- The reactionary nature of international organizations in a time of intense change due to their being used by states to reinforce archaic aspects of sovereignty.

The second step is to identify progress made on peace and security issues in areas outside the UN, to see if they can be transposed to the global arena. Major solutions to peace and security have been found in the European Union and the Conference on Security and Cooperation in Europe. European statesmen thought long and hard about the errors of the Treaty of Versailles and national sovereignty. Their plan was to build a "security community" on a model different than that of "collective security."

> It became recognized that "civilized people" don't have to turn to war to surmount their different interests if they develop: confidence and security building methods; transparent military activities, arms reductions, precise mutual controls; completed by ties of economic and cultural cooperation; and agreements on human rights and political ideology.

A common base of political philosophy and reciprocal methods of cooperation and control have permitted the construction of a European society where it is most unlikely that war would any longer be a tool of political action. However, the third step of transposing this Western model to the world is not easy. Just as happened in Europe, frustration of communal identities leads to ethnic and religious fundamentalism—a root of violence that leads to wars in impoverished countries. Attempts to impose Western models only add to the local sense of humiliation. The lesson from Europe is that this cycle of dissatisfied identities can be broken only by social and economic development that can foster acceptance of the co-existence of different cultures and ideologies (Bertrand 2000: 114).

—The European Union is an innovative governance structure that seems likely to provide a model .... It is neither a multilateral organization nor a national government. But it is a government with governmental responsibilities and constitutional powers that represent a divestment of sovereignty by national governments.

These concepts for the gradual creation of a global regime of peace and security have been paralleled by a number of "third-generation" proposals for supportive organizational transformations that go beyond "little reforms" of the Secretariat toward a "new realism." They include:

- creation of a Council of Economic Security
- replacement of the decentralized system of specialized agencies by a single Commission styled on that of the European Union
- emergence of regional development agencies
- establishment of regional representation to surmount the inconveniences of one-state–one-vote or of a system of weighted voting
- subordinating the principle of universal membership to acceptance of a clear set of principles, and methods of verification and control of their actual application
- elimination of the right of veto in the Security Council and providing the council with a rapid reaction force for intervention
- representation of public opinion through a "world parliament" bringing together representatives of states and of civil society
- extension of the Security Council's membership, and its transformation into a veritable "executive" with social and economic powers (Corps commun 1985; UNA-USA 1987; Bertrand 1988; UNDP 1992).

—What kind of a UN would I like to see for the 21st century? ... World government is just not on: it is not necessary, not feasible and not desirable. This is not to say we can aspire to a world without systems or rules.... The challenge is to strike a balance so that the management of global affairs is responsive to the interests of all the people in a secure and sustainable future. Such management must be guided by basic human values and make global organization conform to the reality of global diversity.... What is needed is an improved system of international agreements and international law and more streamlined international organizations to service and support the cooperation among governments and other key actors.... But even more than this, they need renewal of their political and financial support (Strong 2000: 310).

We need "boundary conditions" to give highest priority at the international level to issues that have a major effect on the security, survival and well-being of the entire human community or major portions of it, so as to protect us from major risks and realize major opportunities. One such condition or principle is that of "subsidiarity," which proposes that the most effective government is the one that is closest to the people affected by specific types of decisions. A number of activities of the UN system could be better handled by other regional or specific-purpose organizations, including non-governmental ones. By the same token, more and more responsibilities of national governments require international cooperation to manage issues single governments can't handle on their own. The UN should concentrate on global issues and give priority to its primary role, which is negotiating, articulating and ensuring enforcement of international legal agreements, dealing with multi-faceted issues, and mobilizing responses to threats to peace and well-being. Security will remain a major preoccupation, as will the growing threat to earth's life-support systems (ibid: 313–18).

The UN of the future must be built around its distinctive attributes: its universal membership, its global mandate, its unique status as a global political forum, and a forum for the development of international law. Governments have made a lukewarm response to the "opening Pandora's box" of fundamental reform issues they do not want to handle. "I'm convinced that opening it and confronting its issues is both necessary and inevitable, or the UN will never be fit to help the world community meet the challenges of the twenty-first century" (ibid: 319).

—"In the United Nations, as in other organizations, members have to strike a balance between their rights and their obligations.... Membership requires an integration of programme decisions and funding commitments, fair burden-sharing among a wider range of rich nations, and a longer term approach to make operational activities more stable and more secure through assured funding" (Commission of GG 1995: 275).

## 4.3 International Financial Institutions and the World Trade Organization

### *4.3.1 Current Status*

The World Bank group and the International Monetary Fund (IMF) were created in 1944 at the Bretton Woods Conference. The original task of the World Bank was to help finance the rebuilding of Europe, but when the Marshall Plan sidetracked this goal, the World Bank was reoriented toward reducing poverty and improving the economies of developing countries that need foreign capital. It makes loans, not grants, to governments (disbursed loans outstanding in 2000 amounted to $119 billion). However, by the 1980s, this task too was partially overtaken by the vastly larger private capital flows, and the question became how poor countries could tap into these new investments. The International Monetary Fund's main tasks are to monitor and guide monetary cooperation between countries, and to facilitate exchange rate adjustments, promote trade expansion, and make temporary loans to states to correct balance-of-payment problems. However, as more and more currencies floated freely and governments deregulated their financial markets, ever-larger amounts of money, aided by advanced information and communications technologies, began to flow across national borders. Rapid shifts led to financial crises in some hundred countries in the last two decades of the 20th century. It is in these circumstances that people talk about the need for "a new international financial architecture."

In the late 1980s, economists, bankers and financial experts propounded the "Washington Consensus." Essentially the idea was to promote "liberalization' meaning to "get the government out of the way of market forces." This became known under the heading of "structural adjustment" programs that the World Bank and the IMF enforced on poorer countries needing and wanting their loans. Countries were to

- cut public spending (and taxes), usually including expenditures on education, health and social services
- eliminate public consumption subsidies (foe example, on basic foods and gasoline)
- privatize state-owned industries and reduce barriers to foreign ownership
- lower interest rates to draw foreign investment
- devalue their currency to encourage exports
- generally end protectionism and encourage free trade.

During the 1990s, new conditions for loans were added under the heading of promoting "good governance." Governmental institutions were to be strengthened and democratized; the rule of law reinforced; and governments were to foster transparency, encourage increased domestic savings, and fight corruption. However, as time went on these programs produced more immiserisation than wealth. International economic experts came more and more to recognize that they know more about reducing government control of the economy that they do about how to help countries to develop, especially when international decision-making is secretive and unrepresentative.

The World Bank is based on member quotas of authorized capital stock, of which approximately half is in subscribed shares and half is on call. In reality, the bank obtains the bulk of its funds from borrowing on the international capital markets, using the callable capital as its security. The World Bank is made up of six parts (the World Bank Group):

- the International Bank for Reconstruction and Development (loans for member states)
- the International Development Association (affordable credits to poorer countries)
- the International Finance Corporation (loans and equity financing to complement private investment, thus promoting the private sector)
- the Multilateral Investment Guarantee Agency (guarantees, i.e. insurance, for foreign investors in developing countries for losses arising from non-commercial risk, such as armed conflict)
- the International Centre for Settlement of Investment Disputes (arbitration and conciliation services)
- the Consultative Group on International Agricultural Research (finance for international agricultural research centres and programs).

Although each of the units is legally, and to some degree, financially distinct, the World Bank president chairs each of them, and each uses the bank's board of directors and executive directors.

For both the World Bank Group and the International Monetary Fund, countries subscribe funds according to their economic strength. Voting power in the governing bodies is linked to the level of subscriptions. In the voting system, voting quotas give 17 percent to the U.S., 16 percent to Japan, 6 percent to Germany, and 5 percent each to France and Great Britain for a total of roughly 39 percent of the votes. For both institutions, each member country (ones ratifying the agreement, usually around 180 countries) appoints one governor and one alternate to the board of governors, and both boards meet together annually. Typically, the governors are ministers of finance or governors of a central bank.

There are two special committees, one on Development (including a Joint Ministerial Committee), and, at the IMF, a Finance and Monetary Committee. They meet together in between the annual board meetings. They oversee current activities and make recommendations to the board. Only countries on the executive boards can appoint members to these important committees. These two executive boards run the day-to-day operations of the bank and the IMF, including requests for financial assistance, economic consultations with member countries, and the development of policy. The executive board of the IMF is composed of the managing director as chair and 24 executive directors, five of whom are appointed by countries having the largest subscription quotas (U.S.A., Japan, Germany, Great Britain and France). The additional 19 are elected every two years by all the other countries, some of which vote in "executive groups." A similar structure exists at the bank. In the Bretton Woods organizations, considerable power is pyramided in the hands of the wealthiest Western countries.

Both the bank and the IMF are independent specialized organizations that maintain formal relations with the United Nations through the Chief Executives Board for Coordination (formally named the Committee on Administration), chaired by the UN Secretary-General, and through mutual representation, consultations and high-level dialogue.

Founded in 1995, the World Trade Organization (WTO) is a successor to the General Agreement on Trade and Tariffs (GATT). GATT was a concession to those who did not want trade to be under the UN, which was the original post-War plan for a still-born International Trade Organization. Over the years, GATT had been able to cut tariff protectionism in half. But there were new forms of protectionism (health, environment, labour regulations, etc.), and neo-liberals wanted a more robust organization.

Not all countries are admitted into the WTO, which insists on legal, legislative and commercial conditions being met. Its 148 members take decisions by consensus, but the real decision-making clout lies in the hands of its quasi-judicial, impartial adjudication tribunals, whose decisions are binding and may include penalties. Decisions are generally observed, because no state can afford to be excluded from the international trade regime.

The main objective of the World Trade Organization is to set and to police rules on trade between countries in goods and services, agriculture, and intellectual property (patents and copyright). Some powerful countries would like to extend this mandate to include competition policy, investments, environmental regulation, public procurement and cultural activities. Independent of the UN, the WTO maintains informal relations through high-level dialogue with other institutions (United Nations Handbook; Fasulo; Florini; Miller 1995; Ubuntu 2004; Porter 1999; Williamson 2003).

### 4.3.2 International Financial Institutions and the World Trade Organization – Criticisms and Proposals

—Joseph Stiglitz's analysis of globalization's discontents also led to a comprehensive series of remedies.

> The most fundamental change that is required to make globalization work in the way that it should is a change in governance. This entails at the IMF and the World Bank a change in voting rights, and in all of the international economic institutions, changes to ensure that it is not just the voices of trade ministers that are heard in the WTO or the voices of the finance ministers and treasuries that are heard at the IMF and the World Bank.... Still, I am not sanguine that fundamental reforms in the *formal* governance of the IMF and the World Bank will come soon. Yet, in the short run, there are changes in *practices and procedures* that can have significant effects (Stiglitz 2003: 226).

Stiglitz therefore proposes that at the IMF there be acceptance of the dangers of capital market liberalization and short-term capital flows. It is the single-minded ideas and practices of neo-liberalism that must be modified. The appropriate way of addressing problems when private borrowers cannot repay creditors is through bankruptcy, not bailouts. There needs to be improved banking regulation adapted to the capacities and circumstances of each country. Improved risk management should be handled through creditors absorbing the cost of insurance against fluctuations. International assistance will be required to provide improved safety nets for agriculture and small businesses in developing countries. Finally, there must be improved response to crises to maintain credit flows and mitigate the collapse in trade through maintenance of stable interest rates. The IMF must return to its task of providing funds to restore aggregate demand.

The World Bank should recognize that "conditionality" has not worked, and should be replaced by "selectivity" that gives aid to countries with proven track records and allows developing countries to focus on priorities instead trying to micro-manage their economies. There needs to be a comprehensive approach to development that encompasses not just resources and capital but a transformation of society that includes education, advanced technological training, economic stability, and equality, as well as growth, new financial institutions, and creation of competition and enterprise.

The WTO needs to balance a) the rights and interests of producers with those of users; b) the trade agendas of both the developing and the advanced countries; and c) major concerns, such as the environment, that go beyond trade (Stiglitz 2003: 236–52).

—Florini forecasts that the IFIs will still be with us in 20 years, but they will operate in a much different fashion. Participation and transparency will be the keys. In general, the IFIs will be obliged to make public more and more information about their data bases, their plans and their decisions, and NGOs will swarm over them to analyze them. New agreements modelled on Europe's Aarhus Convention will help entrench transparency norms at the global level. The Aarhus Convention obliges participating governments to disclose relevant information, be open to public review and consultation, and adopt judicial remedies for non-compliance.

Such conventions could be adopted at the global level in the field of economic information, the environment and health. Governments, international institutions,corporations and civil society will cooperate in agenda setting, and in negotiating,implementing and monitoring agreements. Officials will feel obliged to justify their plans and decisions. The original plan for the International Trade Organization in the 1940s envisaged that NGOs would receive documents, propose agenda items, and observe and speak at conferences, unless specifically objected to on occasion by a majority of members. This should become the norm. Corporate executives, too, will feel the pressure to adopt codes of social responsibility. Under the pressure of transparency, accountability and broader participation, fairness and legitimacy will be added to effectiveness and efficiency as principles of global governance (Florini 2003: 199–208).

—The general principles governing financial flows should be sustainable development and the support of goods and services, not just money trading. Subsidiarity, national autonomy, accountability to citizens, greater United Nations control, and the recognition of social and political rights should also be taken into consideration (Reimagining 2000: 3).

There should be a Currency Transactions Tax, an International Taxation Organization, regional monetary organizations, a World Financial Authority, and an International Independent Debt Arbitration Mechanism under the UN. The IMF should return to its narrow mandate of surveillance and stabilization (ibid: 5).

Ubuntu, Scenario 1: Balanced representation and voting on governing bodies (equal weight of debtor and creditor countries). Restrict policies of IMF to original mandate. Increase transparency of procedures and decisions. Renegotiate agreements with UN so UN can ensure respect for international norms and standards (social, labour, environment, rights). The UN should take steps to ensure the legal primacy of human rights over regulation and agreements regarding trade and investment. Improve coordination and coherence with other international institutions. Scenario 2: Make responsible to the UN General Assembly through ECOSOC. The WTO should provide financing to developing countries to ensure they can fully participate in trade decision-making by having a permanent presence at the WTO in Geneva and at meetings (2004: 10–12).

## 4.4 Specialized Agencies Attached to the UN

### *4.4.1 Current Profile*

Some 14 autonomous agencies have formal relations with the United Nations. Some, such as the International Labour Organization, founded in 1919, antedate the UN; indeed, some have their roots in the 19th century. They are the organizations that make the world go round. They look after the day-to-day, work-a-day relations between states, in areas such as air and maritime transport, postal and telecommunications services, meteorology, health, culture, labour, agriculture and copyright. These agencies include the International Labour Organization (ILO), the Food and Agricultural Organization (FAO), United Nations Educational, Scientific, and Cultural Organization (UNESCO), World Health Organization (WHO), the World Bank Group, International Monetary Fund (IMF), International Civil Aviation Organization (ICAO), International Maritime Organization (IMO), International Telecommunications Union (ITU), Universal Postal Union (UPU), World Meteorological Organization (WMO), World Intellectual Property Organization (WIPO), International Fund for Agricultural Development (IFAD), and the UN Industrial Development Organization (UNIDO).

In many ways, the agencies resemble many of the ministries or departments in a national government, except in the UN system, there is no coordinating authority (such as a cabinet) to make them all work together. The Secretary-General of the UN has no overriding powers. Each agency is founded on its own treaty, and has its own executive committee and governing assembly based on individual departments or organizations within each state. In other words they each have independent, and often competing, bases of legitimacy in the international arena.

"Coordination of these organizations is one of the greatest challenges facing the United Nations" (Fasulo 2004: 159). At the present time, the task belongs to the Chief Executives Board for Coordination (CEBC; formerly the Administrative Committee on Coordination), chaired by the UN Secretary-General. In principle, it was meant to be working better under Kofi Annan. But in the corridors of the UN, the word is that not much has changed. The other agency heads liked to attend the CEBC meetings because Annan was an artful speaker and the font of knowledge. "Sherpas" representing the agency heads now better organize meetings. The UN has made more concentrated effort to work with the agencies and their national bases of support to obtain results, for instance at the Monterrey conference, where more money was obtained for development aid. However, in the much-quoted words of one World Bank president, "We do not need to be 'coordinated,' thank you very much."

## 4.4.2 Specialized Agencies Attached to the UN: Criticisms

—An issue central to the current debates about the effectiveness of development aid is... what to do about the uneven, often poor performance of UN development agencies. Here we have a sprawling "family" that consists of dozens of development agencies, special funds, programs and initiatives that are at least thirty-five in total, many of which have independent mandates and are hobbled by poor leadership and inadequate funding. Rich countries have looked at this highly political mess with despair and have largely retreated from wholesale reform. Instead they have funded agencies they like, such as the UN Children's Fund (UNICEF), and have withdrawn or cut funding to those they do not, such as the UN Educational, Scientific and Cultural Organization (UNESCO) or the UN Industrial Development Organization (UNIDO). Even for those organizations that continue to be supported, the rich countries have tended to cherry-pick projects they like rather than fund the totality of budgets, which in the process undermines the sensible management of budgets and programs (Maxwell 2006: 422).

—The Geneva-based UN Disarmament Commission, The UN Commission on Human Rights, and the UN High Commission for Refugees—each in its own way suffers from sclerosis and needs fixing. Countries whose prime motive is to stall action and prevent any worthwhile initiative seek membership on these bodies. The disarmament agency has ceased to play much of a role and needs a new assignment. Indulging in the worst kind of political horse-trading discredits the human rights group. The refugee organization is dismally underfunded and hasn't taken on the politically difficult issue of dealing with internally displaced persons or environmental refugees... (Axworthy 2003: 257).

—Effective coordination, in particular in the field, is needed. It is governments that are best placed to secure coordination. But they are represented through different ministries and there are few signs they follow coordinated national approaches (Commission on Global Governance 1995: 267–68).

The governing bodies of the funds and programmes adopted the same style as in the UN Assembly, with long meetings, speeches and resolutions as the annual pattern. There are few opportunities for informal collaboration (ibid: 270).

Much of the funding for UN funds and programs is voluntary and comes from a small number of countries. For instance, 10 countries provide 80 percent of the contributions to the UNDP.... A serious drawback to voluntary funding is that it leads to uncertainties. Contributions are pledged on a short-term basis that impedes meaningful planning (ibid 1995: 273).

### 4.4.3 Specialized Agencies Attached to the UN – Proposals

—Ubuntu, Scenario 1: Improve coordination with UN programs, the Bretton Woods institutions, and the World Trade Organization. Scenario 2: Effective responsibility before the UN General Assembly through the ECOSOC. Adequate infrastructure and financing.

—A more modern and efficient mode of governance is clearly required. This includes instituting smaller executive bodies to give continuous guidance to management. For instance, the Global Environmental Facility has more than 100 member-states, but the Governing Board has only 32, each representing a constituency. There are 16 constituencies for developing countries, 14 for industrial ones, and two for Eastern Europe. The countries in each constituency choose a board member and an alternate. New members join an existing constituency. Documentation is sent to all member countries. Each constituency determines its own process of consultationand decision-making (Commission on GG 1995: 271–72).

A new funding system should be designed to combine voluntary short-term funding with negotiated, long-term, burden-shared contributions, linked to the funding needs of approved operational programs (ibid: 274).

This chapter has presented descriptions, criticisims and proposals for change of the United Nation's major organs and its agencies. The next chapter will broaden this analysis to cover the various world-wide policy issues that are challenging the United Nations system. In closing, it must be repeated that those looking for more holistic and cohesive reform proposals can have them at their finger tips by consulting the Internet. Particularly worthy of consultation are:

- *Responsibility to Protect* (www.ciisc-iciss.gc.ca) which is the 2001 report of the International Commision on Intervention and State Sovereignty. It deals with the leading-edge issues of sovereignty, its limits and evolution, and humanitarian intervention.

- *A More Secure World,* the 2004 report of the Secretary General's High Level Panel on "Threats, Challenges and Change", which is a comprehensive analysis of Security issues.

- *Proposal to Reform the System of International Institutions: Future Scenarios* (www.reformcampaign.net). This is the report of Ubuntu, an international NGO, leading the "World Campaign for In-Depth Reform of the System of International Institutions". It is a complete, step-by-step proposal for reforms to the entire UN system.

# 5 Global Issues Requiring Institutional Development

In this chapter we change our focus somewhat to critique some of the major issues of international politics in the context of their requirements for new institutional infrastructures . We continue following the guide outlined in Chapter IV.

Global Issues
1. Peace and security
2. Sustainable development
3. Global democracy
4. Civil society

At the end, to help surmount the rather piecemeal presentation of reform issues in these two chapters, a more elaborate analytical critique is made of two broad-scale, holistic sets of UN reform proposals, that of the High Level Panel entitled *A More Secure World*, and Secretary-General Annan's follow-up report *In Larger Freedom*, both from 2004.

## 5.1 Peace and Security

### *5.1.1 Current Profile*

The UN Charter provides several options for dealing with inter-state conflict. Acting under Chapter VI, the Security Council may try to use various diplomatic and economic measures to bring the parties to settle their differences peacefully. Failing this, under Chapter VII, the Security Council, with the concurrence of the permanent members, may call on members to supply support for military enforcement of the Council's decisions for peace. This has been invoked only twice: once for the Korean War, when the General Assembly passed the "uniting for peace" resolution when the Soviet Union was absent from the Security Council, and once to end the Iraqi invasion of Kuwait. Another option, euphemistically called "Chapter VI and a half," was developed to deal with an increasing number of intra-state conflicts. It includes policies for peacekeeping and peacemaking that have been adopted since the Charter. The Council uses it when it decides an internal conflict poses a threat to international security. The Council asks the parties to accept, or it imposes, international forces between the combatants. The Security Council and the world have been gradually moving toward the concept of humanitarian intervention that has been codified as the "Responsibility to Protect" by the International Commission on Intervention and State Sovereignty in 2001, and adopted by a UN resolution based on the World Leaders summit in 2005.

The United Nations invented peacekeeping to intercede between two warring parties that could agree on the need for outside mediation. More recently, various coalitions of international partners have been cobbled together, usually under the leadership of the United States, to stop international aggressors, as happened in Kuwait and Afghanistan. When belligerents will not stop fighting and it is necessary to intervene for humanitarian reasons or to prop up the state, the UN has turned to new techniques of peacebuilding and humanitarian intervention. This occurred in the Balkans, Africa and Timor, in Southeast Asia. Peacebuilding is accompanied by a panoply of intermediary measures for early warning, fact gathering, inhibiting of war economies, preventive diplomacy, conflict management and resolution, democratic and electoral development, and nation building. When governments will not cooperate with the international political will, a system of sanctions and embargoes may be set up to target the country, or, as was done more recently, its leaders and elites. To add to this agenda, international institutions now must also try to manage international financial, ecological and humanitarian crises arising from natural and manmade catastrophes.

In his 1992 report *An Agenda for Peace*, the then Secretary-General Boutros-Ghali started to codify preventative diplomacy (to stop disputes from becoming violent), peacemaking (use of Chapter VI), and peacekeeping (deploying UN forces between parties to a conflict, with their consent). He added post-conflict peacebuilding (to help rebuild the shattered countries). Boutros-Ghali was also among the first Secretary-Generals to link security to socio-economic conditions, because "poverty, disease, famine, oppression and despair" are breeding grounds for conflict. The Security Council started to change international law in the 1990s by using the Charter's ambiguous support for security and for human rights to override strict considerations of sovereignty, on occasion.

However, conflict management techniques are still half-measures tacked on to the UN Charter. Even peacekeeping, the least intrusive of the UN's conflict resolution techniques, has not received full support of member states. Despite the Charter's permissiveness on this issue, the United Nations has no means for raising a military force of its own. It has to make do with the troops and money provided by members on an ad hoc basis for security operations. And this despite the fact that under Article 43 of the Charter, the original intent was that member states would sign standing agreements with the Security Council to provide armed forces and *matériel*. No agreement was ever signed. *The Agenda for Peace* called for new negotiations so that states would make forces available on a permanent basis as an added means of deterring conflict (1992: 25).

There have been some slight improvements. The UN Department of Peacekeeping has a new headquarters, a staff doubled to around 400, a base of stand-by equipment established in Brindisi, Italy, with enough stock on hand. Some 80 countries have made conditional commitments to supply troops, but only 20 have stand-by capacity. There is a little-known Stand-by High Readiness Brigade, made up of 10 countries (with another 11 observer nations) that have stand-by units available for UN duty. The current reality, however, is that most of the responsibility for peacekeeping is on the shoulders of developing countries, which are furnishing some 70 percent of the troops. Those with the capabilities are no longer contributing, while those without the capabilities are. This is not a very helpful situation in a world with 18 peacekeeping missions underway (circa 2006).

But the UN still does not have the command structures that were also called for in the Charter, or the requirements that have grown up for standby logistics, equipment, and civilian and police support personnel. Missions are thus conducted not only ad hoc, but also usually after the fact. Each security operation is dependent on national political will, and the Secretary-General must go hat in hand to member states to beg for troops and money. This causes a delay in intervention of one to three months—to say nothing of the cases when intervention is refused—with the resulting spread in conflict and increased loss of civilian lives. Of course, the ad hoc, one-by-one nature of the missions leads to a tremendous loss of the competence built up in each deployment. International enforcement coalitions are similarly ad hoc, but also require the leadership of the United States, and, as we have recently seen, may operate outside international law and political consensus. International enforcement loses its legitimacy when those who have the might also have a unilateral power to decide what is right.

The alternatives that have been talked about are not very encouraging. U.S. Secretary of Defense Rumsfeld floated the idea of a standing, multilateral police force or constabulary—led by the Pentagon, but the Iraq experience does not recommend this course. Various elements of the UN do not like the concept or even the language of standing UN military forces. A European Union rapid reaction force would have to carry its colonial past. However, it is likely that NATO and other regional forces will be asked to take over some regional responsibilities. "Contracting out" of peacekeeping responsibilities to "coalitions of the willing" is slow and feeble; giving the responsibility to private contracting firms would cause loss of all sense of control. Both lack legitimacy.

In a seminal article, "Security in the New Millennium", Ramesh Thakur, vice-president of the UN University, traced the development of peace and security concepts. There are now three concepts: national security, human security and global security. National security has just been described. The UN was established to use collective action to damp down inter-state wars and promote development. It has been quite successful. The 20th century required such an organization. With over 250 wars including two world wars and the Cold War the century saw more people killed than in all previous wars in the past 2000 years. Another 6 million have died since the end of the cold war (Thakur 2002: 271).

The shift from the "national security" to the "human security" paradigm transfers the object of security from the state to the individual, from territory to the human, from armament to development. Again, the need is apparent. "Over the course of the 20th century, 30 million people were killed in international wars, but 7 million in civil wars and an additional 170 million by their own governments" (Thakur 2002: 273). The narrow "national" concept of security wastes enormous amounts of wealth and human resources on armaments and the military, while failing to protect citizens from the insecurities of disease, hunger and civil war. In the decade of the 1990s, 2 million children were killed, 1 million orphaned, 6 million disabled – not to mention the emotionally scarred (p. 275). Half the world's governments spend more on undefined military threats than to protect the health of their citizens (p. 275). Of course, they are the most insecure and unstable societies. The shift to human security requires a shift from a culture of reaction ("riot control" Groom and Taylor used to call it) to a culture of prevention. Human security seeks to protect people against threats to life, health, employment, safety, human rights and dignity. As regards the UN, this requires that international humanitarian law be added to efforts for peace and disarmament. Inescapably this leads to a revision of concepts of sovereign impunity, to the necessity to accept humanitarian intervention and the necessity to develop adequate criteria for its application.

Global security is the latest concept to be slowly added to the other two to cover the common vulnerability of all people to such threats as environmental pollution, climate change, state failures, massive migrations, crime and piracy, and biological and chemical weapons etc. By their nature these threats cannot be managed by any state or group of states. Global security demands international cooperation and effective multilateralism (see Trent 2006b; Intriligator 2006).

## 5.1.2 Peace and Security – Criticisms

—In his 2003 report Implementation of the UN Millennium Declaration, the Secretary General noted that the post–September 11 climate of cooperation and consensus on peace and security was seriously eroded by the war against Iraq in spring 2003. The war exposed deep divisions in the international community, with accusations of double agendas. Although the Security Council has since been able to find common ground, the war brought to the fore a host of questions of principle and practice that challenge the UN system. New and potentially more virulent forms of terrorism, the proliferation of non-conventional weapons, the spread of transnational criminal networks and the ways in which all these things may be coming together to reinforce one another are viewed in some parts of the world as dominant threats to peace and security. Questions are being raised about the adequacy and effectiveness of the rules and instruments at the disposal of the international community to confront these new challenges. At the same time, for many around the world, poverty, deprivation, and civil war remain the highest priority. Civilians inevitably bear the cost… (Annan 2003b: 2–3).

A clandestine market for weapons of mass destruction requires more intrusive inspections. Nuclear states have done too little to reduce the symbolic importance of these weapons or reduce their numbers. There are no multilateral means in place to deal with non-state actors. The illicit traffic in conventional weapons requires tighter export controls and identification of sources. Sanctions must become more targeted. Security Council resolution 1373 (2001) imposed binding obligations on all states to take steps to prevent terrorism and its financing, and it established the Counter-Terrorism Committee. All 191 states had submitted first-round reports. But new challenges include ensuring respect for human rights and fundamental freedoms, and strengthening cultural and religious understanding.... Greater efforts must be made, as in the Kimberley Process for diamond identification, to address the economic incentives that establish and maintain war economies, including money-laundering. The process of "naming and shaming" may help in some cases. Providing economic alternatives is necessary in addition to punishment. An effective international response will require addressing war economies at all stages of early warning, prevention, peacemaking, peacekeeping, and peace-building. The countries with strong military capacities that were most vocal in their support of the Brahimi Report on "robust" peacekeeping have been the most reluctant to contribute their forces. We must bridge the commitment gap and the expectations gap (ibid 3–8).

We are in a period of transition from emergency relief and peacemaking to one focused on reconciliation, rebuilding of national institutions, and participation of affected populations (ibid 8).

Globalization has provided new opportunities to those who do wrong. But there is no reason why it should not be exploited by international institutions intent on setting things right (ibid 6).

The problem is that the world paradigm has changed from Westphalian sovereign nations to Global Governance but our political practices are stuck in a post-Westphalian mode (JT).

In this respect, UN members are mired in the status quo, unwilling to challenge the big powers who want to keep the UN emasculated, and reluctant to put up the money and commit the resources (Axworthy 2003: 256).

The UN faces a dilemma. Public expectations for the world body grow with each disaster, but the member states of the UN still have not committed themselves to the fundamental concept of common security... and appear not to support a more effective role for the UN (Canadian Priorities 1995: 25).

In 1991, the UN General Assembly established the United Nations Register of Conventional Arms. No verification procedures were included. It does not require specific types of weapons to be identified. As only about 25 percent of arms are traded, it is not enough to know what a country has imported without knowing its holdings and internal acquisition (ibid 1994: 33).

Are member states willing to provide the kind of support required, including the commitment of military forces under UN command? The UN peacekeeping budget soared from $439 million in 1983 to $3,627 million a decade later.

But a chasm had grown between the UN's task and the willingness of members to pay (despite the fact their own military budgets were infinitely greater). What are the appropriate conditions under which the world community can carry out humanitarian interventions? When do human rights trump sovereignty (Ch. 7 & UDHR versus Art. 2, para. 7)? What are the safeguards to stop aggressive interventions by powerful states using humanitarianism as a cover (Lyons 1995: 57)?

Nuclear proliferation is on the rise. Equipment, material and training, once largely inaccessible, are now available through a sophisticated worldwide network. The 1970 Non-proliferation Treaty relies on a gentleman's agreement that is non-binding and does not include some countries with growing industrial capacity. Some states fail to control exports by their companies. Fewer than 20 percent of the UN's 191 members have signed a protocol allowing broader inspection rights to the International Atomic Energy Agency (Mohamed Elbaradei, Director General, International Atomic Energy Agency, *New York Times* op.ed. 12-02-04).

## 5.1.3 Peace and Security – Proposals

—The circular complexity of the peace problem is exemplified in the following quote: "Global Action's deliberate focus is on violent armed conflict. The world also faces fundamental crises of poverty, human rights violations, environmental degradation, and discrimination based on race, gender, ethnicity and religion. All of these challenges must be met before human security and a just peace can be fully achieved. To meet these challenges many efforts must be pursued; no single campaign can deal with all of them. But efforts to address these global problems can and should complement and support one another" (Thakur 2002: 272).

—By contrast to the Bush doctrine, the concept of global security recognizes the need to create a new global system comparable to the creation of a new world system after World War II, one that would encompass not only security but also economics, politics and other issue areas. This new global system would treat problems of security, both military and nonmilitary, through strengthening existing international institutions or creating new global ones. These new institutions could be built in part on the UN system and its components. They would involve supranational decision-making and authority, with enforcement capabilities, transparency, and accountability, with global perspectives and responses. Participation in the decision process would be through close international cooperation. There would be a prohibition against preemption by any one nation in favour of collective action. Such a system would be preferred to the current system of the U.S. as a hegemonic global power (Intriligator 2006: 18).

—Globalization requires that we go beyond national interests and even protection of human rights toward defense of our common humanity using international institutions as catalysts for achieving our common destiny (Annan 2000).

—A proposal has been made for the creation of a UN Emergency Peace Service that would be a permanent UN formation, maintained at high readiness, with trained, well-equipped personnel available for immediate deployment on authorization by the UN Security Council. This service would be both multidimensional and multi-functional, composed of military, police, and civilian elements for rapid deployment to diverse UN operations.

Ideally, 10,000 to 15,000 personnel would be co-located at a new UN base under a static operational headquarters and two mobile field brigades. Each field headquarters would be assigned sufficient strength to provide robust security elements, as well as a range of skills and services to address human needs. By including a wider range of services within a modular formation, the UN would provide a prompt, coherent response to various contingencies. (A UN Emergency Peace Service 2004).

—There will eventually have to be a standing UN constabulary that can move more quickly on preventative missions, provide an investigative arm for the International Criminal Court, be available for robust duty in protecting UN humanitarian workers or seeing to the dismantling of arms systems… (Axworthy 2003: 256).

—The key principles should be carefully monitored limits on arms production and trade and the reduction and elimination of arms of mass destruction. Institutional initiatives should include a new and upgraded UN Department for Disarmament and Arms Regulation and a permanent forum for the Treaty Secretariats of Nuclear Weapons Free Zones (Reimagining the Future 2000: 5).

A comprehensive light arms control program should include the destruction of seized illicit weapons, regulation of all arms exports, marking weapons at the time of manufacture, and improved records (ibid: 6).

A multi-track conflict prevention action plan would create a Lessons Learned unit in all relevant UN departments, a UN National Office in every state, with conflict oversight as part of its mandate; an International Crisis Prevention and Response Centre; and an International Criminal Court (ibid: 6).

A new Department of Peace Operations would include an Impact Assessment Office to undertake preliminary studies of interventions, an International Peace Operations Centre, and an Ombudsman to accompany peace operations. There would also be an independent Review Tribunal. Enhanced capacity for effective interventions would require a permanent Civilian Police Force, pre-positioned military stocks, rosters of available personnel, and standardized training. Effective operations would also need a standing Force Contributors Committee, a Peace Operations Advisor as chief of staff, a General Staff, and on-the-ground Integrated Task Force commands (ibid: 7–8).

Regarding peacemaking, the problems are legion. To start with, the supposed peacemakers are also the warmongers. The five permanent members of the Security Council account for the vast majority of international arms sales.

—The Nordic UN Project (1991) was the first to link development to security because a stable global system is in the interest of all states. "Development assistance has a preventative role that is crucial to global security" (81–2).

—Such an order (to stimulate peace) presupposes at one and the same time the acceptance of a common political ideology and culture, the bringing into being of an entirely new system capable of satisfying the identity needs of peoples, an arrangement of political units that no longer enjoys absolute sovereignty, and the establishment of a political status for humanity in the form of a global constitution. One can say it is a question of demilitarizing the human spirit" (Bertrand 2000: 7).

—Mohamed ElBaradei, Director-General of the International Atomic Energy Agency, has proposed a six-part plan for tailoring the 1970 Nuclear Non proliferation Treaty to fit 21st-century realities.

- Tighten export controls over nuclear materials with a new binding treaty, a universal control system, and criminalization of persons who assist in proliferation.
- The International Atomic Energy Agency should have the right to conduct complete inspections of all countries.
- No country should be allowed to withdraw from the treaty. At a minimum, an attempt to do so should prompt an automatic review by the Security Council.
- Production of new fuel, processing of weapons-grade material, and the disposal of spent fuel and radioactive waste should be brought under multilateral control, with balances for commercial competitiveness, and assuring supply for legitimate uses. This would include resumption of the Fissile Material Cutoff Treaty, stalled in negotiation for eight years, which would put an end to the production of fissionable material weapons and strengthen security measures.
- The five recognized nuclear states (Britain, China, France, Russia and the United States) should start reducing the 30,000 nuclear warheads still in existence under a verifiable and irreversible procedure, and finally bring into force the long-awaited Comprehensive Test Ban Treaty.
- We must start addressing the root causes of insecurity, and accept that it is not morally acceptable for only some states to possess nuclear weapons for security (New York Times, 12-02-04).

—The Government of Canada should press for the creation of international peace enforcement units based on Secretary-General Boutros-Ghali's ideas for a quick-reaction force composed of national elements—which in turn would be based on volunteers from the regular units of national military forces (Canadian Priorities 1995: 25).

Canada should seek to improve the UN's Register of Conventional Arms by proposing more universal reporting, the prohibition of arms sales to countries that do not report to the Register, improved definitions to include domestic procurement and national holdings, and prohibiting Canadian sales to non-registrants (ibid: 33).

## 5.2 Sustainable Development

### *5.2.1 Current Profile*

The goal of "sustainable" development (which in fact applies to all countries), as defined by the World Commission on Environment and Development, is "to ensure that development and economic growth meet the needs of the present without compromising the ability of the future generations to meet their own needs" (1987: 8).

It assumes that humans have the power to reconcile human affairs with natural laws and to thrive in the process. There is the possibility for a new era of economic growth, one that is based on policies that sustain and expand the environmental resource base. There had been a growing realization that it is impossible to separate economic and environmental issues. Many forms of economic growth occur at the expense of environmental and resources. This, in turn, undermines potential economic development. Poverty is a major cause *and* effect of environmental problems.

Already in 1987, the Commission announced environmental trends that threatened to radically alter the planet. Each year another 6 million hectares of productive dry land turn into worthless desert—roughly the size of Saudi Arabia over three decades. More than 11 million hectares of forest are destroyed yearly—an area about the size of India over three decades. In Europe and America, acid precipitation kills forest and lakes and damages the architectural heritage. The burning of fossil fuels puts into the atmosphere carbon dioxide causing global warming. The greenhouse effect can lead to agricultural production shifts, flooding of coastal cities, and disruption of national economies. The world population recently doubled to 6 billion, and is expected to double again (with 90 percent of the increase occurring in the poorest countries) before stabilizing. This will place another huge burden on the biosphere as we pull more and more raw material from forest, soils, seas and waterways. The same can be said for industrial production, which has grown 50-fold in the past century, with four-fifths of this growth since 1950. Another sort of trend is the growth in manmade and natural disasters: drought-caused crises and starvation; chemical spills and explosions; nuclear reactor burn-downs; unsafe drinking water and urban smog; and land mismanagement, causing immensely destructive floods and mudslides. Such disasters appear to be doubling each decade in recent times (ibid 1987: 1–9).

The Declaration of the UN Conference on the Human Environment, agreed on at Stockholm in 1972, was a groundbreaking soft-law instrument that provided for limitations by governments on activities that adversely affect the environment of neighbors or the world. But there have been other agreements concerning protection of the ozone layer, biodiversity, climate change, pollution of international waters, Antarctica, habitat and species protection, desertification, transboundary movement of hazardous products and wastes, and the placing of arms in space (Strong 2000: 330).

It is easy to get the impression that since the inception of the "sustainable development" terminology, many people have unwittingly set aside concerns about official development aid (ODA). Donor countries give development aid to developing countries, but often with strings attached, such as a requirement to buy goods and services in the donor country, or to follow specific practices such as "good governance."

The total system of those involved includes UN programs (such as the UNDP) and funds, specialized agencies (e.g. UNICEF) and financial institutions (like the World Bank), regional development banks, the bilateral aid programs of wealthier states (such as the Canadian International Development Agency). ODA is bolstered by the contributions of many, many non-governmental organizations (such as Oxfam and Plan International). Still, the amount of aid has declined in the 1980s and 90s, and "conditionality" (the necessity that recipient countries follow the policies dictated by the donors) based on the 'Washington Consensus' has run rampant. Some recipient countries cannot use aid for current expenditures such as teachers' and health workers' salaries. In addition, depressed commodity prices, agricultural and textile protectionism in the North, and continuing debts burdens, as well as a downturn in development finance during the 1990s stifled growth in many developing countries.

According to the *Global Monitoring Report* on the Millennium Development Goals (MDGs) of the UN and prepared by the IMF/World Bank, aggregate income growth between 2000 and 2005 suggested a significant drop in world poverty, perhaps by as much as 10 percent. But progress has been uneven, mainly driven by large pockets of population in India and China but leaving other sectors of these countries and many other countries far behind. The year 2005 was meant to have been a watershed in scaling up aid commitments and deepening debt relief for poor countries. Over \$50 billion was pledged in new commitments by 2010, including a doubling of aid to Africa. A new multilateral initiative will eliminate about \$50 billion of debt, reducing debt servicing of the poorest by \$1 billion annually. The problem is that these are all future commitments and the donor countries have made a habit of reneging on their solemn commitments. "Aid", the Report says, "remains poorly coordinated, unpredictable, largely locked into 'special project grants' and often targeted to countries and purposes that are not priorities for the MDGs" (April 2005).

The question of economic development is, along with collective security, the major issue at the heart of the UN and its North-South divisions. When the UN was founded in 1946 only about 20 of the 51 states were "developing" countries from the south. The Afro-Asian Bandung Conference of 1955 with 29 states and 30 national liberation movements called for the end of colonialism and racial discrimination. The great success of the UN's decolonization programme between 1955 and 1964 increased the number of independent countries by 32. In 1961 the Movement of Non-Aligned Countries was born during the Cold War. Increasingly conscious of their majority within the General Assembly but also of their economic domination by the Western capitalist countries, the developing countries started to exercise their power within the UN. The creation of the United Nations Conference on Trade and Development (UNCTAD) in 1964 lead to the founding of the Group of 77 (now with 132 members), the most powerful block in the Assembly. UNCTAD supported the strategy of autonomous industrial development of southern countries, under the control of public powers, and the substitution of local products for the imports from the advanced economies (Ruiz-Diaz 2005: 20).

An extraordinary meeting of the General Assembly in 1974 recognized "it was impossible to achieve balanced and harmonious development of the international community in the current international economic order" and therefore decreed a "New International Economic Order" (NIEO). Later in the year the declaration on the "Rights and Economic Duties of States" proposed the right of nationalization of foreign investments, the submission of transnational corporations to national laws, the regulation of foreign investments, the right to control capital and financial movements, the right of expropriation of foreign capital, and rights over natural resources and development. However, these pronouncements had only a political value without much obligatory legal force and were undermined by three trends. The advanced economies gradually transferred international economic, social and cultural relations away from the General Assembly and its Economic and Security Council (ECOSOC) and into the hands of the World Bank, the International Monetary Fund and later the World Trade Organization where the Northern countries exercised economic and political control. Second, the end of the Cold War signaled the further economic supremacy of the advanced Northern economies and the gradual ending of governmental regulations. During the 1990 the flows of Official Development Aid were virtually cut in half and the foreign debt of the developing countries rose exponentially. They came to distrust the international financial institutions where they had little representation. In 2003, 20 of the major developing economies including China, India, South Africa and Brazil formed the G20 to try to regain a little negotiating power. In the UN the developing countries fought hard to maintain all the prerogatives of the General Assembly where they have a majority. However, the most important change was Asia's winds of economic change. According to the IMF magazine *Finance and Development*, Asia is the fastest growing region in the world, contributing close to 50 percent of world economic growth, with its GDP exceeding that of the European Union and the United States on a purchasing power parity basis (2006 (June): 1) In August 2006 the Governor of the Bank of Canada, David Dodge made a significant speech calling for the emerging economic powers to be better heard within the IMF (*Le Droit* 22-07-06: a36).

## 5.2.2 Sustainable Development – Criticisms

—"At the UN Environment Programme (UNEP) Nairobi headquarters, however, though greeted politely and given full attention, I could sense the contrast—its lack of ideas, relevance and direction. UNEP does provide information, holds conferences, undertakes different research projects and has a prestigious ministerial forum—all useful undertakings. But as the spark plug for environmental renewal and action commensurate with the seriousness of the issues, it sputters. I saw no chance of it evolving into a worthy competitor of the World Trade Organization in pursuing environmental interests in balance with commercial considerations. To imagine it having any serious influence over nation-states or corporations that pollute with impunity and degrade with disregard is just wishful thinking" (Axworthy 2003: 417).

To attain sustainable development, we require approaches that are both interdependent and integrated. This, in turn, necessitates comprehensive institutional policies and interaction, as well as broad popular acceptance. Yet most of the institutions facing those challenges tend to be independent, fragmented, working to relatively narrow mandates with closed decision processes. The management of resources, the environment and the economy is separated. Confidence in international organizations is diminishing and support for them dwindling. The other great institutional flaw is that the bodies responsible for environmental degradation do not have a policy responsibility to contain it (ibid 1987: 9–10).

At the 1992 UN Rio Conference on Environment and Development, the North refused to help developing countries to pay the costs of complying with new environmental standards (Lyons 1995: 43).

Dissatisfaction with the system of international development runs deep. The UN's development work is marked by overlapping and duplication, limited responsiveness, as well as lack of transparency and accountability.... In practice, the independence of the specialized agencies both from ECOSOC and the Secretariat has been wide indeed. Any blunt attempt to bring them under a single central control would undoubtedly fail, for some of the agencies enjoy more support than the UN itself (Canadian Priorities 1995: 39).

## 5.2.3 Sustainable Development – Proposals

—In an autobiographical memoir on his years as Canadian foreign minister, Lloyd Axworthy concluded with an overview of a possible path ahead for institutional developments in sustainable development, which we may summarize as follows. There are increasing calls for a world environment agency. President Jacques Chirac has made a strong case. Axworthy believes it is a goal to strive for. But many experts are nervous about too great a focus on a new institution that can detract from other immediate issues. David Runnals of the Winnipeg-based International Institute for Sustainable Development suggested some building blocks toward an eventual agency:

- The UNEP should be strengthened with a respectable budget.
- Environmental programs should be bunched under a common administration.
- Sustainable development clauses should be written into trade agreements.
- Greater help must be given to Third World countries for environmental matters.

At the same time, work should begin on the creation of a multi-stakeholder World Environmental Network bringing together governments, civil society and business, sparked by universities, think tanks and NGOs. Governments could provide resources. It should include an international information network, a learning network for students, e-democracy contacts between citizens and parliamentarians, and possibly a global environmental youth corps. It is also necessary to work toward giving some environmental agency sufficient authority, power and resources to hold transgressors to account. That means having the power to require disclosure, verify compliance and ultimately impose penalties after an impartial adjudication, as in the WTO (Axworthy 2003: 417–21).

An institutional change that needs to be made is the establishment, based on UNEP, of a much-strengthened world environmental agency with a status and influence equivalent to that of such international agencies as the World Trade Organization (Strong 2000: 297).

The Canadian government should strongly urge the creation within the UN of a Sustainable Development Security Council with full coordination powers over the specialized agencies. To be credible the Canadian government should create an International Development Advisory Council to assist it in formulating development policy (Canadian Priorities 1995: 39).

The World Commission believed that a) technological means and the carrying capacity of the biosphere can be improved by good management to allow for economic growth; b) widespread poverty is no longer inevitable; sustainable development requires meeting the basic needs of all; a world in which poverty is endemic is prone to ecological and other catastrophes; c) the poor must get their share of resources; d) equity would be aided by participatory political systems and greater democracy in international decision-making; e) those who are affluent must adopt lifestyles (especially energy consumption) more in line with the planet's ecological means; f) population size must be in harmony with the productive capacity of the ecosystem; g) in a world of constant change, changes must be consistent with future as well as present needs (World Commission 1987: 8–9).

"The present challenge is to give central economic ministries the responsibility for the quality of those parts of the environment affected by their decisions. The same holds true for the international agencies responsible for development lending, trade regulation, and agricultural development. They too must take the environmental effects of their work into account" (ibid: 12).

The World Bank can support environmentally sound projects. The International Monetary Fund should support wider and longer-term development objectives, including social goals and environmental impacts. All countries should sign the Law of the Sea, fisheries agreements should stop overexploitation, and conventions should control dumping of hazardous wastes at sea. We need a "space regime." The 1959 Antarctic Treaty should include more signatories, and be strengthened to incorporate mineral developments. The Secretary-General needs to designate a high-level center of leadership in the UN to improve coordination and cooperation. The United Nations Environment Programme (UNEP) should be strengthened to be the principal source on environmental data, assessment and reporting, and as the main advocate and agent for change and cooperation. Its Earthwatch program should be the centre of leadership for identifying, assessing and reporting on risks of irreversible damage. A new international programme is necessary for cooperation among non-governmental organizations, scientific bodies, and industry groups for the independent assessment of critical global risks. To provide the legal umbrella, the UN should prepare a universal declaration on environmental protection and sustainable development, and a subsequent convention (ibid 1987: 18–21).

The Nordic UN Project stressed the importance of a multilateral as opposed to bilateral approach, because of "the absence of commercial and political strings, the broad resource base, and the multisectoral and multidisciplinary character of operations" (1991: 33).

## 5.3 Global Democracy

### *5.3.1 Current Profile and Criticisms*

Many of those who are critical of international institutions believe that a "democratic deficit" is the main cause of their biased policies and inept practices. Although the Charter of the United Nations starts with the expression "We the peoples…," the UN has in fact become the preserve of government officials. All international institutions are, in effect, responsible solely to their member state governments. But governments, even in nominally democratic countries, have done very little to "democratize" their foreign policies and practices. They are still run much as they were under kings and autocrats. In most countries, foreign affairs, defense and diplomacy come directly under the authority of the executive (the president or prime minister and their cabinet and security advisors). There are few public debates, and parliamentarians rarely get a chance to influence or oversee international relations. Parliamentarians do play a limited role through legislative foreign affairs committees in some countries, in general debates about foreign policy in others, and their participation in international parliamentary associations. Still, the public is poorly informed, and consequently most feel they cannot understand or influence the subject. Only on occasion is foreign policy an issue in elections.

At the international level there is no parliamentary oversight, and there are no participatory, elected, representative institutions. And there is very little in the way of public information and responsibility to democratic institutions. Most decision-making, if not by definition profoundly secret, is at least off the record and behind closed doors. In addition, aside from a lack of democracy, the most powerful international institutions are also chastised by their critics for being under the control of a small elite composed of wealthy, powerful countries.

To democratize international politics, some commentators have called for several decades for global democratic institutions. Others, more recent, have proposed democratic practices such as a reinforcement of international law, greater information and participation through civil society organizations, more transparency and pubic knowledge in decision-making, and more direct responsibility and reporting to public institutions.

Those in favor of democratic international institutions are confronted with the reality that more than half the peoples of the world live under authoritarian governments and/or have little or no experience with democratic processes and culture. Just coming up with a representative system would be a formidable task. Their response is to suggest a parliamentary assembly (as in the European Community) or other forms of consultative bodies as a stopgap until the world is better prepared for a democratic regime.

### *5.3.2 Global Democracy – Proposals*

—Stiglitz concludes, "Democratic globalization means that these decisions must be made with the full participation of all the peoples of the world. Our system of global government can only work if there is an acceptance of multilateralism" (Stiglitz 2003: 258).

—Amy Chua believes that democracy in the developing world is often more nominal than real (Chua 2004: 273). Making democracy more than just majority rule, and endowing it with constitutional protection for minorities and property could improve this. But emphasis must be placed on prevention by rethinking the process of democratization. It cannot be achieved just by shipping out ballot boxes and teams of election inspectors. Although it may be difficult to limit the extension of suffrage, as it happened in the West, there may be ways to slow down and stabilize the process. It could start with active participation and legitimate competition in local elections. Legal communities could be strengthened and be made more independent. The West could stop uncritically propping up authoritarian regimes, which should be encouraged to grant more economic and personal freedoms.

—Barber makes extensive proposals for promoting "preventive democracy." These are composed of two parts. The first is protecting national security against terrorists in a manner consistent with liberal traditions and international law, and not by attacking states. Police and intelligence operations should be used to target terrorist agents, cells, networks, financing, camps and weaponry. The goal is to secure America, or any other country, against terrorism without destroying liberty (Barber 2003: 149–54).

The second component is "global democracy-building" both within and among states. It means far more than elections and majority rule. As described by Barber, its characteristics include a patient, long-term approach; a process of local struggle; spreading education and fostering citizenship; building civic organizations; economic development; outside, long-term cooperation, economic support, civic education, and advisors; and international institutions that provide a framework for economic recovery and civic and democratic development (2003: 145–49).

"Preventative democracy" uses a multilateral approach to help seed learning, liberty and self-government to empower the powerless. It starts from a "declaration of interdependence." Second, close civilian cooperation and citizen-to-citizen exchanges are of the essence, using deliberate, lengthy and persistent engagement. Barber claims a start has already been made "led by citizens rather than by governments"—just as in the past, we might add. Third, massive aid must be given to foster education. According to UNICEF good-will ambassador Harry Belafonte, around the world there are 121 million children not in school. Abolishing school fees would be the single-most-effective way to give them opportunity (Belafonte 2004). Fourth, civic organizations and NGOs must selectively engage public opinion using the World Wide Web and publicity campaigns. Fifth, given global interdependence, it is necessary also to foster global citizenship, education, cooperation, law and democracy. Sixth, the U.S. should return to using its weight to promote common rules and law. But it is individuals who must act to become global citizens, not passengers (ibid 155).

—Ann Florini believes that at the global level, "direct electoral systems would be unwieldy." By this we can presume she means that it would be difficult to organize them and to obtain prior agreement on the rules of representation. Also, half the world still has little or no democratic experience. She thinks, however, that the transparency and participation she is projecting would make possible a "highly democratic, albeit non-electoral, system of transnational governance" because it would provide voice and accountability. "Sunlight really is the best disinfectant," Florini claims (2003: 208–9). She argues that we should not confuse the form of democracy with its function. Democracy requires that the people have two things: a voice, and mechanisms for holding officials accountable. "The speed and scale at which decision-making must now take place has outstripped the capacity of purely electoral systems of democracy to cope. If democracy is to survive globalization, we must attend to the free flow of information…. Decision-makers must explain their actions and decisions to the broader public…, and they must allow the public greater say" (2003: 15–16). And, of course, international governmental representatives will still answer to their national electorates.

—According to Dieter Heinrich of the World Federalists, the path to the reform of international institutions centers on the democratization of the United Nations. The first stage is the creation of a consultative Parliamentary Assembly made up of representatives elected by national parliaments. The example has already been set by the European Parliament of the European Union, the parliamentary assembly of the Conference on Security and Cooperation in Europe (CSCE) and several UN agencies. He believes that proposals for an elected citizens' assembly are unworkable at the present time because political will is low and it would take an enormous coalition of social forces to pressure governments. His proposal has the merit of being simple and of relatively little cost. Members would already have legitimacy and moral authority. Since the fall of communism more and more governments have democratic parliaments, and those which do not may just stay away so as not to be "contaminated". However, the heart of Heinrich's argument is that people who speak for citizens will finally be brought into the United Nations, giving citizens a voice within the organization to campaign for full-fledged democracy later on. It would gain leverage on national governments, act as a symbol and help displace the state-centric ideology. Heinrich brushes aside concerns about representatives from authoritarian states and about democratic representatives being under instructions from their parties. Nor does he elaborate much of a strategy for "just bringing a UN Parliamentary Assembly into being" (1992: 18).

—A radical position on global democratization is presented by George Monbiot. He starts from the premise "If we can – as most people do – agree that democracy is the best way to run a nation, it is hard to think of any reason why its should not be the best way to run the world" (2003: 46). However, he wants it to be both an economic and a political democracy. He therefore embarks on a fourfold attack: a directly elected world parliament; a democratized United Nations General Assembly, which captures the powers now vested in the Security Council; an 'International Clearing House', which automatically discharges trade deficits and prevents accumulation of debt; and a 'Fair Trade Organization' which restrains the rich while emancipating the poor (2003: 4). Monbiot believes the people must simply mobilize themselves and "democratically" elect their own World Parliament. He would limit it to 600 seats with world constituencies of 10 million people. Some would straddle national borders, which would make representatives "less parochial". He estimates the election might cost 5 billion $ with annual costs of one billion $ and construction costs of 300 million $. He recognizes it would be necessary to raise funds (perhaps a global lottery) and set up an electoral commission (2003: 84–99). But like many people with broad ideas, Monbiot glosses over such democratic process details as electoral experience and the means and costs of party organization – to take just two examples.

Of course, the authors we have consulted are by no means the only or even the most important people writing about improvements to global governance. They were chosen because they combined an interest in democracy with an analysis of the globalization context. Many others have written about global and UN reform. For instance, the World Commission on Global Governance preceded them. Without saying "no" to democracy, the Commission was circumspect about its support for a directly elected peoples' assembly to complement the General Assembly, or for an assembly of parliamentarians as a constituent assembly to prepare for the people's chamber. Among the problems is the fact that more than half the world presently has no experience with democracy or elections. In addition, a people's assembly would have to have electorates (constituencies) of 12 million people to keep the membership down to 500. This would prevent many countries from having even one representative. The Commission thought it would be best to start, "when the time comes," with parliamentarians acting as a constituent. But nothing should happen (except for the creation of a "Civil Society Forum" and a "right to petition" as in the European Union) until the General Assembly has devised a "revitalized role for itself" (1995: 256–58).

More recently a group called Ubuntu, which presents itself as a "world forum of networks of civil society", held a series of meetings in 2003–4 with representatives of major INGOs specializing in global governance. They formulated a three-step model to move the world toward a more democratic United Nations.

Scenario 1: Create an Inter-parliamentary Assembly to coordinate the work of members of national parliaments. Develop an individual complaints mechanism.

Scenario 2: Establish an independent Assembly of Representatives (World Parliament) with consultative functions within the UN system. Develop a mechanism for consultative World Referendums. Establish new international courts on Human Rights, Economic and Financial Crimes, and Environmental Crimes.

Scenario 3: The United Nations General Assembly (UNGA) would become a two-chamber parliament, composed of a House of the States to represent countries as now, and an Assembly of Representatives elected by universal suffrage. The new UNGA would have authority to adopt binding resolutions with central control over the UN system. A new Peace and Security Council, composed of world regions (permanent member status and the veto would be reviewed and presumably abolished), would be under the supervision of the UN General Assembly. A reconstituted Economic, Social and Environmental Council (ESEC) would have effective control over all financial and trade institutions and UN agencies and programs. These would, in effect, become specialized technical agencies fully integrated into the UN system and accountable to the General Assembly through the ESEC. They would no longer have their own general assemblies or annual conferences. They would hold specific assemblies with actors from all relevant sectors. There would be a new executive mechanism for an interconnected, civil and criminal world legal system, in which the ICJ would have constitutional jurisdiction over all parts of the UN system. Civil society, local governments and international business would have the right to participation in the specific assemblies of the UN and its technical agencies (Ubuntu 2004: 14–15).

## 5.4 Relations with Non-Governmental Organizations (NGOs) and "Civil Society"

*"The legitimacy of civil society organizations derives from what they do and not from whom they represent or from any kind of external mandate. In the final analysis, they are what they do"* (Cardoso Report 2003: 3).

### 5.4.1 The Current Profile

In this section we are not evaluating the concept of 'civil society' as such. It is taken more or less as a given, meaning international non-governmental organizations which have relationships with international institutions. It is the state of that relationship that is under examination here. The Commission on Global Governance pointed out that up until the last two decades, governments and intergovernmental institutions were the main actors in international relations. Gradually non-governmental organizations both national and international (NGOs and INGOs), citizens' movements, transnational corporations, academia, and mass media have taken their place as partners on the international stage as part of an emerging global civil society (1995: 32–35). Often, INGOs have financial resources and operational capacities that are greater than those of the international governmental organizations with which they deal. The exact definition of civil society is somewhat slippery. It is meant to include all non-governmental actors working in the public interest. Generally, governmental and market institutions are excluded as are ones which use violence. One limiting case is that of transnational corporations, whom many consider to be a special category of actor because they are operating in their own interest. However, corporations can and do also operate in the public interest, so on these occasions they can be included in the general definition.

The exponential growth of the world's international non-governmental organizations has been astounding, going from 176 in 1909 to 28,900 in 1993, and now estimated at over 50,000. The take-off period started in the mid-1960s, even in developing countries. For instance, Africa's share of country memberships in INGOs doubled from 8 to 16 percent (ibid: 32). The UNDP claims that 250 million people are now reached by NGOs, as opposed to 100 million in the 1980s. Their rising budget of $7.2 billion is equivalent to 13 percent of net disbursements of official aid (Segaar 2004: 3) Civil society organizations fulfil many functions: channeling the interests and energies of many associations outside government; and offering knowledge, skills, enthusiasm, a non-bureaucratic approach, expertise, a grassroots perspective, voluntary contributions, administrative efficiency, and flexibility—attributes not always found in governmental institutions. For these and other reasons, many international non-governmental organizations have consultative status in ECOSOC and attend UN summits on an ad hoc basis, some having been accorded "major group" status. More and more they are tempted to be active within the ranks of governmental programs and projects. Already in 1999, the annual report of the World Bank stated that the percentage of World Bank approved projects run through NGOs had increased from 25 percent over the period 1987–95 to 50 percent in 1998.

Forman and Segaar summarize the role of civil society organizations in global governance:

> NGOs are now engaged along the entire policy cycle. Their activities include advocacy, rule making, and standard setting; knowledge generation and dissemination; promotion, monitoring and evaluation of treaty obligations; and delivery of social services in communities around the globe. Their contribution to global policy increases pluralism, gives voice to the aspirations of politically marginalized groups, and takes up critical issues that might otherwise not surface on the political radar screen. But rather than being simply voices of advocacy and opposition, they are increasingly engaging government and multilateral organizations as partners in global governance initiatives (2006: 216).

It is not that the degree of penetration by NGOs in intergovernmental decision-making is much greater than 70 years ago (Charnovitz 1997) but rather that the relationship is all-pervasive. NGOs (and corporations for that matter) are much more present, more diverse, and cover more issues. According to Forman and Segaar the relationships have become "political and operational, rather than formal and ceremonial" (ibid 216). Their use of network structure and information technology allows them to mobilize constituencies across the globe. Their influence is flexible. Major examples include networks such as the Coalition for the International Criminal Court, the International Action Network on Small Arms, Jubilee 2000, the Climate Action Network, and the Coalition to Stop the Use of Child Soldiers. They have even moved to counter accusations that they lack transparency by providing annual reports of their finances and assets. Paul Wapner argues that their mechanisms of accountability are greater than those of states or corporations (2002: 197–205).

## 5.4.2 Civil Society: Criticisms

—NGOs and especially their coalitions have clear weaknesses in terms of equity and sustasinability. They lack a clear hierarchy, membership and established organizational and governance mechanisms. Northern NGOs tend to exercise undue influence over agendas and practices. NGOs and even coalitions tend to be issue oriented, have a very fluid constituency and sometimes offer little accountability or oversight. Each member is independent and coalitions tend to dissolve as soon as they reach their goals (Forman and Segaar 2006: 217).

—NGOs have been one important expression of the emerging form of global citizenship. But dominated as they usually are by professional staff and small, somewhat exclusive boards of directors, they are often not very democratic in the way they make decisions or are held accountable. Protests on the streets are another effective way to give people voice, but they are unreliable as a serious source of debate and deliberation. And mass international conferences are never democratic. In the future, one of the most challenging tasks will be to give people a real sense that their voice will be heard (Axworthy 2003: 421).

—"Civil society is therefore much more diverse and fragmented than governments and international organizations. This is, of course, one of its virtues, but it leads to difficulties in providing for the participation of civil society in the official process of governance. Many civil society groups and organizations hold common positions on particular issues, but it is seldom feasible for them to present a united front. Sometimes the very number of small and often fragmented organizations inhibits agreement on common positions, and even governments that wish to accommodate their concerns have trouble doing so" (Strong 2000: 338).

In some countries, governments have seen the organizations of civil society as the political opposition, and their participation on the international scene is seen with suspicion and resistance. As a consequence, international organizations are still predominantly Western in their organization and the Western ethos takes up a disproportionate share of the space. Participation from developing countries has increased dramatically in recent years but the imbalance continues to exist.... Also, they lack the broadly representative character of governments (Strong 2000: 339).

—Civil servants in intergovernmental organizations have been cautious in acknowledging that NGOs can be helpful partners. But since the Rio Conference on Environment and Development, where more than 1,400 were accredited and thousands more participated in the Global Forum, NGOs have increasingly participated in summit conferences.... Policy makers must serve, engage, and mobilize a much wider variety of institutions—and hence to cope with a broader range of interests and operating styles (World Commission on GG 1995: 34).

## 5.4.3 Civil Society – Proposals

—Ubuntu: Civil society should achieve a truly consultative status within the UN General Assembly as well as the IMF, the World Bank and the World Trade Organization. Eventually they should have status with the International Criminal Court to request opinions on a consultative basis (2004: 11–13).

—The "Cardoso Commission" (Secretary-General's Panel of Eminent Persons on Civil Society and UN Relationships) called upon the UN to include "all constituencies relevant to issues" under discussion and not just governments. The General Assembly should accept "high quality independent input" from additional actors. The Security Council too should include presentations by civil society specialists (this was actually done). Structurally, the UN needs to name an Under-Secretary-General in Charge of a new "Office of Constituency, Engagement and Partnership". It would comprise a Civil Society Unit, a Partnership Development Unit, an Elected Representatives Liason Unit, the Global Compact Office, and the Secretariat of the Permanent Forum on Indigenous Issues. At a very practical level, Cardoso called on the UN to appoint 40 specialists to engage the various local constituencies within the offices of resident coordinators within countries (Cardoso 2003: proposals).

—A Consultative Assembly would also be created, with membership drawn from three main types of organizations: transnational firms; trade unions and professional associations; and a range of educational, scientific, cultural, religious, and public-interest organizations (NGOs) active around the issues central to the UN agenda (Reimagining the Future 2000: 2).

The UN must reach out to civil society organizations, give them greater opportunities for effective participation in deliberations, and establish ongoing operational relations with organizations that share common interests. They must be regarded and treated as full partners and not as subordinate actors (Strong 2000: 299). The UN must hear all groups that have a legitimate interest in specific issues. The system of accreditation of qualified NGOs has been useful, but it cuts out participation of less well-organized groups from developing countries (ibid: 339).

—Pending the evolution of a parliamentary or people's assembly within the UN, a start should be made by convening an annual Forum of Civil Society. It would consist of representatives of organizations accredited to the General Assembly, a new and expanded category of accredited organizations, which are presently only in the ECOSOC. They could perhaps discuss items on the General Assembly agenda and would meet in the Plenary Hall of the General Assembly prior to its annual meeting, perhaps preceded by regional Forums. It would be an entry point for public opinion into the UN, and would be quite different from the present annual conference of NGOs (Commission on Global Governance 1995: 257–60).

To enable civil society to activate the UN's potential for preventive diplomacy and the settlement of disputes where the security of people is or could be endangered, a right of petition should be available to international civil society. This would require the creation of an independent Council for Petitions of five to seven eminent persons selected for their merit by the Secretary-General and approved by the General Assembly, preferably created by a Charter amendment. It would be strictly circumscribed in scope by being limited to redressing wrongs that could imperil people's security, and by going through a screening process with clear criteria. Decisions would act as recommendations for action to the Secretary-General and the Security Council. There is a precedent in the Subcommittee on Small Territories, Petitions, Information and Assistance, working with the Special Committee on the Implementation of the Declaration on Decolonization. This committee provided an opportunity for causes to be aired and grievances voiced, and ultimately for action to be taken to advance decolonization. The right of petition would incorporate new voices and provide a practical opportunity to right the massive wrongs that imperil people (Commission on Global Governance 1995: 260–262).

## A Recent Example of a Broad Set of Reform Proposals

Analysis of *A More Secure World: Our Shared Responsibility* (2004)
Report of the UN High-Level Panel on Threats, Challenges and Change
And Kofi Annan's *In Larger Freedom* (2004).

> "*... the most ambitious reform drive in United Nations history ...*" Edward C. Luck (2005).

In 2003, Annan named a High Level Panel on Threats, Challenges and Change to analyse threats to peace, investigate how well existing policies and institutions are meeting them, and recommend changes to provide a more effective collective response. Its report, *A More Secure World: Our Shared Responsibility* (www.un.org/secureworld) outlined six clusters of threats: economic and social including poverty and infectious diseases; inter-state conflict and rivalry; internal war including civil war, state collapse and genocide; nuclear, radiological, biological, and chemical weapons; terrorism; and trans-national organized crime.

The High Level Panel report concluded, first, that the threats are interconnected, and no state acting alone can defeat them. Any threat to one is a threat to all; so all states share an interest in collective security. Second, given the gravity of the threats, the world needs more commitment to prevention and the best preventive strategy is to support development, including the adequate resourcing of the Millennium Goals. In other words, the Panel made a considerable leap by demonstrating the connection between development and security.

The High Level Panel report was followed by the release in January 2005 of the report of the UN Millennium Project. The report, 'Investing in Development: A Practical Plan to Achieve the Millennium Development Goals,' is also known as the Sachs Report after the Millennium Project leader, economist and anti-poverty campaigner Jeffrey Sachs. The Sachs report's central idea is that the eleven remaining years would be enough time to achieve the MDGs—if the global community really started taking them seriously (www.unmillenniumproject.org).

On the basis of the High Level Panel and Sachs reports Secretary-General Annan consulted with governments. His recommendations for a security system that is efficient, effective and *equitable* were synthesized in the Secretary General's report to the General Assembly "In Larger Freedom", published in April 2005 (www.un.org/inlargerfreedom). This package of reforms formed the basis for further negotiations that extended throughout the summer in preparation for a new UN Summit of world leaders to celebrate the UN's 60th anniversary, to review and recommit to the Millennium Development Goals, and to attack institutional reform.

The task of managing negotiations and synthesizing successive versions of a draft Summit "outcome document" fell to Jean Ping of Gabon, President of the General Assembly. After further consultations, he submitted a draft outcome document June 3, a revised version July 22, and another revision August 5 ("Draft Outcome Document of the High-level Plenary Meeting of the General Assembly of September 2005" UN document A/59/HLPM/CRP.1/Rev.2).

Unlike the relatively focused reports of Sachs, the High Level Panel and the Secretary-General, which reflected greater conceptual coherence, the drafting and revision process led to a document that read more like a wish list of the desires of every constituency within the UN.

Enter John Bolton, President Bush's new ambassador to the United Nations, who told envoys to the UN three weeks before the Summit that the United States had 750 amendments to propose that could scrap 400 passages in the Draft Outcome Document that had been negotiated for six months. With negotiations re-opened, Russia and the Group of 77 (G-77, in fact 132 developing states) submitted hundreds more amendments. Final negotiations started on August 29 between a group of 30 representative states put together by Mr. Ping with the aim of drafting a consensus document (www.reformtheun.org Aug. 30, 2005).

Outside observers were hard pressed to know whether the Americans were out to sabotage the process or to negotiate from a position of strength. It seems the latter was the case as Bolton accepted to negotiate on the basis of the Draft Negotiating Document and items such as the Millennium Development Goals were still included. Following the conference, President Bush was at pains to say he endorsed the MDGs. However, the Americans had succeeded in reducing many references: to multilateralism as a fundamental value; to the UN as a main actor with increased resources; to greater use of the International Court of Justice; to enhancement of the General Assembly; and to creating a strategic military reserve for the UN. The U.S. also seems to be having some success in enhancing references to peace and security, international law, the private market, and the obligation of developing countries to provide good governance to attract investment. There was agreement to disagree on 0.7 percent of GNP as a target for development aid and on the language for disarmament. Some states tried to fight back with attempts to include passages affirming multilateralism and rejecting unilateralism, but without success. Members found it impossible to come to agreement on a simple definition of terrorism, on arms of mass destruction and on nuclear proliferation.

If these reports are discussed here, it is not because they are necessarily the best or most elaborate studies of UN reform, but rather to offer the reader a more coherent example of one of the myriad sets of reform proposals commissioned by the UN and others. Once again we will see that seemingly intelligent and timely suggestions have been offered about *what* reforms should be made but without adequate consideration about *how* to get states to adopt them. The world has been offered a road map to reform but no vehicle.

The question posed here is: could these reports have helped bring about the deep reforms that would enable the United Nations and other international institutions to confront the challenges of the 21st century? The Panel's thoughtful study might have been a source of real movement in this direction, but in the end it was not able to attain the high goals the Secretary-General set for it and, in reality, neither the Panel nor Annan confronted the issues of institutional transformation.

The *Secure World* report made far-reaching yet pragmatic proposals. One can only applaud its enunciation of a number of essential principles:

- Credible and sustainable collective security for all in the 21st century must be not only efficient and effective, but also *equitable*. (Let's call it the principle of the third "e.") Although the Report does not define its three terms, we may assume from previous reports that efficiency would refer to stand-by forces, a command structure, good logistics and proper planning. The notion of security being 'equitable' should remind us of the profound meaning behind the expression "peace *and* justice". The Panel suggests that for collective security to be effective, the UN must have common goals with other actors—national, regional, civil society etc. but it must also be able to demonstrate an ability to stop large scale killings and enforce the rule of law.
- The case for collective security rests on three pillars: that "threats recognize no national boundaries, are connected, and must be addressed at the global and regional as well as at the national levels. No state, no matter how powerful, can, by its own efforts, make itself invulnerable to today's threats" (p. 11). Without mutual recognition of threat, there can be no security. We all share responsibility for each other's security (p. 12).
- Threats to global security are interconnected and must be dealt with in a comprehensive manner. The UN's founders also recognized the indivisibility of security, economic development and human freedom.
- The primary challenge for the United Nations is to create a framework for preventive action, including enhanced mediation and sanctions. The first step, however, is to concentrate on development because it is the foundation for sustainable security.
- An effective and principled counter-terrorism strategy must respect the rule of law and the observance of human rights. Effective collective security may require the use of force, but it must start with the rules of international law that must govern any decision to go to war. Otherwise, anarchy will prevail.
- In approaching United Nations reform, it is as important today as it was in 1945 to combine power and principle. Recommendations that ignore underlying power realities will be doomed to irrelevance, and ones based on raw power will not gain the legitimacy required to change behavior.
- The Panel endorses the emerging norm that there is a collective international responsibility to protect people . . . in the event of genocide or other large-scale killing … that sovereign Governments have proved powerless or unwilling to prevent (p. 57).

The report is worth its weight in gold just to have underlined these principles. It is a major step forward in legitimizing new international norms. But it goes on to make significant practical proposals as well. For instance, poverty, infectious diseases and environmental degradation must be dealt with because they constitute conditions from which threats emerge. Criteria are proposed for the appropriate use of military force to fulfill the UN's "responsibility to protect"—seriousness of threat, proper purpose, last resort, proportional means, and balance of consequences (pp. 57–8). For the first time, a clear and acceptable definition of terrorism is suggested for adoption by the UN: "Terrorism is any action … that is intended to cause death or serious bodily harm to civilians or non-combatants, when the purpose of such an act, by its nature or context, is to intimidate a population, or to compel a government or an international organization to do or abstain from doing any act" (p. 49).

The report went on to make detailed proposals to enhance "biological" security and reinforce nuclear non-proliferation. The Panel recognized that the UN Security Council must be more representative of today's world. It put forth two options, models A and B. Model A provides for six new permanent seats without a veto. Model B creates a new category (tier) of eight, four-year, renewable-term seats. There are also proposals to add several new two-year non-renewable seats. The effect of both models on regional distributions would be to add two new (permanent or renewable) seats for Africa, two for Asia-Pacific, one or two more for the Americas, and one for Europe. Both models imply that France and the United Kingdom would give up their permanent seats in favour of one for the European Community but the European region could just add Germany.

The one new structure the report recommends is a post-conflict "Peace-building Commission" to advise on the many difficult tasks of nation reconstruction and to keep world attention focused on the various cases. The UN Economic and Security Council (ECOSOC) should create a smaller executive committee and focus on the socio-economic bases of security. And, more importantly, ECOSOC should transform itself into a development council. Finally, the report proposes steps to set up a new Human Rights Council to regain the legitimacy lost by the UN Human Rights Commission. Recommendations are also made to strengthen the Secretariat, including a one-time review and renewal of personnel.

Kofi Annan's Report: *In Larger Freedom.* Kofi Annan presented his own recommendations for reform of the UN in March 2005. The content of the Secretary-General's report, In Larger Freedom (a title taken from the UN Charter, (www.un.org/inlargerfreedom) was quite similar to that of the High-Level Panel. However, he placed it in the broader UN context and framework of the Millennium Declaration with sections on freedom from want and fear, living in dignity and strengthening the UN. As Secretary-General he knew his report would have to appeal to all the constituencies within his large family to include, for example, women and the environment, so that none would feel left out. Thereby he sacrificed the Panel's focus. He also felt obliged to include many non-structural, policy recommendations such as the need to achieve the target of 0.7 percent of gross national income for official development assistance. At the same time, coming from a CEO, the proposals became more precise projects and included suggested deadlines.

Most of Annan's key recommendations followed almost exactly those of his High Level Panel. However, in some cases they offered more detail. A significant proposal, because it rallied a large number of major players, was the recommendation that the 53-member Commission on Human Rights be replaced by a smaller, standing Human Rights Council. To be elected directly by the General Assembly by a two-thirds majority, it would be more likely to keep at arms length the states with the worst human rights records. The objective was to get rid of the embarrassing "credibility deficit" of the existing Commission whose non-exclusive membership was filled on a rotational, regional basis so that violators of human rights could always find allies to block investigations or condemnations. Annan's proposal would oblige potential members of the Council to declare their full support for the UN human rights regime so it would become a "society of the committed". As an expert, permanent Council it would (in theory) be able to act preventively, respond quickly to crises, follow up on its recommendations, and take action when these are not implemented. If the idea were not seen as an amendment to the Charter, its opponents would not be able to block its adoption without focusing international attention on their own human rights abuses. By 2006 some of Annan's recommendations had been accepted.

Surprisingly, the Secretary-General took the rather unprincipled position of recommending to members that with regard to the Security Council they "consider the two options (of the Panel)… as well as any other viable proposals in terms of size and balance that emerged on the basis of either model". This started a process of haggling about increased representation on the Security Council that almost derailed the whole reform process and ignored the issues of improved efficiency. It can be argued that it was not even the moment to bring up the highly intractable question of the Security Council.

Annan elaborated on the establishment of an intergovernmental Peacebuilding Commission, a Peacebuilding Support Office within the UN Secretariat, and a voluntary standing fund to support it. The Secretary-General noted, "There is a gaping hole in the United Nations institutional machinery: no part of the UN system effectively addresses the challenge of helping countries with the transition from war to lasting peace" (para. 114). He proposed a sub-set of Security Council and ECOSOC members to form a Commission that in the aftermath of war would have the functions of organizing the planning, institution building, financing, coordination, information sharing, and review that are necessary for an effective transition to peace. This general outline was supported by an Assembly resolution at the end of 2005.

Other institutional reforms proposed by the Secretary-General included establishing:

- An International Financial Facility to support an immediate front-loading of official development assistance;
- A worldwide early warning system for all natural hazards;
- A convention on nuclear terrorism;
- A UN civilian police standby capacity;
- A Democracy Fund to assist countries seeking to establish or strengthen their democracy;
- A streamlined agenda and committee structure in the General Assembly;
- A focus on development for the Economic and Social Security Council;
- Charter changes to delete the Military Staff Committee and the Trusteeship Council.

A number of longstanding but mild structural reforms did *not* make it into the Secretary-General's report. Among them are a more powerful environmental agency; the recommendations of His Panel of Eminent Persons on UN-Civil Society Relations (the Cardoso Report); and a smaller, more effective Executive Committee for the ECOSOC. Both his and the Panel's reports also fail to point out that not all threats are global and some of them may be more effectively handled by regional or national security systems.

The third act of what would become almost a tragedy was played out in the negotiations in the summer of 2005 over a draft synthesis document based on the reports of the High-level Panel and the Secretary-General. By this time, the various stages in the report of the Volcker Commission on the Iraq oil-for-food scandal had started coming out implicating both UN personnel and Annan's son. While Volcker also implicated the Security Council among others, it was one more factor that gave the enemies of multilateralism an opportunity to blunt the Secretary-General's thrust towards reform and to deviate his proposals from structures to management.

The following assessment is a comparison of the Draft Outcome Document of August 5, 2005 of the General Assembly (A/59HLPM/CRP.1/Rev.2) upon which the negotiations were made, and the final outcome document of September 13, which was approved by the 154 world leaders attending the largest Summit in history (Trent and Watt 2005a).

## ACHIEVEMENTS:

- The Millennium Development Goals were reaffirmed.
- The Summit recognized new innovative sources of financing to fund development objectives, such as an International Finance Facility or taxing international commerce, e.g. a tax on air travel to be implemented by countries like France.
- The General Assembly accepted the new responsibility for the UN to protect people from genocide, ethnic cleansing and crimes against humanity.

- The UN capacity for peacekeeping, peacemaking and peacebuilding will be strengthened and there is a detailed blueprint for a new Peacebuilding Commission to help war-torn countries.
- The Office of the UN High Commissioner for Human Rights was to be strengthened and the budget doubled.
- The proposal to create a new Human Rights Council was accepted.
- The Outcome Document includes decisions: to create a worldwide warning system for natural disasters; to mobilize new resources for the fight against HIV/AIDS, TB and malaria; and to improve the UN's Central Emergency Revolving Fund for disaster relief.
- It contains, for the first time in UN history, an unqualified condemnation, by all member states, of terrorism.
- There was approval of new, independent auditing and oversight mechanisms for the UN administration. Some new authority over staffing and priorities was accorded to the Secretary-General by the General Assembly, including a cull of obsolete tasks and a one-time buy-out of staff (later blocked by G-77).
- A new Democracy Fund, created prior to the Summit, will strengthen the UN's role in promoting democratic governance in countries around the world.

FAILURES:
- There was an affirmation of old development pledges but without firm, new commitments from the rich. The document failed to break significant new ground on most major issues relating to debt, trade and aid.
- There was no definition of Terrorism because a small number of countries insisted on excluding 'freedom fighters'.
- The Secretary-General was not given the strong executive authority required to manage the UN on a day-to-day basis.
- Criteria for the use of force by the Security Council were not included, which may make the "responsibility to protect" rather toothless.
- The world leaders and diplomats were still not able to reform the Security Council or any of the other organs or structures of the UN.
- There was a failure to affirm a wide range of previously agreed commitments on nuclear proliferation and disarmament.
- The modest efforts contained in preparatory drafts to strengthen environmental governance were stripped from the final document.
- All references to the International Criminal Court were removed.
- Notwithstanding the breakthrough on "responsibility to protect," the document strengthened the sovereignty of nation states at the expense of the human security of the world's citizens.
- The "Sachs programme" of immediate, practical aid was eviscerated.
- There were virtually no reforms of the fundamental institutions of the UN system.

POSTPONEMENTS:

- A comprehensive convention on terrorism was adopted just after the Summit (without a definition).
- The General Assembly needs to "continue consideration of the responsibility to protect populations" (#139).
- Before the Secretary-General can establish a "rule of law assistance unit" he must submit a report to the General Assembly (#134e).
- "We commit ourselves to discuss and define the notion of human security in the General Assembly" (#143).
- The Group of Four (Brazil, Germany, India and Japan) met during the Summit and announced they would submit a new resolution on Security Council reform to the General Assembly. The Assembly was requested to review progress by year-end.
- The new president of the General Assembly, Jan Eliasson of Sweden, was charged with conducting negotiations to establish the Human Rights Council during the 60th session.
- The Secretary-General is to report to the 60th Session on an ethics office, the implementation of management reforms, and budgetary needs.
- The new Peacebuilding Commission was to begin work no later than December 31, 2005. The Secretary-General is to set up a peacebuilding support office within the secretariat and establish a multi-year standing Peacebuilding Fund.

In conclusion, a great deal of the impact of the 2005 UN World Summit would depend on negotiations over the key postponed items. Still, it is worth remembering that until days before the Summit, after the arrival of U.S. Ambassador Bolton with his 450 amendments, it appeared there might not be any final document. However, to reach consensus, statements of principle replaced commitments to action in many passages.

The Millennium Development Goals (MDGs) were still included but many experts believe that the poverty-reduction measures are increasingly falling behind schedule. The big winner under the development heading was the "Global Partnership" programme from the Monterrey Conference in which "development" is always dependent on "good governance" – the new slogan for protection of private property, law and the market economy. The Summit's original thrust, to reinforce efforts to eradicate extreme poverty, seem to have ceded pride of place to making development comfortable for the liberal economy.

Trade, investment, debt, commodities and "quick impact aid" are essentially stand-pat sections based on existing power relations with little innovation. The developed countries showed little real generosity. A paragraph on opening up European and American markets to commodity trade was emasculated (para 29 of the August 5 draft).

Women were one of the few groups from Civil Society who believed they had made gains. After considerable lobbying, gender equality and women's rights were included not just once but under numerous headings. One month after the meeting, the Secretary-General put forth a comprehensive plan for including women in the UN's peace and security efforts.

*COMMENTARY:*
In his address to the World Summit, Secretary-General Kofi Annan concluded, "Let us be frank with each other and with the peoples of the United Nations. We have not yet achieved the sweeping and fundamental reform that I, and many others, believe is required. Sharp differences, some of them substantive and legitimate, have played their part in preventing that …this reform process matters, and must continue." The Final Outcome Document is indeed a half empty glass in comparison with the earlier version. World leaders did not seize the opportunity to reconsider their priorities in dealing with global governance. In its Sept. 15 editorial, the Toronto *Globe and Mail* managed both to give lack-luster applause and to place the blame, "The UN retains the potential to be as effective an organization as its member countries are prepared to let it be".

*PROCESS and CONTENT:*
Annan's report was broad enough to allow member states to 'cherry pick' some items that suited their interests. It allowed the world leaders to ratify an outcome document that some diplomats could claim as progress. But it can hardly be called a systematic overhaul of the United Nations that would allow it to deal with global challenges. For the most part, the proposed changes are adaptations of the 'thumb in the dike' variety. There is no vision of comprehensive transformation for the whole system of international institutions of the 'third generation' variety that would lead to adequate global governance. But, to give Annan his due it must be said he went as far as he could. It is unlikely broader reforms could come from any Secretary-General who is, after all, a public servant of the nation-states.

We are not alone in coming to this conclusion. Writing in the New York Book Review of Feb. 9, 2006, former Under Secretary-General, Brian Urquhart was of the opinion that:

> "Reading the final declaration of the September 2005 summit meeting at the United Nations, which brought 155 heads of state and government to New York, one might reach a similar conclusion about the world in general. International politics, as reflected in the United Nations, in spite of the efforts of Secretary-General Kofi Annan, now largely concern compromise and half-measures. The North-South difference has succeeded the forty-year East-West deadlock as a brake on international policy and action. National self-interest and short-term thinking seem, for the time being at least, to have overcome practical idealism and an urgent sense of common purpose."

As we have already pointed out in the introduction, the 1997–2005 reform process can be instructive in our quest for understanding how to go about reform of the UN. We observed four imbedded obstructions to institutional reform – lack of governmental interest, the distinction between adaptation and transformation, the significance of the political context and actors, and the inbred impediments thrust up by state interests – all of which are central to reformulating a reform process. Let us elaborate a little further by commenting mainly on the High-Level Panel's report because it contained the principles and proposals on which Annan's projects were based. One cannot gainsay the Secretary-General for asking the Panel to focus on security – the basic function of the United Nations. But this narrow focus of reform is just one of several reasons why the *Secure World* and, following it, *In Larger Freedom* were unlikely to succeed. It is not so much what the reports said as what they did not say, and this is principally because of their mandate which had two problems: its source and its content. First, the mandate came from the Secretary-General of the United Nations and not from the Security Council or the General Assembly. The High-Level Panel did not politically implicate the governments of major member states. Nor did it implicate the primary civil society forces that are the main proponents of institutional reform. The Secretary-General apparently did not think he could include civil society representatives or their agenda within the Panel. The outcome was foreseeable.

As regards content, while the Panel's report gave a nod to the interconnectedness of contemporary threats and the concerted actions required of institutions, it did not address the global constitutional issues that face international organizations, ranging from membership and norms to functions and means. There is no content on global democracy and very little on transparency and responsibility. With its insistence on "states being the front line responders to today's threats" so that "greater efforts must be made to enhance the capacity of states to exercise their sovereign responsibility" (p. 22), the report did not noticeably go beyond the sovereignty norms of the Westphalian system, the criticism of which is at the core of civil society demands for global regime change.

The same could be said of two other cornerstones of "alternativist" criticisms of international institutions. The report does not (and was not intended to) deal with the imbalance of policy and representation within international financial institutions or the inherent weakness of ECOSOC. Nor does it offer any hope for providing the UN with its own military capacity for peacemaking. We are still at the stage of States "providing and supporting deployable military resources." There is nothing new here. Because it barely touched the civil society agenda, it did not attract the massive intervention of international non-governmental organizations that would be required to mobilize public opinion and motivate governments.

*TIMING:*

With hindsight, it is clear that the timing was terrible for the reform process because of the split in UN membership over the Iraq invasion and Kofi Annan's leadership being hobbled by the oil-for-food scandal.

As Paul Heinbecker, former Canadian Ambassador to the UN, told me, "The Secretary-General would have required greater lead time and more strategic management to get out himself to the capitals of the world in order to use his prestige to sell his reform package to national leaders – away from the constraining suspicions, hostilities and games of the United Nations diplomatic arena. He would also have needed more time to rally civil society to his cause. As it was, few countries felt pressure from their NGO communities let alone from their broader citizenry to support the overall reforms. Annan might have been able personally to mobilize world leaders if he had been free from oil-for-food allegations to focus on the issue. But without more lead time he still could not have rallied public opinion or civil society. We have learnt from the relatively more focused campaigns for the Landmines Treaty and the International Criminal Court and more recently for the 'Responsibility to Protect' that it takes years to develop public momentum. For instance it took Canada and the members of the Commission four years of dogged effort to convince members of the General Assembly to support the R2P resolution – which nevertheless was warp speed for such a revolutionary idea. Even then, the Canadian prime minister had to telephone some leaders to do some last minute arm-twisting".

As in many other areas of life, timing is everything. While not all exigencies can be foreseen, it is necessary to leave enough time for reform proposals not only to be developed but also to percolate through to political actors and public opinion. Enough time also has to be left to re-schedule activities when there is a negative turn of events such as the oil-for-food scandal. Civil society requires time to mobilize.

*COALITIONS:*

Equally difficult were the structural problems within the UN concerning both attitudes to reform and the need for supportive coalitions. Many of the Permanent Representatives in the UN tend to represent the sovereignty preoccupations of their elites rather than the security interests of the masses. Also, given their conservative preference for "business as usual" (Heinbecker 2005b: 186) the UN Permanent Representatives prefer incremental reforms to structural transformation. Hence we have the twin tendencies to move toward the lowest common denominator, including purely administrative reforms.

They also get tied into UN voting blocks. This is particularly true of the Group of 77 (actually more like 132) developing countries who can be very recalcitrant about change. There is a tendency to be reactive and defensive. With their colonial past, they are understandably cautious when the West tries to gain their support for new ideas on humanitarian intervention like the "Responsibility to Protect", which would entail redefining their recently won sovereignty. They are still more fearful of the intentions of the United States ever since its self-proclaimed war on terror and self-appointed mission to spread democracy. They are very protective of the powers of the General Assembly, which they control with their majority. They can even be leery of proposals from the Secretary-General who is perceived to be at the mercy of the Permanent Five or the U.S. There are also what some diplomats consider to be "spoiler" states such as Libya, Egypt, Cuba, Venezuela and Pakistan that can be very destructive. The General Assembly instinct for consensus-based decisions only strengthens the positions of these countries and encourages lowest common denominator outcomes. For all these reasons the Group of 77 can often block reform.

*THE SECURITY COUNCIL:*

For those hoping for some movement on Security Council reform, the Panel offered the spectacle of a stalemate over two models and Annan refused to endorse either of them. The logjam did not help surmount the fact that changes to structures such as the Security Council requires a two-thirds vote by the General Assembly and no veto by the Permanent Five. More importantly, it is a profoundly divisive issue that stirred up enmities throughout the whole period of negotiation. All the candidates for permanent seats had regional opponents. As Ed Luck points out, "being from a region does not make a Council member representative of its neighbours" (2005: 149).

In fact, Luck found the whole approach by the Secretary-General and the High-Level Panel to be "flawed in its history, diagnosis and prescription" (Luck 2005b: 148). He notes that neither report explained how the Security Council remedies would foster positive reforms; nor did they present the downside risks of unnecessary or misdirected surgery. The reports also neglected to show how possible new permanent members would be any more likely to support humanitarian intervention than present ones. Nor did they provide any precise references to proclaimed new "realities of power" to which the augmented Council was to correspond. There were no proposals for reforming the flawed operating processes of the Council. Luck insists that "the Council's legitimacy comes as much from perceptions of efficiency and effectiveness as from equity" and that "neither report seems to envision much of a place on the Council for smaller member states or even middle powers that have meant so much to peacekeeping, humanitarian affairs and human rights over the years" (p. 149).

*THE TACTICS:*

For the most part, the reports were addressed to member states. A few states such as the "Group of Friends on United Nations Reform", convened by Mexico and including Algeria, Australia, Canada, Chile, Columbia, Germany, Japan, Kenya, the Netherlands, New Zealand, Pakistan, Singapore, Spain, and Sweden said they would take up the cudgels of reform and innovation (Canada, Minister of Foreign Affairs, News Release, Jan. 17, 2005) but they lacked numbers and clout. Aside from such states, the report was reduced to putting all its recommendations in the conditional: "Member States should" do such and such. Such appeals have traditionally fallen on deaf ears. Then the Panel's Report grandiosely proclaimed that "it will require leadership at the domestic and international levels to act early, decisively and collectively…" (p. 12). But, it is the lack of such collective leadership by states that has landed the UN in its current predicament.

This left the Panel to fall back on the Secretary-General to provide the leadership for reform. However, Kofi Annan had repeatedly said it was up to the Member States to promote the fundamental structural reforms that are beyond his jurisdiction. We are in a vicious circle. Nor did it take into account that by 2005, extraneous factors would damage Annan's credibility.

So we are left with the Secretary-General's tactical hopes. He hoped the acrimonious divisions over the 2003 invasion of Iraq would convince the world that reforms are necessary. But here again, the major powers preferred to paper over their differences rather than face the need for change. He hoped that the year 2005, with its summit on the Millennium Development Goals and the decennial outpouring of review articles on the UN's 60th anniversary, would create a wave of support for reform. Given the lack of civil society leadership for Annan's process and the apparent lack of interest of governments, there was little public impetus.

*THE UNITED STATES:*

The question of leadership brings us to the role of the United States. For the four years 2000–04, the UN lived with one of the most unilateralist American administrations in its history. Many of the leaders in the Bush administration were positively anti-UN. The Panel was not blind to political reality, as we saw in its stated desire "to balance power and principle". But, the Panel found itself between the devil and the deep blue sea. If it supported UN principles it was bound to antagonize American neo-conservatives. When it was adamant that the rules of International Law and Article 51 of the UN Charter govern decisions to go to war it confronted the Bush neo-Conservatives' belief that international organizations must not override the sovereign authority of the American constitution. The panel even found a quote from Harry Truman to contradict the Bush U.S. administration: "We all have to recognize—no matter how great our strength—that we must deny ourselves the license to do always as we please," Truman told the UN founding conference.

Washington and its allies have also gone to great lengths to create "Patriot Acts" to empower internal security regulations that were later accused of overriding human rights. "The Bush administration's assault on the Geneva Conventions has caused collateral damage…" (Rosenthal 2004). In response, *Secure World* states that counter-terrorism strategies must not only be effective but also *principled*, and must respect the rule of law and the universal observance of human rights.

Without seeking to irritate the Americans, we can see that the reports contradicted a sufficient number of the Bush administration's international policies to ensure that the United States would not be cheerleaders at the Summit. But there was more. *Secure World* wanted the United Nations to have more and better resources in funding and personnel, to have its own military capacity, and to be able to achieve its Millennium Development Goals. The thrust of the report was to strengthen the UN. President Bush hardly subscribed to any of these goals. It was clear that Kofi Annan was going into the World Summit without the benefit of U.S. leadership and perhaps even with its active opposition. Once again we have seen that little of substance can work its way through the UN system without the blessing or the leadership of the world's leading power. Reformers must work diligently to find American supporters.

Although one tends to hear mostly from critics, the Secretary-General also had his supporters (see Heinbecker and Goff 2005). They thought his broad package of proposals would appeal to different constituencies and allow for logrolling. In any case, there was agreement on the need for change. As the former Canadian Ambassador to the UN, Paul Heinbecker, put it,

> "Some are oblivious or indifferent to the UN's weaknesses, trusting to fate to fix them. Others would just forsake the UN altogether and look to their own strengths in a dangerous age. The first course would condemn the UN to an existence increasingly on the periphery of humanity's vast need. The second course would condemn the world to repeat history in infinitely more dangerous circumstances. The wiser course is to embrace the vision presented by the Secretary-General and adapt the institution …" (p. 186).

We are indebted to the High-Level Panel for the enunciation of an up-dated set of multilateral principles upon which security reforms could be founded:

- Security must be equitable. There must be peace with justice.
- Threats are global and interconnected and must be treated comprehensively through mutual responsibility.
- No state, no matter how powerful, can handle the threats alone.
- Security, economic development and human freedom are indivisible.
- The primary goal is a framework for prevention starting with development.
- Poverty, disease and a degraded environment are conditions from which threats emerge.
- Effective collective security must be based on international law.
- Reforms must be based both on principle and power to attain legitimacy as well as relevance.
- Security must embrace the emerging norm of the responsibility to protect endangered populations.

We can see that it is useful to have thoughtful groups focus their attention on UN reform. We also are indebted to the Panel and Annan for the refinement of criteria for the necessary use of force in humanitarian interventions, a limpid definition of terrorism, and proposals for a new Human Rights Council and a Peacebuilding Commission. However, The narrow, state-centric, focus on security issues in the

High-Level Panel's mandate, aimed at attracting the interest of fearful Western powers, not only failed in this aim, but also relegated to the sidelines potential civil society supporters. Without trying to be all things to all people, a UN reform program has to be well-enough conceived and sufficiently fundamental to deal with the problems of globalization.

The commitment to multilateralism of member states, while weak, would appear to be alive. The reform process gave us the state of play in the present decade. Perhaps Ed Luck was right when he concluded, "The current reform process tested the member states commitment to the organization and found it to be fundamentally sound, if as shallow and self-serving as ever" (Luck 2005b: 412).

# 6 The Reformers

The issue of institutional reform and innovation is familiar territory for numerous NGOs, research institutes, and academics. In addition to those who work within multilateral institutions on internal reform, a large number of individuals and groups have pursued similar projects from the outside. As various aspects of globalization make their way to the forefront of the global agenda, the number and intensity of efforts to understand how the international institutional framework needs to be adapted have been increasing. These individuals and groups aim to influence a process of change in international institutions to make them more effective, efficient and democratic, and also to improve their capacity to fill identified gaps and to meet new and emerging challenges presented by globalization.

Their research and advocacy focuses on everything from micro-level reform in specific institutions to transformational innovation of the international financial institutions (IFIs) or the creation of new institutions such as a world environment organization. Some conservative UN abolitionist groups (such as the U.S.-based Heritage Foundation and Cato Institute) are some of the noisiest groups working to "reform" the UN system by trying to weaken its present capacity and authority. This section, however, presents groups that are working to foster innovation in order to *strengthen* an existing system of governance, and increase the capacity of institutions, or create new ones, to meet new and emerging challenges.

## 6.1 The Main Areas of Reform

Work and advocacy by individuals and groups in the realm of reform and innovation are growing in major areas of research and advocacy:

i) *General Reform Proposals:* Address reform of the entire UN system and its various conceptual components, including these:
   - promoting and enhancing "global governance"
   - democratizing the existing UN system
   - establishing effective sustainable development governance
   - enhancing and implementing existing instruments to advance human rights, including women's rights
   - establishing some sort of corporate governance structures
   - internal reform efforts by notable individuals, such as the Secretary-General

   Note: Many organizations dealing with general reform proposals also include efforts to reform specific institutions. Examples can be found in the table below.

ii) *Specific Reform Proposals:* Address reform of specific institutions within the existing UN system, including these:
   - reform of the Security Council
   - reform of the International Financial Institutions: the World Bank, International Monetary Fund, World Trade Organization, regional development banks, and the Bank for International Settlements

In addition to the continuing work of individuals and groups in these areas of reform and innovation, many meetings, conferences and other gatherings have also brought together experts and advocates to bring forward the reform agenda. The tables below outline efforts of the recent past and present in these categories. The tables mention meetings that have also significantly affected the movement for reform and innovation in the international arena. Because the number of reform efforts and activities are burgeoning, this list is likely far from exhaustive.

(For additional information on those seeking to reform global governance, see the Helsinki Process: Survey of Global Commissions and Processes," Helsinki 2003, at www.helsinkiprocess.fi/netcomm/imqlib/24/89/hc komissio.pdf, and www.reformwatch.net.)

TABLE 2: Reform Efforts Targeting Overall System

| **Who/What** | **Activities** |
|---|---|
| Commission on Global Governance http://www.itcilo.it/english/actrav/telearn/global/ilo/globe/gove.htm | This commission was made up of 28 individuals chosen because of their influence and past work in the area of global governance. Its final report, *Our Global Neighbourhood*, was released in 1995 (Oxford University Press, 1995). |
| The South Centre http://www.southcentre.org/ | The South Centre was created as a result of the report of the South Commission, and continues to support action-oriented proposals for reform favouring Southern interests. Their major policy publication regarding general reform is *For a Strong and Democratic United Nations: A South Perspective on UN Reform* (The South Centre, 1996).<br>They have also recently released a book on the UN-corporate relationship, *Development at Risk: Rethinking UN-Business Partnerships*, in collaboration with the UN Research Institute for Social Development (http://www.unrisd.org). The book is available through the South Centre website. |

(*continued*)

TABLE 2 *continued*

| **Who/What** | **Activities** |
|---|---|
| La Trobe University (Australia) with the Toda Institute (Japan/ Hawaii) and Focus on Global South (Thailand) | These three research institutes collaborated in a study called the Global Governance Reform Project. The major product of their work, *Reimagining the Future: Towards Democratic Governance* (La Trobe, University 2000), is a result of three years of meetings and exchanges led by the three institutes. The report is available at http://www.toda.org/publications/book_series/reimagining%20_the_future/reimagining.html. |
| The Alliance for a Responsible, Plural and United World http://www.alliance21.org/en/proposals/summaries/global2.htm | The Alliance is a consortium of individuals and groups working through the medium of continuing thematic and regional "workshops." Each workshop has produced a proposal paper, which continues to be updated through a series of meetings, workshops and conferences. The proposal paper for global governance offers 36 concrete proposals. |
| Independent Working Group on the Future of the UN http://www.library.yale.edu/un/un1e.htm | This working group was convened by the Ford Foundation at the request of Secretary-General Boutros Boutros-Ghali. Its final report, *The United Nations in its Second Half-Century* (Yale 1995), is available at http://www.library.yale.edu/un/un1e3co.htm. |
| PHP Research Institute http://www.php.co.jp/english.html | Four researchers (Tatsuro Kunugi, Makoto Iokibe, Takahiro Shinyo and Kohei Hashimoto) at this Japanese think tank co-authored a book called *Towards a More Effective UN* (PHP Research Institute, 1996). |
| World Campaign for In-Depth Reform of the System of International Institutions http://www.reformcampaign.net | In this campaign, prominent individuals and organizations are promoting reform of the UN system through a series of consultations and presentations at venues where civil society is present (most notably at the 2002 World Summit on Sustainable Development and Porto Alegre World Social Forum). The campaign's manifesto, "World Citizen Legislative Initiative," will be submitted to the General Assembly to call for a World Conference on Reform of the System of International Institutions. |

(*continued*)

TABLE 2 *continued*

| Who/What | Activities |
|---|---|
| Ubuntu www.ubuntu.upc.es | Ubuntu defines itself as a World Forum of Networks of Civil Society. The group includes networks and organizations working on the democratization of the system of international institutions. The group has held two constitutive meetings to define its mandate and operational directions, and it plans to meet every one or two years. It is a forum for debate and discussion among civil society members. (Ubuntu spearheaded the *World Campaign for In-Depth Reform of the System of International Institutions*—see above.) |
| World Federation of United Nations Associations http://www.wfuna.org/what/mdgcampaign/index.cfm | In collaboration with the North-South Institute, the World Federation of United Nations Associations leads the Global Millennium Campaign in which civil society addresses the need for the UN system to innovatively meet the Millennium Development Goals (as outlined in the 2000 UN Millennium Summit). Their most recent report, *We the Peoples: 2003 – A Call to Action for the Millennium Declaration* is available at http://www.wfuna.org/document.cfm?documentID=42. |
| New School of Athens Global Governance Group info@globalgovgroup.com | This group functions within a tripartite dialogue of academics and political representatives, business and civil society. Like Plato's Academy it seeks to bring together the opposing visions of the World Economic Forum (Davos) and the World Social Forum (Porto Allegre). The report of its major 2006 conference, "Beyond the Millennium Declaration: Embracing Democracy and Good Governance", can be found at www.globalgovgroup.com |
| Civicus http://www.civicus.org | This international alliance promotes citizen participation and action worldwide. Civicus organizes a World Assembly every few years (www.civicusassembly.org), where citizens can gather to exchange learnings about how to strengthen governance and legitimacy of civil society organizations globally. |

(*continued*)

TABLE 2 *continued*

| Who/What | Activities |
|---|---|
| World Federalist Movement http://www.wfm.org now Citizens for Global Solutions in the U.S. | The World Federalist Movement is an international umbrella group for organizations (including national-level federalist associations) working to create democratic global governance institutions.<br>It functions through individual campaigns and projects directed at specific institutions, including the Campaign for an International Criminal Court. |
| Secretary-General Kofi Annan | Kofi Annan has addressed reform since taking office in 1997 with his proposal of a "two-track" reform program. This aimed to streamline the work of the many UN agencies, funds, departments and programs.<br>Annan's reform efforts are articulated in his reports to the 57th and 58th General Assembly sessions: *Role of the UN in Promoting Development in the Context of Globalization and Interdependence* (A/57/96) and *Implementation of the UN Millennium Declaration* (A/58/323). These reports are about the need to address the fundamental legitimacy of many multilateral institutions, whereas Annan's first efforts were more administrative in nature.<br>In the later part of his mandate he created a High Level Panel to analyze security reforms in preparation for the 2005 World Leaders Summit at the UN. |
| Montreal International Forum http://www.fimcivilsociety.org/g02/ | Following a first "World Civil Society Conference" in Montreal in 1999, Montreal International Forum organized in 2002 the Global Conference on "Civil Society and the Democratization of Global Governance" where civil society actors gathered to create innovative strategies to build democratic governance.<br>Montreal International Forum, primarily organizes regular meetings, forums, symposia, etc., to look at civil society participation at a variety of multilateral institutions (including NATO, la Francophonie, and the Commonwealth). Forum internationale de Montréal also organized G05 in 2005. |

(*continued*)

TABLE 2 *continued*

| Who/What | Activities |
|---|---|
| One World Trust http://www.oneworldtrust.org | One World Trust has launched Charter 99 to raise the profile of the UN Millennium Summit, where the Charter was presented.<br>Another of this group's ventures is the Global Accountability Project, a large-scale evaluation of how open and receptive global organizations are to the internal demands of their members and to the external demands of individuals and groups who are affected by the organizations' daily operations. |
| State of the World Forum www.worldforum.org | This network of global leaders and thinkers meets every year to exchange ideas and develop innovative solutions to emerging global challenges. It is driven by the principle of "transforming conversations that matter into actions that make a difference." Meetings are thus translated into specific projects, which are called strategic initiatives. |
| Commission on Globalization http://www.commissionon globalization.org | Convened at the 2000 gathering of the State of the World Forum, this commission aims to function as a global network of key world leaders working for democracy at the global level. The commissioners and co-chairs meet annually to discuss potential actions for reforming institutions in order to address issues related globalization. |
| First Canadian Conference on UN Reform | Held in Montreal, Canada, in March 1995 by the United Nations Association in Canada, this conference considered priority issues for reform in light of the UN's 50th anniversary. The conference addressed overall reforms as well as the need to reform and create specific institutions. |
| Secretary-General's Panel of Eminent Persons on Civil Society and UN Relationships (Cardoso Commission) http://www.un.org/reform/panel.htm | Kofi Annan convened this 12-person panel as part of the UN reform process to recommend how civil society can better be integrated in the existing UN system. Fernando Enrique Cardoso, a former president of Brazil, was the panel's chair. The panel used a variety of means to determine ways to improve civil society engagement, including a survey of organizations and a series of consultations and meetings with civil society groups. |

(*continued*)

TABLE 2 *continued*

| Who/What | Activities |
|---|---|
| Citizens for Global Solutions (formerly Campaign for UN Reform) http://www.globalsolutions.org/ | This U.S.-based group works to educate Americans about global issues and to lobby U.S. decision-makers about foreign policy. It also performs a research function through its World Federalist Institute, which creates proposals to strengthen and reform the UN. |
| Women and Development Organization http://www.wedo.org | The Women and Development Organization's Gender and Governance program works to increase the number of women that hold decision-making power in the United Nations system, as well as to reform the way the structure views and treats women. This initiative is part of the Women and Development Organization's 50/50 Campaign: Get the Balance Right!, which has been most aggressive at the Commission on the Status of Women.<br>The Women and Development Organization generally works within the UN system, and is strongest at advocacy and lobbying through larger NGO coalitions. |
| UN Reform Center http://www.unreformcenter.org/ | This organization works to generate proposals through three means: sponsoring and/or publishing research monographs, books and papers; public forums and university-based conferences; and its website.<br>Each year the center publishes a set of proposals for UN reform, called the Handbook of Recommendations. The center attempts to implement these through coalition work and advocacy. |
| United Nations Association of the United States of America (UNA-USA) http://www.unausa.org/issues/unreform.asp | UNA-USA has had a continuing focus on UN reform, most notably in the last decade through its U.S.-based advocacy for the International Criminal Court, and through occasional gatherings and papers on the United States' role in the reform process. Executive Director of Policy Studies Jeffrey Laurenti has had a particularly strong presence in UNA-USA's efforts through his papers, articles and commentary on Kofi Annan's various efforts, as well as on the need for reform of specific institutions. |

(*continued*)

TABLE 2 *continued*

| Who/What | Activities |
|---|---|
| Forum on the Future of the United Nations System, Vienna, 1995 | This forum was convened in 1995 at the request of Secretary Genearal Boutros Boutros-Ghali to occur during the first regular session of the Administrative Committee on Coordination (ACC). Its goal was to promote dialog between executive heads and prominent chairs of commissions on various aspects of UN reform. ACC's role was to solidify political support for continued resources for the UN so it could meet new challenges. ACC also offered a forum for exchanging ideas on reforming management and increasing cost-effectiveness. |
| Campaign for a more Democratic UN http://www.camdun-online.gn.apc.org/ | The Campaign for a more Democratic UN's objective is to create a People's Assembly to represent world citizens within the UN system. Although the "United Nations and Peoples" is their ultimate aim, they also advocate for increased democratization of other UN organs, including through representation of civil society organizations.<br>This group holds regular conferences on democratizing the UN. It has also produced papers and reports that are used to pressure high-level UN panels. |
| United Nations Project at the World Policy Institute http://www.worldpolicy.org/projects/un/about.html | This broad-reaching project convenes expert round tables, symposia and panels, in addition to its advocacy activities with U.S. decision-makers.<br>Its most relevant reform efforts are in the policy area, where the project's experts contribute both at the Secretariat and General Assembly levels. |
| Global People's Assembly Movement http://acpc.org | This U.S.-driven group aims to create a global parliamentary assembly, preferably within a reformed United Nations. The movement is an outcome of the solidarity resulting from people's assemblies held all over the world.<br>The San Francisco People's Assembly lead other groups to organize the UN Charter Review Conference, in 2005 in San Francisco. |

(*continued*)

TABLE 2 *continued*

| Who/What | Activities |
|---|---|
| World NGO Conference, Montreal, Canada, 1999 | Inspired by the report of the Commission on Global Governance, this 1999 conference brought together decision-makers in NGOs and civil society networks to share and formulate strategies for civil society to more effectively participate within the UN system. |
| International Facilitating Group on Financing for Development (IFG) http://www.interaction.org/development/finance | This group was established in April 2002 from among the NGOs that worked in the UN Financing for Development (FfD) conference held in Monterrey, Mexico, that same year. The group continues to monitor governments and international institutions and their implementation of the commitments made in Monterrey. It works to move the FfD agenda forward on the issue of reforming global governance. |
| Carnegie Endowment for International Peace: Managing Global Issues Project http://www.ceip.org/files/projects/mgi/mgi_home.ASP | This research project compares the mechanisms, processes and roles of various international actors in the management of global problems. One of the main activities of the project is information exchange among scholars and interested individuals through a comprehensive online database of information on management of global issues, as well as through monthly seminars. The other main project focus is preparation of a book called *Managing Global Issues: Lessons Learned*, formulating policy recommendations based on comparing what kind of governance measures worked best in various scenarios. |
| Global Policy Forum (www.globalpolicy.org/reform) | UN Reform represents one of the policy programmes on which the Global Policy Forum (GPF) concentrates. In addition to being an impressive clearinghouse of reform-related research and information, GPF conducts research and advocacy within larger mandates of coalition-based work to strengthen international law. GPF organizes both large-scale conferences and smaller consultations and meetings. GPF is the prinicipal organizer of the NGO Working Group on the Security Council. |

(*continued*)

TABLE 2 *continued*

| Who/What | Activities |
|---|---|
| Centre for Global Studies (University of Victoria) http://www.globalcentres.org | In the governance program area, the Centre for Global Studies associates research and formulate policy recommendations for reforming local, national and international governance structures to allow them to manage the "deficit" in governance left by new global actors dealing with new global challenges.<br>Most notably, the globalization and governance program is undertaking a series of projects to develop proposals for reform of international institutions. |
| Parliamentarians for Global Action http://www.pgaction.org | Parliamentarians for Global Action is a network of 1,350 members of Parliament from 111 elected national legislatures. The organization works to advocate within the wider UN system for its principal values. Recently, it has been advocating for the ratification of the International Criminal Court, and the need for an enabling environment in which sustainable development governance can proceed. |
| Citoyens du Monde http://citmonde.free.fr/ | This France-based group seeks a People's Parliamentary Assembly and the creation of a new World Federal Authority to which nations would transfer elements of their sovereignty in order to effectively address problems emerging from *globalism*.Its main activities are distribution of a quarterly news bulletin, and research regarding the promotion of federalist culture. |
| Research Centre for Global Governance, Brazil | Inspired by the needs outlined in the Commission on Global Governance's report, the Research Centre for Global Governance is a think tank that seeks articles and papers from citizens all over the world. It aims to consolidate all contributed research and present it at a future world conference on global governance (as recommended by the Commission). UN reform is one area of research and study identified by RCGG. |
| Programme on World Governance (Miguel Servet college of Higher European Studies) | This program involves 11 European universities, as well as the European Agency for Culture (UNESCO), that promotes and coordinates a work program, including a two-year program of six seminars hosted by various universities. The resulting recommendations on world governance were to be presented at a conference in Brazil in 2005. |

(*continued*)

TABLE 2 *continued*

| Who/What | Activities |
|---|---|
| Centre for War/Peace Studies www.cwps.org | The CW/PS is a global governance and peace-oriented NGO incorporated in the United States in 1977. Its current main focus of activity is a campaign to promote UN reform, in particular, the promotion of a weighted voting procedure for the General Assembly and the adoption of a taxing procedure on international exchange transactions (Tobin Tax) as a means of funding the UN. As an additional activity, the CW/PS is offering its assistance with their advocacy efforts in New York to other international civil society organizations active in the field of global governance and UN reform. |
| Global Progressive Forum (Brussels 2003) http://www.pes.org/GlobalProgressiveForum/content.asp | This public forum was held at the European Parliament and convened policy makers, civil society leaders, trade unions, business and academia from around the world. It consisted of three round tables on development issues, global policy issues, and global governance. The last round table discussed international institutional reform in considerable detail. |
| EFFORTS FOR CORPORATE GOVERNANCE | |
| Alliance for a Corporate-Free UN http://www.corpwatch.org/campaigns/PCC.jsp?topicid=101 | A campaign with a secretariat in the U.S.-based organization CorpWatch, the Alliance for a Corporate-Free UN is an international coalition that is pressuring the UN to forgo formal relationships with corporations (through initiatives such as the UN Global Compact) and spend more time counterbalancing institutions inherently involved in engaging the corporate sector, such as the WTO. |
| World Economic Forum http://www.weforum.org | The World Economic Forum (WEF) is an international organization with a membership representing companies and businesses from around the world. It is striving to establish world corporate governance. In particular, WEF's Global Governance Initiative is monitoring the Millennium Development Goals to identify means of cooperation among actors (including corporations) to realize the goals. The Corporate Governance Dialogue is a multi-year series of workshops that promote discussion among leading corporate representatives and experts to generate models of corporate governance. |

(*continued*)

TABLE 2 *continued*

| **Who/What** | **Activities** |
|---|---|
| UN Global Compact http://www.unglobalcompact.org | The UN Global Compact represents Kofi Annan's attempt to address the crucial relationship between multinational corporations and the prospects for development in poor countries.<br>In this cooperative venture, businesses publicly commit to actively promoting the core values of the UN in human rights, labor and the environment. |
| EFFORTS FOR SUSTAINABLE DEVELOPMENT GOVERNANCE | |
| United Nations University (Institute of Advanced Studies), in collaboration with University of Kitakyushu (Japan) and Japan Foundation Centre for Global Partnership http://www.ias.unu.edu/binaries/NYPrepComReport3.pdf | The main result of this collaborative project was a report to inform the Third Preparatory Committee Meeting of the World Summit on Sustainable Development. The report, *Study on International Environmental Governance Reform*, stresses the need for international environmental institutions to reflect the link between environmental problems and underlying economic and social issues.<br>Several proposals are put forth, including the creation of overarching institutions, such as a world environment organization, or a clustering of elements of present-day multilateral environmental agreements. |
| World Resources Institute http://www.wri.org | The World Resources Institute (WRI) produces research on the interaction between human society and the environment from a multi-disciplinary perspective. One of their main objectives is to provide institutions with information and proposals for policy and institutional change that is amenable to sustainable development.<br>WRI's 2003 World Resources Report, *Decisions for the Earth: Balance, voice, and power*, provides a strong case for governance reforms as a necessary element in slowing global environmental problems. This report was produced in collaboration with UNEP, UNDP and the World Bank. |

(*continued*)

TABLE 2 *continued*

| Who/What | Activities |
|---|---|
| Stakeholder Forum for Our Common Future http://www.stakeholderforum.org/ | Stakeholder Forum was organized immediately after the 1992 Rio Earth Summit to engage relevant actors in the U.K. Its focus became increasingly international as the 10-year review of the Rio Summit's Agenda 21 approached (World Summit on Sustainable Development). Stakeholder Forum is monitoring the implementation of the Millennium Development Goals, bringing together all relevant stakeholders identified in Agenda 21 to increase their ability to influence decision-making. |
| World Summit on Sustainable Development, Johannesburg, 2002 | The World Summit on Sustainable Development (WSSD), the 10-year review of the 1992 Rio Earth Summit, in Johannesburg, had a lengthy preparatory process that allowed for civil society organizations active in all different realms (environment, development, human rights, etc.) to contribute.<br>The agenda to reform international institutions to better address sustainable development was strongly represented in the WSSD process, most notably under the organization of the World Federalist Movement and Stakeholder Forum. The reform issues being raised at the WSSD are described in "Reforming International Institutions" (http://www.earthsummit2002.org/es/issues/Governance/FDoddsCh5.rtf), a chapter of *Earth Summit 2002* by Felix Dodds (Executive Director of UNED-UK). Other relevant resources regarding WSSD and governance issues can be found at http://www.earthsummit2002.org/es/issues/Governance/governance.htm.<br>The Johannesburg Plan of Implementation includes strong references to the need to strengthen the international institutional framework for sustainable development. |

TABLE 3: Specific Reform Proposals

| Who/What | Activities |
|---|---|
| Joseph Stiglitz | As former Chief Economist at the World Bank and Nobel Prize laureate, Joseph Stiglitz's public criticism of the policies of the IFIs has been a powerful source of legitimacy for those advocating their reform. Stiglitz himself has said that he does not condone shutting down the IFIs, but he is a strong proponent of their fundamental reform. Stiglitz argued his case for reform of the IFIs and the U.S. Treasury in his book *Globalization and its Discontents* (W. W. Norton & Company, 2002).<br>Aside from his individual efforts, and because of his reputation as a respected economist, Stiglitz's departure from the World Bank is considered to be a living illustration of the legitimacy of critics' demanding reform of the IFIs. |
| International Forum on Globalization http://www.ifg.org | The International Forum on Globalization (IFG) is a think tank of about 60 prominent scholars, economists, researchers and writers who publicly oppose the "global system" of economic globalization and challenge the "takeover of global governance by transnational corporations and the international trade bureaucracies." IFG associates regularly meet and speak out against the structure and activities of the IFIs. Prominent associates include Maude Barlow (Council of Canadians), Walden Bello (Focus on Global South), Jerry Mander (IFG), and Vandana Shiva (Foundation for Science, Technology and Ecology). |
| NGO Coalition for an International Criminal Court http://www.iccnow.org | This network of over 2,000 NGOs worked to ensure a fair, independent and effective International Criminal Court (ICC). The Rome Statute establishing the ICC was adopted in July 1998 after two years of work on the draft statute. This NGO Coalition coordinated by the World Federalists, was involved in the process from the beginning (it was established in 1995). Their advocacy made significant contributions on gender crimes and the role of the independent prosecutor.<br>The Coalition continues to monitor the implementation of the Court, including on the national level in ratifying and non-ratifying countries, and to act as an information portal. |

*(continued)*

TABLE 3 *continued*

| **Who/What** | **Activities** |
|---|---|
| Bretton Woods Project http://www.bretton-woodsproject.org | The Bretton Woods Project works for increased transparency and civil society participation in the IFIs by encouraging information exchange and debate, and by acting as a watchdog and media informant on IFI activities. It publishes a bimonthly digest of key IFI activities and monitors their management, policy reforms and major projects. |
| General Assembly Working Group on Security Council Reform | Since 1993, this working group has been reviewing Security Council reforms in two "clusters." Cluster 1 looks at Council membership, including expansion, the veto and voting; cluster 2 looks at increasing the transparency of the Council, in particular its working methods and decision-making process. The group's annual reports are available at http://www.globalpolicy.org/security/reform/reports.htm. |
| NGO Working Group on the Security Council http://www.globalpolicy.org/security/ngowkgrp/index.htm | This consortium of NGOs, convened by the Global Policy Forum, seeks to influence the Security Council. While it started in the mid-1990s with the focus of reforming the Council, its efforts have shifted to dialogue and interaction with Council members by establishing a good track record of contributions by NGO representatives with an expertise in the Council. The working group now regularly contributes to the Council's functioning, often working with the non-permanent members. |
| International Commission on Intervention and State Sovereignty (ICISS) http://www.dfait-maeci.gc.ca/iciss-ciise/menu-en.asp | The International Commission on Intervention and State Sovereignty (ICISS) was established by the Government of Canada to explore the highly debated issue of the "right to humanitarian intervention," as it was raised in the case of Kosovo and Rwanda. ICISS explored when and how intervention should be an option, and who can authorize such a decision to act. The Report's findings imply reform in many of the UN's structures, including the Security Council, the Secretariat, and the General Assembly. The commission's report, *The Responsibility to Protect*, is available at http://www.dfait-maeci.gc.ca/iciss-ciise/report2-en.asp. In addition to the existing research on the topic, ICISS also embarked on consultations with NGO representatives, policy makers, academics and other important actors in 10 world cities. |

(*continued*)

TABLE 3 *continued*

| Who/What | Activities |
|---|---|
| Panel on United Nations Peace Operations http://www.un.org/peace/reports/peace_operations/ | Initiated in light of the international community's late response to significant humanitarian crises throughout the 1990s, this panel was convened. In August 2000 it released its findings—called the "Brahimi" Report, named after its chair, Mr. Lakhdar Brahimi, the former Algerian Foreign Minister and UN representative. Reforms outlined in the Brahimi Report target the Department of Peacekeeping Operations and more strategic planning around missions, including rapid response. |
| Halifax Initiative http://www.halifaxinitiative.org | The Halifax Initiative is a coalition of Canadian organizations working in environment, development, human rights and social justice. NGOs formed the Halifax Initiative in 1994 to ensure that reform of the IFIs was on the agenda of the 1995 G7 meeting.<br>The Halifax Initiative's goal is to transform the present international financial system through research, education, intense advocacy efforts, and alliance-building. The group has also created the NGO Working Group on Export Development Canada in recognition of the importance of export credit agencies in the IFIs. |
| Citizen's Network on Essential Services http://www.challengeglobalization.org/html/otherpubs/advocacy.shtml | Working from the premise that services providing healthcare, water, education and electricity should be universal, this network works on the local as well as global level. Globally, this network support citizens' groups that are working to democratize the IFIs. The network identifies the process through which IFIs affect the provision of essential services without legitimacy. It also offers critical analyses of their policy choices. |
| Reinventing Bretton Woods Committee http://www.rbwf.org/ | This committee regularly brings together government officials, members of international organizations, and other actors involved in global financial activities to discuss building a stable and flexible financial architecture.In addition organizing regular consultations, the committee is a resource for information and policy analysis, and it is an intermediary between the IFIs, governments, the private sector, and private creditors. |

(*continued*)

TABLE 3 *continued*

| Who/What | Activities |
|---|---|
| International Financial Institution Advisory Commission (Meltzer Commission) | This U.S. Congress commission was convened in 1999 on a short-term basis to evaluate the IFIs— in particular, the U.S contribution to IFI activities. Their final report (March 2000, U.S. Joint Economic Committee) is available at http://www.house.gov/jec/imf/meltzer.htm |
| New Economics Foundation http://www.neweconomics.org | This independent think tank envisions a "new economy based on people and the environment." The New Economics Foundation has challenged the role and activities of the IFIs in various ways, most notably in its 2000 report, *"It's democracy, stupid": The trouble with the global economy – the United Nations lost role and democratic reform of the IMF, World Bank and WTO,* available at http://www.neweconomics.org/gen/uploads/doc_89200002723_3028pdf%20nef.pdf |
| Jubilee Research http://www.jubileeresearch.org/ | Jubilee Research is a program of the New Economics Foundation. Growing from the international campaign for G7 countries to cancel developing countries' debts (known as Jubilee 2000), Jubilee Research is continuing the campaign's research on international debt and finance. It urges its readers to use its information to advocate for debt cancellation.<br>One of its main objectives is to democratize multilateral institutions (the IFIs) to make them more transparent and accountable to citizens through advocacy. |

The above table provides a good sample of the efforts to reform and innovate the international institutional framework, but it does not include the many individual scholars, activists and practitioners who contribute to the growing reform movement. This is because it is not within the scope of this book to include what would be a very long list. However, it is useful to note that some prominent individuals have dedicated a lot of energy to the reform agenda, either through scholarly contributions or advocacy.

## 6.2 Some Conclusions about Current International Reformers

The main conclusions that may be drawn from the list of current reformers are that the issue of reform and innovation of the international institutional system has become a priority issue for civil society, and that NGOs from most sectors are dealing with the issue in some capacity. Kofi Annan also gave internal reform new life, putting the spotlight on the need for fundamental reforms (after the immediacy of the financial crises of the 1980s had been dampened).

Most heartening is the coalition and alliance-building that has occurred among NGOs, coordinating their efforts and increasing their possibility of success. Evidently, groups working with different stakeholders have identified common causes (most notably to criticize and pressure the IFIs to modify their practices, and in the move to establish an International Criminal Court). Continued, focused pressure from such alliances may eventually lead to more fundamental widespread reform. Also very positive is the importance that has been placed on dialogue and the exchange of ideas in the process of innovation. Symposia, conferences, forums and panels on various aspects of reform have sprung up all over the world. They are engaging audiences that that are often seen to be the biggest obstacles in meeting the challenges of globalization, such as the corporate sector.

Parallel to the positive elements of fostering dialogue runs the risk that though a lot of discussion is underway, there is little impetus for concrete action. This is most evident among research institutes and the smaller, "visionary" organizations that focus on reform. Their research and input is important to foster innovative ideas. However, it is presently unclear how they fit into the international movement toward reform—they are more like satellites revolving around bigger coalitions. Much discussion and research is being duplicated in these satellite groups that are less connected to larger networks.

Another concern is the legitimacy of major civil society organizations, whose participation is often seen as a testament to the increasing democratization of international institutions. While some groups envision a "People's Assembly" representing "world citizens," questions have also been raised whether active NGOs themselves represent the element of democracy for which advocates for reform are looking. Northern NGOs and individuals are also significantly more powerful, due to higher access to resources, than are their Southern partners. This again raises the question of how legitimate present coalitions are, and whether they really are accountable to a larger populace than any other actor in the international arena. Much of the civil society reform activity originates in the U.S. and U.K.

Overall, increased coordination of existing efforts (including among larger campaigns) is probably the most important next step for reforming the international institutional framework.

# 7 Seeking a Path Toward Transforming the UN

*"Building an efficient and enduring system of international cooperation will be expensive, but it will be less expensive than creating and maintaining a system of nuclear deterrence was. If properly conceived, cooperation will also yield far greater benefits.*

*Harmonizing diverse interests, perceptions, policies, and actions in a dynamic world will never be easy. But it can best be achieved democratically, within a constructive multilateral framework of shared responsibility and mutual accountability."*

(Mihaly Simai, *The Future of Global Governance, Washington,* 1994, United States Institute of Peace Press).

## Introduction

In this study it has been shown that globalization has caused many problems that affect all humanity, and that exceed the capacities of individual countries or even regions to deal with the new challenges. Policies and institutional capacities must be globalized to deal with these worldwide threats, and we have seen that many groups and individuals are working toward this goal. It has also been shown that there are a plethora of ideas available about *what* policies and institutional changes are required to reform the world. Paul Kennedy's eloquent *The Parliament of Man*, based on informed and judicious historical scholarship, serves us up another recipe of "muddling through" when it comes to the future and reform. He is in agreement that doing nothing is impossible, given humankind's needs for better cooperation and governance. But he insists, "The world organization is, by its very nature, so complex and massive that a single recipe for improvement would be absurd. Reforms will, or should, come piecemeal" (2006: 277). The question is how? Relatively little attention has been given to the question of *how* to choose among the competing proposals and how to bring about the reform of international organizations—or what we have called the modernization of multilateralism. The conclusion of this book addresses this question.

First, the lessons learned about the development of international institutions are synthesized. Second, it is understood that the transformation of international organizations cannot happen in a cocoon. As has been noted, the context in which organizations operate is of crucial importance. The next step is to analyse developments in international relations that will have to precede or accompany the modernization of multilateralism. These world restructurings include a new balance of power in which more countries share the burdens of world leadership; development of a sense of global community; re-engagement of Americans in the spirit of multilateralism; and creation of a new, more balanced image of the United Nations.

It is then time to turn to the primary issue, the process for modernizing multilateralism. In addressing the issue of how to bring transformation about, the principal proposal is for INGOs to create sections of their association dedicated to institutional reform. These sections would coalesce in a "campaign coalition". One of its first initiatives would be sponsoring a "constitutional discourse" on the principles of global governance required to modify the Westphalian sovereignty system. Then we turn to the core of our proposals addressing the issues of how a 'campaign coalition' for the transformation of the UN can be created, organized, led and financed. But such an effort needs to be motivated and mobilized so we end with an appeal to democratic principles.

## 7.1 Lessons Learned

As we reach the end of our journey, let us pause to recapitulate the main lessons about how international organizations have evolved.

1. *The reform of the UN is not an exclusive 'either-or', once and for all issue*. Rather it is an inclusive 'both-and', continuing and long-term process. It is not about reforming global governance "perhaps" through the UN or "perhaps" outside it. There is, and always will be, just one legitimate, universal forum for international relations, just as there will always be alternate venues for distinct global objectives. The modernization of multilateralism cannot be a one-time, make-or-break activity. Rather it is both a continuing, incremental activity within the UN that makes one achievement at a time, and also a long-term, fundamental process beside the UN. Just as we strive to develop intentional reform and learning within the UN, so we must work on creating an independent, standing, transformational mechanism beside the UN – with the support of 'like-minded' states. Both "tinkering" and "rethinking" are on the agenda. Transformation cannot be restricted to one issue like security, rather it must allow a successor organization to cope with globalized problems beyond borders in such fields as health, ecological overload, economic disparities, law and order, social mobility, trade and finance, and human rights. It is not about protecting individuals or states, but both. It is not a question of de-legitimizing states but of getting them to accept and participate in global governance. Sovereignty is not to be obliterated but transformed. And it is not just about the policies and organizations of global governance but about its norms and principles, rights and obligations. Innovation in reform includes both idealism and realism, because each is the raison d'être of the other.
2. *Multilateralism is still the world's best bet* for now and the future. Citizens, governments, corporations, and civil society—need international institutions. Effective multilateralism must be based on mutual respect, complex learning and

global legitimacy, all of which require being representative of the world. The year 2003 proved that only collectively do we have the capacity and the legitimacy to deal with peace and security issues, terrorism, nation rebuilding, human rights, international law and order, social justice, protection of the environment, and the global commons. No single state or combination of states has the authority or the knowledge to seek resolutions to these issues for the long term. Just to take one issue, the editor of the *Australian*, Tom Switzer, summarized in 2004 the new lessons that have dissipated some illusions that existed at the beginning of the invasion of Iraq: 1) international containment would still seem to be superior to pre-emptive wars against "rogue states" (not necessarily for terrorism); 2) democracy is not an easily exportable commodity—it depends on the conditions; 3) the scope of American power is not virtually limitless, and the United States cannot impose its will and leadership across the globe.

3. *Modernized international institutions will be able to cope with a changed global environment and the challenges of the 21st century.* The UN is still struggling to cope with the issues of the 1960's such as nuclear proliferation, the ethics of intervention, reconciliation between members' degrees of resources and their representation, and the dilemmas of human rights (Padelford, in chap. 3). Current institutions are struggling to deal with the impacts of globalization such as international crime, pandemics, pollution, the wealth-poverty gap, cultural conflict, terrorism etc., to say nothing of increased demands for equity, transparency, responsibility, representation and participation. Their managerial competence is always under attack. Recalling the roles and functions of international organizations, we can note that the UN is rarely able to take the lead on peace and security issues, and has been displaced as a social and economic arena by the World Bank and the International Monetary Fund. Although the UN system is still predominant in norm creation, humanitarian aid and training, nation-building and global functional services, it cannot protect international law, human rights, the environment or the global commons. A revitalized institution will have the personnel, financial and military capacities to carry out its mandates and be effective enough to be the focus of powerful ministers and executives. We are imagining a different institution from that understood by Innis Claude in the 1960s. In comparison to his strictures, we now know that a new UN will have to encourage *and* inhibit, be useful *and* strong, be able to accommodate *and* impose (see chap. 3).
4. *The critique of international organizations should not blind us to their almost miraculous achievements.* They are humanity's crown jewel. Given the nature of the nation-state system in which they have evolved, given the context of war, conflict and rivalry of the past two centuries, it is astounding that humanity has been able to create world institutions during the same revolutionary period. Because of international organizations, international exchanges and communications proceed relatively smoothly on any given day – despite terrorism,

warfare and crime. Because of them, states talk more than they fight. Because of them, human rights, women's equity and sustainable development are kept on the international agenda. Because of them most countries have already signed international treaties and conventions that condemn most of the world's evils. The lack of implementation is due to a lack of political will in the member states, not in the UN secretariat.

5. Time and again, our *international organizations have proven they cannot reform themselves*. The reasons are manifold. There is no political will among their members. Due to built-in interests and habits, transformation of human institutions is always long and arduous. Nation-states concentrate on their own national interests. Politicians and diplomats are so busy managing the system that they have little time to think about its reform. Because of a lack of information, most citizens in most countries are unaware of the nature of international institutions and politics, and therefore feel uninvolved and incapable of influencing the global future. We have seen that, alone, the Secretary-General can not bring about reform and the member-states will not. Civil society is only beginning to pick up the slack. But most of all, the problem is quite simple:

   > These reform studies and recommendations have become something of an industry, and the fact that actual reforms have thus far been minimal is not for a lack of ideas but for lack of political will and a sufficient degree of consensus among member governments (Strong 2000: 289).

6. *International institutions are highly context-specific*. They are constituted by victorious powers, which have a built-in bias to protect the institutional status quo that favors them. So *any plan to change them must recognize the realities of international politics* and seek to surpass them. Reforms and innovations must be representative of the world. In creating a third generation of international institutions, we must look for a 'constitutional' process that is driven by political debate and is not simply a response to crisis. It must be a determined effort to manage the future, rather than respond to the past. Such a debate over basics can only be organized by political entrepreneurs who are able to influence both national and international politics. Among the realties of the present system are the need to re-engage Americans, both Washington and the people, in the modernization of multilateralism; the awful overload of the globe's carrying capacity; the multiplication of actors, power coalitions and groupings whose interests must be considered by the process; and the rapidly changing, complex turbulence of our times.
7. *The world is strewn with the skeletons of noble ideas for "perpetual peace,"* dating from the time of Emmanuel Kant, in the 1790s. Everyone has his pet ideas about specific reforms. *The primary question now is how multilateralism will be modernized* if powerful interests lack the will and the people lack the know-how. The lessons from the 19th century, as well as from recent international reforms, are revealing. They tell us we must all be involved in

reform—individuals, associations, civil society writ large, business and labor, parliamentarians, churches, academics and philanthropists. Individuals, associations and popular movements can take the lead and work through a campaign coalition. They can create activist partnerships with like-minded states to change ideas and then institutions. They can use their widespread networks to lobby governments to do what some leaders would like to do if they felt the public was with them. They can use their knowledge to promote interest in the media and the public through stimulating debates and hard-hitting information campaigns. George W. Bush may have helped by demonstrating in a highly visible manner the dire need for effective multilateralism.

8. *A transformation process that will succeed will have to be driven by an organization that is competent, inclusive, open and knowledgeable, one that is used to working in both the international and national sectors.* Political problems and the building of convergence must be addressed within the states as well as internationally. Recent international innovation has been produced by 'campaign coalitions' of international non-governmental organizations (INGOs). These groups are capable of normatively inspired, long-term projects. Current research shows that there is an international opportunity in the global governance system for skillful entrepreneurs to help direct and guide the process of modernization. Such a process requires massive momentum and mobilization, which must entail democratic goals to attract participation. Once consensus is reached, it is likely more governments will come on board to be the eventual architects of change. In the end, the coalition must bring all interested parties together to forge the structures and politics of the future.

## 7.2 Setting the Context for Institutional Modernization

One of the major observations we made of Annan's efforts to reform the UN (as well as of previous reform efforts) was the extraordinary significance of the "context" in which the attempted reforms are proposed. It is useless to beat one's head against a stone wall. At a minimum the context must be permissive, at a maximum supportive. Of the barriers to reform, we have observed four that demand thought and action. It would be helpful if there were more burden sharing on the international scene, if there were a feeling of cooperation, if at least some leading powers were on side, and if public opinion strongly supported international organizations. First, to help minimize Washington's unilateralism, Americans need to be reassured that they are not carrying the world's problems alone. Second, there has to be a sense of world community in whose name a transformed UN can legitimately act. As the sense of world community grows, so will the demands for effective global governance. Third, we have repeatedly seen that there are more than enough global challenges that will require the collaborative efforts of the world's most powerful country and its most legitimate international actor. Every effort must be made to win back the favour of the American people who have traditionally admired the UN. Fourth, people are not going to waste time on an organization that is not respected. We all know that the UN has black marks against its name but its reputation is not as tarnished as some of its ideological detractors claim, so its image must be shined up.

### 7.2.1 Creating a New Balance of Power

*"The other nations have a similar responsibility to take the new challenges seriously and to treat them as something beyond the sole responsibility of America. The major nations are all dependent on the global economic system. They are all threatened if ideology and weapons run out of control. The challenge is to build a viable international order without the impetus of having survived a catastrophe"* (Kissinger 2006).

As a preparation for the modernization of multilateralism, the first step is for other countries to attract the attention of the United States by sharing global responsibilities with it.

> "Yet, even the United States, the only state with multidimensional sources of power in the evolving international power structure, cannot act unilaterally or construct a political and institutional structure that meets the criteria formulated by U.S. leaders for the post-Cold War era. The burden of sustaining a new order based on the rule of law and intent on eradicating the worst forms of poverty, conserving the environment, and accomplishing a broad range of security tasks is far too heavy a burden for any one country to bear...Sharing economic burdens and political power in the key institutions of collective security will thus occupy a prominent place on the future reform agenda" (Simai 1994: 352).

If everyone agrees that no one state alone can respond to global challenges, then Washington should not have to bear most of the burdens and costs of international security. Arguably, other states are not doing their share.

If we are to move toward stable international peace and security in the aftermath of the September 11, 2001, "attack on America," the cooperative struggle against terrorism must be pursued. But there must also be a fundamental return to the notion of a balance of power requiring continuous investment in security resources by America'a allies. This is not to introduce a new arms race, but simply a better international balance of power and responsibility. Other strong states must develop the capacity to send autonomous, air-transported brigades or divisions to the world's trouble spots, along with the sea and air logistical support to keep them supplied. It appears that even a peaceful country like Canada understands the logic of this situation and is re-equipping its armed forces, Australia too. Europe is also moving ahead on international forces.

In addition, a number of like-minded countries might consider forming a standing global security coalition to deal with international crises on behalf of the UN. This standing coalition would be a training ground for multinational forces, and a stopgap until the United Nations develops improved decision-making and military capacities that will allow it to fulfil its security mandate. Ad hoc coalitions simply forestall more imaginative institutional reforms. But, in the meantime, a better balance of power will develop a better working relationship with the United States.

There is already a partial model for such a coalition in the form of what Amitai Etzioni has dubbed the "Global Antiterrorism Authority." Etzioni points out that almost all the countries in the world joined the coalition after September 11, 2001, including countries that had previously aided terrorists. Fifty states, including Arab countries, often working in collaboration with the American Central Intelligence Agency (CIA), arrested suspected terrorists. Many countries made rapid, synchronized changes to domestic laws. The European Union introduced a community-wide arrest warrant. By 2003, the U.S. had established a semi-military presence in at least 137 countries, and had divided the world into five military commands, each under a four-star general. Despite the war in Iraq, this antiterrorism maintained a degree of legitimacy because it met the "interest-convergence test," with most countries seeing it in their interest to comply. Also, it was recognized the U.S. had exhausted all other courses of action in response to bin Laden's open call for a holy war against the United States which had claimed 270 lives and 6,500 wounded prior to September 11, 2001. His "holy war" thus contravened the moral values of a growing world opinion of attentive publics.

However, the "Global Antiterrorist Authority" suffers from many limitations, as Etzioni also points out. It is ad hoc and unlikely to become institutionalized in its present form. It is not the result of a democratically deliberated common purpose. Rather it has been "formed, led, managed and largely financed" by the Americans (Etzioni 2004: 103–109). As such, it does not respond to a shared "balance-of-power test" that would release the Americans from acting as a "globocop." Nor does it make other countries feel less dominated. While it demonstrates what sovereign nations can do when they believe it is in their interest to cooperate, it is only a temporary, short-term expedient that cannot be seen as an alternative to the legitimacy of international institutionalization.

Even this limited support for a "security coalition" should not detract from a major lesson of recent American foreign initiatives – war is increasingly less functional as a tool of international relations. Decision-makers have to see military operations as a limited tool that must be complemented by peacebuilding, nation building and developmental activities. More specifically, as Jennifer Welsh has pointed out,

> "The 9/11 attacks were swiftly followed by an awesome display of American military power against the Taliban regime in Afghanistan. But did this application of military prowess translate into a political solution that the U.S. preferred? According to the first finance minister of post-Taliban Afghanistan, Ashraf Ghani, U.S. power proved necessary but insufficient. A much more intangible phenomenon, legitimacy, was needed to bring about a political settlement. It was only the United Nations, in the form of the Secretary-General's special representative, that could create the conditions for political stability. This, too, is reality" (2005: 244–45).

In Iraq, the Untied States was criticized for not adequately planning and preparing for the post-war rebuilding of the country. Again it had to turn rapidly to the UN for assistance. So, yes to broader coalitions that can help the UN with international security as a short-term stopgap, but with the full understanding that it must be linked to efforts such as the new Peacebuilding Commission. But, of course, proposals for security are themselves only a short-term palliative that needs to be bolstered by much more serious efforts to build a genuine sense of global community.

## 7.2.2 Toward global community

> *"So you can't have a coherent view of national interest today without a coherent view of the international community"* (Prime Minister Tony Blair, *The Globe and Mail,* 27-05-06).

> *"The notion of community is deeply embedded in the normal psyche of many countries. Surely we need to start by redefining* the boundaries of *our communities and recognizing their new global dimensions"* (Maxwell 2005: 423).

A second precursor to the establishment of new international norms to replace the Westphalian nation-state system is the creation of a sense of world community. It is not just a question of imagining new institutional constructs. Rather, it is a question of getting a majority of people and of states to believe that sovereign interests can best be protected by global cooperation. That means overcoming national trepidations, which only a sense of community can achieve.

Thinking about change, especially the notion of creating a new level of international community, is very convoluted. Karl Deutsch presented some of the most detailed thinking and empirical research on the concept of community. He proposed that a community exists when a people have learned to communicate with each other and to understand each other because a complementarity of messages is transmitted rapidly and accurately—that is, with a minimum of cost, loss, effort and distortion. Based on a common culture, a community is more integrated than a society, which is essentially an economic construct formed by an intense division of labour and the cooperative production of goods and services. There is a third element of community: the political elites. They must come to belief that mutual problems are best resolved and their aspirations attained by an improved, collective political capacity (Deutsch 1967: 87–107).

These three notions of cultural community, economic society and available elites, give us three possible measures of degrees of community. In an earlier study, I used these criteria to help answer the question: what proportions and what elements of national populations are available to support or accept a transfer of their country's political power to a global level of governance (Trent 1995a)? This study found that while there was an international economic society, it was narrowly concentrated and superficial, and, because of a lack of equity, it hampers community rather then promoting it. Except for a very thin stratum of society, there was little evidence of a sense of community because most communication is still national in scope. Political elites generally have retrogressed into nationalism rather than embracing common issues.

One of the primary tasks is to produce more equity by reversing the recent trend toward a greater gap between rich and poor. Contrary to most thinking, this is a political and not an economic task. In a seminal article Ted Lowi has traced the links between economics, community and politics (Lowi 2005). He recalls that Schumpeter claimed that the success of capitalism undermines the social institutions that protect it and that Adam Smith stressed the social need for a sentiment of justice. While there seems little doubt that capitalism is the most efficient system for producing wealth, insufficient attention had been paid to its costs. As a revolutionary force, Lowi points out, capitalism undermines traditional authority and established social order, thus augmenting social destabilization, poverty and inequality. A competitive market economy is the "mortal enemy of good citizenship" and loosens the bonds of community, because the strict logic of marginal costs pushes proprietors to forsake the civic virtue of fair salaries and environmental stewardship. Without compensating rules, graduated taxes and welfare, the gap between rich and poor will continue to widen. "The corollary is that government coercion of good citizenship, through rules applied equally to all and enforced uniformly, would equalize the cost, provide a closer approximation of the true cost of capitalism, and keep the field of competition flat…" (Lowi 2005: 11). Relative to the search for stability and community in a period of turbulent globalization, the conclusion is clear that we need more and better governance not only to improve communal bonds but also economic competitivity.

Given the present international climate, dominated by a recalcitrant U.S. government and a global business agenda, perhaps the best we can do in the short run is to struggle to achieve the UN's Millennium Development Goals (MDGs) and ensure that the additional commitments in foreign aid in the Monterrey Accord are forthcoming. Unfortunately, we already know we are falling behind on the MDG goals and the World Bank says we require an additional $50 billion annually. The only likely way of succeeding is through the mobilization of civil society. The World Federation of United Nations Associations was right in seizing the initiative through its "We the peoples..." program. But a world press campaign is also needed.

### 7.2.3 Re-engaging the Americans

> *"It is ironic, and grossly unfair, that these poorest members should be in effect subsidizing the richest. I am sure that if the American people fully understood this situation, they would not tolerate it" (Strong 2000: 327).*

When one considers ways of re-engaging Americans in the multilateral enterprise, it is no surprise that we start with several strikes against us. As a rule, big powers are not enamored of international organizations. The George W. Bush administration, in particular, has shown its disdain for the United Nations. Conservative Republicans who have been controlling Congress and American foreign policy are generally opposed to the world organization. A growing "imperial elite" has interests in a militaristic foreign policy. The influence of the Department of Secretary of State, which was more sympathetic to multilateralism, appears to have waned. Lest one think this exaggerates the situation, perhaps it is best to hear the arguments from the horse's mouth, so to speak. David Brooks of the New York Times leaves little doubt about the depth, even the ideological passion, of the right wing opposition to international organizations.

> "John Bolton is just the guy to explain why this vaporous global-governance notion is a dangerous illusion, and that we Americans, like most other people, will never accept it.
>
> We will never accept it first because it is undemocratic. It is impossible to set up legitimate global authorities because there is no global democracy, no sense of common peoplehood and trust. So multilateral organizations can never look like legislatures, with open debate, up or down votes and the losers accepting majority decisions.
>
> Instead they look like meetings of unelected elites, of technocrats who make their decisions in secret and who rely on intentionally impenetrable language, who settle differences through arcane fudges. Americans, like most peoples, will never surrender even a bit of their national democracy for the sake of multilateral technocracy.
>
> Second, we will never accept global governance because it inevitably devolves into corruption. The panoply of UN scandals flows from a single source: the lack of democratic accountability. These supranational organizations exist in their own insular, self-indulgent aerie.
>
> We will never accept global governance, third, because we love our Constitution and will never grant any other law supremacy over it. Like most peoples (Europeans are the exception) we will never allow transnational organizations to overrule our own laws, regulations and precedents. We think our Constitution is superior to the sloppy authority granted to, say, the International Criminal Court.

> Fourth, we understand that these mushy international organizations liberate the barbaric and handcuff the civilized. Bodies like the UN can toss hapless resolutions at the Milosevics, the Saddams or the butchers of Darfur, but they can do nothing to restrain them. Meanwhile, the forces of decency can be paralysed as they wait for the "international community".
>
> Fifth, we know that when push comes to shove, all the grand talk about international norms is often just a cover for opposing the global elites' bêtes noires of the moment – usually the U.S. or Israel. We will never grant legitimacy to forums that are so often manipulated for partisan ends" (14-04-05).

Still, this is by no means the whole story. There is also a strong opinion in favor of multilateralism in the United States with which one can cooperate. To do so requires sharing the burdens of international security, but it also requires understanding Washington's legitimate grievances with international organizations and its search for responses. After helping to build international institutions in the post-World War II period, the U.S. became increasingly angry at the cold-war anti-Americanism of the developing countries it had helped to become independent. This aversion had grown to a full-fledged antagonism by the time the neo-conservative Republicans came to power.

> The financial crisis brought on by the United States' action was more than a challenge to the financial status of the United Nations, however. It was also part of an ideological attack on multilateral organizations by the Reagan administration, which had taken office in 1981 and was driven by a deep resentment against the loss of control that the United States had suffered all during the 1970s when the developing countries, backed by the Soviet Union, had rammed the New International Economic Order (NIEO) through the General Assembly. The NIEO was viewed by American neo-conservatives, who dominated the administration, as international sanctioning of the state control of economies and a raid on first-world treasuries (Lyons 1995: 46).

It is instructive to remember that by 2006, the United Nations and other international institutions, such as UNESCO, have been under attack within the United States for almost a quarter of a century. American elites think that if there is no respect or gratitude toward the United States, why should the U.S. show any toward others (Nye 2002: 157)? This, plus the swing to neo-conservatism, started a wholesale re-evaluation of the role of international institutions at a time when the U.S. was becoming the world's one mega-power. One result was the attack on the UN bureaucracy and budget in the 1980s, which clipped the institution's wings, and, perhaps, promoted efficiency. The sentiment of animosity was once again inflamed in 2002, when the U.S. was voted off the UN Human Rights Commission.

According to a second strand of American thinking, international institutions in general, and the United Nations in particular, should not overrun national sovereignty, even if this concept must evolve in the aftermath of globalization and of the September 11, 2001, terrorist attack. International Law is subservient to the U.S. law and Constitution. Hence, the U.S. prefers institutions with weighted voting or with consensus voting, which, in effect, permits a U.S. veto in all debates. Also, weighted voting allows the United States and the other advanced economies to control the international financial institutions to which they have shifted more and more of the UN agenda. The consensus voting on budgets that the U.S. forced on the UN in 1985 was the price it exacted for paying its dues at that time.

A third difficulty, one that does not fly, is that some in the U.S. perceive that although it provides 22 percent or about 400 million dollars of the UN's regular annual budget of 1.8 billion dollars it may not be getting the most value for the dollars it contributes. It therefore wants a more dominant voice in the UN's management and administration. Americans would probably be pleased to learn that the U.S. has the number one spot in taking 22.5 percent of the UN's procurement contracts totaling 331 million dollars in 2005. Indeed, along with its various agencies in New York, the UN contributed about 3.2 billion dollars annually to the city's economy in the 1990's, according to former Mayor Rudy Giuliani.

A fourth area of grievance is American frustration with UN decision-making procedures. One-state–one-vote procedures do not satisfy the richest, most powerful country in the world with its population of 300 million (unlike the micro-states, with their fewer than 500,000 inhabitants). In 1985, before it accepted the consensus vote compromise, the U.S. was asking for voting procedures to be modified to give greater weight to major contributors. The man that President Bush named in 2005 as his envoy to the United Nations, John Bolton, at one time let it be known he thought the Security Council only needed one permanent member – the United States (*New York Times editorial* 9-03-05).

One can see why some Americans are frustrated. The large numbers and disparate sizes and interests of the members, combined with unmanageable debating and voting procedures, inhibit the UN from developing and sticking to a set of priorities. A myriad of little sovereignties paralyzes the organization. One ambassador can drag out or kill a resolution or project. Blocking groups can delay any issue. Agencies often work alone and refuse to be "coordinated" by the UN Secretariat. There is also a belief in Washington that the UN is not transparent and responsible, so that giving too much power to global institutions would mean a loss of democracy. A lot of American grievances about international institutions hold water and are shared by other countries and must be dealt with in a serious manner if broad-based American support is to be rejuvenated.

Nevertheless, it is always a danger to see the United States as a seamless whole and it would simply be a mistake to assume that all Americans are opposed to multilateralism, or that a future American government might not once again turn in that direction. In the American election campaign of 2004, the Democratic candidate, John Kerry, was already talking about "internationalized" actions, "shared responses" and "collective" policies, while renouncing "unilateralism" (Pfaff 2004).

Recent publications have shown that although U.S. foreign policy is dominated by a vocal and active, conservative, Republican minority, a large majority of Americans would still seem to prefer collective international action. At the end of 2004, the Chicago Council on Foreign Relations carried out the latest in its series of American foreign policy opinion surveys dating back to 1974. It studied 1,200 randomly selected members of the public and 450 foreign policy elites. Some 40 percent of the elite considered "strengthening the United Nations" as a "very important goal", up 12 percent from 2002. The number of leaders who cited "maintaining superior power worldwide" as a very important goal fell from 52 percent in 2002 to 37 percent in 2004. Large majorities of both the public and leaders opposed states taking unilateral action to prevent countries from acquiring weapons of mass destruction but support such action if the UN Security Council approves. As regards international treaties, 87 percent of the public and 85 percent of the elite would favour the terms of the Comprehensive Nuclear Test Ban Treaty, 76 percent of the public and 70 percent of the elite said they support U.S. participation in the International Criminal Court, and 71 percent of both groups said they back U.S. participation in the Kyoto Protocol. Two-thirds of the public and three-quarters of the foreign policy leaders agreed that, in dealing with international problems, Washington should be more willing to make decisions within the UN, even if it means that its views will not prevail. This highly reputable study gives us a far different perspective on American public opinion than the world has come to expect. It is time to re-engage the American majority.

According to a BBC world opinion survey, both the UN and its reform enjoy considerable support not only in American public opinion but also around the world. An average of 64% of the 23,500 polled around the world (including the U.S.) between November 2004 and January 2005 said they wanted to see a reformed UN becoming "significantly more powerful in world affairs" (21-03-05) (http://news-vote.bbc.co.uk/mpapps/pagetools/print/news.bbc.co.uk/hi/americas/4362709.stm).

Friends of the United States, whether they are governments or civil society organizations, must encourage U.S. policy makers and public opinion to return to multilateralism as the dominant idiom of American foreign policy. Statecraft and lobbying will be necessary to target all branches of American government, potential allies among civil society leaders, and public opinion.

> The survey shows that there is fertile ground for presentation of the case for multilateralism. The electorate can see that unilateralism provokes hostility and has enormous financial and other resource costs, that unilateralism is an expression of fantasy and multilateralism the counsel of realism. There is a clear contradiction between the neo-conservatives' views about U.S. military dominance and general American belief in freedom and democracy. It is clear that deterring terrorism and easing conditions that breed terrorism require international cooperation. Multilateralism is a necessary condition for the safety and security of Americans... "Imperialism and democracy are at odds with each other", the *Economist* wrote, "The one implies hierarchy and subordination, the other equality and freedom of choice... Empire is simply not the American way" (Langmore 2005).

If friendly diplomacy is to be effective, the rest of the world must not arrive empty handed. As we have just seen, other states must make the required and continuing investment in the provision of international security forces. These globally available forces will provide for burden sharing and legitimacy, reduce the risks of exposure, and distribute the costs of security operations that no country can handle alone. In the United States there are strong voices for a broader interpretation of American leadership responsibilities:

> The biggest challenge for the United States is not how to win the next military encounter but how to conduct itself so that other nations will willingly accept its leadership. The most effective way to make other countries comfortable with U.S. military power is to demonstrate that America has their best interest at heart, too. They will not be impressed by the offer of a kind of Pax Americana in which Washington makes the world safe for everyone on its own terms (Editorial, The New York Times in the IHT, (4-03-02).

Amitai Etzioni thinks the Republican administration of George W. Bush may have learned some lessons about the value of multilateralism. He believes that when the U.S. and Britain had to return to the UN to seek its endorsement just months after their invasion of Iraq, it reversed the earlier debacle and "turned into one of the United Nations' greatest victories, significantly enhancing its stature and normative power and reinforcing its position as the source of global legitimacy… The longer run trend will strengthen multilateral institutions…." (Etzioni: 114). For instance, the U.S. has found it needs multilateral help in dealing with the Middle East, Iran and North Korea. So the time may be ripe both to reengage Americans and to undertake some of the institutional reforms that would attract them and many others. For instance, one must ask if it is any longer reasonable for a multitude of micro-states to have the same weight in the UN as China, India, Russia and the United States. The world community must start to face the issues of membership and voting and the broader question of sovereignty as has already been suggested by a number of voices (Szasz 2001, Schwartzberg 2004).

Finally, reformers will be able to ally themselves with the American foreign policy elites who have been supporting multilateralism for a number of years. They claim that multilateralism will help American foreign policy by strengthening its soft power, reducing accusations of arrogance and worries about American power, making the U.S. less vulnerable, promoting international order and cooperation, and reducing temptations to construct alliances against the U.S. (Nye 2002: 156–9, U.S. Commission on National Security 2001). Still even these potential allies believe that not all multilateralism is good and only those aspects that benefit American foreign policy are viable.

To respond to the considerable forces arrayed against international institutions and their continued development, we require a concerted global reform movement to cooperate with allies in the United States to bring the above arguments to the

American people. Such arguments must also include an improved image of international organizations.

### 7.2.4 Creating a New Image of the World and the United Nations

> "Perhaps the most important reminder from collective action theory is the importance of creating the right climate of opinion – that is, a culture in which lack of progress is unacceptable. There is an opinion job here not just for diplomats but also for civil society" (Maxwell 2005: 423).

It would indeed be foolhardy to take on the task of reforming a country or the world without thinking first about the people and making sure they understand the task at hand. Long-time international advisor Maurice Strong is categorical: "Revitalizing international institutions will not be possible without a much broader understanding and more positive appreciation of the role of the United Nations and other multilateral organizations (2000: 310)". After two decades of negative media reporting on governmental institutions (corrupt, bloated, incompetent, uncaring bureaucracies) public opinion has also been turned off.

Although our aim is not to "save the United Nations," the UN is the one international institution that is best known by the public. It will be difficult to rally the public to an interest in modernizing multilateralism if there is a black cloud and a lot of misinformation hanging over the international organization people think they know. And we do have to take public opinion into account.

> Because attentive publics often are not swayed by whatever the political leaders claim to be the right course, public opinion does play an important role in foreign policy. Hence the importance of convincing the various publics, and not just their political representatives, of the merits of one's case (Etzioni 2004: 111).

While there are still vast sectors of the world population with little or no access to information, the size of the "attentive public"—those who are concerned by global affairs—is growing. This is due not only to increased education and worldwide communications but also to a wider potential for political participation. There are even some indications that we are witnessing the beginnings of a shared moral sense favoring the protection of the environment, the United Nations, and the reallocation of wealth (Schwartz & Bardi; Pew 2002; Waltzer; Harbour).

A broad historical perspective tells us that the UN is unique because it includes everyone in the world (universality), and it has a capacity to deal with global problems through its functional agencies. It is represented in more than 140 cities throughout the world and has links to corporations, civil society, scientists and academics. It has gradually developed procedures for multilateral decision-making and peacekeeping, and has been the impetus behind the formation of global values (Alger 1995: 33–4).

In *The Parliament of Man*, Paul Kennedy offers a well-reasoned explanation of the UN's importance that bears repeating. "Without the actions and existence of the world organization, humankind would be a lot worse off than it is today, warts and all. It would be much more fragmented, and countries would be much less understanding of others, and much less capable of taking collective action in the face of grave crises" (2006: 285).

Because of the UN and its structural underpinnings, Kennedy continues, aside from the fact we have made terrible mistakes, it is also true that we have established:

- A central place to assemble, raise a common budget and empower international mechanisms;
- A world secretariat to coordinate needs and requests;
- A security body that can be summoned day or night in the event of emergencies;
- An international early-warning, assessment, response, and coordination mechanism;
- Powerful international financial instruments;
- Myriad agencies to help poor and medium-income economies;
- Bodies to respond to the needs of women and children;
- An international human rights regime;
- International monitoring of the environment (p. 286–7).

"Can any intelligent person hold that such cooperative progress or, rather, efforts to reverse the damage – can be done without international agencies" (2006: 288).

To get this information out to the world requires a concentrated and coordinated campaign. Much, but not all, of the criticism of the UN is a matter of perception and image. Images are often made by the media and by interests that have a hobby-horse. Good PR requires a structured campaign that directs specific messages to specific audiences and is capable of rapid response. Not only must there be a campaign to present the logic and benefits of multilateralism in a globalized world, but the United Nations needs friends to carry out a large-scale public relations campaign on its behalf. The United Nations cannot defend itself all alone. Organizations, like individuals, are best defended by others. In concrete terms, this means that those countries that call themselves "Friends of the UN" and NGOs that support multilateralism must coordinate their activities to stand up for the UN in the international court of public opinion. They must provide the means for forming opinion and for standing up to those who are spreading false and misleading communications. But, a concentrated PR will probably also require the coordination of a campaign coalition.

## 7.3 A Process for Modernizing International Institutions

*It is not because it is difficult that we are afraid to act; it is because we are afraid to act that it is difficult* (Seneca).

The aim of this last section, based on all the preceding analysis, is to answer the questions of *how* we can go about the process of modernizing international institutions and *who* should lead the charge. The method is to use a deductive process to arrive at a number of practical principles for moving ahead with the modernization of multilateralism.

This study has shown nine reasons for requiring a new, civil society forum dedicated to promoting global reform:

1. Successive world crises have shown the need for legitimate global institutions.
2. International organizations have proven incapable of reforming themselves.
3. Governments are proving unwilling to take the initiative.
4. Historically, the impetus for world institutional reform has come from civil society.
5. There have been plenty of studies, but they lack focus, relevance and coherence.
6. There is an urgent need for a platform for debate and consensus building.
7. Creative ideas need to be connected to political mobilization by civil society.
8. Public opinion on global governance is ill informed and unprepared.
9. The world has been transformed, but global institutions have not kept pace.

### 7.3.1 Campaign Coalitions

The hypothesis being promoted here is that it will require what has come to be known as a "campaign coalition" based on international, civil society associations to develop consensus and undertake the long-term coordination of all the partners interested in the modernization of multilateralism and, specifically, the transformation of the UN system. Because this issue is the core of our study on 'how' to modernize the UN, let us approach it by answering three questions. What are the principal characteristics of campaign coalitions? What are the advantages of creating such a forum? And, what are some of the difficulties that must be recognized and dealt with?

### 7.3.2 The Characteristics of a Campaign Coalition to Restructure the UN System

Like all new initiatives, it is helpful to learn what we can from the experience of others. Sidney Tarrow's *The New Transnational Activism* is a structured analytic compendium of many of the studies that have been made of international advocacy groups. We learn that the integrated international economy, and relatively easy communication and travel have made it more and more possible for nongovernmental actors with different but complimentary aims to form collaborative alliances. However, coalitions are hard work, especially ones that must be maintained across borders.

Based on recent research, there are five sets of factors that will help coalitions to form and endure: careful definition of a common interest and a compatible set of tactics; mutually trustworthy representatives; credible commitments by the member organizations; management techniques for tension resolution; and selective benefits for the member organizations (Tarrow 2005: 165). Inter-cultural trust is especially difficult to establish and depends on a continuing process of mutual socialization. A first and contentious step is defining procedures for debates and decision-making. It may be, for instance, that cooperation can be maximized by the coalition becoming a distinct organization with independent staff, membership and fund-raising. Procedures must also be in place that allow representatives to voice concerns at difficult moments. Overtime, a new collective identity must be formed that goes beyond initial issues and allows the campaign coalition to weather inevitable storms. A coalition dealing at the highest levels of international politics on the issue of the reform of intergovernmental organizations will inevitably have to engage heavily in the "politics of expertise". Even if it uses a mix of routine negotiations and contentious politics, it will still have to work hard to avoid possible disjunctions between the coalitions' elite relationships and the engagement in local politics by its member organizations.

According to Tarrow, the internationalism that shapes coalitions is a triangular structure of opportunities, resources and threats. It is composed of new, dense networks and a growth of institutions and regimes. This structure provides the opportunity space within which actors can attempt to control globalization and advance human rights. He has found that to influence international affairs, grassroots activists must imbed their issues in domestic cleavages and frame them in ways that matter to their compatriots. More specifically, however, the mechanisms of diffusion of the messages all have their drawbacks for which coalitions must allow. Established networks of trust are surer and more durable but their reach is limited. The Internet has greater reach but its impact is thinner. Mediated diffusion gives the brokers leverage over the content of the message. But, to start with, the opportunities must be used and Tarrow shows both the highs and lows of international advocacy. "Transnational campaign coalitions are the surest sign that enduring networks of activists and advocates can have an impact on global governance" (2005: 205). But also,

> "Campaign coalitions are unglamorous, require constant negotiation, engage in education and lobbying and seldom protest, and usually focus on concrete and often technical objectives. Many collaborate with institutional and governmental elites, requiring compromises that can disappoint the hopes of their more ardent supporters. But some

including the landmines coalition, the European anti-GM movement, and the coalition that derailed the Cancun summit have proved remarkably successful" (2005: 207/11).

## 7.3.3 Some Advantages of Campaign Coalitions

Campaign coalitions can pool their resources and produce solidarity to gain joint political influence. They combine a narrow focal point and high intensity of involvement with long-term collaboration, thereby gaining flexibility and common identity to persist. There is even proof of their capacity to initiate new organizational forms. Moreover they can choose specific targets and combine contentious and negotiated forms of action. Campaign coalitions can open up new opportunities by analyzing changes in their milieu and initiating spirals of action and reaction. They can also shift their activity from one venue to another, as opportunities permit. Mutual support across borders opens up worldwide pressure points. Umbrella organizations can create informal working groups to focus efforts and speak with greater force. Successes such as the Kyoto Protocol, the defeat of the Multilateral Agreement on Investment (MAI), and the Ottawa Landmines Treaty show that when activists are determined and well organized, and when they can collaborate with groups of "like-minded" states and international organizations, and when they put together political opportunities and resources, more durable fusions of international and domestic efforts can result (Tarrow 2005: 172).

> "That is why campaign coalitions, which are less exciting than short term event coalitions and have narrower ambitions and more concrete issue-foci than federated coalitions, may be the wave of the transnational future. Their focus on specific policy issues, their minimal institutionalization, their capacity to shift venues in response to changing opportunities and threats, and their ability to make short-term tactical alliances according to the current focus of interest make them among the most fruitful strategies for transnational collaboration" (Tarrow 2005: 179).

## 7.3.4 Some Difficulties for which Transnational Coalitions must Prepare

As well as all the advantages that have been mentioned, campaign coalitions also have costs and must be prepared to expend resources to maintain themselves. Changing circumstances can deflate or even erase the original enthusiasm of some members. Or purist members who are aggrieved by compromises may turn away or maybe try to compete with the coalition. Procedures must be in place to allow members to express their grievances but too much tolerance for marginal members can make a coalition implode. On the other hand, some members may contribute more and expect higher benefits. Changing circumstances may inhibit a member from meeting its commitments so it must be given time to prove itself. It would seem that a coalition dealing with UN reform would have to pay special attention to managing north-south relationships. All in all, it would seem that both coming together and growing apart are best dealt with by personal relationships and political skill.

Campaign coalitions that are in intensive relationships with partner states, corporations or international organizations may find themselves "caught between a rock and a hard place" when it comes to trying to satisfy politicians and bureaucrats as well as their members. European experience would suggest that at the very least a coalition must avoid making entanglements or becoming dependent on any one or even several agencies. In any case, it is true that transnational activity is heavily dependent on outside forces. For instance, analysts of transnational activism note that security and environmental issues and also climate change have local-global connections where local concerns and interests will often trump transnational commitments. When it comes to protective instincts we return to our national roots and it is well known that people are very "NIMBYISH" (not in my back yard) when it comes to the environment. Sometimes one has to work through cumulative local actions. Even so, one might be accused of simply putting new wine in old bottles. What it will take for a campaign coalition is to forge new political identities and new democratic practices out of the fusion of the local and the global.

Finally, there is always the danger of being derailed by current world events. The 9-11 attacks on the United States should have brought President Bush to turn toward the international institutions for a mutual attack on terrorism – which he did, at first. But then national protective instincts, ideology and American military might brought him to turn inwards and declare war on the "Axis of Evil". However, within months of the attack on Iraq, he was back at the UN's doorstep – but not before he had declared it irrelevant. All these rapid-fire events inevitably had a harmful effect on all Kofi Annan's carefully made plans for reform. A coalition working for the transformation of international institutions is thereby warned that it is not a straightforward process. When it comes to the modernization of the UN, politics is the name of the game. Part of the game is to have a diversified, long term plan that permits the coalition to weather political storms.

The coalition we are proposing would bring together analysts, knowledgeable citizens and researchers with practitioners and representatives of governments, civil society and the private sector. It will use informal "second track diplomacy" to bring the expertise of civil society to cooperate with parliamentarians, governments and the United Nations to strengthen initiatives for the renewal of global institutions. The forum will be part of an institution-building, constitutional process. As with any process, it will not produce one-day miracles—any more than did the Congress of Vienna or that at Philadelphia—but it will coordinate the international debate by bringing together disparate and isolated discussions from around the world.

This independent coalition would cooperate with the United Nations, and would serve to focus public opinion, offer a platform for creative ideas, and, through debate, prepare proposals. One objective is to prove that the research is right: that it is not necessary to have a major crisis in order to move states to re-evaluate their common interests. The forum could pave the way for reform by pre-establishing areas of consensus. Along the way, it might even be able to spark some smaller areas of reform in on-going institutions. These goals suggest that, if successful, such a forum may lead to an on-going series of conferences.

The global reform campaign coalition would be a center for thought and discourse, a "parliament of ideas." It would bring the expertise of civil society to cooperate with the United Nations to strengthen reform initiatives. It would be a platform for the presentation and analysis of innovative ideas for the reform of international organizations. Then they move on to tough lobbying and pressure politics.

The coalition would have to be a knowledge-based body. The principle participants would have an active knowledge of either the management or the critical analysis of global institutions—people who both favor and oppose current trends in globalization. Among the participants would be researchers, present and former international practitioners (outside their official capacities), representatives of international NGOs, parliamentarians, business and labor leaders, authors and columnists, leaders of international movements and governance projects, and international aid and development workers. It would be a multi-stakeholder meeting of all those with a demonstrated interest in global governance.

## 7.4 How: Creating a New Consensus – A Constitutional Discourse on Global Politics

In the present context, it seems that to broaden and deepen the current UN emphasis on institutional change, the first priority is to place on the international agenda a public discourse on the constitutional principles that should underlie institutional transformation. The sections on international change and on current international politics in this study lead to the conclusion that the world is in the midst of a fundamental transformation from a "Westphalian," nation-state system to a global political system combining state, non-state, and supra state actors (see also Lyons & Mastundano 1992). This requires rethinking our world political system. Our current political structures are not capable of coping with the problems and opportunities of globalization.

One is forced to agree with Simai that, "major disagreements exist about which direction future institutional changes should take… there is no grand design" (1994: 349). That is why an elaborate process of discourse is not a luxury but a necessity. The analysis in this study points to a need for two complementary processes for the modernization of multilateralism: one to initiate a fundamental constitutional discourse and the other to create forums for the debate of incremental, structural reforms. There is no necessity that one precedes the other. Indeed, they could be accomplished together.

Thinking about the reform of the United Nations and other international organizations is constitution-making by another name. The studies of institutional reform should be accompanied by an analysis of the total international context in which they will have their place, the major principles and norms they should foster, and the relations among the institutions, as well as between them and the world population they are to represent. As Edward McWhinney states in *Constitution Making,* "Law cannot exist in isolation from society" (1981: 135).

A public discourse would enrich the UN's studies by bringing to bear a wider array of world political and constitutional expertise. Fostering participation in institutional innovation by constitutional, democracy and international relations specialists, as well as by philosophers and futurologists, should meld with the UN's new, open political culture. This new UN openness has been exemplified by Canada's initiative to invite non-Council members to address the Security Council, the Arria Formula for the Security Council to consult civil society, the Secretary-General's Global Compact with business, and new initiatives for recognizing and working with international non-governmental organizations and other representatives of civil society such as the Cardoso Report. So, a constitutional exercise would fit the new era of the UN but it must be established with or without the official blessing of the Organization.

As one of our colleagues has said, if we want to support the UN's institutional debate we must write the "Federalist Papers" of the 21st century. These new "Global Governance Papers" will require both expertise and wisdom to create criteria for developing a consensus to construct our global political system for coming decades.

But it must be emphasized that this is an exercise in constitutional discourse or pre-constitutionalism, which sets out to analyze and prepare the elements of a consensus on principles, aims, conditions and context that decision-makers and the public will want to take into consideration.

> A pre-condition for any politically viable exercise in constitution-making is a prior political consensus – on the part of the society for which the constitutional charter is intended, or at least its dominant political elites – as to the main goal values and policies of that society in the future (McWhinney 1981: 134).

It requires astute political thinking, because we know that the ideals and values that inspire any set of rules and structures will soon be ignored in the rough and tumble of democratic politics. We must project into the future the implications for political dynamics of today's integrated but divided world – democratic and authoritarian, rich and poor, technologically advanced and developing. In our real world we will need both long-term vision and short-term plans. It is in this fractured context that we must re-imagine traditional constitutional fundamentals. "Constitutional systems must always include an in-built quality of change" (McWhinney 1981: 132).

At present, when we consider modifying international institutions, we think, for instance, about better representation on the Security Council and constraining the veto, more balanced economic institutions, democratic influences, inter-agency coordination, humanitarian intervention, and the responsibility to protect. However, this is only the icing on the cake. We must broaden our perspective to think in terms of political ideals and fundamental values and objectives; rights and obligations of membership and citizenship; recognition, participation and representation of individuals, peoples, wealth, territories, and cultures; duties and rights of majorities and minorities; democratic and electoral forms; political and civic mobilization; weighted voting; structure, linkages and balances between executive, legislative, judicial and administrative functions and institutions; power structures, limits, and checks and balances a possible federal regime; inter-institutional coordinating mechanisms; relationship of political institutions to the population, however defined; responsibility and accountability of power structures and leaders; civic education and information and communication processes; judicial institutions and legal enforcement and sanctions; resources and revenues; social services and equity, economic development; etc. The length of the agenda alone should convince us of the need for a global constitutional discourse. But the process is complicated by the need to proceed in a complicated series of stages.

It is not sufficient to just define new institutions; we must also imagine, to the best of our ability, the conditions in which the institutions will exist. Our mission is to use these age-old constitutional concepts to reformulate the goals of international institutional reform and use these goals to recast the traditional constitutional notions that were developed for national societies. We must ask ourselves: are we dealing with just another phase in human evolution or are we at a fundamental turning point when we must reimagine a new style of global politics?

This is no academic exercise. What successful business would undertake a significant merger or take-over without a debate among its managers and board of directors, a research analysis of the field of business, the advice of expert consultants, careful investigation of the synergies of the combined organization, a study of the present and future market, and an analysis of the competition and eventual approval at the annual meeting? What modern government would consider creating a new ministry or agency without lengthy pressures from within the party and the policy community, commissioned research studies, debates within the public service management, consultations with public policy experts, public consultations, opinion polls and focus groups, and serious policy debates within cabinet? And what leading countries were ever founded or undertook institutional reforms without enormous constitutional debates among their intellectuals and citizens? Why should it be any different when we are considering the reform of the major institutions of global governance?

We now turn to the question of who should form such a network and how it should be structured?

## 7.5 Who: The Question of Leadership

Now that the need for a coalition has been established and its nature described, there remains one question: *how* can the process of modernizing multilateralism be initiated? Who will organize and fund the "modernization of multilateralism reform movement"? Let us proceed by a process of elimination.

- Leadership will not come from the great powers. Studies show us they want the greatest degree of latitude to follow their own will in international politics. The more effective multilateral institutions are, the more they tie the hands of the powerful. Even if they provide international stability, this appears to be secondary to their national interest. The postwar multilateral leadership of the United States was a one-of-a-kind situation, not the rule. Bush has said that he wants to be free to follow his own drummer.
- The dozens of finely crafted UN reform proposals that have led nowhere prove that we cannot depend on member states to be the great innovators. There are ample reasons. States and their diplomats, the ones we call "UN hands," are run ragged just managing international relations. They have no time to think about reforming them. In addition, as memories of World War II fade, the will for collective action has given way to self-interest. Countries look after their national interests first. Still multilaterally oriented countries should help the global reform movement by concentrating on the UN rather than setting up rival groups.
- UN professional personnel, though acutely aware of their organization's shortcomings, are national nominees and international public servants. They do not have the clout or liberty to initiate a reform movement. But they can be excellent advisors.
- Who else has the scope and the power to promote global governance? Corporations have the wealth, the power and the motivations. But usually governance is a marginal topic for them and their interest in UN reform is narrowly based and short-lived, at best. Business associations in America and Europe have shown they are capable of crafty political action and long-term strategies. But they do this only when it affects their interests—mainly their profit margins. Although some corporations might be interested because they want to see stable international markets, history rarely shows the business community leading political transformations. One specialist on business-government relations recently concluded, that by definition, public policy is not the primary business of firms; therefore, business managers tend to be reactive, following the lead of others in deciding to get involved with policy issues. Besides, to enjoy legitimacy, such an initiative must be developed by "disinterested" persons and organizations—ones that do not have tangible ideological or financial motives and are not beholden to particular states or capitalist enterprises.

- What about the academic community, which does show a vital interest in this issue? Research institutes and academic specialists have already demonstrated that they are capable of leading "second-track diplomacy." For instance, they founded the Asia-Pacific Economic Council, which eventually became a political institution. But academia it is not broadly representative, and it tends to have little practical experience or political competence. Academics should be of the game but they cannot be the game. Although some individuals might play a leading role even beyond their academic research, as a community they do not have the organizational structures or the mandate from their members to initiate a political movement. The same is true of some interested and wealthy foundations that offer crucial support but cannot take political leadership.
- Foundations have played a major role in research and reports on the reform of international organizations. Often they have been responsible for whole series of studies, conferences, and other initiatives. Primarily, however, they do not have a mandate to spearhead political action. They also have their rules, policy objectives and closed-end time frameworks that limit their flexibility. Also, most of the affluent foundations come from developed Western countries, and even if they have a hands-off policy, their money might be suspect in certain parts of the world.
- Finally, we have already seen that there are trends by some actors to avoid the UN as much as possible and, instead, to promote specialized summits, institutions, coalitions, and regional organizations. It is unlikely that any of these alternative, semi-institutional instances will have any interest in UN reform.

The best candidate for sustained leadership of a movement to transform the UN is the organized capacity of civil society. We have seen that in the 19th century, disinterested philanthropists, leading citizens, budding NGOs and social movements, academics and international lawyers, etc., aided and abetted by like-minded governments, took the lead in reforming international governance and developing new institutions. We have also seen that since the founding of the UN 60 years ago, the only major structural transformation, the founding of the International Criminal Court, was inspired by a coalition of International Non-Governmental Organizations (INGOs) and brought about (once again) by a collaboration between "like-minded governments" and the INGOs representing civil society. They must do so again. Nor am I alone in coming to this conclusion. In his study on the *Future of Global Governance*, Mihaly Simai noted the multiple, important functions of the civil sector; "NGOs are increasingly needed as forces of independent and innovative political thinking and as champions of pluralism and democracy. The future vitality of international multilateralism depends on NGOs continuing to place critical issues on the global agenda and mobilizing national publics to ensure that collective action is taken and programs implemented (1994: 348).

The man with the most experience on the subject also agrees. In an interview on the BBC on 15 Sept. 2005, Kofi Annan stated,

> "You have no idea of how we work with civil society and the NGOs. They can lead and say things I cannot say. There are times we don't like what they say or do and times when they don't like what we say or do and there are moments when they are ahead of us. They can lead and say things I cannot say. We cannot operate in the field without our essential partners, the NGOs."

Annan's quote underlines the crucial strengths that civil society can bring to the cause of UN reform. Its diversity in numbers and composition, including International Non-Governmental Organizations, intellectuals, journalists, religious groups and so on, reflects the complexity of society. Its amazing growth in numbers worldwide makes it a force to be reckoned with. Its experience in local development and in the trenches of international politics gives it a full panoply of practical, national and specialized knowledge to bring to the table. Its very diversity is a guarantor of its autonomy of mind. The obvious fact that it is obedient to no single interest, gives it a fairly broad sense of responsibility. It is truly international in scope. And, most of all, the great INGOs are Janus-faced: they look out on international politics as an experienced player and inward toward national politics where they can mobilize the populace and lobby the government and opposition.

In the Introduction, we defined civil society as it is used in this study as associational life in national and international non-governmental organizations that are concerned with global issues, international institutions and the question of global governance. International studies of civil society have depicted it more specifically as being: a part of society distinct from states and markets that is aimed at advancing common interests and facilitating common action; an arena for public deliberation, rational dialogue and the exercise of active citizenship; and often in the realm of service rather than self-interest; and a breeding ground for attitudes of cooperation, trust, tolerance and non-violence (Edwards 2004, Keane 2003, see Introduction). These are exactly the qualities that would be required to move along the debate on the transformation of the UN. Under the organizational conditions we have described in the last two sections, INGOs also can fulfill the role of an 'epistemic community' to accumulate the consensual knowledge required for rethinking the Organization by developing common beliefs, causal understanding and defined criteria for UN transformation that must sustain social action (p. Haas 1992). Being from outside the Organization, they have the distance required to question accepted wisdom while still being close enough to an understanding of UN realities because of their day-to-day activities (Keohane 1988).

While it is hard to find perfect human beings, civil society leaders have developed three additional aptitudes that make them a good choice for leading UN reform. First, while politicians are generally activated by power and executives by profit, association leaders normally are motivated by doing good. Second, over time, they have become highly knowledgeable in their international field of interest. They not only have a deep understanding of their special domain, say the environment or human rights, but they also develop expertise in operating within the multilateral system. Third, while NGOs must learn to deal with 'real politick', they must also be responsible to their very morally oriented members. Thus, as leaders, they are not foreign to the use of power and profit, but the leash placed on them by their motives and their members limits their implication.

However, Cerny (2006) introduces a series of warnings that must absolutely be taken into account as we try to insert pluralism into a global governance context. When you have competitive organizations it may lead to increased conflict and disorder if not somehow counteracted by other structural and political constraints. There may be anarchy rather than accommodation. Also, the tendency of individuals to "free ride" on the activities of groups and to have multiple or overlapping loyalties may undermine coherent participation. Second, interest groups tend to be inherently undemocratic in their internal workings, as Michels (1962) also contended.

> "Even when a group starts out as a democratic association, the necessities of managing the group and competing with other groups means that strategic and even tactical control, including financial control, is increasingly ceded to elites *within* the group. Therefore the interaction of these groups with others will ultimately be determined to a large extent by the self-interests of the groups' leaders, especially their interests in organizational and personal survival and maintaining their own status – something they have in common with the leaders of other groups" (Cerny 2006: 106).

In these cases, mutual accommodation would lead to oligopoly. If groups act as a 'closed corporation', relationships of 'clientelism' and 'patronage' can arise linking the groups to the ruling bureaucracy. Furthermore group politics might well lead to greater inequality among groups and their goals, which can often be zero-sum in nature so that when one group wins, others lose. A group possessing more relevant resources is likely to control outcomes (Cerny 2006: 106–7).

There must be a pluralism-reinforcing playing field that provides opportunities for people to associate, internalize pluralistic practices, coalition-build, and have an influence on power. Liberal-democratic nations have played that role by creating a political milieu that maintains a sort of stable coexistence. The question for us is whether these conditions can be gradually recreated at the global level?

There are two pre-conditions for the existence of pluralism: a genuine plurality of socio-economic forces and a supportive structural/institutional environment. However, and according to Cerny this is crucial, these structures may exist (liberal-democracy) or there must be the possibility of generating them through proactive politics of "political entrepreneurs". In other words, liberal-democracy did not just happen by a miracle. It was the sum total of thousands of self-limiting interests, politicians and political thinkers interacting over generations. "The key to this process is the role of individual and group actors in intervening, managing, manipulating, reshaping, and reconstructing both plurality and pluralism. Thus pluralism is what *actors* make of it" (Cerny 2006:108–9) Thus also, the political entrepreneurs must have the capacities to counteract opposition from the authorities or opposing economic and social forces. In other words they must be able to compete in the continuing tension between institutional-administrative forces and individual, liberal and pluralist forces (cf. "the conflict between powerful elites and human needs", Burton 1979: 32, above). The capacity to act as a group would appear to be crucial.

Not all the characteristics of civil society fit the perfect leadership profile for the modernization of the United Nations system. We have already noted Edwards' warnings that there are dangers of cooptation, of exaggeration of political importance, of "loonies and paranoids", and of narrowness of purpose and constituency that can lead to illegitimacy, lack of accountability and external dependence (Edwards 2004, see Chapter 1). Thakur also recognizes the policy-making functions of NGOs but adds that not all are "good ones". "We must confront, address and redress the problem of unelected, unaccountable, unrepresentative, and self-aggrandizing NGOs" (Thakur 2002: 278). These criticisms need to be taken very seriously. While heads of international associations are usually ethically motivated, they can become entrapped in their own end game. Often they are limited by their own normative narrowness, that is to say, if you don't accept my rules and precepts then the only way for you is the highway. This obsession with one's own values and specialized goals leads to a desire to control one's own space (no matter how small) and hence to exaggerate its importance. That's why some NGOs give the impression of being run by loonies and paranoids. In a return to the old saw about the "enemy you know", they are just as ready to attack a brotherly association that has a difference of opinion on some obscure value, as they are to cooperate for common goals. This is one of the two major Achilles heels of any potential civil society reform movement.

The other is the problem of cooptation. In a sense, INGOs find themselves in a "catch-22" situation. If they do not cooperate with governments, corporations and international agencies then they risk not being part of the international game. If they do, they risk being co-opted. But behind this continuous danger lurks something worse: a feeling on the part of some NGO leaders of only being truly validated when they are on the same playing field as the "big boys". Often it seems as though they get more satisfaction out of being invited to a 'high-level meeting' to discuss some policy matter with relatively limited significance than to investing time and energy in the building of a reform movement that will impact all policies for generations to come. The desire to want to 'be on the inside' can also be a justification for accepting grants, and invitations and funding for "important" meetings. The slippery slope to perdition is paved with the good intentions of being an insider and paradoxically gives sense to the expression "external dependence".

The amorphousness of civil society would be a guarantor of disinterestedness but it could also pose a barrier to constructive action. As one experienced practitioner has observed,

> Civil society is therefore much more diverse and fragmented than governments and international organizations. This is of course one of its virtues, but it leads to difficulty in providing for the participation of civil society in the official processes of governance. Many civil society groups and organizations hold common positions on particular issues, but it's seldom feasible for them to present a united front. Sometimes the very number of small and fragmented organizations inhibits agreement on common positions... (Strong 2000: 338).

Maurice Strong also points out that even though a disproportionate share of civil society organizations still have Western roots, developing countries' participation has dramatically increased. And many of the INGOs have resources that exceed those of UN agencies. Therefore, he believes, civil society must be a partner of international organizations, despite their drawbacks.

The World Social Forum appears to becoming more interested in institutional reform. It is the largest gathering of civil society organizations, with more than 150 represented on its Council. At recent planning meetings, its representatives announced that the January 2005 meeting in Port Alegre would start providing concrete answers to problems for "another possible world." The forum wants to find ways to influence governments' choices with concrete responsibilities and practices. In 2005, the World Social Forum took on themes other than globalization, including peace and security and reform of international financial institutions and the United Nations. There is going to be a coordination space to set up a common agenda (IPS 2004).

This might be the catalyst for getting its members to create wings of their organizations specializing in institutional issues. These could be brought together by the few INGOs, such as the World Federalists, that have shown leadership and know-how in coordinating civil society in campaign coalitions.

## 7.6 How: Funding – Sources and Balance

When it comes to international reform initiatives, funding is always an issue. It has to be clearly independent and squeaky clean. Proposals will not be accepted if they are seen as coming from one country (or countries) or one set of financial interests. No INGO will be willing to let its independence be eroded by suspicion of being at the hire of some paymaster. The best way of funding the Forum would be through a "participation tax" levied on membership fees. Another possibility is the voluntary creation of a special "institutional reform" sections with their own budgets in participating INGOs. The funds so raised would be pooled in a coalition reform budget, overseen by a coalition Council. Once such funding assures the independence of the coalition's deliberations, then other sources of funding from host countries, corporate sponsorships and advertising, and foundation grants could be solicited. The diversity would assure both the appearance and reality of independence. NGOs are always complaining that they are not sufficiently listened to. In part, this is because they do not give themselves the organizational muscle and finances to develop long-term, experienced spokespersons.

In some senses, money can be an excellent leveller and energizer. Once one makes a financial contribution, a desire to ensure its productiveness follows. A common membership contribution (according to means) would give civil society a common objective and some real clout in the area of institutional reform. The crucial aspects about funding are its stability and—especially—its diversity, which provides legitimacy. Foundations and like-minded governments might also aid the cause. The cost of meetings could be partially offset by registration fees and government sponsorships. Contributions might come from national reform coalitions.

The greatest difficulty for civil society could be the necessity of putting water in its wine. Most voluntary organizations are based on sets of norms and values. They do not take kindly to compromise. Although it might start as a civil society reform forum, eventually a continuing forum to modernize multilateralism would succeed only if it were able to represent all the types of stakeholders that make up the global community. Some civil society organizations would not much like their prospective bedfellows.

So not only the tenants of the status quo block innovation in international institutions. There is also the ineffectiveness of the highly varied contingent of reformers who are weakened by infighting, and a lack of coordination and focus.

To say that a great variety of birds are flying around in the reform aviary is an understatement. Perched on top are the realist eagles, who only believe in process reforms to improve inter-state relations by making international organizations a little more efficient and less onerous. Bureaucratic penguins, which strut around guarding the institutions they know and love, often support them. Nearby are the woodpeckers, who demonstrate their knowledge of the status quo by pecking away endlessly at minute administrative and financial process reforms, seldom raising their heads to see the forest for the trees. The sharp-eyed owls do see the big picture, and at the drop of a pen will write soul-satisfying, far-sighted plans for fine new institutions that never see the light of day because there is no action plan for getting from here to there. Of a similar stripe are the red-breasted idealists, who reject anyone's reforms that do not include all their cherished politically correct values. They are much like the do-gooder storks who love bringing their world-saving packages of policies to any conference that will invite them. The parrots crying their wish lists of desirable reforms make a great racket but don't fly very far. And then there are the cardinals, dressed up in the finery of their noble visions of democracy-now, who seem unaware that half the aviary just wants bread and water first.

Irony and exaggerated characterization aside, it is probably true that the world needs far-sighted visionaries who can set the agenda for the future. But we also need to find a way to bring the various sorts of reformers together so that differences can be debated and perhaps overcome, and effective paths to the future elaborated.

But such is the nature of governance and institution building. Here is a challenge worthy of citizens and associations who are worried about the negative aspects of globalization and recognize that reformed world institutions are a necessary step to a better world. It is a noble goal, but it is also workable and doable.

## 7.7 Practical Ideas on How to Transform the United Nations System

Let us try to bring the foregoing proposals about how to transform the UN system together in one brief package.

1. To answer the question of *how* to reform international institutions, we should proceed from knowledge of past and present efforts to transform international politics, and then by logical deduction and a process of elimination of options.
2. History tells us there have been several major influences on the nature and evolution of international organizations. These include technological, economic and military challenges, which create the demand for change; international movements and non-governmental organizations, which are motors of transformation; the personnel of international institutions, who are connoisseurs of evolution; great social and political leaders, who are activators of change; and international events and crises, which trigger great modifications.
3. On rare occasions, political leaders are inspired by world crises to transform international organization. They do this while maintaining their dominant status, and based on their perception of international techniques that work. More generally, the reform of international institutions has been determined by a combination of exceptional individuals, the insistent ideas and political pressures of international non-governmental organizations (INGOs), and the expertise of international public servants, often in alliance with a few concerned states.
4. The evolution of international organizations is moved ahead by continuing debates at international technical, scientific and humanist conferences, as well as by the development of new forms of international consultation and decision-making through experimentation and imitation. Conferences help develop organizational techniques and psychological aptitudes for multilateral situations.
5. INGOs have learned that they can move governments in the direction of increased multilateral cooperation through judicious influence and continuous political pressure, and by leading the way.

6. If we want reform and innovation in international organizations, we should not wait for an international crisis or expect major powers to offer their leadership.
7. We learn similar lessons from the sociology of change within societies. Major social transformations are a response to change in the socio-economic and technological environments. What is required to respond to these changes is transformation of the national regime. This includes procedures and personnel, composition, structures, value system, and processes of conflict and cooperation. Agents of change include portions of the elites, social movements, and pressure tactics to mobilize opinion for change.
8. We are moving into new territory when we think about international regime change. One direct analogy between national and international societies is the European Union. It shows the importance of far-sighted leaders, the spillover effect of a step-by-step approach, the need for INGOs to counter conservative special interests, and the need to bring along public opinion (an example is the Franco-German Friendship Treaty and its student exchange programs).
9. We are in new territory, so we must be creative. Power elites are generally in favor of the status quo, both because they must defend established interests, and because they are too preoccupied with managing the system to think about changing it. But traditional elite analysis does not fully take into account the complexity of modern society, with its multiplicity of alternative elites that exercise influence and leadership at different levels. For instance, on the international scene, certain former and present international public servants and national politicians and NGO leaders see the need for change. It is not just a question of power structures but of public information and the mobilization of public and elite opinion to put the issue of regime change on the political agenda.
10. To transform international institutions, the issues are so profound that you cannot just count on concerned groups and specialists to provide brilliant ideas and lobby leaders. Alternative leadership groups, those wanting transformation, must also provide platforms for their ideas, develop consensus, attract the media, change public opinion, and influence national priorities. They must create a global reform movement aimed at reinforcing the effectiveness and legitimacy of international organizations.
11. These alternative elites must start by answering the question "why"? Why bother to reform international institutions? The answer is because we must transform the Westphalian *inter-national* system, based on national sovereignty, to allow for the evolution of a *global* system that can confront the global challenges that threaten all humanity, beyond national frontiers.
12. What does institutional reform include? Agendas vary, but most would encompass these: a) a constitutional debate about the meaning of multilateralism, including forms of membership and participation, the basic rights and responsibilities of world citizens, and the rule of law; b) the composition, roles, functions and coordination of global assemblies, councils, agencies and secretariats; c)

methods of decision-making; d) socio-economic, financial and environmental management of the world; e) rules of humanitarian interventions in sovereign states; f) a security regime that benefits all countries, big and small; g) the resources and institutional infrastructure for aid and development; and h) global peacekeeping and peace-building capacity. We need long-term, sustainable reform leading to the creation of fundamental, global institutions—not adhockery, not personnel, not policies, and not administration.

13. Who will lead the reform process? We must learn from the past, and proceed by a process of elimination.
    - Leadership will not come from the great powers. Studies show us they want the greatest degree of latitude to follow their own will in international politics. The dozens of finely crafted UN reform proposals that have led nowhere prove that we cannot depend on member states to be the great innovators. UN professional personnel do not have the political clout or liberty to initiate a reform movement. Business associations do this only when it affects their interests—mainly their profit margins. What about the academics? As a community they do not have the organizational structures or the mandate from their members to initiate a political movement. The same is true of some interested and wealthy foundations. Parliamentarians play only a limited role because of their responsibilities to their national constituencies and parties.
    - The only significant option left to reform global governance is to mobilize the collective forces of civil society: international non-governmental organizations (INGOs) and global social movements in a campaign coalition. Although we came to this conclusion by eliminating other alternatives, we do not endorse a process of exclusion. In fact, the INGOs will likely be able to use the help and even the leadership of some scholars, present and former international public servants, parliamentarians, business people, foundations, and like-minded political leaders from middle powers.
    - One option that is not viable is a "benevolent," unilateral hegemony enforced by a dominant power such as the United States, or even a small, self-appointed group of democratic countries that think they can guide the world. People espousing such courses of action have not realized we are no longer living in the colonial environment of the 19th century. At the beginning of the 21st century, we find ourselves with global challenges, 192 independent states, and an international system based on norms of human rights. The task of global governance is to surmount the contradictions between these three facts of life. Some states may require international assistance, but they will not accept tutelage. Only multilateral institutions can deal with the complexity of global problems and the requirement of international legitimacy to intervene in sovereign states.
14. Civil society has many advantages that recommend it as the leader of the global reform campaign coalition. It is global (50,000 NGOs and INGOs with

increasingly transnational membership), relatively "disinterested," and is reasonably accepted by all the stakeholders. Civil society also has expertise, can raise funds, and can mobilize national and international influence.

15. To a growing degree, civil society is aware of its capacities and responsibilities. Leading "coordinators" are starting to appear, as we have seen in the Johannesburg conference on sustainable development and the International Criminal Court. "New diplomacy" came to the fore when middle powers joined INGOs and dedicated social movements to bring about both the Ottawa treaty on landmines and the Treaty of Rome on the International Criminal Court. More recently, the Porto Alegre World Social Forum is reported to be reorienting itself to attain specific reform goals.
16. Given the significance of civil society, and particularly of INGOs for the global institutional reform coalition, it is important to note that civil society has characteristics that a reform process will have to take into account. These include fragmentation, a normative orientation toward entitlements and not obligations, a lack of focus on institutional issues, a poorly informed public, a tendency to be single-issue groups rather than having global concerns, and a leadership that is sometimes protective of its turf. The campaign coalition must be designed to surmount these difficulties and manage the sensitivities of INGOs:
    - Reform will not be achieved overnight just because there is a need and some farsighted people believe in it. Global governance reform is a long process (with perhaps some short-term victories). It requires a sustaining structure.
    - The global governance reform coalition will work best if it is sustained over the long haul by a consortium of major INGOs working with each other and with other interested individuals and groups.
    - There need to be regular international forum-conferences to provide a platform for competing ideas on global governance, to work toward the development of agreement on priorities for institutional reforms, and to mobilize public opinion and political will for their achievement.
    - The reform coalition should start as a "second-track diplomacy" led by a combination of academics, political leaders, philanthropists, parliamentarians, diplomats and UN hands, working with major "coordinating" INGOs.
    - The reform coalition can be financed by a combination of foundations and countries hosting the forums. Some corporations in the UN Compact might wish to advertise at the conferences. But the basic requirement is that major INGOs take leadership of the institutional reform movement by establishing global governance sections of their associations and by dedicating a small proportion of their membership dues to the institutional issue.
    - If the coalition is to last, it will have to equip itself with a global governance reform assembly and a council. Both must be open to all interested and competent parties, and be regularly renewed by election. They will create a permanent secretariat, which, along with standing working groups on

institutional issues, will move the analysis and mobilization of multilateral reform ahead between the forums. They will include and be supported by national coalitions for global governance reform.

- Once the coalition is established and starts attracting attention from politics, business and the media, the INGOs and their initial allies must be prepared to open the reform movement to all interested stakeholders, including the business community and like-minded governments. Reform cannot be seen to be the purview of any country, group or sector of society. Reform will succeed only once it has attracted the leading edge of all major sectors of society.
- To satisfy the sensitivities of civil society, the global reform coalition must be a) open to all interested and knowledgeable parties; b) transparent in its decision-making; c) responsible to its members and the public; d) accessible in the five continental regions; and e) a consortium, not a monolith.

Institutional reform will be an ongoing, step-by-step process. A structured Global Governance Reform Coalition anchored in leading INGOs must sustain the reform process through vicissitudes. This will not be a straight path. It will be necessary to keep in mind the goal of creating global institutions, based on human rights and eventually on democratic procedures, to allow humanity as a whole to effectively manage global problems.

To this end, we need to harness the collective energies of civil society to keep up the pressure and momentum for reform. The movement starts with the willing and the interested. It has to use crises, not succumb to them. It builds by increments but must be directed by global goals. The Global Governance Reform Coalition will be recognized as legitimate if it is molded in the image of the world it wishes to create.

## 7.8 Mobilizing for Democracy

The keen observer will have noticed that in all these proposals for institutional transformation one link is missing: a social goal, a set of values that is capable of mobilizing broad public support. The proposal (no. 11 above) that the aim of reform is to transform international organizations so that they will be able to cope with global problems is correct, but it lacks passion. It is only enticing for those who accept rational, egghead reasoning. It does not say what sorts of organizations are required. Also, when we see that to make reform work requires not only leadership and alternative elites but also public opinion and social movement support, it is clear that broader motivation is required. Historically, democracy has been the great mobilizer. Throughout this book we have seen that current world governance is unrepresentative, exclusive, closed and unjust. These are problems that cry out for democratic solutions. But just how will democratic goals fit into the reform process?

The issue of international democracy has been discussed for some decades now. Many of those who are critical of international institutions believe that the main cause of their biased policies and inept practices is their "democratic deficit". Most of the analysts reviewed in this book recognize that in the context of globalization, world problems provide strong motivations for democratization at the international level. I have found at least 16 INGOs like South Centre, Civicus, Campaign for a more Democratic UN, and Global People's Assembly Movement that promote democracy as part of their strategy (Trent 2006a: 9–10). And this does not include comparative research centres like IDEA, or international efforts such as the Community of Democracies piloted by Madeline Albright. Purposely excluded are agencies for promoting democratization within transitional and developing countries because they are not always keen on democratizing international institutions. Nevertheless, it is clear there is a strong movement toward international democracy.

However, in practice, it is difficult to conceive that we could move directly to global democracy at the present time. The value objectives for global reform include democracy as just one among many desired goals – and by no means the most immediate or urgent in comparison with surmounting hunger and poverty. Similarly, among all the proposals for changing international organizations, democracy takes second place to other more practical and relevant steps such as humanitarian intervention, sustainable development, equity for women or reforming the Security Council. As we have seen, most of the studies and commissions on the transformation of the United Nations are technical in nature, dealing with their norms and structures. So, we have some reformers dealing with technical realities while others promote democratic objectives. Often one type of reformer ignores the other. The danger is that by excluding each other, both may be lost. All this brings forth the question of how can we square the circle? How can democratic values be introduced at the global level and how can democratization be included in the development of global governance?

Before going further, it is necessary to specify what is meant by 'democracy' (for a detailed study and references see Trent 2006a). During the last half century a great deal of emphasis has been placed on what is called the 'electoralist' or 'process' definition. It insists the central feature of democracy is the competition for governmental power based on inclusive participation in fair and regular elections and backed up by civil and political liberties such as freedom of speech and association, that are sufficient to insure the integrity of participation (Schumpeter 1950, Dahl 1971). Left out of this definition are two other equally important features: opposition to concerted power and the need to develop an effective democratic culture.

It is thus necessary to include in the definition 'elite autonomy criteria' and 'wealth differential criteria'. These criteria reflect the need to insure, first, that there is a dispersal of power so that opposing groups have sufficient resources to compete in politics; and, second, that a lack of wealth does not exclude any category of citizens from the possibility of participating (Etzioni-Halevy 1993, Tourraine 1991). In a presentation at the 2006 World Congress of the International Political Science Association, Vidar Helgesen, president of the Institute for Democracy and

Electoral Assistance (IDEA) insisted that democracy is about more than elections. One must instill a democratic culture and this is a long-term proposition. Democracy is inherently local, growing from within. Imposed frameworks will be dismantled. Democracy is about politics and power, not just about electoral techniques. It is a value and end in itself. Although democracy cannot be exported ready-made, local actors can be supported internationally (koskag@idea.int). Timothy Ash of Oxford agrees: "It's better for people to find their own paths to freedom and our job is to support them in the ways they want" (*Globe and Mail*, 4-08-06: A13). This extended definition is of vital importance because it tells us that it is wrong-headed to think democracy has been instilled just because you have an election. In the short run, precipitate elections can often lead to a populist cacophony and conflicting demands that can increase the dangers of violence and even destroy political regimes (Chua 2003–4). Equally it tells us that developing democracy at the global level is not as simple as setting in motion a process for a People's Assembly. That is why Ash believes "The right conclusion is strange but true: A little democracy is a dangerous thing – so let's have more of it" (ibid). We need to enhance democratic values in all countries.

But, all this is just the tip of the iceberg when it comes to reasons for not being able to proceed immediately with global democratic reforms. As we have seen, we are confronted by the reality that more than half the people of the world live under authoritarian governments and/or have little or no experience with democratic processes and culture. Just coming up with a satisfactory electoral system in present circumstances would be difficult if not impossible. Ann Florini believes that at the global level, "direct electoral systems would be unwieldy." She thinks, however, that the transparency and participation she is projecting would make possible a "highly democratic, albeit non-electoral, system of transnational governance" because it would provide voice and accountability. "Sunlight really is the best disinfectant," Florini claims (2003: 208–9). She argues that we should not confuse the form of democracy with its function. Democracy requires that the people have two things: a voice, and mechanisms for holding officials accountable.

Without saying "no" to democracy, the World Commission on Global Governance was circumspect about its support for a directly elected peoples' assembly to complement the General Assembly, or for an assembly of parliamentarians as a constituent assembly to prepare for the people's chamber. Aside from half the world presently having no experience with democracy or elections, a people's assembly would have to have electorates (constituencies) of 12 million people to keep the membership down to 500. This would prevent many countries from having even one representative. The Commission thought it would be best to start, "when the time comes," with parliamentarians acting as a constituent. But nothing should happen (except for the creation of a "Civil Society Forum" and a "right to petition" (as in the European Union) until the General Assembly has devised a "revitalized role for itself" (1995: 256–58).

But there are also plentiful reasons for insisting on the need to move toward democratic objectives in global governance. Foreign policies are still run much as they were under kings and autocrats. Especially in parliamentary countries, foreign affairs, defense and diplomacy come directly under the authority of the executive (the president or prime minister and their cabinet and security advisors). There are few public debates, and parliamentarians rarely get a chance to influence or oversee international relations. The public is poorly informed, and consequently most feel they cannot understand or influence the subject. In international institutions there is no parliamentary oversight, and there are no participatory, elected, representative institutions. There is very little in the way of public information and responsibility to national democratic institutions. Much decision-making, if not profoundly secret, is at least off the record and behind closed doors. The most powerful international institutions are under the control of small economic and political elites of wealthy, powerful countries.

So we see that there are lots of reasons to desire democratic global institutions and lots of reasons to be skeptical about the world's capacity to move ahead with this noble endeavor right away. To democratize international politics, some commentators have long called for the introduction of global democratic institutions. Others, more recently, have proposed democratic practices such as the reinforcement of international law, greater information and participation through civil society organizations, more transparency and more direct responsibility and reporting to public institutions. If one refers back to Chapter 5 and the issue of global democracy, one will find that we do not lack for creative suggestions about how to promote global democracy. The question is how to proceed?

The authors we have consulted have reminded us that in some ways we are in a global situation akin to the historic conditions prior to national revolutions. Under the impact of globalization policies, the wealth gap is now the central problem. The cause is rampant capitalism without any democratic safeguards. The common root of most world problems from terrorism to environmental degradation is savage economic exploitation without the political balance to protect the common good. "The historical symmetry that paired democracy and capitalism within societies and made the democratic nation-state the free market's most effective regulator, humanizer and overseer has gone missing" (Barber 2003: 158). Too few people control too much economic and political power. Barber believes global capital is completely unchecked, which breeds anarchy, nihilism, and violence. One of the reasons it is so difficult to get people on the same wavelength about the provision of collective goods is that:

> With the private sector ever more powerful and the wealthy ever more isolated from the rest of society, governments find themselves unable to compel those with money to help pay for such basic public needs as defence and police functions, economic infrastructure, environmental protection, or a social safety net (Florini 2003: 3).

In pre-revolutionary China, France and Russia the aristocracy was so isolated from what was going on with the common people that they were able to say "let them eat cake" if they do not have bread. Once again, elites are flying so high above the heads of ordinary citizens that they either do not know or do not want to know the difficult circumstances in which ordinary people live.

The raw facts are illuminating. During 2003 alone, the world gained 111 new *billionaires*, to bring the total to 587 (*International Herald Tribune* 1/03/04). According to a study by Merrill Lynch and Capgemini, in 2005 there were 8,700,000 millionaires in the world. At the same time there were 85,400 very rich persons in the world with fortunes over 30 million dollars. During the year 2004–5, their numbers increased by 10.2% (*Agence France-Presse/Le Droit* 21-06-06). But, how do they compare with the people at the other end of the economic scale? Even in the powerhouse of globalization, the United States, the Economic Policy Institute tells us the heads of large corporations pocketed 262 times more than employees in 2005. The gap has been increasing over the long-term: the CEOs gained 24 times more than employees in 1965 and 71 times more in 1989 – just before globalization took off in the 1990s and CEO income skyrocketed with it. And no wonder: in the year 2004–5 the income of the heads of the 2000 largest American corporations increased by 20% while the minimum salary in the U.S. remained unchanged at $5.15 for the previous nine years (*Agence France-Presse/Le Droit* 25-06-06). The annual World Economic Survey of the UN's Department of Economic and Social Affairs reminds us that inequality in incomes between rich and poor countries is also growing. In 2005, the average U.S. citizen had an income 27 times greater than the average Nepalese. In 1950 the difference was only 19 times as great (*Reuters/Globe and Mail* 1-07-06). Even growth is inequitable. In the 35 year period from 1965 to 1999, of 95 developing countries surveyed, 28 suffered a decline in GDP per capita, and 46 others did not even double their GDP (which they would have done with a growth rate of 2 percent annually (UN 2000: 122).

In such circumstances, it is no wonder that some authors face us with the choice of reform or revolution. If this study opts for evolution, it is partly because the author is Canadian and partly because history confirms to us the heavy cost in violence, conflict and loss that was inflicted on the people by the countries that opted for revolution. Great Britain avoided revolution with the help of relevant elites, but it took time. Nearly 60 years were necessary to get child labour laws because they were opposed by mine and mill owners who argued it was a "human right" for children to work!

But, as we have seen, there is reason for optimism. Existing hierarchies are being challenged by new economic powers and by new coalitions of transnationally linked interest and value groups. States, acting alone can no longer control policy outcomes. Trends in transnationalization are opening up unprecedented possibilities to shape global change. If civil society entrepreneurs can be put to work "globalization is increasingly what actors make of it" (Cerny 2006: 110). If I believe we can do better, it is not because of wishful thinking but because we have a structural situation that is different. We now have thousands of competent, knowledgeable and organized NGOs that can give leadership to the reform agenda.

But they need a plan not only about how to transform international institutions as outlined above but also one that sets motivating goals. Our authors clearly indicate that the goal of democracy must be one of the aims of reformers. The cumulative research they have presented points to the conclusion that our world problems have one major cause. Too few people control too much economic and political power. This is surely a democratic issue. Neither globalization nor international organizations are the causes of poverty, infant and maternal mortality, the wealth gap, pollution, unemployment, and illiteracy. Rather they are the result of those who mastermind globalization and inter-governmental relations. We are talking about the governments of rich, mainly Northern states, major corporations, the wealthy elites and their allied media. It will not be easy to change their orientations. Thus, institutional modernization must be buttressed and inspired by a public appeal to democratic ideals to overturn an unjust, immoral and oppressive international system.

Whatever can be said against democracy, the facts are that for three decades after the Second World War democratic politics produced not only freedom but also wealth and welfare in pluralist societies of multiple, reasonably balanced stakeholders. Leftists and Marxists eventually brought about an over-dependence on the state, which in turn engendered the neo-conservative reaction. Corporations and rich manipulators turned to the lawless conditions of a globalized world to make their fortunes on the backs of poor countries in an international system they controlled. In the long run, as Lowi says, only political democracy can bring about a fair international system. What sort of process can we suggest that will bring together the various proposals we have just seen into a coordinated movement toward democracy? Let us assume that we start by enunciating the goal of global democracy from the outset. One also presumes that there will be an ongoing, multilateral pursuit of peace and security. After that, it is likely the various steps toward democracy will alternate between sequential and overlapping modes, depending on strategy and opportunities.

### 7.8.1 Eight Steps Toward Global Democracy

*Pluralism*: If I am correct in concluding that the principal momentum for the modernization of the UN and other international institutions must be supplied by civil society in general and INGOs in particular, then the absolute minimum for their increased influence is a pluralist international system. Therefore the first task of civil society entrepreneurs is to ensure the maintenance of the present open system of international relations with counterbalancing actors that preclude monopolistic players.

*Transparency*: While it is hardly sufficient in and of itself, transparency – that is, open, non-secretive meetings and access to information – is not only an important aspect of democracy but is also a sine qua non of participation and responsibility.

Transparency in national governments and inter-governmental organizations is crucial to the effectiveness of pluralism. Civil society should reinforce its demands for transparency and play off one agency or level of government against another in a continuing effort to set standards and provide examples.

*Civil Society*: If civil society is to play a leadership role in transforming international organizations then it must make an active decision to do so and must take proactive initiatives to give itself the means to become effective. As outlined above, this means essentially that INGOs must create institutional reform sections and devote a portion of their revenues to a reform movement. Expertise and autonomous finances are essential to success. As researchers have pointed out, we now have the luxury of multiple points of global governance in which influence and leverage can be exercised – but only if civil society provides itself with the organizational capacity to take advantage of the openings.The leadership of civil society is itself a step toward global democracy.

*Democratization*: Globalization opens the door to the spread of learning about liberty and self-government around the world. A multilateral consortium of citizen-to-citizen exchanges of long duration must lead it. Civic organizations and NGOs should, in addition, make sure there is a massive aid and publicity campaign. Happily there are already many groups with active campaigns along these lines. The more effective democracies there are in the world, the more rapidly we can progress toward global democratic institutions.

*Ongoing Institutional Transformation*: There are some examples of reforms in the UN, such as the new Human Rights Council and the Peacebuilding Commission. There is one example of transformation, the resolution in September 2005 concerning the international "Responsibility to Protect" civilians in danger. Every effort must be made to provide effective criteria for operationalization of this new principle by the Security Council. It is a first step toward taming the principle of sovereignty. Beyond this, the self-interested behaviour of governments, reinforced by the unilateralism of the U.S., makes one rather sanguine about prospects for fundamental transformation of the UN. There is, it seems to me, one good possibility. It is the "Binding Triad" proposal for weighted voting in the General Assembly (Szasz 2001, also Schwartzberg 2004). The idea is to give each vote a triple weighting according to sovereign autonomy, population and financial contributions. The proposal is easy to operate, inexpensive to initiate and offers advantages to all the stakeholders in the UN. The General Assembly would become a force to be reckoned with, democratic principles would be introduced and the UN would become more effective.

*Petitions and Referendums*: The Commission on Global Governance recommended the use of public petitions to the UN and other international organizations. The European Union has demonstrated how effective they can be. Petitions and the parallel idea of global referendums would be precursors to democracy. The cost of investment in each one would be repaid in democratic learning, international visibility, and global symbols.

*Courts and Law*: While, at present, international law is weak and can hardly be claimed as a basis of multilateralism, we do know that the rule of law and independent courts are an imperative foundation for democratic liberties and stability. The European Court and Charter of Rights have shown how effective law can be both in leading democratization and also in securing citizen rights. The creation of the International Criminal Court was an example of how effective a mobilized civil society can be. We should move ahead with demands for an International Human Rights Court and a Court of the Environment.

*A Democratic Parliamentary Assembly*: Assuming some progress in each of the preceding steps, many of the present roadblocks to a people's assembly at the UN would be neutralized. As has been proposed, one can envisage moving ahead with an advisory Parliamentary Assembly of representatives of national parliaments as a first step. If necessary, it could start with representatives of recognized democracies.

## 7.9 The World Cannot Go On Like This

To close, let me make a brief summary of the book's argument. The state of the world is untenable. As presently constituted, the international system is undemocratic, out-of-date, immoral, ineffective and unsustainable. Northern countries, in particular, should be embarrassed enough to want to work to transform the system – even if it must be said that leaders of developing countries often do little to help their own people.

The countries of the South and citizens everywhere are, for the most part, excluded from deciding on foreign affairs and their global future, which are dominated by the rich and the powerful. Resources and wealth are transferred to the rich from the poor who live in squalid conditions. There is no need for this oppressive state of affairs. There is more than enough to go around but the corporate managers and owners keep grasping a greater and greater share. Needless to say there are also many public-spirited business people. Nothing is black and white but the basic trends are exactly as described. And, more and more, 'riot control' rather than prevention is used to keep the poor in their place. Sooner or later the pressure cooker will burst. Some people, riding high on their wealth or their fundamentalism, don't care. But thoughtful citizens should, especially when they now know that the financial and political institutions invented almost a century ago are used like crutches to prop up this unfair system.

Globalization has brought in its wake economic growth but also disparity and interdependence, caused by bull-in-the-china-shop capitalism and technological transformation unconstrained by political and social reform. Underneath it all we are despoiling our forests and waters, abusing our resources and climate, and polluting our environment. These are all facts, not ideological fervor. When I started the research and writing, I had little idea how unjust things are, not only for international institutions but also for the whole world.

The flip side of the coin is also true. The world of the state is untenable too. We cannot flinch from another series of facts. The out-dated notion of national sovereignty, where each government thinks it can do what it wants, now undermines the nascent global system. The United Nations was created by a post-war desire for collective action to promote peace and development. It's no longer the case. National leaders, supposedly acting in the name of the people, but really protecting their own interests, operate on a narrow and out-dated concept of national security. From President Bush's unilateralism in the name of constitutional sovereignty, to President Mugabe's destruction of opponents and minorities in the name of national sovereignty, to China's blocking Security Council action in Darfur to protect its access to Sudan's oil – all of them put self-interest ahead of UN collective security or human rights. There is a little blue sky on the horizon following the General Assembly's support for the principles of humanitarian intervention for the "Right to Protect" civilians being harmed by civil conflict. But we have a long way to go before the Security Council develops criteria for putting the principles into practice and we start to transform the UN from an inter-national organization into a global one capable of dealing with global problems.

However, given the reality that it is national sovereignty and national self-interest which themselves block all possibility of modernizing the United Nations, to whom can we turn to transform our international institutions? Only one group has the competence and resources to influence government and public opinion both at the national and international levels. This immense group is composed of the large transnational associations (INGOs) and the rest of civil society. Such leading NGOs as Greenpeace, Doctors Without Borders, the Helsinki group, Red Cross, the World Federalists, Oxfam, Amnesty International, the International Crisis Group, Care and Save the Children have become household names. They have demonstrated that they have the capabilities, the specialized knowledge, and the altruistic reputation to lead governments and the public on the long complex journey to global transformation. They have the potential but not yet the organizational will and muscle to do the task.

But it is not just its new structural presence on the international scene that presupposes a transformational role for civil society. History shows us that it was leading citizens and groups, not governments, who were primarily responsible for the origin and evolution of international organizations. Governments react to threats and opportunities. Civil society entrepreneurs act on foresight and principle. Democracy and human rights cry out for such leadership. The UN requires transformation before already visible crises burst forth with disastrous effects for our integrated world where all are vulnerable. International relations theorists tell us there is now an opening for civil society action. Not only have INGOs become legitimate, recognized international actors, but the current confluence of the global system opens up opportunities for influence at the multiple locales and levels of global governance. Will civil society entrepreneurs seize the opportunity? Will they mobilize public opinion to oppose international domination by the few and seek more representative global institutions and governance?

*"Why do nations so furiously rage together, and why do the people imagine vain things? The kings of the earth rise up, and the rulers take counsel together against the lord... Let us break their bonds asunder and cast away their yokes from us... The trumpet shall sound, and the dead shall be raised incorruptible, and we shall be changed" (Charles Jennens & Georg Frideric Handel, 1742).*

---

John Trent is a Fellow in the Centre on Governance of the University of Ottawa and former Secretary General of the International Political Science Association.
11 Williamson Rd., Chelsea QC Canada J9B 1Z4 jtrent@uottawa.ca (819) 827-1025

Monika Rahman is a an international researcher, and law student at McGill University, Montreal.

# References & Bibliography

Albright, Madeleine (2003). "Think Again: The United Nations," *Foreign Policy*, 09-9-03.

Alger, C. F. (1995). "The United Nations in historical perspective," in *The United Nations System: The Policies of Member States* (chap. 1), Gene M. Lyons, Chadwick F. Alger and John E. Trent, Tokyo, United Nations University Press.

Alston, Lee J., Thrainn Eggertsson and Douglass C. North (eds.) (1996). *Empirical Studies in Institutional Change*, Cambridge, Cambridge University Press.

Anheiner, H., M. Glasius, & M. Kaldor (eds.) (2001). *Global Civil Society*, Oxford, Oxford University Press.

Annan, Kofi (1997). *Renewing the United Nations: A Program for Reform*, Report of the Secretary-General, United Nations, General Assembly, A/51/950.

——— (1999). "Two Concepts of Sovereignty," *The Economist*, 18 Sept: 49–50.

——— (2000). *Preventing War and Disaster: A Growing Global Challenge: Annual Report of the Secretary General*, DPI/2058.

——— (2002) "Role of the United Nations in promoting development in the context of globalization and interdependence," Background Information, Agenda Item 96, Sept.

——— (2003a). *Annual Report to the General Assembly*, New York, United Nations.

——— (2003b). *Implementation of the United Nations Millennium Declaration: Report of the Secretary-General to the General Assembly*, A/58/323.

——— (2004). *In Larger Freedom: Towards Development, Security and Human Rights*, Report of the Secretary-General, http://www.un.org/largerfreedom, 25-3-05.

Appiah, Kwame Anthony (2006). *Cosmopolitanism: Ethics in a World of Strangers*, New York, W. H. Norton.

Archer, C. (2001). *International Organizations* (3rd ed.), London, Routledge.

Archibugi, Daniele (ed.) (2003). *Debating Cosmopolitics*, London, Verso.

Archibugi, D., D. Held, and M. Kohler (1998). *Re-imagining Political Community: Studies in Cosmopolitan Democracy*, Cambridge, Polity Press.

Archibugi, Daniele (1992). "Models of International Organization In Perpetual Peace Projects," *Review of International Studies*, 18(5): 295–317.

Armstrong, D., L. Lloyd and J. Redmond (1996). *From Versailles to Maastricht: International Organizations in the Twentieth Century*, Basingstoke, Macmillan.

Aron, Raymond (1966). *War and Peace: A Theory of International Relations*, New York, Praeger.

Assembly 2000. *Renewing the United Nations and Building a Culture of Peace*, New York, Interreligious, International Federation for World Peace.

Axworthy, Lloyd (2003). *Navigating a New World: Canada's Global Future*, Toronto, Alfred A. Knopf, Canada.

Axworthy, Thomas S. (2003, February 27). "Muscular Multilateralism," Speech to the annual seminar of the Conference of Defence Associations Institute, Ottawa.

Badie, Bertrand & Alain Pellet (eds.) (1993). *Les relations internationales à l'épreuve de la science politique: Mélanges Marcel Merle*, Paris, Économica.

Barlow, Maude and Tony Clarke (2001). *Global Showdown: How the New Activists are Fighting Global Corporate Rule*, Toronto, Stoddart.

Barber, Benjamin R. (1995 with a new introduction, 2001. All references to the 2001 volume). *Jihad vs. McWorld: Terrorisms Challenge to Democracy*, New York, Ballantine Books.

Barber, Benjamin R. (2003). *Fear's Empire: War, Terrorism, and Democracy*, New York, W. W. Norton.

Beigbeder, Y. (1987), "Reformes administratives et structurelles des Nations Unies," *Revue Études internationales*, xviii(2) 1987: 353–69.

———(1992). *Le rôle international des organisations non-governementales*, Brussels and Paris, Bruyland & L. G. D. J.

Belafonte, Harry (2004). "School fees in Africa: Where the West can open the *classroom* door," *International Herald Tribune*, op. ed., 1-03-04.

Bertrand, Maurice (2000) 3rd ed. *L'ONU*, Paris, Éditions La Découverte.

Bertrand, Maurice (1988). *The Third Generation World Organization*, Dordrecht, Martinus Nijhoff.

Best, G. (1999). "Peace conferences and the century of total war: The 1899 Hague Conference and what came after," *International Affairs* 75(3): 619–34.

Birdsall, Nancy (1998). "Life is unfair: Inequality in the world," *Foreign Policy* 111 (summer): 76–93.

Boli, John & George Thomas (eds.) (1999). *Constructing World Culture: International Non-governmental Organizations Since 1875*, Stanford, Stanford University Press.

Boulding, Kenneth E. (1985). *The World as a Total System*, Beverly Hills, Sage.

Brierly, J. L. (1946). "The Covenant and the Charter," *British Yearbook of International Law*, 23: 83–94.

Boot, Max (2001). "The Case for American Empire," *Weekly Standard 7*, no. 5, Oct. 15: 27.

Boutros-Ghali, Boutros (1992). *An Agenda for Peace*, New York, United Nations.

——— (1999). *Unvanquished: A U.S.-UN Saga*, New York, Random House.

Boyd, Andrew (1964). *United Nations: Piety, Myth and Truth*, Hammondsworth, Penguin.

Brzezinski, Zbigniew (2005). *The Choice: Global Domination or Global Leadership*, New York, Basic Books.

Brooks, David (2005). "Loudly, With a Big Stick", *New York Times*, op-ed, 14-4-05.

Brown, Seyom (1992). *International Relations in a Changing Global System*, Boulder, Westview Press.

Bull, Hedley (1977). *The Anarchical Society: A Study of Order in World Politics*, London, Macmillan.

Burton, John (1979). *Deviance, Terrorism and War: The Process of Solving Unsolved Social and Political Problems*, London, Martin Robin.

Cameron, Maxwell A. (2002). "Global civil society and the Ottawa Process: Lessons from the movement to ban anti-personnel mines," in Andrew F. Cooper et al, op. cit.

Canada. Department of Foreign Affairs and International Trade. Centre for Foreign Policy Development. (2003, February 18). "Perception of the Security Council as an Instrument of American Foreign Policy." Speaker: Dr. James Sutterlin. *The United Nations and the Security Council: Central or Sidelined?* (expert round–table, netcast). Ottawa. Retrieved July 30, 2003 from http://www.dfait-maeci.gc.ca/cfp-pec/library/acuns-netcasts-en.asp

Canada. (2003a). "Canadians in the World: Canada and International Organizations," Department of Foreign Affairs and International Trade. Retrieved October 5, 2003 from http://www.dfait-maeci.gc.ca/ciw-cdm/orgs-en.asp.

*Canadian Priorities for United Nations Reform* (1995). Proceedings from the First Canadian Conference on UN Reform, Montreal, UN Association of Canada, in Fawcett and Newcombe op. cit.

Cardoso Report (2003). The Secretary-General's Panel of Eminent Persons on Civil Society-UN Relationships (www.un.org/reform/panel.htm).

Caron, David B. (1993). "The Legitimacy of the Collective Authority of the Security Council", *American Journal of International Law*, (87): 552.

Cerny, Philip G. (2006). "Plurality, Pluralism and Power: Elements of Pluralist Analysis in an Age of Globalization", in Rainer Eisfeld (ed.) *Pluralism: Developments in the Theory and Practice of Democracy*, Opladen, Germany, Barbara Budrich Publishers.

Cerny, Phillip (1995). "Globalization and the Changing Logic of Collective Action", *International Organization* 49: 595–625.

Charnovitz, S. (1997). "Two Centuries of Participation: NGOs and International Governance," *Michigan Journal of International Law*, 18(2): 183–286.

Chemillier-Gendreau, Monique (2005). « Pour une organisation de la communauté mondiale », *Le Monde diplomatique*, Sept: 22–3.

Childers, Erskine with Brian Urquhart (1994). *Renewing the United Nations System*, Uppsala, Sweden, Dag Hammarskjold Foundation.

Chua, Amy (2004). *World on Fire: How Exporting Free Market Democracy Breeds Ethnic Hatred and Global Instability*, New York, Anchor Books.

Claude, I. L. (1966). *Swords into Ploughshares: The Problems and Progress of International Organizations*, London, University of London Press.

Coate, Roger A., W. Andy Knight & Andrei I. Maximenko (2005). Requirements of mutilateral a governance for promoting Human Security in a Postrodern-era in W. Andy Knight (ed). Adapting the United Nations to a Postmodern Era.

Coleman, James (1990). *Foundations of Social Theory*, Cambridge, Harvard University Press.

Commission on Global Governance (1995). *Our Global Neighborhood*, New York, Oxford University Press.

Cooper, Andrew F., John English and Ramesh Thakur (eds.) (2002). *Enhancing Global Governance: Towards a New Diplomacy?* Tokyo, United Nations University Press.

Cornelius, Wayne A., Philip L. Martin and James F. Hollifield (1994). *Controlling Immigration: A Global Perspective*, Stanford, CA, Stanford University Press.

Corps commun d'inspection (1985). *Quelques réflexions sur la réforme des Nations unies*, A/40/988, New York, United Nations.

Cox, Robert W. (1992). " Multilateralism and World Order", *Review of International Studies*, 18(2).

Cox, Robert W. (1983). "Problems of Global Management," in T. T. Gati (ed.), *The U.S., the UN and Management of Global Change*, New York, NYU Press.

Crisp, Jeff (2001). "New Issues in Refugee Research," Geneva, UNHCR. www.unhcr.ch/refworld/pubs.

Culpeper, Roy and Caroline Pestieau (1996). *Development and Global Governance*, Ottawa, North-South Institute.

Cushman, John H. (2003). "Terror Alert is Raised to High," *The New York Times*, 03/12/22.

Daalder, Ivo H. and James M. Lindsay (2003). *America Unbound: the Bush Revolution in Foreign Policy*, Washington, Brookings Institution Press.

Dahl, Robert A. (1972). *Polyarchy: Participation and Opposition*, New Haven CT, Yale University Press.

Davidson, George (1986). "United Nations Financial Emergency," New York, mimeo.

Davis, Lance and Douglass North (1970). "Institutional Change and American Economic Growth: A First Step Towards a Theory of Institutional Innovation," *Journal of Economic History*, 30(1): 131–149.

Davies, N. (1997). *Europe: A History*, London, Pimlico.

De Senarclens, Pierre (1988). *La Crise des Nations unies*, Paris, Presses universitaires de France.

Deutsch, Karl W. (1968). *The Analysis of International Relations*, Englewoods Cliffs N.J, Prentice-Hall.

Deutsch, Karl W. (1967). *Nationalism and Social Communication*, Cambridge, Mass., MIT Press, 2nd ed.

Dingwerth, Klaus & Philipp Pattberg (2006). "Global Governance as a Perspective on World Politics", *Global Governance* 12(2): 185–203.

Dodge, David (2006). The Right Policies for Today's Global Economy", Speech to Chile-Canada Chamber of Commerce, Ottawa, Bank of Canada, www.bankofcanada.gc.ca.

Donini, Antonio (1988). "Resilience and Reform: Some thoughts on the processes of change in the United Nations," *International Relations*, ix(4).

Dowty, Alan and Gil Loesher (1999). "Changing norms in international responses to domestic disorder," in Raimo Vayrynen (ed.), *Globalization and Global Governance*, Lanham, MD, Rowman and Littlefield.

Durch, W. J., and B. M. Blechman (1995). *Keeping the Peace: The United Nations in the Emerging World Order*. Washington, Henry L. Stimson Center.

Eastby, J. (1985). *Functionalism and Interdependence*, Lanham, MD, University Press of America.

Easton, David (1953). *The Political System: An Inquiry into the State of Political Science*, New York, Alfred Knopf.

*Economist* (1993). "A survey of multinationals," 27 March 1993: 5–6.

*Economist* (2003). "The poor who are always with us," a UN, World Bank, IMF, OECD Situation Report, July.

*Economist* (2004). "High Level Panel and Security Council Reform," 22 July 2004.

Edgar, Alistair D. (2002). "Peace, justice, and politics: The International Criminal Court, 'new diplomacy,' and the UN system" in Andrew F. Cooper et al, op. cit.

Edwards, Michael (2004). *Civil Society*, Cambridge, Polity Press.

Edwards, Steven (2003). "UN's 'sloppy' security costs lives in Iraq: report," *Ottawa Citizen*, 22-10-03.

Ehrenberg, John (1999). *Civil Society: The Critical History of an Idea*, NY, New York University Press.

Eisfeld, Rainer (ed.) (2006). *Pluralism: Developments in the Theory and Practice of Democracy*, Opladen, Germany, Barbara Budrich Publishers.

Etzioni, Amitai (2004). *From Empire to Community*, New York, Palgrave MacMillan.

Etzioni-Halevy, Eva (1993). *The Elite Connection: Problems and Potential of Western Democracy*, Cambridge, Polity Press.

*A Fair Globalization: Creating opportunities for all* (2004). Report of the Commission on the Social Dimensions of Globalization, Geneva, International Labour Organization.

Falk, Richard, R. Johanen and Samuel Kim (1993). *The Constitutional Foundation of World Peace*, Albany, State University of New York Press.

Falk, Richard, S. Kim and Samuel Mendlovitz (1991). *The United Nations and a Just World Order*, Boulder, CO., Westview Press.

Falk, Richard A. (1977). "Contending Approaches to World Order", *Journal of International Affairs*, 31(Fall/Winter): 171–98.

Fasulo, Linda (2004). *An Insider's Guide to the UN*, New Haven, Yale University Press.

Fawcett, Eric and Hanna Newcombe (1995). *United Nations Reform: Looking Ahead After Fifty Years*, Toronto, Dundurn Press.

Ferguson, Niall (2001). "Clashing Civilizations or Mad Mullahs: The United States between informal and formal empire," in *The Age of Terror: America and the World After September 11*, Strobe Talbott and Nayan Chanda (eds.), New York, Yale Center for the Study of Globalization and Basic Books.

Florini, Ann (2003). *The Coming Democracy: New Rules for Running a New World*, Washington, Island Press.

Forman, Shepard & Derk Segaar (2006). "New Coalitions for Global Governance: The Changing Dynamics of Globalization", *Global Governance* (12): 205–25.

Frachon, Alain and Daniel Vernet (2003, April 16). "Le stratège et le philosophe : qui sont les néoconservateurs qui jouent un rôle essentiel dans les choix du président des États-Unis?" *Le Monde*.

Fuchs, Doris A. & Friedrich Kratochwil (eds.) (2002). *Transformative Change and Global Order: Reflections on Theory and Practice*, Munster, Lit Verlag.

Fuchs, Joseph (1993). *Moral Demands and Personal Obligations*, Washington, D.C., Georgetown University Press.

General Assembly (1986). G18 Report, Official Records, 41st session, Supplement No. 49 (A-41-49), New York, United Nations.

Gillinson, Sarah (2004). *Why Cooperate? A Multi-disciplinary Study of Collective Action*, London, Overseas Development Institute, Working Paper 234.

Gilpin, Robert (2001). *Global Political Economy*, Princeton, N.J., Princeton University Press.

Glennon, Michael J. (2005). "Idealism at the U.N.", *Policy Review*, 129 (Feb.–Mar.): 3–13.

Godoy, Julio (2005). "Rough Row Breaks Out on Diversity", Other News, Robert Savio/IPS, soros°topica.email-publisher.com 14-3-05.

Gonzalez, Enric. (2003, April 14). "War in Iraq: The new American century? More than a war: Iraq is the litmus test for the United States' plan to transform the power balance in the Middle East," *El Pais*.

Goodrich, Leland and Edvard Hambro (1946). *Charter of the United Nations: Commentary and Documents*, Boston, World Peace Foundation.

Gordenker, L. and T. Weiss (1998). "Devolving Responsibilities: A Framework for Analysing NGOs and Services," in Tom Weiss (ed.), *Beyond UN Subcontracting: Task-Sharing with Regional Security Arrangements and Service-Providing NGOs* (pp. 30–45), Basingbroke, Macmillan.

Graham, Bill (Hon). (2003, June 13). "Notes for an address at the 16th Annual Meeting of the Academic Council on the United Nations System," New York. Retrieved July 30, 2003 from http://webapps.dfait-maeci.gc.ca/minpub/Publication.asp?FileSpec=/Min_Pub_Docs/106272.htm&Language=E

Groom, A. J. R. and P. Taylor (eds.) (1975). *Functionalism: Theory and Practice in International Relations*, London, University of London Press.

Haas, Ernst. (1964). *Beyond the Nation-State: Functionalism and International Organization*, Stanford, Stanford University Press.

Haas, Ernst (1997). "Reason and Change in International Life: Justifying a Hypothesis", *Journal of International Affairs*: 209–40.

Haas, Ernst (1990). *When Knowledge is Power: Three Models of Change in International Organizations*, Berkeley. University of California Press.

Hass, Peter M. (1992). "Introduction: Epistemic Communities and International Policy Coordination," *International Organization* 46(1): 1–35.

Hancock, Graham (1989). *Lords of Poverty: The Power, Prestige, and Corruption of the International Aid Business*, New York, The Atlantic Monthly Press.

Hankey, Lord (1946). *Diplomacy by Conference: Studies in Public Affairs 1920–1946*, London, Ernest Benn.

Harbour, Frances V. (1995). "Basic Moral Values: A Shared Core," *Ethics and International Affairs* 9: 155–170.

Hauss, Charles (1996). *Beyond Confrontation: Transforming the New World Order*, Westport CT, Praeger.

Helgesen, Vidar (2006). "Institutions and Beyond: Making Democracy Sustainable", paper presented at the 20th World Congress of the International Political Science Association, Fukuoka. Stockholm, Institute for Democracy and Electoral Assistance (IDEA), www.idea.int.

Held, David and Anthony McGrew (eds.) (2002). *Governing Globalization: Power, Authority and Global Governance*, Oxford, Polity Press, Blackwell Publishers.

Held, David (1995). *Democracy and the Global Order: From the Modern State to Cosmopolitan Governance, Cambridge University Press.*

Heinbecker, Paul & Patricia Goff (eds.) (2005). *Irrelevant of Indispensable? The United Nations in the 21st Century*, Waterloo, Ont., Wilfrid Laurier University Press.

Heinbecker, Paul (2005b). "The Way Forward", in Heinbecker & Goff, *Irrelevant or Indispensable?* op. cit.

Heinrich Böll Foundation (2002). *The Jo'Burg-Memo: Fairness in a Fragile World – Memorandum for the World Summit on Sustainable Development*, Berlin, Germany. Retrieved October 24, 2003 from http://www.boell.de.

Heinrich, Dieter (1992). "The Case for a United Nations Parliamentary Assembly," Amsterdam, World Federalist Movement.

Hemleben, S. J. (1943). *Plans for World Peace Through Six Centuries*, Chicago, University of Chicago Press.

Hinsley, F. H. (1967). *Power and the Pursuit of Peace*, Cambridge, Cambridge University Press.

Hoffe, Otfried (2001). "A subsidiary and federal world republic: Thoughts on democracy in the age of globalization," in *Global Governance and the United Nations System*, V. Rittberger (ed.), Tokyo, United Nations University Press.

Hoffman, Stanley (1978). *Primacy or World Order: American Foreign Policy Since the Cold War*, New York, McGraw-Hill.

Hoffman, Stanley (1965). *The State of War: Essays on the Theory and Practice of International Relations*, New York, Praeger.

Hoge, Warren (2005). "U.S. Lobbies Security Council on Darfur", *International Herald Tribune*, 20-1-05.

Holloway, Steven (2000). "U.S. Unilateralism at the UN: Why Great Powers do not Make Great Multilateralists," *Global Governance* 6: 364.

Holmes, John. (1986a). "The United Nations in Perspective." *Behind the Headlines*, 44(1): 13.

Holsti, K. J. (1985). *The Dividing Discipline: Hegemony and Diversity in International Relations*, Boston, Allen & Unwin.

Ignatius, David (2003). "Some day France will learn the error of its ways." *The Ottawa Citizen*, column from the Washington Post Writers Group, 20-05-03.

Independent Advisory Group (1993). *Financing an Effective United Nations*, New York, Ford Foundation.

Independent Working Group on the Future of the United Nations (1995). *The United Nations in its Second Half Century*, New York, Ford Foundation.

International Commission on Intervention and State Sovereignty (2001). *The Responsibility to Protect*, Ottawa, International Development Research Centre.

International Criminal Tribunal for Rwanda (1999, May 21). "Kayishema and Ruzindana convicted of Genocide." ICTR/INFO-9-2-184 (press release, non-official, for media information only), Arusha, Tanzania.

International Institute for Applied Systems Analysis (2002) "Achieving Sustainable Development: The 21st Century Imperative," *Options*, spring.

International Press Service (2004). Other News, Robert Savio/IPS, soros topica. email; Stefania Milan, "New World Social Forum: New Opportunities," 06-04-04; Gustavo Gonzalez, "Americas Social Forum: Global Forum to Move and Improve," 30-07-04.

Intriligator, Michael D. (2006). *Issue Paper: The Threat of Insecurity: Are we Meeting the Challenge*, The New School of Athens op.cit.

Jacob, P. E., A. L. Altherton and A. M. Wallenstein (1972). *The Dynamics of International Organization* (2nd ed.), Homewood, IL, Dorsey Press.

Jolly, Richard, Louis Emmerij, & Thomas G.Weiss (2005). *The Power of UN Ideas: Lessons from the First 60 Years*, United Nations Intellectual History Project, New York, City University of New York Graduate Centre, www.unhistory.org.

Johnston, David (2003). "In debate on antiterrorism, the courts assert themselves," *The New York Times*, 03-12-19.

Judt, Tony (2003, August 15). "Its own worst enemy," *The New York Review*. pp. 12–17.

Kaldor, Mary (2003). *Global Civil Society: An Answer to War*, Cambridge, Polity Press.

Kaplan, Morton A. (1967). *System and Process in International Politics*, New York, Science Editions (1st edition 1957, John Wiley & Son).

Kaufmann, Johan, Dick Leurdijk and Nico Schrijver (1991). *The World in Turmoil: Testing the UN's Capacity*, Dartmouth College, The Academic Council on the United Nations System.

Kaul, Inge, Pedro Conceiçao, Katell Le Goulven and Ronald U. Mendoza (2003). *Providing Global Public Goods: Managing Globalization*, New York, Oxford University Press.

Kaul, Inge and Katell Le Goulven (2003). "Institutional Options for Producing Global Public Goods," in Kaul et al., op. cit.

Keane, John (2003). *Global Civil Society*, Cambridge, Cambridge University Press.

Keck, M. E. and K. Sikkink (1998). *Activists Beyond Borders: Advocacy Networks in International Politics*, Ithaca, Cornell University Press.

Kennedy, Paul (2006). *The Parliament of Man: The Past, Present, and Future of the United Nations*, Toronto, HarperCollins.

Kenworthy, L. S. (1995). "The Increasing Role of Regional and International Organizations." *Catching Up with a Changing World: A Primer on World Affairs* (chap. 9). Kennett Square, Pennsylvania: World Affairs Materials.

Keohane, Robert O. (2002). "Governance in a partially globalized world" in D. Held and A. McGrew (eds.), *Governing Globalization*, op. cit.

Keohane, Robert O. (2002b). *Power and Governance in a Partially Globalized World*, New York, Routledge.

Keohane, Robert O. (1990). "Multilateralism: An Agenda for Research", *International Journal*, xiv(4).

Keohane, Robert O. (1988)."International Institutions: Two Approaches", *International Studies Quarterly* 32(4).

Keohane, Robert O. and J. S. Nye (1971). *Transnational Relations and World Politics*, Cambridge, MA, Harvard University Press.

Keohane, Robert O. and J. S. Nye (1989). *Power and Interdependence* (2nd ed.), New York, Harper Collins.

Khagram, Sanjeev, Kathryn Sikkink, & James Riker (2002). *Restructuring World Politics: Transnational Social Movements, Networks, and Norms*. Minneapolis: University of Minnesota Press.

Kille, K. J. and R. M. Scully (2003). "Executive heads and the role of inter-governmental organizations: Expansionist leadership in the United Nations and the European Union," *Political Psychology* 24: 175–198.

Kissinger, Henry A. (2006). "American strategy and pre-emptive war", *International Herald Tribune*, 14-04-06.

Klein, Nomi (2005). "The Rise of Disaster Capitalism", Other News, Roberto Savio/IPS, soros.c.topica.com/maadqwtabgdoDb7zlPfb/, April 19.

Koenig-Archibugi, Mathias (2002). "Mapping global governance," in *Governing Globalization*, pp. 46–69, Held and McGrew, op. cit.

Kothari, Rajni (1974). *Footsteps into the Future*, New York, Free Press.

Knight, A. W. (ed) (2001, 2005). *Adapting the United Nations to a Postmodern Era: Lessons Learned*, 2nd edition, Houndmills, U.K., Palgrave Macmillan.

Knight, A. W. (2000). *A Changing United Nations: Multilateral Evolution and the Quest for Global Governance*, New York, Palgrave.

Knight, A. W. (2002). "The Future of the UN Security Council," in *Enhancing Global* Governance, Andrew Cooper et al., op. cit.

Krasner, Steven (ed.) (1983). *International Regimes*, Ithaca, Cornell University Press.

Krasno, Jean (ed.) (2004). *United Nations: Confronting the Challenges of a Global Society*, Boulder, Lynne Rienner.

Kratochwil, F. and J. Ruggie (1994). "International Organization: A State of the Art on the Art of the State," in, F. Kratochwil and E. Mansfield (eds.), *International Organization: A* Reader (pp. 4–19), New York, Harper Collins.

Krause, Keith, W. Andy Knight and David Dewitt (1995). "Canada, the United Nations, and the reform of international institutions," in *The United Nations System: The policies of member states* (chap. 4), C. Alger, G. Lyons and J. Trent, Tokyo, The United Nations University Press.

Krugman, Paul (2003). "Whose opinion counts," *The New York Times*, 03-3-17.

Krugman, Paul (2003a). "Telling it right," *The New York Times*, 03-12-19.

Kuhn, Thomas S. (1969). *The Structure of Scientific Revolutions*, Chicago, University of Chicago Press.

Kung, Hans (1998). *A Global Ethic for Global Politics and Global Economics*, New York: Oxford University Press.

Kupchan, Charles A., Emmanuel Alder, Jean-Marc Coicaud and Yuen Foong Khong (2001). *Power in Transition*, Tokyo, United Nations University Press.

Lachapelle, Guy & Stéphane Paquin (eds.) (2005). *Mastering Globalization: New sub-states' governance and strategies*, London, Routledge.

Lachapelle, Guy and John Trent (eds.) (2000). *Globalization, Governance and Identity: The Emergence of New Partnerships*, Montreal, Les Presses de l'Université de Montréal.

Ladd, W. (1840). *An Essay on a Congress of Nations for the Adjustment of International Disputes Without Resort to Arms*, London, Ward.

Langille, H. Peter (2002). *Bridging the Commitment–Capacity Gap: Existing Arrangement and Options for Enhancing UN Rapid Employment*, Wayne, NJ: Center for UN Reform Education.

Langmore, John (2005). *Dealing with America: The UN, the US and Australia*, Sydney, University of New South Wales Press.

*Le Monde diplomatique* (2005). « Enquête sur la réforme des Nations unies », 618 (Sept.): 18–23.

Lesnes, Corine (2004). "Les dirigeants de l'ONU sont mis en cause dans plusieurs affaires," *Le Monde*, 3-04-04.

Lowi, Theodore J. (2005). "Politics, economics, and justice: Toward a politics of globalizing capitalism", in Lachapelle & Paquin (eds.), *Mastering Globalization*, op.cit.

Luck, Edward C. (2005a). "The UN Security Council: Reform or Enlarge? in Paul Heinbecker and Patricia Goff (eds.) *Irrelevant or Indispensable: The United Nations in the 21st Century, op.cit.*

Luck, Edward C. (2005b). "How Not to Reform the United Nations", *Global Governance*, 11(4): 407–414.

Luck, Edward C. (2003). *Reforming the United Nations: Lessons from a History in Progress*, New Haven, Academic Council on the United Nations System.

Lyons, F. S. L. (1963). *Internationalism in Europe: 1815–1914*, Leiden, A. W. Sijthoff.

Lyons, Gene M. and Michael Mastanduno (1992). *Beyond Westphalia: International Intervention, State Sovereignty, and the Future of International Society*, Hanover, NH, the Rockefeller Center, Dartmouth College.

Lyons, Gene M. (1995). "Competing visions: Proposals for UN Reform," in *The United Nations System: The policies of member states*, C. Alger et al., op. cit.

MacMillan, Margaret (2002). *Paris 1919*, New York, Random House Paperbacks.

Maghroori, Ray & Bennett Rambagh (1982). *Globalism vs. Realism: International Relations Third Debate*, Boulder, Westview Press.

Malone, David M. (2004). *The UN Security Council: From the Cold War to the 21st Century*, Boulder Co., Lynne Rienner Publishers.

Malone, David M. and Y. F. Khong (eds.) (2003). *Unilateralism and U.S. Foreign Policy: International Perspectives*, Boulder, CO, Lynne Rienner.

Malone, David (2002). "The new diplomacy at the United Nations: How substantive?" in *Enhancing Global Governance: Towards a New Diplomacy* (chap. 3), Andrew F. Cooper et al., op. cit.

Mansbach, Richard W., Yale H. Ferguson and Donald E. Lampert (1976). *The Web of World Politics: Nonstate Actors in the Global System*, Englewood Cliffs, N. J., Prentice-Hall.

Martin, Hans-Peter and Harald Schumann (1997). *The Global Trap: Globalization and the Assault on Democracy and Prosperity*, London, Zed Books.

Matthews, Jessica T. (2000). "The Information Revolution," *Foreign Policy* 119 (spring): 63–5.

Maxwell, Simon (2005), "How to Help Reform Multilateral Institutions: An Eight-Step Program for More Effective Collective Action", *Global Governance*, 11(4): 415–424.

McWhinney, Edward (1981). *Constitution-Making: Principles, Process, Practice*, Toronto, University of Toronto Press.

Mendlowitz, Saul H. (1977). "The program of the Institute of World Order", *Journal of International Affairs*, 31(Fall/Winter): 259–66.

Merle, Marcel (1987). *The Sociology of International Relations*, Leamington Spa, UK, Berg Publishers.

Michels, Robert (1962). *Political Parties: A Sociological Study of the Oligarchical Tendencies of Modern Democracy*, New York, Crowell-Collier.

Miguel Servet College of Higher European Studies (2004). Programme of "World Governance," Paris.

The Military Balance, 2002–2003 (2002). Table 26. The International Institute for Strategic Studies, London, Oxford University Press.

Miller, Morris (1998). "Beyond Aid: Cooperative Approaches to Achieve Effective International Programs for Poverty Alleviation," www.management.uottawa.ca/miller.

Miller, Morris (1995). "Globalization: Structural Adjustment on a Planetary Scale," *Futures Research Quarterly*, 11(3): 53–88.

Mitrany, D. (1965). "The Prospects of Integration: Federal and Functional," *Journal of Common Market Studies* 4(2): 119–49.

——— (1975). *The Functional Theory of Politics*, London, Martin Robertson.

Monbiot, George (2003). *The Age of Consent: A Manifesto for a New World Order*, London, Flamingo HarperCollins.

Moravesik, Andrew (1999). "A New Statecraft? Supranational Entrepreneurs and International Cooperation," *International Organization* 53(2): 267–306.

Morden, Reid (2003). "Spies, not Soothsayers: Canadian Intelligence After 9/11," *Commentary*, Ottawa, Canadian Security Intelligence Service, No. 28.

Morgenthau, Hans J. & K. W. Thompson (1985). *Politics Among Nations: The struggle for power and peace*, 6th ed., New York, Knopf, (1st. ed. by Morgenthau published in 1948).

Mulligan, Shane and Peter Stoett (2000). "A Global Bioprospecting Regime: Partnership or Piracy," *International Journal* 55(2).

Multilateralism and the United Nations (1987). *Journal of Development Planning*, No. 17.

Murphy, C. N. (1994). *International Organization and Industrial Change: Global Governance Since 1850*, Cambridge, Polity Press.

Nafziger, Wayne, Frances Stewart and Raimo Vayrynen (2000). *War, Hunger and Development: The Origins of Humanitarian Emergencies*, New York, Oxford University Press.

Najam, Adil (2004). Tufts University, Presentation at Ubuntu Seminar, Barcelona, March.

National Intelligence Council (2004). The 2020 Project, "International Institutions in Crisis", NIC 2004-13, based on consultations with non-governmental experts around the world.

Nau, Henry R. (2005). "Bush's Classic Conservatism", *International Herald Tribune*, 29-03-05.

Nayyar, Deepak and Julius Court (2002). *Governing Globalization: Issues and Institutions*, Policy Brief No. 5, Helsinki, United Nations University World Institute for Development Economics Research.

Newhouse, John (2003). *Imperial Amercia: The Bush Assault on the World Order*, New York, Alfred A. Knopf.

New School of Athens (2006). *Conference Book: Beyond the Millennium Declaration: Embracing Democracy and Good Governance*, Athens, Global Governance Group, www.globalgovgroup.com.

*New York Times* (2003). "The Padilla Decision," editorial, 19-12-03; "Nuclear Mirage" editorial, 2-06-03.

Nicholas, H. G. (1962). *The United Nations as a Political Institution*, London, Oxford University Press.

Nicholson, H. (1969). *Diplomacy*, London, Oxford University Press.

The Nordic UN Project (1991). *The United Nations in Development: Reform Issues in the Economic and Social Fields*, Final Report of the Nordic UN Project, Stockholm.

North, Douglass C. (1990). *Institutions, Institutional Change and Economic Performance*, Cambridge, Cambridge University Press.

Nye, Joseph S. Jr. (2002). *The Paradox of American Power*, New York, Oxford University Press.

O'Brien, R., A. Goetz, J. Scholte and M. Williams (2000). *Contesting Global Governance*, Cambridge, Cambridge University Press.

O'Neale, John and Bruce Russett (1999). "The Kantian Peace: The Pacific Benefits of Democracy, Interdependence, and International Organization 1885–1992," *World Politics* (52) 1: 1–37.

Oldstone, Michael B. A. (1998). *Viruses, Plagues and History*, New York, Oxford University Press.

Ostrom, Elinor (1990). *Governing the Commons: the Evolution of Institutions for Collective Action*, New York, Cambridge University Press.

*Ottawa Citizen* (2004). "Pope urges new world order in annual New Year's message," 3-01-04.

Padelford, Norman J. and Leland M. Goodrich (1965). *The United Nations in the Balance: Accomplishments and Prospects*, New York, Frederick A. Praeger.

Panel of Eminent Persons on United Nations – Civil Society Relations (Cardoso Report) (2003). United Nations, New York.

*Partners for Peace: Strengthening Collective Security for the 21st Century* (1992). New York, United Nations Association of the United States of America.

Pentland, Charles (1992). "International Organizations and Their Roles," in *Perspectives on World Politics* (pp. 242–9), R. Little and M. Smith (eds.), London, Routledge.

Pew Research Centre (2002). *Global Attitudes Survey*, http://people-press.org.

Pfaff, William (2004). "How Kerry's foreign policy might look," *International Herald Tribune*, 06-03-04.

Pines, Burton Y. (1984), *A World Without a UN*, Washington, The Heritage Foundation.

Plumptre, Tim (2004). "New Rules of the Board Game: The Changing World of Corporate Governance and Its Implications for Multilateral Development Institutions," Ottawa, Institute on Governance.

Porter, Tony (1999). "Representation, Legitimacy and the Changing Regime for Global Financial Institutions," paper prepared for the annual meeting of the Canadian Political Science Association, Hamilton, Ont., McMaster University.

Power, Samantha (2005). "Réformer les Nations unies: pour nous sauver de l'enfer", *LeMonde diplomatique*, Sept.

Preston, Richard (2002). *The Demon in the Freezer*, New York, Ballantine Books.

Prestowitz, Clyde (2003). *Rogue Nation: American Unilateralism and the Failure of Good Intentions*, New York, Basic Books.

Price-Smith, Andrew T. (1999). "Ghosts of Kigali: Infectious Disease and Global Stability at the Turn of the Century," *International Journal* 54(3).

Puchala Donald J. and Roger A. Coate (1988). *The State of the United Nations, 1988*, Hanover, NH, The Academic Council on the United Nations System.

——— (1989). *The Challenge of Relevance of the United Nations in a Changing World Environment*, Hanover, NH, The Academic Council on the United Nations System.

Ratner, Steven R. and Jason S. Abrams (2001). *Accountability for Human Rights Atrocities in International Law: Beyond the Nuremberg Legacy*, Oxford, Oxford University Press.

Reed, James (2002). "Why is the USA not a like-minded country? Some structural notes and historical considerations," in *Enhancing Global Governance: Towards a New Diplomacy* (chap. 4), Andrew F. Cooper, et al., op. cit.

*Reimagining the Future: Towards democratic governance* (2000). La Trobe University, Australia, Toda Institute, Japan, Focus on Global South, Thailand.

Reinalda, Bob (2001). *International Conferences at the Heart of International Organizations*, Canterbury, ECPR.

——— (2003). *The Evolution of Public and Private International Organizations Before 1919*, Paper prepared for the 19th World Congress of the International Political Science Association, Durban, South Africa.

Reinalda, B. and B. Verbeek (eds.) (1998). *Autonomous Policy Making by International Organizations*, London, Routledge.

Reinsch, P. S. (1911). *Public International Unions: Their Work and Organization*, Boston, Ginn and Co.

Report of the Group of Experts on the Structure of the United Nations System (1975). *A New United Nations Structure for Global Economic Cooperation*, E-AC.62-9, New York, United Nations.

*Responsibility to Protect*, see International Commission on Intervention and State Sovereignty.

Richardson, L. (1999). "The Concert of Europe and Security Management in the Nineteenth Century," in H. Haftendorn, R. O. Keohane and C. A. Wallander (eds.), *Imperfect Unions: Security Institutions Over Time and Space* (pp. 48–79), Oxford, Oxford University Press.

Rittberger, Volker (ed.) (2001). *Global Governance and the United Nations System*, Tokyo, The United Nations University Press.

Rivlin, Benjamin and Leon Gordenker (eds.) (1993). *The Challenging Role of the UN Secretary General*, New York, Praeger.

Rivlin, Benjamin (1991). "The Rediscovery of the UN Military Staff Committee," Occasional Paper No. IV, City University of New York, Ralph Bunche Institute, The Graduate School.

Roberts, Adam (1999). "The role of humanitarian issues in international politics in the 1990s", *International Review of the Red Cross*, 81: 19–43.

Roberts, Adam and Benedict Kingsbury (eds.) (1995). *United Nations, Divided World: The UN's Roles in International Relations* (2nd ed.), Oxford, Clarendon Press.

Rocher, Guy (1969). *Introduction à la sociologie générale, Tome 3, Le changement social*, 2nd ed., Montreal, Hurtubise HMH.

Rock, Allan (2006). "Present at the Re-Creation: Reflections on the Reforming of the United Nations for the 21st Century", Lecture to the University of Ottawa Alumni, MaRS Centre, Toronto, April, Canada-UN@international.gc.ca.

Roodman, David M. (1998). *The Natural Wealth of Nations: Harnessing the Market for the Environment*, New York, Norton.

Roodman, David M. (1999). "Building a Sustainable Society," *State of the World 1999*, New York, Norton.

Rosenau, James (2002). "Governance in a New Global Order" in David Held and Anthony McGrew (eds.) op.cit.

Rosenau, James (1990). *Turbulence in Global Politics: A Theory of Change and Continuity*, Princeton, N.J., Princeton University Press.

Rosenthal, Andrew (2004). "Legal Breach: The Government's Attorneys and Abu Ghraib," *The New York Times*, Opinion, Editorial Observer, 30-12-2004.

Rothkopf, David (2005). *Running The World: Inside Story of the National Security Council*, N.Y. Public Affairs.

Ruggie, John G. (ed.) (1993). "Multilateralism: The Anatomy of an Institution," in *Multilateralism Matters: The Theory and Praxis of an Institutional Form*, New York, Columbia University Press.

Ruggie, John G. (1998). *Constructing the World Polity: Essays on International Institutionalization*, London, Routledge.

Ruiz-Diaz, Hugo (2005). "Une tribune pour les pays du sud", *Le Monde diplomatique*, (sept.): 20–1.

Russell, R. and J. E. Mather (1958). *A History of the United Nations Charter: The Role of the United States 1940–1945*, Washington, The Brookings Institution.

Russett, Bruce and John R. O'Neale (2001). *Triangulating Peace: Democracy, Interdependence and International Organizations*, New York, W. W. Norton.

Russett, Bruce, Barry O'Neill and James Sutterlin (1996). "Breaking the Security Council Logjam," *Global Governance*, 2(1): 57–78.

Sachs, Jeffrey D. (2005). *The End of Poverty: Economic Possibilities for Our Time*, New York. Penguin.

Sachs, Jeffrey (2000). "Globalization: A New Map of the World," *The Economist* 24 June: 81–3.

Sallot, Jeff (2003, June 14). "Canada calls for UN Reform," *Globe and Mail*, Retrieved June 15, 2003, from http://vancouver.indymedia.org/news/2003/06/52658.php.

Schemeil, Yves (2003). *Trade, Environment and Intellectual Property: Lessons from the Past*, paper prepared for the 19th World Congress of the International Political Science Association, Durban, South Africa.

——— (2003a). "Expertise and Politics: Consensus Making Within the World Bank and the World Meteorological Organizations," in *Decision-Making in International Organizations*, Bob Reinalda and Bertjan Verbeek (eds.), London, Routledge.

Scholte, J.A. (2000). *Globalization: A Critical Introduction*, Houndsmills and Basingstoke: Palgrave.

Schumpeter, Joseph A. (1950, 1962). *Capitalism Socialism and Democracy*, 3rd. ed., New York, Harper Torchbook.

Schwarz, Shalom H. and Anat Bardi (2000). "Moral Dialogues Across Cultures: An Empirical Perspective," in Edward W. Lehmann (ed.), *Autonomy and Order: A Communitarian Anthology* (pp. 155–179), Lanham, MD, Rowman and Littlefield.

Schwartzberg, Joseph E. (2004). *Revitalizing the United Nations*, Institute For Global Policy, World Federalist Movement, New York and Den Haag.

Scott, N. (1985). "The Evolution of Conference Diplomacy," in L. Dembinski, R. O'Regan and J. Björklund (eds.), *International Geneva 1985* (pp. 40–51), Geneva, Payot.

Seara-Vazquez, Modesto (2003). *A New Charter for the United Nations*, Huajuapan de Leon, Oaxca, Mexico, Universidad Technologica de la Mixteca.

Segaar, Derk (2004). "The Evolving Roles of NGOs in Global Governance", New York, Centre on International Cooperation, May.

Simai, Mihaly (1994). *The Future of Global Governance*, Washington DC., US Institute of Peace Press.

Simoni, Arnold (1972). *Beyond Repair: The Urgent Need For a New World Organization*, Don Mills, ON, Collier-Macmillan Canada.

Slaughter, Anne-Marie (2004). *A New World Order*, Princeton, Princeton University Press.

South Centre (1996). *For a Strong and Democratic United Nations: A South Pers–pective on United Nations Reform*, Geneva, the South Centre.

South Commission (1990). *The Challenges to the South: Report of the South Commission*, New York, Oxford University Press.

Sprout, Harold and Margaret (1962). *Foundations of International Politics*, Princeton NJ, D. Van Nostrand.

Spruyt, Hendrik (1994). *The Sovereign State and its Competitors: An Analysis of Systems Change*, Princeton, NJ, Princeton University Press.

The Stanley Foundation (1994). *The UN System and NGOs: New Relationships for a New Era*, Muscatine, Iowa, Stanley Foundation.

Stein, Michael B. (1990). *Canadian Constitutional Renewal, 1968-81*, Kingston, Institute of Intergovernmental Relations, Queen's University.

Sterling, Richard (1974). *Macropolitics: International Relations in a Global Society*, New York, Alfred A. Knopf.

Stewart, Frances and Sam Daws (2000). *Global Challenges: An Economic and Social Security Council at the United Nations*, London, Christian Aid.

Stiglitz, Joseph H. (2003). *Globalization and its Discontents*, New York, W. W. Norton.

Strange, Susan (1996). *The Retreat of the State: the diffusion of power in the world economy*, Cambridge, Cambridge University Press.

Strong, Maurice (2000). *Where on Earth Are We Going?* Toronto, Alfred A. Knopf Canada.

*A Study of the Capacity of the United Nations Development System* (1969). DP-5 (the Jackson Report), Geneva, United Nations.

Szasz, Paul C. (2001). *Alternative Voting Systems in International Organizations and the Binding Triad Proposal Improve Genera Assembly Decision-Taking*, Monograph No. 17, Centre for UN Reform Education, New Jersey.

Tarrow, Sidney (2005). *The New Transnational Activism*, Cambridge, Cambridge University Press.

Taylor, Paul (1999). "The United Nations in the 1990s: proactive cosmopolitanism and the issue of sovereignty," *Political Studies* 47: 538–65.

Taylor, Paul (1999a). "The United Nations and International Organization," in J. Baylis and S. Smith (eds.), *The Globalization of World Politics: An Introduction to International Relations* (chap . 14) New York, Oxford University Press.

Thakur, Ramesh (2002). "Security in the new millennium," in *Enhancing Global Governance: Towards a New Diplomacy* (chap. 15), Andrew F. Cooper et al., op. cit.

Tourraine, Alain (1991), "What does Democracy Mean Today?", *International Social Science Journal*, 129: 259–68.

Trent, John E. (2006a). "Democracy and the Reform of International Institutions," paper presented at the 20th World Congress of the *International Political Science Association*, Fukuoka, Japan, July 9–13.

Trent, John E. (2006b). "How well are we dealing with the challenges of insecurity?", Report to the New School of Athens, op.cit.

Trent, John E. and Fergus Watt (2005a). *United Nations World Summit Conference on Development and Reform (Millennium + 5): Media Backgrounder*, Ottawa, World Federalist Movement – Canada.

Trent, John E. and Fergus Watt (2005b). *United Nations World Summit: Major Achievements, Failures, Postponements*, Ottawa, World Federalist Movement – Canada.

Trent, John E. (2004). "Governing Global Security", Report on Session 2 to the Global Governance Group, Athens.

Trent, John E. (2003). "International Institutions: The Case for Innovation and Reform," paper presented at the 19th World Congress of the International Political Science Association, Durban, South Africa, July 2003; published in *Canadian Foreign Policy* 11(1) 2004: 3–30.

Trent, John E. (1995). "Foreign policy and the United Nations: National interest in the era of global politics," in C. Alger et al., *The United Nations System*, op. cit.

Trent, John E. (1995a). "The United Nations Between Status Quo and Utopia", in Madesto Seara Vazquez (ed.), Las Naciones Unidas a los cincuenta años, Mexico, Fondo de Cultura Económica.

Trent, John E. (1993). "L'acteur en politique internationale: Parfois plus bête que méchant", in Bertrand Badie & Alain Pellet (eds.), op.cit.

Ubuntu (2004). "Proposals for Reform of the System of International Institutions: Future Scenarios" Barcelona, Technical University of Catalonia, www.reformwatch.net.

United Nations Association of the USA (1987). *A Successor Vision: The United Nations of Tomorrow*, Final Panel Report, United Nations Management and Decision Making Project, New York, UNA-USA.

*United Nations Handbook (2006)*, Wellington, New Zealand Ministry of Foreign Affairs and Trade.

*United Nations Handbook 2002*, Wellington, New Zealand Ministry of Foreign Affairs and Trade.

United Nations (2005), *60 Ways the United Nations Makes a Difference*, New York, UN, DPI/2405.

United Nations (2004). *A More Secure World: Our Shared Responsibility*, Report of the Secretary-General's High-Level Panel on Threats, Challenges and Change, New York (www.un.org/secure world).

United Nations (2001). *Report on the World Social Situation*, New York.

United Nations (2000). *World Economic and Social Survey: Escaping the Poverty Trap*, New York.

United Nations (1986). *Report of the Secretary-General on the Work of the Organization*, New York.

United Nations Development Programme (1992 and 1993). *Human Development Report*, New York, Oxford University Press.

*A United Nations Emergency Peace Service: Protecting Civilians, Preventing Genocide and Crimes Against Humanity* (2004). Peter Langille, University of Victoria, British Columbia, Centre for Global Studies and David Krieger, Santa Barbara, California, Nuclear Age Peace Foundation.

*UNU Report: International Environmental Governance*, Tokyo, United Nations University.

U.S. Department of Defence (2002). *Nuclear Posture Review*, The Pentagon, http://www.globalsecurity.org/wmd/library/policy/dod/npr.htm.

U.S. Office of the National Security Advisor (2002). *The National Security Policy of the United States of America*, The White House, Retrieved October 24, 2003, from http://www.whitehouse.gov/nsc/nss1.html.

U.S. Office of the President (2002). *National Strategy to Combat Weapons of Mass Destruction*, The White House, http://whitehouse.gov/news/releases/2002/12/WMDStrategy.pdf.

Urquhart, Brian and Erskine Childers (1990). *A World in Need of Leadership: Tomorrow's United Nations*, New York, The Ford Foundation.

——— (1992). *Towards a More Effective United Nations*, Uppsala, Dag Hammarskjold Foundation. www.Vatican.va/holy_father/john_paul_ii/messages/peace/documents/hf_jp-ii_mes2003, 1-01-04.

Valaskakis, Kimon (2006). *Issue Paper: Are Present Global Institutions Still Relevant?* New School of Athens op. cit.

Valticos, N. (1985). "International Labour Standards and the World Community," in *International Geneva*, L. Dembinski et al., op.cit.

Wallerstein, Immanuel (1979). *The Capitalist World Economy*, Cambridge, Cambridge University Press.

Waltz, Kenneth (1979). *Theory of International Politics*, Menlo Park, Addison-Wesley.

Waltzer, Michael (1994). *Thick and Thin: Moral Arguments at Home and Abroad*, Notre Dame, IN, Notre Dame University Press.

Wapner, Paul (2002). "Defending Accountability in NGOs", *Chicago Journal of International Law* 3(1):197–205.

Weinberg, Steven, (2003). "The Growing Nuclear Danger," *The New York Review*, 18-07-03.

Weiss, Thomas G. (2005). *Overcoming the Security Council Reform Impasse: the Implausible versus the Plausible*, Occasional Paper No. 14, Berlin, Friedrich-Ebert-Stiftung.

Weiss, Tom and L. Gordenker (eds.) (1996). *NGOs, the UN and Global Governance*, Boulder, CO, Lynne Reinner.

Wheeler, Nicholas J. (2000). *Saving Strangers: Humanitarian Intervention in International Society*, Oxford, Oxford University Press.

Wilenski, Peter (1991). "Reforming the United Nations in the Post-Cold War Period," in M. R. Bustelo and P. Alston (eds.), *Whose New World Order?* Sydney, The Federation Press.

Willamson, John (2003). "From Reform Agenda to Damaged Brand Name: A short history of the Washington consensus and suggestion for what to do next," *Finance and Development*, Washington, IMF.

Wiltshire, Kenneth (2001). "Management of Social Transformations: Introduction," *International Political Science Review* 22(1): 5–11.

Wolfensohn, James (2002). "There is no wall," quoted in *The Washington Post* and *International Herald Tribune*, 13-03-02.

Woolf, Leonard (1916). *International Government*, 2nd ed., London, Allen & Unwin.

World Bank (1997). *World Development Report: The State in a Changing World*, Washington and New York, Oxford University Press.

World Bank, *Global Poverty Report*, www.worldbank.org/poverty/library/G8_2000.htm.

World Bank (2000). *World Development Indicators.*

World Bank (2003). *World Development Indicators.*

World Campaign for In-Depth Reform of the System of International Institutions (2004). *London Declaration*, Barcelona, Ubuntu.
World Commission on Environment and Development (1987). *Our Common Future*, Oxford, Oxford University Press.
Young, Oran (1994). *International Governance: Protecting the Environment in a Stateless Society*, Ithaca, Cornell University Press.
Youngs, Gillian (1999). *International Relations in a Global Age: A Conceptual Challenge*, Cambridge, Polity Press.
Zedillo, Ernesto (ed.) (2005). *Reforming the United Nations for Peace and Security*, New Haven, Yale Centre for the Study of Globalization.

# Index